Modern and Site Specific

The Architecture of Gino Valle, 1946–2003

Pierre-Alain Croset and Luka Skansi

LUND
HUMPHRIES

This edition of *Modern and Site Specific: The Architecture of Gino Valle, 1946–2003* published by Lund Humphries in 2018

Lund Humphries
Office 3, Book House
261A City Road
London EC1V 1JX
UK
www.lundhumphries.com

This is a revised and abbreviated version of the Authors' previous book, *Gino Valle*, published in Italian by Electa Architettura in 2010 and again in 2014

ISBN: 978–1–84822–277–9

Translation from Italian to English: Stephen Piccolo (Transiting sas)

The publishers and the authors gratefully acknowledge the support of Xi'An Jiaotong-Liverpool University (Suzhou, China) for funding the translation from Italian to English (Grant Research Development Fund Ref. No. RDF-14-01-05)

Front cover: Low-cost housing complex at Giudecca, Venice, 1980–86.
Photo: Alessandra Chemollo, 2018.

Back cover: Gino Valle in front of the hot springs complex in Arta Terme.
Photo: Fulvio Roiter, 1964.

Copy edited by Pamela Bertram
Designed by Luka Skansi and Jacqui Cornish
Set in Arnhem Pro and Eurostile
Printed in Slovenia

The publisher and the authors gratefully acknowledge the support of Studio Valle Architetti Associati, Dottore Ennio Brion, the Politecnico di Torino, and the Fantoni Furniture Company.

fantoni

Contents

Foreword by Joseph Rykwert   4

The Modernity of Gino Valle: Craft, Landscape and Architecture as Testimony   7

1   **Formative Experiences and Early Works (1946–51)**   59

2   **Return from Harvard (1951–58)**   73

3   **A Contextual Brutalism (1953–61)**   89

4   **From the Zanussi Offices to 'non-architecture' (1957–70)**   105

5   **Monument to the Resistance and Foundation Architecture (1959–67)**   121

6   **A First Synthesis (1961–78)**   137

7   **Large Building Complexes (1967–82)**   157

8   **Industrial Objects and Pictorial Gestures: Towards an Architecture of Pure Relationships (1972–96)**   167

9   **Low-cost Housing (1975–95)**   193

10   **Reusing, Restoring, Restructuring: Architecture as Brand (1977–99)**   213

11   **Constructing 'pieces of city' (1983–2003)**   231

12   **Urban Design and Public Buildings (1984–2003)**   247

13   **Complex Volumes and Blocks: Office Buildings (1985–2003)**   269

14   **The Architect of Major Urban Transformations (1991–2003)**   291

Biographical Notes   311
List of Works   313
Bibliography   328
Index   343
Illustration Credits   352

Foreword
Remembering Gino Valle

In introducing Pierre-Alain Croset and Luka Skansi's definitive monograph on Gino Valle and his work, something in the nature of a memoir might justify my presenting it to the English reader.

My first memory of Gino Valle is of his act of generosity: we were both at a summer school organised by CIAM, the *Congrès International de l'Architecture Moderne*, in Venice in 1952, and as a translator/student I was put up at a very cramped local youth hostel. Gino shared a sparse but more amenable flat in Campo Santa Margherita with his sisters Nani (who was to work with him and who later married another Venetian architect, Giorgio Bellavitis), and Lella (the youngest, who would marry Massimo Vignelli; they would go on to run the enormously successful New York design studio which, many years later, would be responsible for the graphics of the subway system there, as well as a vast variety of graphic and industrial designs).

All that was in the future. In the meantime, the Valles offered me the use of a spare bed in their apartment where I spent the rest of that Venetian stay. Since we were an easy-going household, it became the beginning of a friendship with the whole family. Much as I would later admire the Vignellis' work, it was Gino's architecture I found immediately entrancing. He had returned from a spell in the Jenbach concentration camp (of which he memorably said: 'architecture is easy; surviving a concentration camp is difficult') to studies in Venice – and after the spell at Harvard which gave him a personal insight into transatlantic doings, he returned to his native Friuli and joined Provino, his architect father; after he died the office would become his and he continued to work there for the rest of his life.

Of course, it was the sense of being worldly-wise, familiar with the international situation, yet rooted in his home town, in its ways, speaking its dialect – the same spoken by the masons and carpenters who put up his buildings – which gave his work some of the dialectic power that allowed him to operate with ease on the international scene. But it also bound him to the site of his work: the scaffolding was his second home.

Attachment to site and the builders' work had always been evident: and that was what I could sense in those first visits to his buildings: the Town Hall at Treppo Carnico, the Savings Bank at Latisana and the first instalment of the Zanussi offices seemed more interesting than what I had seen published of the work of most of his contemporaries. I was able to publish them in the monthly *Architecture and Building* (long since defunct). Towards the end of the 1950s I had been invited to teach at the Hochschule für Gestaltung in Ulm which had uneasily taken on the mantle of the Bauhaus and where I found myself at odds with its rather dry analytic-semiotic approach. Asked to contribute to one of their commemorative publications I demurred, explaining that my approach was rather different from that of most of my colleagues. But they insisted – we were all people of goodwill, after all.

As I expected, my contribution was turned down and I therefore took my typescript (which has since been published in several versions and other languages) to Udine which was my first stop south and showed it to Gino, who read through it. 'Of course, you are quite right', he said when he finished it, 'but if I were you I wouldn't publish it. When I say that sort of thing to any of my colleagues they treat me as a madman ...'

But publish it I did, and it became another link between us.

Meanwhile I had moved to the Royal College of Art which fortunately had an exhibition gallery in its very new building, but no exhibition programme as yet; and that allowed me to arrange an exhibition of Gino's drawings as well as photographs of executed buildings, and he was invited to deliver the RIBA Annual Discourse. The photographs were important since an English critic had published the drawings for the Rex-Zanussi works with a comment that Italians produce splendid projects which do not get built. And although no British commissions followed this otherwise very successful Anglo/Scottish visit, during this time he met Jack Coia, the last surviving partner of Honeyman and Keppie – Charles Rennie Mackintosh's office – as well as his two junior partners, who would show themselves to be splendid architects, Andrew Macmillan and Isi Metzstein.

It was sometime after this that at lunch in Giò Ponti's house (I had been working for some time on the monthly journal he founded and edited, *Domus*), somewhat ruefully, Ponti said that although I had been insisting to him on how good an architect Gino Valle was, he had taken no notice, and he now agreed – and wanted to make amends. Although I thought a generous publication in *Domus* would do that, Ponti insisted that it would be inadequate. He therefore sent me down to Udine with a photographer and the results of our visit were indeed published in *Domus*, as were his other later projects.

His very assured later work consolidated his stature and he continued building beyond the end of the century – and as long as his health permitted. Of the later work, the Palazzi di Giustizia in Padua and Brescia, the Theatre in Vicenza or the development of the University of Padua all bear witness to his continued civic engagement – as do, sometimes paradoxically, his buildings for corporate clients, which include the two shopping centres, one in Milan, the other just north of Rome. There is too, triumphantly, the redevelopment of the industrial quarter at Portello near the Fair area in Milan, now paved in a Michelangelesque reticulated fan pattern which has appropriately been named Piazza Gino Valle.

In all that work, as in his life, he was very much seconded by his wife, Piera, and there was consolation in his last days that he would be able to hand over his office to a sympathetic successor – his son Piero, who has now become the third architect Valle in Udine.

Joseph Rykwert
2018

The Modernity of Gino Valle: Craft, Landscape and Architecture as Testimony

For Gino Valle, architecture could not exist unless it was *built architecture*. He thought of his craft as an absolute commitment, designing as an incessant daily practice, sketching as a tool of thought prior to communication. In over 50 years of his professional career, from his degree thesis in 1948 to his death in 2003, his attitude to architecture did not change; it was centred on a passionate curiosity and an extraordinarily open mind, but at the same time fully focused on the concrete, real problems of constructed architecture: analysis of the programme, control of costs, skilful use of construction systems, correct insertion in the context. He liked to 'find things', citing Picasso as his artistic model,[1] but at the same time this forceful experimentalism was associated with a refusal to take *a priori* avant-garde positions.

From the outset, he was absolutely aware of his expertise and creativity as an architect, but he was never satisfied, and strived even in the final projects to improve his sensibility and his work. While his attitude and work ethic were marked by coherence and continuity, the many completed works bear witness to a surprising variety and heterogeneity: town halls and banks, factories and monuments, office buildings and residences, courthouses and shopping centres, in Udine and the smaller cities of Friuli and the Veneto, but also in big cities like New York, Berlin, Paris, Rome, Milan.

In terms of both quantity and quality, the oeuvre of Gino Valle stands out as one of the riches of Italian postwar architecture. The profound originality of many of his most successful buildings soon brought Valle to the attention of critics, starting in 1955 with his first published project, in *Casabella-Continuità*,[2] as an exceptional talent and a singular figure on the European architecture scene. This positive critical response remained constant over the years, though Valle's refusal to take ideological positions led many critics to label his work as 'impossible to classify' and 'heterodox'. Valle himself was very lucid about the apparent difficulty experienced by many critics when they tried to fit his work into pre-set 'critical cages': with a taste for polemics, he said he was very irritated by those 'critics who want to classify the work of architects, believing they can do so by taking shots to the left and right, as if they were out hunting. For these involuntary but chronic blind men, I am and wish to remain like an Indian with a feathered headdress, visible from a distance but impossible to catch'.[3] In effect, he was never 'caught' and never entered the 'star system' of contemporary architecture, in spite of the fact that he had produced large, internationally acclaimed

(*left*) Gino Valle at the solo show held at the Royal College of Art, London, 1964. In the background, images of the pillar of Arta Terme.

buildings during his career. Neither 'local' nor 'global', he seemed most at ease designing small buildings scattered in his native territory, and in one-to-one dialogue with the protagonists of international architectural culture.[4] An atypical figure of Italian design culture, which was accustomed to enforcing strict categorisation of 'professionals' and 'intellectuals', Valle was an erudite, refined designer, but also profoundly anti-academic and anti-dogmatic. In his conception of the profession as '*grande artigianato*'[5] he felt closer to Alvar Aalto and the culture of pragmatism of the English-speaking world than to the figure of the *homme de lettres*, Le Corbusier. He loved concreteness, precision, the physical character of his work, and therefore rejected the worldly rituals of the architectural establishment, irritated by the linguistic pedantry of his colleagues at the university, intolerant of intellectual dishonesty in architects and a tendency not to take responsibility for the quality of projects.[6] Esteemed for his authenticity, his design talent and the expressive intensity of his constructed works, he was supported by a few critics and historians, such as Reyner Banham, Joseph Rykwert, Kenneth Frampton and Manfredo Tafuri, and appreciated by architects such as Vittorio Gregotti, Álvaro Siza, Rafael Moneo, Luigi Snozzi and Boris Podrecca, who saw Valle as a 'travelling companion'.[7]

This book springs from the need to document, in all its fullness and rich variety, the whole of Valle's work and design activity. After the publication in 1989 of the only complete monograph,[8] there have been very few critical surveys: the first issue in 2000 of the monograph, *Lotus Navigator*,[9] covered the design activities of Gino Valle in the 1990s, while specific aspects of the work were illustrated in three posthumous exhibitions at Treppo Carnico ('Gino Valle in Carnia') and Ferrara ('Da, chez, from Gino Valle') in 2005, and in Udine ('Gino Valle: progetti e architetture per Udine, 1948–2003') in 2007.[10]

This new book sets out to reveal new insights to the oeuvre and figure of Valle, due to the discovery of important documents in the archives of the studio in Udine, which have never previously been

taken into account. Two documentary sources have provided fresh light on Valle's work. The first is the archive of Provino Valle, Gino's father and his first 'mentor', which has been found to contain many drawings by Gino, some made prior to his graduation from the Istituto Universitario Di Architettura of Venice (IUAV) in 1948. This body of drawings demonstrates intense, significant activity inside his father's studio, conducted in parallel with his studies, and thus reveals a substantial autonomy in the making of linguistic choices. These documents offer a glimpse of a precociously 'mature' and 'independent' designer[11] well before 1952, when Gino, returning from Harvard after a year of specialisation in City and Regional Planning, founded Studio Architetti Valle with his father and his sister Nani. The second documentary source has to do with the more 'private' part of the Valle archives (letters, manuscripts, photographs, written and sketched notes), which sheds light on certain less familiar aspects of his activity and personality, in particular the relations with Anglo-Saxon design culture, his activity as a product designer, his interest in urban planning as a discipline and not just as a practice, his university teaching, his relationships of friendship and intellectual exchange with certain figures of Italian and international culture.

This book is based on a particular narrative structure, organised into 14 theme chapters and 22 descriptive profiles of a selection of individual works.[12] The book does not take the form of a *catalogue raisonné* of the works, with in-depth analyses of the complex process of design development and a critical interpretation of the constructed buildings. This type of historiographic reading, though legitimate for the analysis of individual works, does not seem appropriate for the work of an architect like Gino Valle, which is particularly heterogeneous and wide-ranging, versatile and open. Instead of describing the differences (of language, programme, scale, but also context) that mark the individual works, differences at times so striking as to make us wonder if the works were made by the same architect, rather, it seems more important to reconstruct the network of relationships between the projects and the constructed works. Valle often insisted on the temporal continuity of his design activity: 'I consider my job an uninterrupted labour, a continuous flow. The design and the projects are part of this whole … The project set aside is at times picked up again, returned to the temporal flow, ceasing to be an interrupted architecture and moving once again in pursuit of achieved architecture.'[13] This temporal flow of Valle's design activity did not proceed in a linear way, but was crossed by a series of thematic threads that were explored in certain projects, then put aside and later returned to, or mixed with each other to construct new syntheses. The thematic chapters that pace the chronological narrative of Valle's work, then, are designed to reveal the network of relationships – at times, secret or deeply repressed – that exists between the individual works of architecture, demonstrating how a single theme – of form, typology, construction, function – can give rise to buildings with very different results from a linguistic standpoint. This thematic approach thus corresponds to the need to produce lines of interpretation that go beyond architectural language, and thus beyond an apparent lack of 'stylistic consistency' of which Valle's work was often accused.[14] Each chapter introduces the coverage of one or more buildings grouped by themes, and as a whole, the book simultaneously offers two interpretations of the work: while the thematic chapters illustrate the project context in which the constructed works of architecture were developed, the presentation of the selection of individual buildings reveals the material and spatial dimension of the architecture as a physical thing, a functional organism, notwithstanding the temporal process of its design.

This particular narrative structure corresponds to a critical choice, with the aim of directing the reader towards an understanding of one fundamental characteristic of Valle's architecture: the fact that it possesses certain specifically tactile and spatial qualities that can be perceived only in the experience of a real visit, and do not lend themselves to representation only through drawings and photographs. As happens with the works of Loos, Aalto or Siza, a visit to a building by Valle often

Treppo Carnico City Hall, 1956–58.

reveals a large gap between the visual and formal characteristics conveyed by photographs and the sensorial qualities of the experience of the actual space. To assist readers in imagining these specific tactile qualities and in perceiving the particular character of the building in the suitability between function and image, the descriptive texts of the profiles of the individual buildings are presented in the narrative of a visit: since they focus on certain salient moments of 'tactile experience'[15] of the architecture – in particular the paths of approach and of internal layout – these texts as a whole should provide an anthology of spatial experiences of Valle's architecture, both inside the buildings and in the relationship between building and context.

The importance of spatial experience was explicitly acknowledged by Valle:

> to start with, yes, I am a visual person, because I judge and also need to work with the hands to find something. However, what I find has another type of communication, which is what interests me … when I am in a room I am not interested in having the carpet over there or a painting hanging on the wall: I am not interested, I don't look. I am interested in the contents of the environment, not the form. In a room, I can feel good, or not: but this is completely independent of visual factors. In other words, I sense what is there under the leaf, not what you see.[16]

With these very words, Valle alluded to the relationship between his particular way of experiencing a space – 'sensing' it more than 'seeing' it – and the type of content and spatial quality he wanted to achieve in a work of architecture. Among the critics who have been most attentive to these particular tactile qualities of Valle's architecture, Joseph Rykwert aptly describes how 'the strongest impression left on the visitor by his constructions … is the awareness that walking through them, in any direction, one is always led into a succession of appealing and engaging spaces – and that this is truly an effect that is hard to attribute to signs coming from the tangible surfaces'.[17] Valle effectively insisted in his architecture on the qualification

Spatial experiences and paths in Valle's architecture: city hall of Casarsa, 1966–74.

of the elements to be walked through – ramps, staircases, entrances, corridors, passages, place of relation between spaces – while the spaces in which to remain were often marked by a certain formal neutrality. One of the most significant examples might be the city hall of Casarsa della Delizia, designed starting in 1966 and completed in 1974. If we look at the drawings and photographs, we see only a certain geometric complexity in the plan – three squares shifted on their diagonal axes – an apparently 'humble' expression of simple 'industrial boxes', yet, on visiting this building, one is immediately struck by the clarity of the paths and by a sensation of deep familiarity with the domestic scale of the architecture. This gap between image and experience is particularly evident in a series of buildings by Valle that seem to be inspired by the principles of Minimal Art, precisely because they shift the attention of the observer from the formal qualities of the object to the relationships between

object and environment. In the administrative centre of Pordenone (1972–82), for example, a visit reveals a surprising quality when walking through a system of open zones typical of authentic urban space, qualities that cannot be glimpsed by seeing only the photographs, which seem to suggest only a Gestaltist perception of the large elementary volumes. Among all the more recent buildings, perhaps the headquarters of the Deutsche Bank in Milan (1997–2005) offers the greatest perceptional surprises, especially in terms of the role this architecture plays in the surrounding urban setting and with respect to the Bicocca complex, and in the treatment of the base in shiny black stone that produces singular reflection effects as one gradually changes the vantage point.

Ascribing more importance to the contents of the experience of habitation and the spatial dimension rather than to the visual values of architecture, Valle demonstrated remarkable similarities to the design

Spatial experiences and paths in Valle's architecture: Headquarters of Deutsche Bank Italia, Milan, 1997–2005.

attitude of Alvar Aalto, though this affinity of thought never translated into direct linguistic or stylistic resemblance. What Valle discovered very early on in Aalto turned out to be decisive for the development of his anti-formalist conception of architecture:

> I have always loved Aalto; I remember seeing for the first time, in 1951 in Chicago, photographs of the city hall of Säynätsalo that had just been built, and was unknown to me. I understood a fundamental thing, namely Aalto's tendency towards the non-form, which is the key for interpretation of his architecture. I understood the discourse of non-form back then, and afterwards it always interested me: to arrive, that is, not at the form you see as the work of man, but at something that is derived from nature, that is *not read as form but only as space, and you use it only as space*.[18]

This complex and in some ways paradoxical discourse on 'non-form' represents one of the problematic nuclei of Valle's design activity. Already in 1958 Joseph Rykwert, in an essay published in the pages of *Architecture and Building*, had noticed the 'only indirectly programmatic' character of Valle's architecture, in which the elegance of a solution 'is the result of a general exploration of the problem being examined, and has nothing to do with the application of preconceived formal notions'.[19] Later, in an essay from 1963 published in the magazine *Zodiac*,[20] Giuseppe Mazzariol took up Rykwert's observation on the profoundly empirical approach of Valle to projects, proposing the identification of anti-formalism as 'the most evident characteristic of the architectural production of Gino Valle', to interpret as an 'explicit message in the whole oeuvre of the architect from Udine'. This anti-formalism was not to be considered an aesthetic category, according to Mazzariol,[21] connected with the linguistic character of the work, but as a moral category, linked to the personality of Valle as an artist and an intellectual:

> Valle's antiformalism is first of all a fundamental component of his moral personality; *he is a convinced layman* ... There is a claim always present in Valle's architectural action which might simply be defined as a desire for liberty, to get beyond schemes, to apply formulas to new contents to demonstrate, with open-minded intelligence, their efficiency or lack of timeliness.[22]

This 'desire for liberty' has often been cited by critics as one of the most characteristic features of Gino Valle's thought and design activity. Germano Celant, on this subject, spoke of a 'subjective adventure, without restrictions',[23] and it is no coincidence that Valle willingly used the term 'testimony' borrowed from the vocabulary of phenomenology, because he thought it was 'the most suitable to name, or more precisely to describe, what has been and continues to be'[24] his work. Celant also proposed listening to certain verbal 'testimony' of Valle, related to given projects, to demonstrate how his architecture was based on

View of the installation of the exhibition *Gino Valle Architetto* at the Basilica of Vicenza, curated by Pierre-Alain Croset in 1989.

an experience lived 'personally', always open and ready to 'overflow its boundaries'. As an example, Valle wrote that

> the hot springs facility at Arta represents an autobiographical discourse, since I spent my summers in Arta as a child. Therefore, my intervention at the spa has a storybook reference, the Castle. There I deliberately chose the reference to the castle and immersed myself in the theme with great confusion, though I found my way out of it, in the end, and it was an important experience. For the red house [the house on Via Mercatovecchio] in Udine the same reasoning applies: here it is the filtered memory of medieval Udine, with its wooden houses.[25]

Although this autobiographical dimension should be prudently assessed to avoid historiographical misunderstandings,[26] the written and oral statements of Valle also represent for us a fundamental documentary resource which helps to reconstruct an interpretative path through his drawings, and in particular the personally made sketches, and identify the network of ideas and themes that connect the projects and the completed works to each other.

How Valle communicated his design thinking was complex and often contradictory. On the one hand, he felt the need to conserve large shadowy areas in his work, significantly asserting that 'mystery is important for me and should remain what it is by definition: something that cannot be explained, but the hunt for mystery is the motivation of the work. This is the obscure zone'.[27] When faced with critics' questions, Valle was not always loquacious, and he explained his reticence and silences by comparing the trade of the architect to that of the chef: 'I am a great chef, and like all great chefs, I have my tricks and my secrets. I can only explain the mechanics of the operative process to you.'[28] This reluctance was not only connected with a certain characteristic reserve, but also had to do with several deeper mechanisms of his creativity that Valle did not want to make too explicit.[29] On the other hand, he

could not stand excessively 'literary' interpretations of his work, and therefore he willingly narrated the evolutionary process of a project, especially where the constructive choices were concerned, with very clear and concrete explanations. He did this at public conferences, university lectures and in interviews, but also during works visits: while it is true that Valle wrote very little compared to other Italian architects of his generation like De Carlo, Gregotti, Gabetti or Rossi, his many oral statements can be seen as a precious resource offering insights to the passions and stimuli that went into his architectural thinking. Another oral source of information that has been useful to us comes from the people who lived and worked with him: first of all Piera Ricci Menichetti,[30] his wife since 1961 and a partner of Studio Valle, and thus the most precious witness on a design level and a human level, and his son Pietro Valle,[31] now both owners of Studio Architetti Valle in Udine, which takes the legacy of Gino forward with the group of trusted staff,[32] but

Poster for the exhibition *Studio Valle* at the Royal College of Art, London, 1964.

also with architects who worked in association with the studio: Giorgio Macola[33] in Venice and Paris, Mario Broggi and Michael Burckhardt[34] in Milan.

One of the most singular aspects of Valle's personality regards the extreme variety of the formal, compositional, but also layout and construction solutions explored during the preparation of a project. The drawings archive reveals, in many cases, surprising design variations, some of which are quite the opposite of the final solutions, which Valle explored without any a priori exclusions, as if to verify the correctness of the final choices starting with the multiplication of the original hypotheses, while in other cases radical changes reflected a desire to challenge apparent certainties. Among the most spectacular examples illustrated in this book, we can recall the three projects for the Zanussi offices (1957–61), the two projects for the Arta spa (1960–64), the series of as many as eight projects for the Rinascente headquarters in Milan (1967–72), the settlement variants for the administrative centre of Pordenone (1972–82) and the headquarters of Deutsche Bank at

Milan-Bicocca (1997). In an interview in 1970, Valle described this 'open' and 'experimental' way of designing:

> I never know where I will end up when I start a project … and you never know what the results will be like. This is what interests me. I know nothing, absolutely nothing about what will happen when I begin a project. I never envision anything. I find it, and this interests me very much. And the older I get, the more experience I have, the better I understand that this is my job, to find things.[35]

The drawings effectively demonstrate the complexity of Valle's procedure through the design materials, a way of proceeding that Fulvio Irace has compared to that of a diviner who

with crafted tools probes the roughness of the land to renew the miracle of discovery. A tactile experience of the place and of architecture

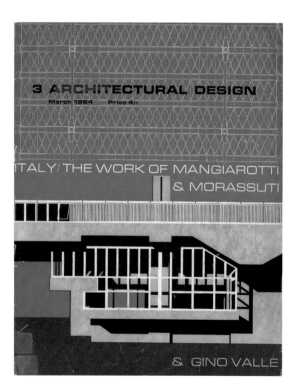

Cover of *Architectural Design* (March 1964) with the stylised image of the facade of the Zanussi offices, an issue entirely devoted to the work of Mangiarotti-Morassutti and Valle.

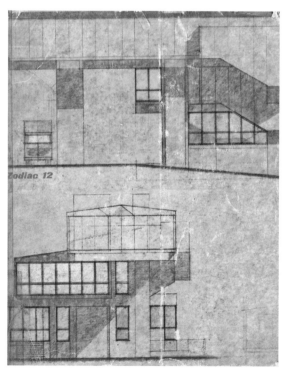

Cover of *Zodiac*, 12 (October 1963), with drawings for the Zanussi offices at Porcia.

requires long passage inside the suspensions of design, a capacity to linger, to dawdle, maybe only to catch one's breath for a final leap forward, that of the finished product. Nevertheless, it is clear that precisely in the digressions of that design by wandering we can find the most authentic essence of his approach to architecture.[36]

Irace correctly recognises, in this avowedly experimental attitude, but one that is also strongly rooted in the place and its productive conditions, the affirmation of a figure of the architect 'a thousand miles away from the figure of the ascetic prophet that remains the most fitting metaphor of the avant-garde architect today'.

Nevertheless, we should be careful about interpreting the portrait Valle offered of himself as an 'architect who never envisions anything beforehand'. While it is true that Valle's buildings often display marked and significant differences from one another, also in the same time period, the differences can nearly always be explained

in rational terms. For Valle, 'never envisioning anything' did not mean starting over from scratch each time. Over the years and with more experience, in fact, Valle had achieved certainties, above all: his insistence on 'finding things' as his centre of interest was profoundly linked to a constant interest in the relations between architecture and environment, building and landscape, project and place. This interest in, and sensibility for, the environment had been cultivated in Valle ever since childhood, during long bicycle rides with his father who encouraged him to observe the Friuli landscape; it was further stimulated (while at Harvard in 1951) by reading a text by Patrick Abercrombie[37] on the practice and experience of Chinese Feng Shui, which thereafter became a 'fetish' text and companion, mentioned in many interviews.[38] Undoubtedly inspired by Feng Shui, Valle associated the experimental attitude of 'finding things' with a sensitivity to the specific characteristics of places and he explained this way of acting by using an evocative metaphor: 'when I

The comments of Reyner Banham regarding the Vriz tower ('Tall Block in Trieste') in *The Architectural Review*, 742 (1958).

Cover of *Casabella*, 519 (December 1985) with drawing of the entrance arch of the IBM offices at La Défense, Paris (detail).

start a project, I start to go scratching around the place. And with experience, I have learned more and more how to have the nose for scratching, like a dog that finds truffles. I go scratching until I find something, like extracting it from the earth. The more experience I gain, the more truffles I find!'[39]

This quote partially corrects Valle's previous statement of 'absolutely not knowing what will happen' when he started a project. This rather ideological assertion was actually contradicted by some interesting experiments he conducted over the course of the 1960s and 1970s on the possibility of a 'reproducible' architecture, linked to the use of prefabricated construction parts (the Zanussi standard warehouse and equipped axis, the Valdadige schools). And in spite of his often harsh criticism of a recognisable brand image promoted by many contemporary architects,[40] in the last 15 years of his career he had accepted, in a clearer way than previously, the principle that different projects could develop as variations and evolutions of the same theme, as demonstrated, for example, by the variegated series of large office complexes in the 1980s and 1990s.

On various occasions, Valle had also tried to clarify lines of continuity present in his work: the first was in 1960, when *Casabella* included an assessment of the first ten years of activity of Studio Valle;[41] the second came in 1965, when he was invited to deliver the Annual Lecture at RIBA in London;[42] a third was in 1970, in the form of a long interview for the magazine *Zodiac*.[43] Many years later, in 1992 Valle wrote an autobiographical note to accompany a nomination form for an important international architecture prize.[44] This document seems to suggest that Valle had attempted to identify a thematic core, a red thread that could sum up all of his complex design research. Valle stated, in fact, that all his architecture had been constantly oriented towards the pursuit of a language 'profoundly rooted in the thing itself, specific to place and circumstance', and that each new project had contributed to enrich his 'storehouse of experience' all the way to reaching the Zanussi offices (1957–61) as the 'first mature work, unifying language and place in a single architecture'.[45] In this significant document, Valle no longer spoke of the

need to 'start over from scratch each time', though he did acknowledge, as in previous statements, that after the success of the Zanussi offices, he went through a profound methodological and expressive crisis that coincided with the design of the city hall of Jesolo (1962), which was never built. This profound crisis represented the only true discontinuity and break in his path of research, leading to a completely new line of work which Valle himself called 'non-architecture', conceived for industrialised buildings that could exist in any place but would have 'a language clear and coherent in form and material'.[46] Therefore this crisis turned out to be very productive, prompting Valle to return 'with a deeper vision' to his original interest in the relationship between language and place, arriving at the more mature works of the 1980s that 'replaced steel with stone' and 'do not reflect the space of the immediate past' but seek contact with the 'tacit traces of a cultural place covered by centuries of habitation'. Valle concluded by presenting his latest works 'in stone' not as a break with the previous works, but as the result of a slow, continuous evolution: 'With each project Valle continues to sharpen his sense, his ability to scratch and dig beyond the patina of the immediate past to discover an architecture coherent in form, material and space, which does not represent the place but is the place in all its qualities.'[47]

This 'symbiotic relationship between the language of architecture and the specific qualities of the place' therefore represents the most authentic character of continuity to be found in his work. This forcefully contradicts one of the most widespread clichés among critics, who, faced with the difficulty of classifying a production seen as 'unclassifiable',[48] have ended up using the presumed eclecticism of Valle as an alibi for the failure to attempt any hypothesis of overall critical interpretation. It also contradicts another historiographical misunderstanding that arises in the proposal of observing, in the works of the 1980s, and in particular the projects for Venice, New York and Paris, the rise of a 'second manner of Valle' that apparently makes a break with the previous works.[49] This attempt to force a subdivision of Valle's output into multiple 'periods' does not seem pertinent if we observe the individual works of architecture with their contexts and the design methods effectively applied by Valle, which often link together works done even in very separate time periods. Therefore the interpretations proposed by Manfredo Tafuri in 1985, indicating a 'new manner of great interest, also on a methodological level',[50] starting with works like the housing in Venice-Giudecca and the office complex in Paris-La Défense; by Pierluigi Nicolin in 1989, seeing a passage from the 'well-known experimentalism of Valle' to a 'second manner' with respect to which 'the categories applied to explain the previous works no longer make sense';[51] by Francesco Moschini in 1991, who believes that Valle 'only in the most recent works' has gone beyond a (supposed) 'conception of the autonomy of the architectural object to understand it instead inside a shattered *ordo urbis* in which the works of architecture reflect each other as parts of a purely arbitrary metropolitan system';[52] but also by Vittorio Gregotti, much later, in 2005, who saw a late focus, 'starting perhaps with the Bicocca project in 1987', on Valle's part regarding 'the theme of urban design in recent years', in contradiction to the entire career of the architect 'entirely oriented towards the physical consistency of architecture as a finished object, though with the rightful exceptions of Pordenone or Venice',[53] would all seem to be controversial.

Nevertheless, it is clear that Valle's figure has yet to be sufficiently analysed in historical terms. One of the goals of this book is to demonstrate not only the deep contiguity of his work with certain important themes approached by international architectural culture, but also and above all to reveal the particularities and complexities of the ways in which he gave concrete expression to these themes in the individual works of architecture. There are qualities that, seen in terms of single chapters or single projects, are not immediately discernible: Valle's work, finally gathered and seen as a whole, inserted in the historical conditions of the discipline and seen in its light, begins to reveal its own surprising richness, its many facets and its historical value.

Valle's output, as we have seen, has been taken into consideration by a number of illustrious critics and historians, though only in an episodic manner. In most cases a linguistic interpretation

has prevailed, which is insufficient to understand the complexity of his work. Rather than constituting opportunities for an overall in-depth examination of his career, Valle's works are often used by individual authors to construct other 'histories', and drawn into preordained historical-critical discourses, outside the specific context of the biography of the architect. But Valle's work deserves to be explored as a whole, because it makes it possible to reveal the historical importance of themes and experiences of research that have been only partially appreciated or insufficiently explored in the narratives of a general character of recent historiography. Just consider, for example, the fact that any history of prefabrication in Italy cannot be separated from the long research conducted by Valle in the industrial field (here we can cite the work for the facilities of Zanussi, Scala, Fantoni, Bergamin, Eco), in the residential field (IACP in Udine, Giudecca) or in the area of scholastic design (the Valdadige experience). At the same time, an exhaustive history of urban planning in Italy cannot help but address his research in many 'guideline plans' in the 1980s and 1990s, or the paradigmatic responses to the issues of shopping centres and large-scale projects in the constructions at Milan-Portello and Rome-Bufalotta. A similar statement could be applied to his activities in the field of product design: though the architect himself did not 'love' it and repeatedly took his distance from the world of industrial design, he made an important contribution, as demonstrated by the objects he designed for Solari and Zanussi, as acknowledged by many critical works and retrospectives, since the start of the 1960s.[54]

Though the figure of Valle has not been an important reference point in narratives of Italian postwar architecture,[55] it is interesting to notice, on the other hand, the extent to which some of his projects have promoted, immediately after their completion, a reaction of critics who have underlined their particular meaning and, in some cases, historical importance. Besides the already mentioned contributions of Samonà and Tentori, one of the first cases of praise of the figurative and spatial nature of Valle's work can be found in the words of Bruno Zevi, published in 1959 in the magazine *L'Espresso*. His interpretation of the results of the competition for the monument to the Resistance at Udine is explicit: Valle's proposal is seen as 'dramatic and brilliant' as a sophisticated and in many ways unique response to the 'symbolic concern' the event of the Resistance prompted in the Italian postwar artistic and architectural context. Zevi, by way of Valle's project, underlined how 'an event like the Resistance is best evoked with abstract forms', without 'the almost nauseating abuse of symbols' of current practice, recognising the highest value of the work precisely in the complexity of the proposal: 'the project's merits lie in the fact that it resolves a difficult urban planning problem' while at the same time it 'has situated the celebrative and ceremonial place at the centre of the monument, and no longer in a space surrounding the monumental object'.[56]

On multiple occasions from the late 1950s to the mid-1960s the young Valle was noticed by English architectural culture, which was particularly critical of Italian architecture at the time, first of all by Reyner Banham on the pages of *Architectural Review*.[57] Both the Zanussi offices and the Vriz tower in Trieste were hailed as rare and therefore promising results arriving from the Italian context in the 1950s and 1960s, because they avoided that tendency which the English critic defined as the generalised Italian ideological practice of a 'return to the good old days before the Modern Movement'.[58] Not by chance, Banham compared the Vriz tower to the Torre Velasca of the group BBPR, praising it as a more coherent and refined operation of insertion of contemporary architecture in historical urban contexts, with respect to the tower in Milan. Joseph Rykwert, in the first in-depth analysis of the work of Valle in an international magazine, constructed his essay around the same critical keys as Banham:[59] he described the output of Studio Valle as 'superlative and tenacious', particularly when considered inside the 'trivial and aseptic historicism' found in the language of Italian contemporary architects. A less acute but still significant assessment of the work of Valle was supplied by another English critic, Kenneth Frampton, in his famous essay 'Prospects for a Critical Regionalism' in 1983.[60] Rather than focusing on the nature of Valle's refined contextualism,

which was far from linguistic and iconic, Frampton proposed comparing the work of the architect from Friuli – seen through certain early works like the Quaglia house at Sutrio, the Zanussi offices and the Arta spa – to the work of Utzon, Ungers, Gregotti, Fehn and Scarpa, putting it into historical context in the by-then famous framework of the 'regionalist' tendency of an entire generation of European architects in the postwar era that in Frampton's view were critical of the phenomena of universalisation of architectural language.

Manfredo Tafuri devoted short but extremely interesting observations to two distinct moments in Valle's career. Observing the Zanussi offices, Tafuri recognised the ability to 'masterfully' approach the theme of the image of the industrial client, inserting Valle in a much larger context of 'high Italian professionalism' – together with Viganò, Figini-Pollini, Caccia-Dominioni – which he considered 'courageous' and an alternative 'to the tormented appeals of Italian high architectural culture': for Tafuri, the value of Valle's first work lies in the 'anti-intellectualism content with its correct and confident insertion in the world of production', while 'the geographically peripheral position [of Valle], but in direct contact with concrete clientele, distances him from the reigning ideologies but also from the autobiographical vogue'.[61]After all, Tafuri was one of the first to notice the positive results of Valle's research in the field of urban design, for which he expressed praise.[62]

While the architectural work connected with urban themes over the course of the 1980s was widely covered on the pages of *Casabella* directed by Gregotti, the study of the constructive aspects of Valle's buildings on the part of Sergio Poretti comes as a surprise. It is significant that his history of construction in postwar Italy concludes with an appreciation, in historiographic terms, of the housing at Giudecca: an emblematic complex, in Poretti's view, that recovers and at the same time reinterprets the Italian tradition of construction, in which the architect is still able to supervise the worksite and the construction processes, and through them governs the final results of the project:

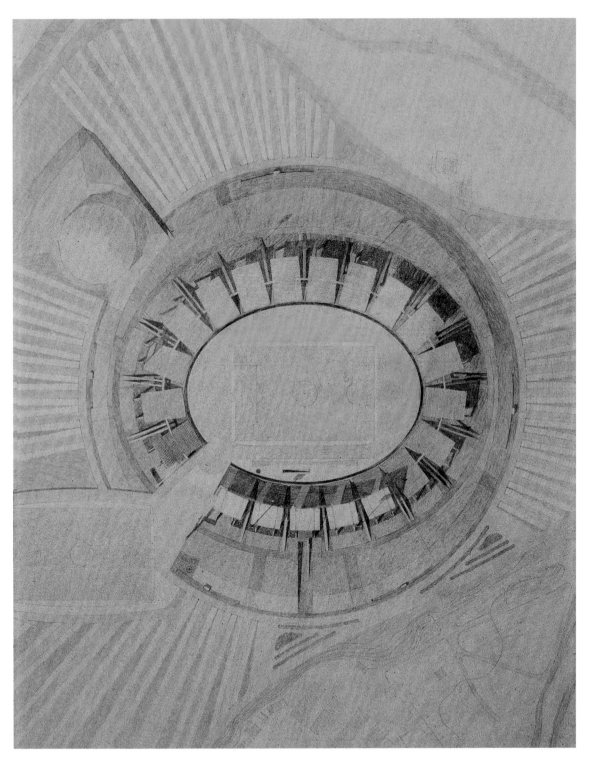

Competition project for the Udine stadium, 1971. Coloured pencils on heliographic copy
(drawing by Alfredo Carnelutti).

The authentically load-bearing masonry of exposed brick and the clearly displayed system of basic elements of the masonry construction underline the vital survival of traditional masonry in the present phase. The precision of the construction elements and their assembly, the brick – never split – that functions as a module, the prefabricated pieces in reinforced concrete that form architraves, thresholds, handrails, eaves, grafted into the masonry volume and kept perfectly flush with the outer surface, introduce a timely note of abstract, scientific precision in the crafted construction.[63]

Construction, prefabrication, linguistic freedom, a never transitive contextualism, urban meaning of architecture, management of complex

processes and professionalism are the themes that coexist, always in different ways, in the work and design methods of Gino Valle – a coexistence that makes the historiographical interpretation of his output more problematic, and does not permit the nonchalant use of the parameters generally available to understand and to explain its wealth and multiple branches. In this sense, Boris Podrecca, in a commemoration of the architect after his death, recognised the work and the attitude of Valle as clearly in contrast with the 'official' culture of Italian architecture: 'The empirical behaviour of Gino Valle and his "antidogmatic commitment" have for almost half a century contributed to a vital disquiet, without rigidity, in the Italian landscape marked by extreme stylemes … From my subjective viewpoint, he was

the most important and lively Italian architect of the Modern in the post-war era.'[64]

Besides providing documentary evidence to the most significant part of an immense oeuvre that lasted over fifty years, this book sets out to emphasise the many topical aspects of Valle's production, both in terms of methods and project practices, and in terms of specifically architectural phenomena: many of the works remain relevant and topical, a quality that can be directly related to the importance assigned by the architect to the temporal dimension of the design experience. One distinctive trait of his works was their way of indirectly conveying, in an anti-ideological and non-programmatic way, his qualified contribution on many of the central questions for international architectural culture after World War II: the relationship between new architecture and place; the use of prefabrication as a meaningful constructive language; the dialogue between architecture, geography and landscape; the role of the architectural project in urban transformation, with the renewed relationship between architecture and urban planning; the proposal of an architecture of great semantic value conveyed to motorists in motion; the ability to act on complex processes of urban transformation. Therefore the book presents an imaginary dialogue between the 'viewpoint of the producer' and the 'viewpoint of the user'[65] that encourages getting beyond a linguistic or excessively fragmented reading of the single works, precisely to show how exemplary and singular, in the postwar history of European architecture, is the work of Valle as a whole.

Nevertheless, it is clear that only through more specific analytical studies, necessarily more limited in their field of investigation, will it be possible to bring out the complexity of a design process, reconstructing in a necessarily detailed way the phases that lead to a given formal expression and to the concrete construction of the building.[66] Thanks to the documentary resources of the Valle archives, though they are composed of heterogeneous and varied materials, a further expansion of knowledge of the work of Gino Valle will be possible in the future.[67]

To conclude this essay, we present seven themes of interpretation that cross specific aspects of Valle's personality, his way of working, his thought, his conception of the profession and the experience of the architect, relying to a great extent on archival documents. Through this, we hope to stimulate a new generation of historians and critics to propose interpretative hypotheses that are no longer based on 'ideological' readings and labels, but instead on the comparison of archival sources and constructed works, recalling a precious bit of advice from Sandro Marpillero: 'The relationship between Valle and his work was like a bonfire ... and yet, it is in the constructed architecture that the enigma of Valle's work is stored. A work never willing to be exploited, nor easy to understand without crossing it in person, through its internal variants and surprising resonations.'[68]

(*left*) Zanussi offices in Porcia, 1957-61. Southern facade towards the Pontebbana road.

Valle with his father Provino, late 1940s.

Architect, Craftsman, Designer, Intellectual

In various ways, Gino Valle was representative of the 'cultured professional' typical of Italian post-war architecture, and he often remarked on how he had been influenced, beginning his activity as an architect, by the profoundly pragmatic view his father Provino had of the profession.[69] Accompanying his father to worksites since childhood, he had acquired a taste for building but also understood the importance of the concrete relationship with clients, because his father had transmitted to him the conviction that 'the architect is he who transforms into stone the needs, dreams and money of the priest, the banker, the bourgeois, and so he has a great responsibility, because those needs and dreams become stones, which remain in time'.[70] Actually this stated continuity with the work of his father happened only in terms of professional ethics, and was quickly contradicted after Provino's death in 1955, when Gino found himself in the condition of having 'destroyed all of my father's clients with my attitude, which was different'.[71] His relationship with clients, indeed, was different, and he spoke of them in critical, even brutal terms, asserting the need to 'educate, coerce' the client, because the latter 'is always wrong, because if that were not the case he wouldn't need you. If the architect fails to give the client something more than what was expected, more than what he knows about, he might as well not be an architect, because he is useless, his work becomes an automatic thing, like industrial production.'[72] Already during his training Valle had been through discontinuous and contradictory experiences, far from any reassuring 'continuity' with the professional activity of Provino: a short but lively artistic activity that made him the protagonist of certain exhibitions on a local and national level, but also a traumatic period of wartime imprisonment in Germany that taught him to 'conserve respect and self-esteem to be able to respect others'[73] and to survive with the job of a 'mechanical designer' in a factory that made motors. In his youth these experiences had a deep impact on Valle in the formation of his expertise and abilities

as an architect, in complementary ways: while the experience of the 'painter' developed an exceptional capacity for visual observation and sensitivity to the characteristics of places, lighting and proportions, the experience of the 'mechanical designer' taught him an extraordinary precision in draughtsmanship while offering initial contact with the processes of industrial production.

Another decisive factor was the year spent on a postgraduate course in City and Regional Planning at Harvard, which allowed Valle not only to widen his cultural horizons, but also to better identify the central motivations of his professional activity. In spite of the high level of specialisation of this American training, Valle never became an 'urbanist'. A series of letters sent from the US to his sister Nani[74] offers a very interesting glimpse into the intellectual and professional relationship between Gino and his sister, but also of his particular mood during the stay in America. Very critical of the Harvard academic establishment, in these letters Valle conveyed the image of a 'poor student planner' who envied his sister 'as an architect' who had stayed in Udine to develop the projects begun prior to Valle's departure: 'I can't wait to get back to my red studio, even if there may be a brawl [or fight] because you also are a big boss.'[75] In these letters they also discussed project solutions in detail, especially for the Istituto Tecnico in Udine, whose design was proceeding after winning a competition in 1950, demonstrating how concerned Valle was about controlling the work of the studio from a distance, but also how central architectural projects were for him, rather than urban planning.[76]

After having interrupted relations with his father's clients, Valle managed to find himself a

(*right*) Gino and Nani Valle, late 1940s.

new clientele in the world of industry, first as a consultant product designer, with rapid success: with the company Solari starting in 1954 (Compasso d'Oro award in 1956 for the Cifra 5 electric clock, and in 1963 for the alphanumeric flap displays), and with Zanussi starting in 1956 (Compasso d'Oro in 1962 for the Rex 700 stove). Valle later stopped designing products, even stating that the activity of the 'designer' had never interested him as such.[77] At the start of the 1950s the young architect, however, found himself in a different situation. Having refused by ethical choice to work for the private real estate market which, in a period of growth, offered many possibilities for professional advance, he had to find an activity that would guarantee the economic survival of the studio without sacrificing his freedom, both in the choice of clients and in the assertion of his own convictions. Product design represented just such an opportunity, and Valle also knew how to nurture a demand for quality in this industrial clientele. In this way, he was able to establish a lasting relationship with an industrial client and to influence his choices which led to opportunities in the field of architecture. The case of Zanussi is a good example of such a relationship, since Valle was effectively able to extend his role as a consultant to provide interventions at all levels related to the corporate image: from the design of objects to that of production plants and other facilities (offices, service centres, warehouses).

The idea of a labour of 'qualificazione' or 'upgrading' has often been called into play to describe Valle's activity in the industrial field, but it is important to observe the way such qualification focused as a priority not on the design of the object, but on that of its production processes. Pier Carlo Santini was one of the first to point out how important it was for Valle to know how to move 'inside the system and in the relationships of production of the system', in such a way as to understand which things 'had to be done better' to 'represent a communication that would make

Gino and Nani Valle meet Ernest Hemingway, 9 April 1954, Ristorante Friuli on Piazza XX Settembre in Udine.

the structure advance'.[78] Whether it was for a refrigerator or a factory, Valle therefore identified upgrading with an action of modernisation and rationalisation of the production process: for example, where product design had previously been assigned to an external consultant, Valle introduced the significant innovation of an in-house design division as part of Zanussi; where, in an internal construction firm, production had previously been made with 'artisanal' means, for the first time he proposed using prefabricated parts from external industrial construction firms, achieving decidedly better results in terms of economics and in terms of functional flexibility.

Valle developed the most lasting and productive relationships with private clients, first with 'family'-owned industries and companies of the initial economic 'boom' like Zanussi, Fantoni and Bergamin, and later with large multinational corporations like IBM and Olivetti, and also Banca Commerciale Italiana and Deutsche Bank, to the point of becoming one of the leading 'specialists' in the design of office buildings in Europe. However, he also worked for public clients, both in the small rural towns of Friuli and in more important cities like Venice, Brescia, Vicenza and Padua, which offered the opportunity to combine architectural and urban design. Though Valle himself often spoke of the need for an architecture that was 'produced honestly, as an honest trade or an honest craft',[79] the portrait drawn of him by Tafuri still seems excessive, when he speaks of an 'anti-intellectualism content with its correct and confident insertion in the world of production', asserted by Valle in

(*top*) Solari alphanumeric split-flap displays showing departures in the TWA terminal of JFK Airport in New York (early 1960s); (*bottom left*) Solari alphanumeric split-flap displays (1960), the parts of a line of information, conceived for separate installation; (*bottom right*) Design for Solari: Cifra 3 (1966).

(*top*) Dator 6 horizontal (1958); (*middle*) Dator 10 (1961); (*bottom*) Cifra 5 (1954).

response to the 'tormented appeals of Italian high architectural culture'.[80] Though referring mainly to the Zanussi offices completed in 1961, this quotation seems symptomatic of how many critics have artificially constructed the false myth of Valle only as a 'builder' and 'craftsman', far from the image of the artist-intellectual of many protagonists of that so-called 'high culture' of architecture in Italy. Valle did not feel the need to assert his identity as an 'intellectual'[81] separate from that of the architect, and for this reason he preferred to take part in the disciplinary debate with constructed buildings rather than written essays. Nevertheless, he did not shirk his responsibilities as an 'intellectual' when he stated what he thought in an absolutely direct and at times brutal way, disrupting the rituals based on codes of silence of academic and professional culture.

A systematic analysis of his large library proved very useful in shedding light on the breadth of his intellectual curiosity, with a particular focus on literature and poetry, the Anglo-Saxon empirical philosophers, and the history of art. The experience of solitude that went together with his character as a diffident, restless and secret intellectual was fundamental to his work as an architect, as we read in a letter to Piera Ricci Menichetti in which he wrote about the 'many jobs I have done alone, with tremendous passion',[82] and even more in this other singular confession:

I nurse, I nurse work, I am crazy and I am seriously crazy. I have always scorned the artist as such and I'm in it up to my neck, at this point when someone survives himself, he is an artist, he is a monster. There is so much hard, cruel force in me and all this has a meaning, I paint strange colours on panels, all lovely, glued on blockboards, but they seem to be blurred, they don't convince me, there is something wrong, and the colours bring them alive, it is a still ambiguous life, it is like opening a small glimpse into mystery, but they are mine, they are myself, there can be no doubt of that, I hate them savagely to make them live, they are mine, my creatures.[83]

In Valle's Workshop

Studio Valle in Udine, since the early 1950s, was organised as a modern crafts workshop,[84] a place of production and training for young staffers, but also a place of cultural reference. The

Studio Valle, in the Bisaro building on Viale Venezia.

description of the workplace, its organisation, the professional figures and objects it contained, can offer precious information. The first was the 'red studio' on Viale Venezia, at the base of the Bisaro apartment building which was completed in 1950 and contained within a rectangular prism. Federico Marconi[85] joined the studio in 1955, when Provino was still working there, a 'silent, vigilant personality who watched the rise in the profession of his children Gino and Nani with a combination of pride and concern'.[86] Marconi remembers that there were only four drawing tables at the time: the innermost was occupied by Gino, the others by Nani Valle and the English architect Donald Appleyard,[87] while in the sector towards Viale Venezia stood Provino's table and the 'computation and estimates department, commanded by the geometer Umberto Sgobaro'.[88] Marconi confirms that the new ideas brought by Gino from the US had 'changed the cultural climate of Studio Valle, previously marked by a traditional, reassuring

physiognomy, above all for the Carnic clientele that represented the most solid base for the work of the studio in the field of planning and public works'.[89] In this same period, Francesco Tentori, who had met Valle in 1952 in Venice during Le Corbusier's lecture at the CIAM summer school, began to frequent the studio. Eight years younger, Tentori recalled how, for him and a small group of architecture students from Friuli, Gino and Nani constituted a point of reference during their studies. The place in the studio that fascinated him most was the mezzanine, which contained a library with many magazines and a corner with seating for conversation: 'When I was in Udine, on my own or with one or two friends, I would go to the studio to ask Gino something or with the pretext of wanting to look at a magazine. We would go up to the mezzanine, greeting Gino's father who went on working, without answering, and we would sit in the armchairs to converse.'[90] The fact that the studio library was an abundant resource was a legacy from Provino's studio, so much so that Gino remembered not only making use of it during his studies, but also astonishing Samonà and Scarpa when he showed them 'my father's old magazines, where there was Wright, or Scharoun, or Neutra, practically unknown'.[91] Studio Valle was therefore a culturally up-to-date place and Tentori narrates that in 1959, when he was a young member of the editorial staff of *Casabella* studying recent architecture of the United States, it was Valle who advised him:

> By now Wright belongs to the past of architecture, so if you have a passion for American architecture, why don't you focus on Louis Kahn? And he sang the praises of the art gallery in New Haven and the plan for Philadelphia. He told me about a recent issue of *Architectural Forum* and was the first to tell me about *Perspecta*, the magazine of Yale University ... and this is just one example of how much I owe, as a student to a mentor, to Gino Valle. He taught without making it weighty, like a conversation between friends.[92]

(*right*) Competition project for the Monument to the Resistance of Udine, 1959, urban placement (drawing Alfredo Carnelutti).

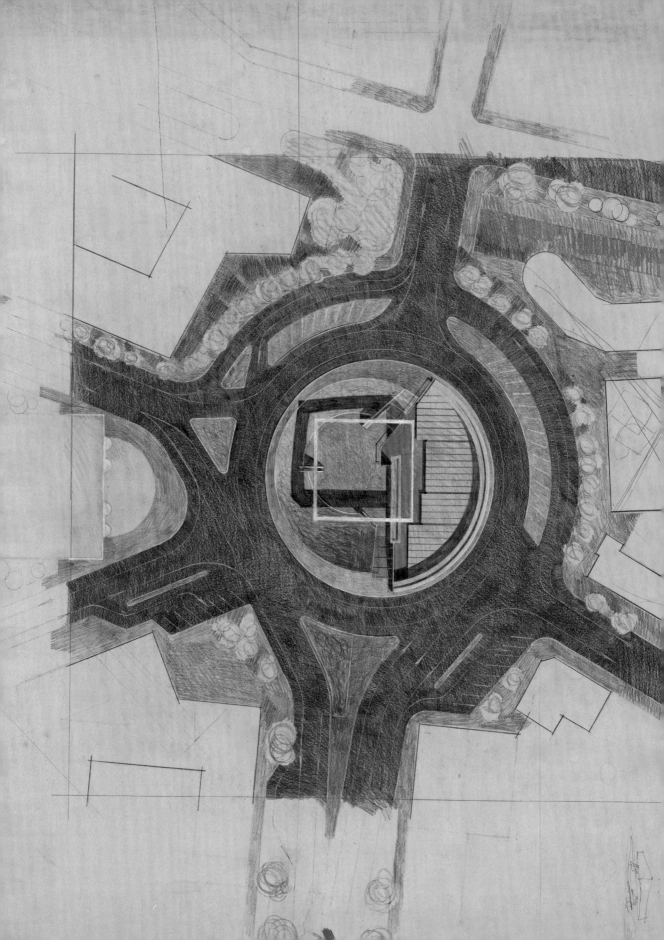

Valle in the studio on Piazza 1° Maggio in Udine, 1982.

A photograph of the studio on Viale Venezia was published in 1964 by Joseph Rykwert to illustrate a feature on recent works in the magazine *Architectural Design*.[93] During those same years, Nino Tenca Montini, an architect from Udine, worked in the studio as a student,[94] and he remembers that 'being an intern of Studio Valle was different from an apprenticeship in an architectural practice today', just as the working tools were different, 'with the "boss's" wooden drafting table, the Kuhlmann drafting tables with counterweights, the shelves, the filing cabinets for drawings, the Olivetti electromechanical adding machine and typewriter [...]; with the pencils, rapidographs, tracing paper and Swedish paper, the Dia-Master and "radex" copies to scratch with a blade, oil paints spread on the back of the tracing paper with cotton'.[95] In the same remarks, Montini remembers the great importance of the precision of drawings, which had to be made 'quickly and well, with the precise purpose of serving for the construction, done in a very close relationship between studio design and reality, covering technical and economic aspects, without ever sacrificing experimentation, seeking "coherency" and efficiency, fundamental characteristics of the

architecture of Gino Valle'. To this end, a decisive role was always played by staff with a background in technical drawing: Tenca Montini recalls Alfredo Carnelutti, Nelson Zizzutto and Adelchi De Cillia, and sees the later presence in the studio in Udine of their sons Marco [Carnelutti], Francesco [De Cillia] and Robert [Zizzutto] as 'a continuity that is also a guarantee of the quality of the architecture in itself'.

While the intensity of the work steadily increased towards the end of the 1960s, Studio Valle always remained a small 'artisanal' structure, with the drafting table at the centre of every activity. Even in the 1980s, with the advent of very large worksites far from familiar contexts of work, Valle's way of operating did not change, as he preferred to open associated studios in Milan, Venice and Paris[96] rather than to greatly increase the number of staff in Udine. Valle had already experienced the possibility of working in the United States in 1965–68, becoming a partner of Unimark International founded by Massimo Vignelli and Bob Noorda, although the projects he worked on, a residential tower in Chicago and a factory in Denver, were never built.[97] In 1970 the studio, combined with Valle's home, moved to Piazza Primo Maggio in an arrangement that underwent additions as the volume of work increased. Alessandro Rocca has described the architectural characteristics of this small, rural building, originally constructed in 1580, as 'almost little more than a tollhouse of bygone days' that became the centre of life and work of Gino, his family and his staff.

> In the portico, decorated by a rainbow by the painter Carlo Ciussi, there were two simple, identical rustic doors, one painted red for the studio, the other blue for the house. The two doors led to a village formed by a series of small additions made over time situated around a courtyard, a leftover space transformed into a garden. [...] The centre of the studio was on the lower level of the main house, behind the portico; a sequence of large rooms occupied by drafting tables [...]. On the walls and tables,

and on the floor, an anthology of photographs, newspaper clippings, sketches and drawings, written notes; objects of study and affection that accumulated in keeping with the progress of ideas, memories and projects. Nothing picturesque, no compositional gestures, simply the anarchic depositing of traces of a continuous exchange between outside and inside, between Valle and others, between professional identity and the most personal facts of everyday life.[98]

Among these 'personal facts of everyday life' design sketches stood out, made on a daily basis and scribbled on the margins of project panels, but also on scraps of paper, the back of envelopes or concert programmes, without ever taking on any fetish value for Valle: 'Maybe because I have a past as a painter, and therefore modesty about the signed product. I use a piece of paper and then I turn it around, I try to exorcise these sketches and not make them become products, because they are a tool.'[99] Unlike Álvaro Siza, he said he never made sketches directly on site: 'I make them afterwards, and using them as memory, they serve to make the project, to recall the places and spaces already physically and mentally measured'[100] during the first visit to the project location. Valle therefore directly associated the experience of the hand drawing with the visual and tactile experience of the place and of architecture, and he saw his sketches as 'written notes, like the travel sketches of Le Corbusier: calligraphic, natural, not academic'.[101] He continued these remarks with a telling description of the various types of drawings produced during the design process:

> The sketch winds up, for habit and experience, becoming something on scale. After that I begin to draw up, with ruler and square, the project coordinates. In case of quick implementation one passes from the handmade sketch to the construction of the geometry. I lay out the project in scale and if I can manage to do it all I already have a definite version, and I hand it over to my staff and we proceed. In other cases I have my collaborators develop it, and I continue to go back to it, correcting things, making sketches on their drawings ... Then the process moves from an initial phase, that of the presentation of the project itself, with the famous coloured drawings of Studio Valle that then remain hung on the wall for months and years, and serve as drawings of self-reassurance ... So they are not realistic drawings, but caricatures of the project. At a certain point the celebrative drawing arrives, which serves to sell the project to the client. It represents another stage: it becomes a system of communication with the client who has to understand the project and become our accomplice, establishing a dialogue with the project.[102]

Valle made many drawings and continuously reworked his projects, and his conception of the lifespan of the project as an 'uninterrupted flow' had some affinities with the design method of Carlo Scarpa, though with very different results.[103] In an essay from 1975, Francesco Dal Co and Mario Manieri-Elia interpreted Valle's habit of lengthy reworking of projects as a desire to 'test their wear over time'.[104] This acute observation can be applied generally: perhaps there is a correlation between this 'temporal wear' of the project, measurable in the 'labour' of Valle in pursuit of the final solution, and the ability of the work to last in time and to age well.[105] When talking about the long gestation of works, Valle used the metaphor of a difficult childbirth:

> The detachment of the drawings from the table, the end of the exorcisms, of the dubious reassurances, the start of the unstoppable movement towards the worksite, is the first trauma, joyful on the surface; the test tube says yes, the angel has gone: life begins. But before the creature can emerge from the womb, from the stroller, go to school, live on its own, there is such work, such labour, seeing the score become matter for the first and last time, and each time.[106]

Gino Valle and the Arts

One of the salient characteristics of Valle's work is the focus on the space defined by the architecture. By space we mean the construction of a perceptive and sensitive experience of architecture through visual and tactile tools. This sensibility covers both the insertion of the building in a given landscape – and thus the construction of an environment of architecture on a visual level – and the physical determination of the crossings and places defined by the architecture – i.e. the construction of physical, visual and tactile experiences.

One of the courtyards of the Bergamin offices, Portogruaro, 1988–91.

This particular sensibility of Valle also came, above all in certain cases, from his affinity with the artistic universe. This was an interest nurtured since childhood, which cannot be confined to a given direction or a specific artistic movement. As his career evolved, Valle enriched his knowledge of contemporary artistic experiences, drawing on them for stimuli and ideas in an indirect way for his projects. These experiences came from the widest range of contexts, which as in the case of architectural stimuli were intercepted in keeping with his own propensities, again without the filter of 'official cultures': Valle paid close attention to the lively local scene (in both Friuli and Venice from the 1950s to the 1970s), but also the national context and certain international circles, especially in America; at the same time, there were friendships with artists and curators (Vedova, Dino and Afro Basaldella, Zigaina, Ciussi, Celant) and various experiences with exhibition design (the Venice Biennale in 1974 and 1976, Vedova's exhibition at Museo Correr in 1984).

He was prompted to cultivate this passion – which immediately shifted into an intrinsic part of his way of working – by his father Provino, through the practice of drawing and watercolour painting. 'For me this experience meant a lot, it made me know nature, sense sunlight, measure space.'[107] Not only exercises of representation of mountain landscapes, but also cityscapes and portraits, always oriented towards the pursuit or the knowledge of pictorial techniques for the definition of objects in space. In the same interview, Valle remembered the summers in Rome, as a child, when 'I looked at Rome as if it were a landscape, making drawings of things or excavations that struck me'.[108]

The 'amateur' depiction of landscapes, bodies and figures developed, briefly, into a true vocation. His precocious career in painting dated back to the early 1940s and focused on the breakdown of naturalistic forms to create abstract figures, taking its cue, in particular, from the early paintings of Mondrian: 'I think of the first Mondrian, still linked to Expressionism. I was oriented in that direction: I put landscapes to memory and constructed spaces.'[109]

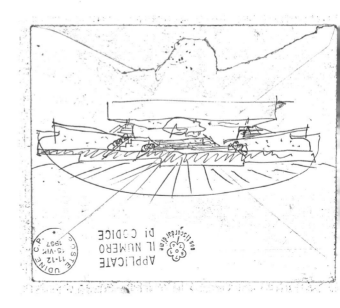

Monument to the Resistance in Udine, sketch on envelope, 1967.

Valle's main interest, however, was the relationship between the object and its perception: 'It has been said that Duchamp rejected the physical figure to seek its contents. This interests me very much because it is a discourse I have delved into for a long time, and which I am clarifying. To start with, yes, I am a visual person, because I judge and also need to work with the hands to find something. However, I do not look at what I find with the eyes, what I find has another type of communication, which is what interests me. The solution is not in the data, it is in the relationship with the data.'[110] So Valle never started with an a priori figurative intent, but 'found' the figures during the process of design development, in relation to a given context: this phenomenon of genuine discovery of the figures in creative work – independent of any rational decision – was made possible by the high degree of formal indetermination Valle conserved in the project development, and above all by the exceptional wealth of his visual culture. So the work of drawing triggered surprising mental associations with

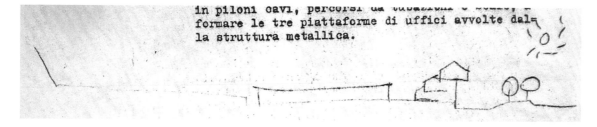

in piloni cavi, percorsi da tubazioni e canali, a
formare le tre piattaforme di uffici avvolte dalla struttura metallica.

Section and landscape relations of the Zanussi
offices, sketch, 1960.

heterogeneous visual materials, in a process of slow sedimentation.[111] The 'found' figures are thus inserted in the landscape, reinterpreting it, or granting it new visual values: their form is filtered by 'storybook' stimuli (the Arta spa), signs in the territory in the style of Ed Ruscha (Geatti warehouse and showroom), abstract geometric sculptures of great chromatic (Dapres plant, Bergamin warehouses) or graphic force (IBM Distribution Centre, IBM tower in Rome), with a visual impact and conceptual relations that are particularly close to the experiments of Land Art in America. The meaning of these buildings, in fact, does not lie in the figurative quality of the architectural object – in the end, they are conventional geometric forms – but in the thought behind it, i.e. the discreet modification of the landscape, the relationship established between context and artifice, nature and abstract shapes, rapid movement of observation and object.[112] According to Valle, colour, a basic feature of these architectural interventions in the territory, is not 'used to make architecture', with the risk of becoming 'an object of fashion and therefore of hasty consumption', because for him 'colour should be interpreted in relation to the landscape, a constant in all my works'.[113]

The works of architecture that come to terms with the urban setting also have similarities, on a conceptual level, to some of the most avant-garde artistic experiments of the same period. First of all, the Resistance monument in Udine, built around a true empathic dramaturgy, between the movement of the observer and the definition of

the monumental space, in some ways foresees the spatial thematics of Richard Serra. The monumental place is a zone opened in urban space that is conquered and contemplated with the senses, in an utterly conceptual relationship with the work. The places of memory invented by Valle are abstract and conceptual as well: the project for the victims of Piazza della Loggia in Brescia, the tomb of Pasolini, the project for the setting of the monument of Piazza Vittoria in Bolzano.

Secondly, there are the 'cuts' and 'excavations' made on certain works of architecture in Udine in the 1970s, such as the INA building on Via Marinelli, the project for the palace of the Cultural Associations on Via Manin, or the Chiesa and Manzano houses. In these projects violent manipulations are performed on consolidated architectural figures (the apartment building, the single-family house, the palace) almost without originality, located inside urban space. An attempt – not distant from the manipulation of buildings done by Gordon Matta-Clark in the 1970s – to grant immaterial and conceptual force to a real landscape, in the critical interaction between manipulated object and environment. As Alessandro Rocca suggests, regarding certain projects in the Carnic Alps, it is 'an attribution of meanings and potentialities to the place of the project that forecasts … the most operative concept of the site-specific that is so widespread in modern and contemporary art'.[114]

The examples could continue since this is a constant in Valle's output. He frequently collaborated with sculptors like Dino Basaldella (on the Bank of Latisana, and the Monument to the Resistance) or painters like Giuseppe Zigaina (on the city hall of Treppo Carnico) and Carlo o

Ciussi (on the bank in Azzano Decimo, and the Valle house on Piazza Primo Maggio), called upon not to embellish his architecture, but to transform surfaces into 'matter' or volumes into sculpture. He had similar relationships with the landscape designers George Gyssels and Ippolito Pizzetti, who were fundamental for Valle to construct an ulterior character of the spaces he designed.

One other fundamental relationship was the long collaboration between Valle and Alfredo Carnelutti, who, starting in 1956, was the graphic designer and draughtsman in the studio.[115] A figure described well by Tenca Montini, as a

great painter, draftsman, a master of perspectives created using his own unique methods to complete work quickly and to make the process of constructing the image less boring and more intuitive ... Carnelutti's perspectives are great geometric and pictorial inventions that undoubtedly had a positive

effect on those who had to look at them to judge a project. At the same time, narrating its force, they provided a preview of the poetic world of the project.[116]

Carnelutti's drawings – in certain cases true works of painting – besides offering a tool of presentation of projects to clients, served to grant visibility to the spatial and landscape focus of Valle's architecture: a sort of pictorial testing of the experience of the space, or as Valle said in a famous statement: 'I refer [through the drawing] to the idea of touching the space, touching it directly, having a concrete experience of it.'[117] In an interview in 2000, Valle recalled how, after the death of Alfredo Carnelutti in 1984, he found himself painting the drawings to present the offices at the Défense: 'I went back twenty years and again realized that when you paint the drawings, spontaneously, taking the colours a bit as they come, the goal is always to be able to touch the space. To sense the "colour of the air" (as Carnelutti put it, in an apt expression in Friuli dialect); this is what makes you feel the depth of the space.'[118]

Geatti plant at Terenzano, 1973–74.

Environment, Landscape, Context, City

During his long career, Valle paid constant attention to the relationship between architecture and the environment. First of all, he developed a particular sensitivity and ability to interpret the specific characteristics of the open landscape, exercised since childhood through an intense exploration and observation of the Friuli landscape. The feeling of belonging to one's land, also manifested in the everyday use of the Friuli dialect, nevertheless never coincided with a position of cultural closure or regression, since Valle cultivated true cultural cosmopolitism, nurtured by an erudite family, his studies and encounters at Harvard, his travels and continuing updates on international architectural production. This interest and sensitivity to the relationships with the environment would later drive his action as an architect above all in anthropological terms, as the ongoing reference to the text by Patrick Abercrombie on the practice and experience of Chinese Feng Shui would seem to bear out:

> The Chinese have always thought of the countryside as their home. This is why they have attempted to create a harmony between human intervention and natural characteristics, to bring out a new, composite landscape, a complex fusion of art and nature [...]. The words Feng Shui mean 'wind-water', since it was believed that the final form taken by mountains and valleys was the result of the shaping force of wind and water; but this concept has been enormously expanded, so that: 'in each place there are special (natural or artificial) topographical characteristics that indicate or modify the spiritual breath of the universe'.[119]

Chinese gardens were an important reference point for Valle, their importance first discussed with Angelo Masieri, and later with his friend, the landscape designer Ippolito Pizzetti. Chinese gardens, since they are enclosed, establish a clear relationship between the world 'inside' and the world 'outside', and what interested Valle was precisely the fact that 'these relationships between the two worlds are very important, and their difference represents a very beautiful aspect of the architecture'.[120] The relationship with the environment, described in anthropological terms in Abercrombie's text, was interpreted by Valle in more topographical than visual terms: 'I always start from the belief that I must in any case build in a place that already exists, where there are other things. And with respect to these other things my buildings offer a front and a back, suggesting directions of access and modes of use.'[121] This way of doing things was clearly asserted in the city hall of Treppo Carnico, closed at the sides to open towards the valley, in the Zanussi offices that 'turn their back' on the street to open towards the production facilities, but also in the Fantoni offices, with a linear footprint that is overturned at the position of the entrance. The buildings for Zanussi and Fantoni are also good illustrations of Valle's focus on a geographical relationship with the environment: in the Zanussi building, the offices are oriented along the east–west axis and open towards a horizon of mountains, beyond the production sheds, while the Fantoni offices are inserted in the valley parallel to the flow of the Tagliamento,[122] so as to avoid creating a barrier in the landscape. This geographical relationship with the environment also arises when establishing the ground level, a ditch is often excavated around the building, making it appear as if it had grown out of the ground.[123]

In 1958, Joseph Rykwert was the first to point to the relations between Valle's work and the local culture of Udine and Friuli, though he later observed that 'if traditional forms of construction appear, it is always in an unusual context, and in contrast, rather than agreement, with the environment'.[124] Giuseppe Mazzariol focused instead on the way Valle established a critical relationship between environment and architecture, saying that he 'never paid attention to the exterior or characteristic aspects of the environment on the level of mere custom, apparent tradition, evident symbols, of everything – in short – that has already been

Fantoni industrial complex, Osoppo, 1972–96, view of the 'cabins' for storage of chipboard materials.

published as an element of folklore'.[125] Valle's work in Carnia effectively developed in terms of a refined relationship between modern design and contextual character. Just as Rykwert refused to reduce Valle's work in Carnia to a 'vernacular' interpretation, instead saying that the work 'belongs to the more vast and valid lineage of occidental architecture, without localisms',[126] Alessandro Rocca has recently proposed the definitive inclusion of these works of architecture 'in the register of the important Italian works of the 1950s and 1960s'.[127] Giovanni Corbellini,

on the other hand, has observed that the centrality of the relationship between architecture and environment was undoubtedly a

non-banal relationship continuously reinvented by Valle, creator of projects closely linked to contextual characteristics and memory, but also of abstract gestures marked by a powerful constructive autonomy in tension with the surroundings, the existing features and the landscape.[128]

In typewritten notes from 1966, Valle explained the importance of the relationship with the environment in an even more concise way: 'let's try to define the quality in the object–environment relationship, not in the object per se',[129] after which he lists a series of places to demonstrate that this relationship has always existed ('Feng Shui, Roman aqueduct, Venice, medieval hilltop city, Siena, San Marco, San Pietro'). In the same notes, he pointed to exemplary works of modern architecture in Italian historical centres (from the Rinascente of Albini in Rome to the Venetian projects of Wright, Gardella and Le Corbusier), problematically concluding that there existed a 'genesis of the psychosis of the environmental insertion in historical centres'. With the construction of the Vriz tower in Trieste in 1957, openly 'modernist' and therefore in clear controversy with the Torre Velasca of BBPR in Milan, Valle took a clear stand of opposition to the 'psychosis of the environmental insertion' intrinsic to Italian postwar design culture.[130] Later, from 1963 to 1975, his projects in the historical centre of Udine are interesting precisely because they present different ways of establishing a meaningful critical tension between new architecture and historical context. This renewed focus on the urban dimension of architecture emerged in the 1980s – in the construction of individual works like the addition to the Comit headquarters in New York or the school in Berlin, but also in the design of true 'pieces of city' like the housing at Giudecca or the office complex at the Défense, and through new ways of associating urban transformation of large abandoned industrial areas and urban voids with the installation of public buildings, office buildings and shopping centres in Padua, Brescia, Vicenza, Milan – succeeding in achieving a symbiosis between urban planning and large-scale architectural design.

Arta Terme, the entrance 'pagoda'.

The pillar of Arta Terme during construction, 1964.

To understand the overall quality of Valle's attitude towards the environment, the landscape, the context and the city, the notion of 'critical regionalism' proposed by Kenneth Frampton is undoubtedly still valid, not as a movement or a trend, but as a strategy of resistance of architecture to 'mediate the impact of the universal civilization with certain elements indirectly derived from the characteristics of a particular place'.[131] For Valle, the feeling of belonging to his 'land' in Friuli[132] was never effectively translated into a form of naturalistic imitation, because his works of architecture, not reconciled with the formal values of the environment, demonstrated that 'to really be contextual' one cannot 'exclude modern design'.[133]

Towards a Linguistic Interpretation of the Architecture of Gino Valle

Valle's linguistic sources do not represent citations of objects, but become momentary 'interlocutors', never exclusive: a single project, in fact, can have multiple linguistic references during the course of its gestation, leading to solutions that are at times radically different from one another (see, for example, the projects for the Vriz tower in Trieste, the Zanussi offices or the Rinascente). At the same time, the 'external' stimuli are constantly reinterpreted and remixed, reaching the point of constructing their own narrative and form. In-depth comparative analysis of the individual works or groups of works makes it possible to reconstruct the multiple references explored by Valle during the course of his long career, and the methods with which they are imported and deformed in his work: for a careful, painstaking philological operation, it will suffice to leaf through the collection of over fifty years of the leading Italian and international architecture magazines, still lined up on the shelves of the studio, observing the countless bookmarks and notes the architect inserted in them over time. Torn and folded magazines, which along with books, catalogues and brochures were everyday working tools, were never considered in terms of fetishism. Rather than analysing the sources from which Valle extracted the visual and conceptual materials of his work, what counts here is an understanding of the ways these materials were processed in relation to the specific problems posed by a new project.[134]

Valle clearly had an extremely open attitude in his linguistic choices: unlike many of his contemporaries, he never attempted to impose a unique personal and constant language that would be clearly recognisable from one work to the next. To describe this particular preference for diversity found in all his work, Francesco Dal Co has used the apt metaphor of the 'linguistic baggage' of Valle that 'is formed starting with suggestions absorbed without differentiation from the tradition; this baggage does not reach the point of ossifying – or of being exalted – in a rigorously defined style, since the architect wanders eclectically through history, without settling on definitive points of reference, also on an ideological and methodological plane'.[135] If Valle manifested an exceptionally wide range of external suggestions in his work – from a house by Paul Rudolph to a cornice by Sullivan, a photograph of the Aswan Dam to a structural model by Buckminster Fuller, a section sketch by the Smithsons to the memory of a building by Álvaro Siza – this 'omnivorous' ability was always directed towards the development of an original, specific formal solution. Speaking of this personal 'linguistic baggage', Valle preferred to use the metaphor of the 'cellar' where one 'descends, to pull out stuff':

> Architecture is narration and making architecture is also a way of inventing stories for ourselves that come from a complex process of creativity, contaminations and associations of memories. In the end, when you start to design, at a certain point you go down to the cellar to pull out stuff, and 'old things' can also surface spontaneously in relation to a certain design opportunity. I believe that the project is constructed precisely with these precious 'archaeological finds' from the repository of memory ... The essence of the work is that the things stored in our personal warehouse should not get lost along the way, and should constitute our experience and our creativity.[136]

These languages 'taken from the cellar' immediately start to be deformed in the course of the project development, modified to obtain spatial and contextual relations or, in many cases, to pursue specific architectural images. Speaking of the Giudecca housing, for example, Valle stated that the image pursued was that of 'transforming, practically as metaphor, this heap of bricks that was the cement plant into another heap of bricks; in other words, from the ground there arose this new organism, this new Golem'.[137] Valle's architecture is often also composed of organic figurations, to which he attributed precise metaphors coming from utterly private stimuli, granting each building a specific character: like the 'nose' of the Deutsche Bank, the overhanging volume that breaks up the massive character of the building; the 'ears' that mark the entrances to the Bergamin warehouse in Istrana or the IKEA store at Bufalotta; or the fact that the buildings have to have their 'belly' and their 'back', namely a skeleton that closes on one part and welcomes on the other, a teaching Valle often repeated to the many students in his courses.

Sandro Marpillero has proposed making reference to Wittgenstein's 'language-game' in an attempt to describe Valle's design approach in general terms, apparently oriented towards exploration of the 'possibilities of "variance" present in linguistic procedures' and of the 'difference that can be instituted with a certain statement, within the system of internal and external rules of a certain "language-game"'.[138] Without delving further into the merits of a specifically linguistic analysis, it seems interesting to consider this particular tension that evidently returns often in Valle's work: a tension between the assertion of a rigorous rule – typological, constructive, geometric – and the introduction of 'variances' and 'differences' not perceptible as 'isolated signs' but as products generated by the rule itself.

Commercial building on Via Mercatovecchio, Udine, drawing by Alfredo Carnelutti 1963.

Giovanni Corbellini instead focuses on certain characters of 'ambiguity' in the youthful work of Valle, proposing the extension of this comment to other, also later works: 'This interest in the hybrid, the contradictory, the mutable represents one of the most vital demonstrations of the realism of Valle.'[139] Undertaking a tectonic interpretation of the Quaglia house, Corbellini identifies, for the right reasons, contradictions in the attempt to display and at the same time disguise the structure and material presence of the building. Considerations that cannot help but come from another reflection on the role of the various parts, in a gap between the image of the house and its structural essence: 'An ambiguity that holds our attention and produces minimum, continuous detours, playing by subtly confirming and contradicting our expectations as observers.'[140]

At this point, all these critical interpretations seem to make clear that the so-called 'eclecticism' of Valle should be seen in positive terms, restoring the methodological value the term had for the philosophers of the Enlightenment.[141] The continuing enrichment of the 'linguistic baggage' of Valle does not, in fact, correspond to any systematic or programmatic order, but seems to be the result of encounters with the diversity of languages directly stimulated by project opportunities. This dialogic capacity of architecture was explored by Valle in particular in the more recent works, revealing affinities with the work of James Stirling. The same taste for play, the same ability to feel at ease in the vast world of architectural tongues and dialects, seem to characterise the design attitude of both, though with profound differences: where Stirling used the tool of literary citation, making reference to a poetics of the collage of heterogeneous linguistic materials, Valle operated through allusions and evocations, reworking his formal reference with great freedom to the point of also obtaining radical transfigurations.

Pluralism and experimentalism were salient features of Valle's character, and he enjoyed playing at 'changing identity'.[142] Rather than imposing his 'own' identity, his 'authorial' mark, what was

Veranda of Romanelli House, Udine, 1952–53.

important to him was to leave behind testimony of the interpretation of a place, a situation, a context, referring himself on many occasions to his very personal interpretation of a famous aphorism of Kahn: 'The place expects you to discover what's already there. But it has to be found, because up until then the place does not exist. As Kahn would have put it, "the project is what a place is waiting for".'[143] His interest in not being recognised as an 'author' is also shown by an acute remark on architecture in the 1990s: 'In my view, what is happening in the field of architecture is that precisely architecture is moving towards the timeless ... Architecture should be invisible, i.e. perfectly natural, i.e. produced by the environment and history.'[144] And Valle concluded: 'At the end of a conference in Lausanne, Luigi Snozzi told me: "one of my students asked me whom he should look at"; I told him to look at Gino Valle, and he replied: "but Gino Valle is hard to copy, because he always changes". I told Snozzi: "you should have answered: because Gino Valle does not exist".'[145]

Architecture as an Art of Montage

The deep realism of his character led Valle to fully explore, in different moments of his career, the theme of prefabrication, becoming one of the protagonists of postwar architecture in Italy in the field of design research within the limits posed by serial production. This was a theme that had its own logical and compositional autonomy, calling for a type of design that operates through the assembly of components produced away from the worksite, not through the invention of new forms.

Valle's interest in this theme came early on and reached its first significant synthesis in the multiple solutions produced for the Zanussi plants, both in the field of the organisation of design processes (the creation of the 'Industrial Design Unit') and in that of architecture (the various Rex factories, the standard warehouses, the equipped axis of Porcia) – a complex experience, with Zanussi, that contributed to convincing him that architecture in general comes from the relationship between the 'culture of the designer' and the 'culture of production'. The approach to this type of assignment had confirmed Valle's conviction that from the outset design thinking meant thinking about construction,

and developed starting with knowledge of the real possibilities of construction systems.[146] According to Valle, the responsibility of the architect is to establish a critical relationship between two cultures with diverging interests: design culture and building culture. While the quality of the individual products – from the traditional brick wall to pre-stressed beams and prefabricated walls – can be objectively assessed, the quality of the final 'edified product', as Valle asserted at a conference on 'Rationalization of production', is 'a matter of relation between the objects that go into a project', and the quality of the relation 'cannot be objectively determined a priori'. Only the architect, then, is responsible for the 'quality of the relation', notwithstanding the quality of the individual components, because it is he who has to 'use production, select from it, demand something more of it, establishing the relationship between project and production'.[147]

In the 1960s Valle began working with the manufacturer of prefabricated parts, Sipre, developing certain types of precast panels in reinforced concrete, one of which went into the solution for the Zanussi warehousing system: the panels were designed to make it possible, with a few simple formal strategies, a visual variety in

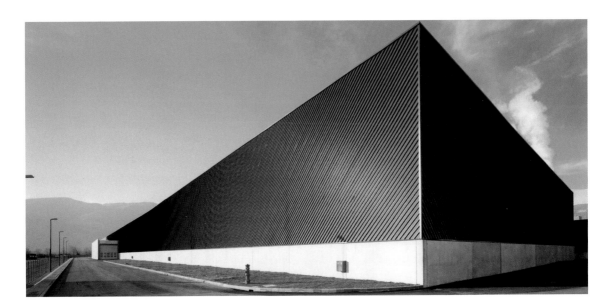

Fantoni industrial campus, Osoppo. Finishing division, 1999–2000.

the process of assembly.[148] These were heavy but non-structural panels that formed the enclosure of sheds, the roofing instead being supported by a light metal structure. In this sense Valle operated in a radically different way from the experiments of the same period by Mangiarotti, Morassutti and Zanuso in the field of industrial architecture, who focused on the design of the structural members (pillars, beams), which took on a central expressive role in their works. While in these works the parts became structural figures, 'large design objects', Valle instead thought about the architectural meaning of enclosures composed of prefabricated materials. Gregotti has proposed an original reinterpretation of the relationship between Valle's activity as an architect and that as a designer, which share a specific 'architectonic quality': the design objects (the parts of Rex stoves, the clocks for Solari, the furniture for Fantoni), for Gregotti, possess an 'architectonic quality' that is recognised as specific to the 'tradition of the modern', as opposed to the contemporary tendency to think of architectural objects as enlarged 'design' objects, in their pursuit of an aestheticising form. Gregotti goes on to say: 'It is this presence of architecture in the object that allowed him, I think, also for cultural attunement, to construct a series of industrial buildings that are exemplary in their apodicticity, their refined morphological simplicity without simplification.'[149] Gregotti then underlines Valle's close relationship with the production systems of the parts, interpreting his industrial sheds as the result of a logical design procedure that attempts, through simplicity, to somehow escape from the authorial condition that would instead characterise the attitude of a designer. In this sense, the reduction of the details to a minimum, with the resulting disappearance of the looming presence of the author, were Valle's response to the objectives set by the Zanussi company itself, namely the formal and dimensional coordination of the appliances. Annalisa Avon also observes how the partnership between Valle and Zanussi 'unfolded in terms of concrete realism ... In it we can see the lack of interest in research as a private pursuit, the acceleration of the process of image consumption, a substantial economy of figurative means'.[150]

With the Geatti, Dapres and Bergamin facilities, Valle further developed the industrial 'boxes', on the one hand inserting the theme of colour, while on the other erasing any tectonic clues – the enclosures became continuous, no connection was shown between structure and panelling, there were no joints – taking these objects to the verge of abstraction, without materiality and a sense of 'scale'. But it is in the relationship with the Fantoni company, which lasted for over thirty years, and for whom the architect created a true industrial 'campus' in Osoppo,[151] that we can appreciate the most successful range of experiments in the field of the assembly of prefabricated parts. The growth of the factory and its productive specialisation was matched in parallel by the achievements of Valle for the individual segments of the large complex: again in this case, the particular forms of the large enclosures (the 'cathedral', the warehouses, the wood deposits, the showroom space, the auditorium, etc.) were determined above all by the functions they contained and the production lines of the factories.

Going beyond the specific theme of industrialised construction, the issue of construction and the central importance of the worksite was fundamental in Valle's thinking. Through certain aphorisms he offered a theoretical conceptualisation of the relationship between 'design' and 'implementation'. Speaking of the execution of an architectural work, Valle used the analogy of the musical 'score' – the definitive drawings of the building – as a system of notation for production, picking up the definition of Nelson Goodman of the analogy between architecture and music as 'allographic' arts.[152] He thought of the worksite, ideally, as the ultimate time of ripening of architecture, a ripening similar to that of a musical composition during rehearsals. The music analogy also turned out to be pertinent on another level: like a musician who imagines his composition not as an abstract structure but as a structure of relations between concrete sounds, Valle took the physical, tactile and optical properties of the materials utilised into account, to imagine the spatial experience of the building. In this sense Valle again referred to Goodman in a lecture at IUAV in 1994:

Arti Grafiche Chiesa facility, 1959–60.

The musician does not imagine the score as an abstract structure, but as a structure of concrete relationships between sound and time; so the architect has to know the physical, visual and tactile properties of materials to be able to imagine the spatial experience in the construction … The instruments of the project are instruments that demand all our force, our personality, our culture and knowledge. The life of the architect is a continuous effort to bear witness through form, without ever being able to possess it.[153]

The use of standardised materials, however, was not limited to constructions in the industrial sector. Public works with representative functions – such as the city hall of Casarsa, the project for the theatre of Udine, the Olivetti offices in Ivrea – were also made through the skilful design of the assembly of prefabricated parts, and explored for their expressive potential. In particular, in the works of the 1980s and 1990s Valle developed a continuous modification of construction typologies, which he explored, mixed and refined answering to the various functional needs to be addressed. His approach was totally nonchalant, combining an outstanding talent for montage with an ability to recycle construction systems, typological options and formal relationships between the structural and panelling components.

This recycling, indicated by Valle himself as one of his explicit design approaches, was in some ways one of the foundations of his way of operating. In the interview with Marpillero, Valle compared himself to Buster Keaton, who in the *The Navigator* uses objects in an utterly anomalous and innovative way (a coffee pot that moves an ocean liner, a ship's boiler to make coffee, his own body in a diving suit that becomes a boat): 'he thus redefines the use of things and transforms their most obvious past into a possible present'.[154]

Lecture by Le Corbusier, *A propos de Venise*, at Ca' Giustinian, Venice, during the CIAM summer school, September 1952. In the audience, third row, Carlo Scarpa (centre), Valle between John Myer and Donald Appleyard and, to the right, Nani Valle. In the first row, seated on the ground, Gerard Philippe, Giancarlo De Carlo and Luciano Semerani.

A Master without Masters

Though he taught for over forty years in a range of different schools, influencing entire generations of students, Gino Valle never wanted to assume the role of a true master, because the idea of founding a school of disciples was just the opposite of his free, open way of thinking and designing, and therefore also of teaching. His idea of teaching was closely linked to his experience as a non-conformist student and autodidact. Valle said he had not had 'relationships of the master-student type with anyone',[155] since he saw his teachers at IUAV like Scarpa, Samonà or Albini, namely the generation of Italian architects connected with the CIAM, as more like 'uncles', points of reference who had 'indicated a professional path of construction'.[156] In the United States in 1951–52, he had a chance to meet some of the great masters of the Modern Movement, but he did not feel awe in the presence of Wright, 'with whom it was impossible to have a dialogue' or Gropius, judged as 'too compliant', although Valle would have liked to stay with Mies in Chicago, 'to fight with him a little, and also because I am convinced that he is the greatest master. He was the one that imparted the most subtle and least personal teachings.'[157] From the letters sent to his sister Nani during his stay in America, a self-portrait of Gino emerges that is utterly irreverent regarding the prestigious institution: 'We scorn everyone and make fun of Harvard'[158] where 'they are all sheep and stare at us as if we were rare beasts'.[159] Valle probably did not get much from Gropius, as his remarks on the

Valle at the design seminar organised by Carlo Aymonino at IUAV on the Saffa area (Cannaregio), Venice, 1979: from left, Nani Valle, Peter Eisenman, Carlo Aymonino, Rafael Moneo, Valeriano Pastor, Carlo Magnani, and (from behind) Vanna Fraticelli.

Valle at the seminar in Ulm, 1965.

universities.[163] He finally accepted a position as visiting professor at Harvard in 1971, an experience lived with enthusiasm,[164] in spite of the difficulty of having to 'spend one week here and one week there … true madness. But it was something that keeps you alive.' After this experience, he turned down the offer to remain definitively at Harvard as a full professor, because a teaching post had opened up at IUAV in Venice:[165] he held that position for four years, before winning the chair in 1976, and continuing to teach there until his retirement in 1994.

Valle's academic career met with many difficulties in Italy. After the stimulating experience as an assistant at the CIAM summer school in Venice, from 1952 to 1954, he became a lecturer in the course of Applications of Descriptive Geometry at IUAV (1954–55), before the brief experience in 1963–64 as coordinator of the advanced course in Industrial Design at the Istituto statale d'arte in Venice, the only course in Industrial Design in Italy at the time, and a period in 1964–67 as a member of the Education Working Group of ICSID.[166] Just as his activity as a product designer was tactically used by Valle as a way of obtaining architecture commissions, so his thinking in the field of design education was useful in formulating his position on the training of architects. Directly reporting the conclusions of the important ICSID conference in Bruges on design training, in 1964 Valle asserted that 'only designers, qualified as professionals or researchers, will be able to teach design in schools … Design teachers should continue their professional activity, and be encouraged to do so.'[167] Defending the need to associate teaching with professional endeavour, Valle confirmed a position taken by the CIAM congresses in the postwar period, especially at Bergamo[168] in 1949. Though he was personally supported by Samonà who had invited him in 1965 to take part in the examination for a lecturing post, Valle met with resistance and distrust at IUAV due to the fact that he represented the figure of a 'professional' rather than a 'researcher'.[169] To obtain a position as lecturer in Elements of Composition he had to repeat the exam during which he had clashed with Raffaello Fagnoni, then at the height of his power as dean of the School

latter's teaching would seem to bear out ('Yesterday Gropius did a Bauhaus lecture that stank of old warehouse stock'),[160] as would the story of their first meeting: 'So at a certain point he says: "Why don't you go see the Graduate Center?" Reply: "I live there, and luckily I have a room facing south," and he catches the drift and changes the subject.'[161]

The year spent at Harvard was decisive in reinforcing Valle's self-awareness as an 'international' architect, distant from and distrustful of Italian academic debates, which seemed too narrow in his view: 'a circular autoculture that fed on itself, incapable of taking a look around and understanding things'.[162] He remained on good terms with his Harvard classmates, especially Jacob Driker and George Skrubb, and regularly welcomed students from MIT as collaborators in the studio in the 1950s, though later he turned down several invitations to teach in prestigious American

of Architecture of Florence, after having appealed to the Consiglio Superiore della Pubblica Istruzione.[170] The text of Valle's appeal, based on the reconstruction of how he had approached the theme of the lecture, contains some interesting statements on the principles of modern design education, principles that were later put into practice in his teaching at IUAV.[171] After having asserted that 'one danger for the freedom of the architect is eclectic vagrancy, the citation of forms borrowed from masters without having understood their merits', Valle concluded that the job of architecture schools was to 'train fully responsible architects, eliminating the gap between school and reality', and that their responsibility was therefore 'to understand and act, training ranks capable of bridging this gap and requalifying the profession of the architect'.[172]

In his teaching at IUAV Valle effectively attempted to resist this split between school and reality, encouraging students to base their design activity on the concrete experience of places, paths, the effects of light on materials, spatial values, in keeping with a phenomenological approach to architecture. After a number of years of teaching fourth-year students, in the 1980s he decided to focus on first-year students because they were 'fresher' and not yet deformed by the institution:

> I get more out of the first-year students than those of the fourth year: when you say that something is something, they believe you, while the others look suspicious. They say to themselves, 'who knows what Gino Valle means by that?' For the first-year students you are the big brother, the father, the uncle, not necessarily the teacher. So they look at you as someone who gives them something, or that knows something more than they do, or has more experience than they do. But they have to look at you as a person, not an institution.[173]

Valle, speaking of this first year, often used the term 'initiation',[174] reminding us that to become an architect it is necessary to learn 'to have a "compass" in the eyes, as Michelangelo said, to measure space with the eyes':[175] for this reason, he based his teaching on exercises of observation of places and spaces, which then had to be described with drawings and stories, before doing a small 'real project in a real place'. Ippolito Pizzetti, whom Valle had invited as an adjunct professor to join him in the first-year programme, described this pedagogy well: 'One day in Venice, during a lesson, Gino Valle told the students that a project that has consistency, even before being drawn, has to be narrated [...]. The medium doesn't matter [...] what counts is to translate one's own intuition through an expressive medium – that clump or start of movement that has formed inside us in the contact and relationship with the place.'[176]

Valle liked to teach in this rather unorthodox way, with few texts to read and to discuss in the classroom, often in an improvised way, and many drawings the students had to make and comment on with the greatest freedom, even at the risk of causing outbursts of rage and fierce criticism: 'The ladies and gentlemen who come here should consider themselves indicted, they must speak the truth.'[177] Valle was very demanding and always addressed the students directly, spurring them on to find their own means of expression, to achieve their own space of freedom, so that they could one day become 'responsible architects'.[178] Though he based his teaching on his own experience as an architect, he considered school a total alternative to professional practice, as he confessed in the last year of his teaching career:

> After 23 years at IUAV and almost 50 years of professional practice, I am still an amateur, if by amateur we mean a person who takes risks, cognizant or not [...]. But I seek and do not want certainties, creative work is a private affair. The profession and the academy touch the public, and have to take that into account. I confess, I have been and am a virtuous professional; I cannot say that I have been a virtuous academic. I have given all the time to the students and almost nothing to the institution, and I apologize for this to my colleagues and my assistants, who will never advance in their careers.[179]

Gino Valle, 1966.

Notes

1 'The architect, in fact, should be the one who finds things. In the end it is a bit like the discourse of Picasso. Picasso was the personality who managed most completely to bear witness to his own span of life. He always worked to find and was ahead of all the others ... he always searched. This, in my view, is exactly what an architect should do.' See Vittorio Magnago Lampugnani (ed.), 'Gino Valle. Dal luogo alla casa', *Domus*, 692, March 1988, pp.18–24.

2 Giuseppe Samonà, 'Architetture di giovani', *Casabella-Continuità*, 205, April–May 1955, pp.19–23.

3 'Sandro Marpillero intervista Gino Valle da New York', *Lotus Navigator*, monograph on Gino Valle, 1, 2000, p.88.

4 It is interesting, on this subject, to cite the critical judgment of Fulvio Irace, who sees Valle as 'one of the last masters of the "Italian way" to architecture as a global practice of transformation of the world: an attitude that cannot be repeated, that has not had reflections in the other exponents of European culture', concluding that 'Valle has been the most "international" of our architects: yet this has not prevented him from constantly essaying the nature of places, their history, their geography'. See Fulvio Irace, 'Gino Valle (1923–2003)', *Abitare*, December 2003. Vittorio Gregotti has also clearly observed the very personal position of Valle in this dialectic between

local character and international focus: 'This character of natural connection with international architectural culture, without sacrificing his very personal critical regionalism, penetrates all his work as an architect, also precisely when he focuses on specific contexts.' See Vittorio Gregotti, 'Gino Valle', in Nico Ventura (ed.), *Da, chez, from Gino Valle*, exh. cat., MusArc, Ferrara, 2005, pp.13–14.

5 'Designing and building architecture is always a battle. And that is part of the fun, the game of the profession, which as far as I'm concerned is the best job in the world, because you really do have fun, you have to stay alert. It is a sort of big craft.' See Gino Valle, 'Il mestiere più bello del mondo', in Giorgio Ciucci (ed.), *L'architettura italiana oggi. Racconto di una generazione*, Laterza, Bari, 1989, pp.275–90.

6 Valle did not accept the excuses made by architects in the face of the difficulties of design work: 'The aim of any project is to produce construction, good or bad; if it is bad [...] the responsibility lies only with the designer, because the project is the fundamental element [...]. If the project is bad the responsibility lies with the designer, due to ignorance or laziness or bad faith, and the cause is never the cost, never the regulations, never the culture of the client, never the political conditions.' See Gino Valle, talk at the conference 'Razionalizzazione della produzione e gestione edilizia in rapporto al risparmio energetico',

Abano, 23 February 1980, published in Atti del convegno, Consorzio regionale IACP, Veneto, 1980.

7   With his cultural and publishing activity during the 1970s and 1980s, Gregotti played an important role in the promotion of Valle. In 1975, as the director of the Visual Arts section of the Venice Biennale, Gregotti invited Valle to replace Scarpa as its main exhibition designer; in 1979 he promoted the exhibition on the architecture of Valle at the Padiglione di Arte Contemporanea in Milan (See *Gino Valle. Architetto 1950–1978*, Edizioni Pac and Idea Editions, Milan, 1979); in 1982, he launched his editorial directorship of *Casabella* with a cover and a long report dedicated to the Giudecca project in Venice (see *Casabella*, 478, 1982). In a recent publication, the Roman architect Carlo Melograni (a year younger than Valle) acknowledges the uniqueness of Valle as 'the best architect of his generation' (Carlo Melograni, *Architetture nell'Italia della ricostruzione: Modernità versus modernizzazione 1945–1960*, Quodlibet, Macerata, 2017, p.329). Podrecca interprets Valle as 'the most important and lively Italian architect of the Modern in the post-war era', but at the same time as a 'loose cannon who has never been forgiven by the doctrinal and mired Italian architecture scene for having built so much and so well'. See Boris Podrecca, 'Gino Valle 1923–2003, Ein Requiem', *Architektur-Aktuell*, April 2004, p.6.

8   Pierre-Alain Croset, *Gino Valle. Progetti e architetture*, Electa, Milan, 1989.

9   'Gino Valle', *Lotus Navigator*, December 2000, with an important essay by Alessandro Rocca ('Valle ultimo. Fabriche, uffici e frammenti di città', pp.4–23) and a long conversation between Gino Valle and Sandro Marpillero ('Sandro Marpillero intervista Gino Valle da New York', pp.62–89).

10   The exhibition 'Gino Valle in Carnia' (Treppo Carnico, 2 July – 25 September 2005, which then travelled around Europe) and the exhibition catalogue (edited by Elena Carlini, Navado Press, Trieste 2005, with essays by Giovanni Corbellini and Alessandro Rocca) represented the first serious attempt at an in-depth critical interpretation of a particular group of works. The exhibition 'Da, chez, from Gino Valle' (MusArc of Ferrara, 28 October – 11 December 2005) and the corresponding catalogue (edited by Nico Ventura, MusArc, Ferrara, 2005, with writings by Nico Ventura, Vittorio Gregotti, Amerigo Restucci, Alessandro Rocca), presented an anthology of photographs, with a selection of original drawings of the projects in Milan for Deutsche Bank and Portello. The exhibition 'Gino Valle: progetti e architetture per Udine, 1948–2003' (Galleria d'Arte Moderna, Udine, 16 February – 31 May 2007) documented unbuilt works with original drawings, while a video by Ennio Guerrato represented the completed works. At the time of the exhibition, the book *I costruttori del Novecento. Gino Valle a Udine* (ed. Pierre-Alain Croset, Mazzotta, Milan, 2007, was published, a small guide to the constructed works, together with a discussion of the difficult relationship between Valle and his city.

11   In an interview in 1992, Valle recalls how, after his return from imprisonment in Germany, his father was so happy that he granted him wide responsibilities in the studio: 'I had returned, I was 22 years old, I was overbearing.' See Giovanni Vragnaz, 'Intervista a Gino Valle', *Piranesi*, 1, January 1991, pp.26–47.

12   This specific narrative structure was used in the 1989 monograph, organised in 18 theme chapters and 39 profiles of constructed buildings, and later in the 2010 monograph (Pierre-Alain Croset and Luka Skansi, *Gino Valle 1923–2003*, Electa, Milan, 2010), with 16 chapters and 57 profiles (50 buildings and 7 projects that were not built).

13   Gino Valle, 'L'architettura come pratica progettuale', *Casabella*, 450, September 1979, pp.12–13.

14   In 1979, tracing back through essays published on the work of Valle, Germano Celant was able to identify, in the writings of the various authors, a 'subtle but continuous intolerance of presumed "shortcomings" of coherency and harmony, symmetry and synthesis, of which his architecture was accused'. See Germano Celant, 'Al limite dell'avventura', in *Gino Valle. Architetto 1950–1978*, pp.8–9.

15   See the well-known observations of Walter Benjamin: 'Tactile appropriation is accomplished not so much by attention as by habit. As regards architecture, habit determines to a large extent even optical reception. The latter, too, occurs much less through rapt attention than by noticing the object in an incidental fashion.' Walter Benjamin, *The Work of Art in the Age of Mechanical Reproduction* (trans. J.A. Underwood), Penguin, Harmondsworth, 2008[1936], Chapter XV.

16   Maria Bottero and Giacomo Scarpini (eds), 'Intervista a Gino Valle', *Zodiac*, 20, December 1970, pp.94–115.

17   Joseph Rykwert, 'Gino Valle architetto', *Gino Valle. Architetto 1950–1978*, pp.6–7.

18   Maria Bottero and Giacomo Scarpini (eds), 'Intervista a Gino Valle', pp.94–115, italics in the original.

19   Joseph Rykwert, 'The Work of Studio Architetti Valle', *Architecture and Building*, April 1958, pp.121–39.

20   Giuseppe Mazzariol, 'Gino Valle', *Zodiac*, 12, October 1963, pp.165–91.

21   Mazzariol therefore made a clear distinction between the concept of the 'anti-formal' and that of the 'informal' used by Francesco Tentori in an essay in 1960 (Francesco Tentori, 'Dieci anni dello Studio Architetti Valle', *Casabella*, 246, December 1960) to connect given linguistic characteristics of Valle's architecture to the currents of 'informal painting': Mazzariol considered this definition of 'informal architecture' as 'too extensive and in any case not always pertinent'.

22   ibid., italics in the original.

23   Germano Celant, 'Al limite dell'avventura', pp.8–9.

Valle in Salem (Massachusetts), winter 1951–52.

24   Gino Valle, 'L'architettura come pratica progettuale', pp.12–13.

25   Germano Celant, 'Al limite dell'avventura', pp.8–9.

26   Valle's attitude, in fact, seems very distant from the 'autobiographical' obsession that characterised a part of Italian postwar architectural culture, and in particular the figure of Aldo Rossi. See Manfredo Tafuri, *Storia dell'architettura italiana 1944–1985*, Einaudi, Turin, 1986, in particular the chapter 'Il "caso" Aldo Rossi', pp.166–71.

27   Gino Valle, 'L'architettura come pratica progettuale', pp.12–13. In the same text, with a forcefully self-analytic character, Valle quoted from a well-known poem by T.S. Eliot: 'Between the conception / And the creation / Between the emotion / And the response / Falls the Shadow / Life is very long' (T. S. Eliot, *The Hollow Men*, in *Collected Poems*, 1909–1935, Faber & Faber, London,

pp.89–90), concluding: 'This is the problem: I find myself in the shadow that falls between conception and creation, like a schizophrenic mother' – Valle refers here to the discomfort he feels when he has to 'separate himself' from a project – 'and this has forced me to be an architect who builds a lot'.

28   'Gino Valle. Dal luogo alla casa', pp.18–24.

29   For a discussion of this point in greater depth, see the introductory essay 'L'avventura soggettiva', in Pierre-Alain Croset, *Gino Valle. Progetti e architetture*, pp.13–15, where, as an example of 'overlooking' of Valle, two significant buildings were discussed, works that were never photographed or listed, namely the school of Sutrio and the Chiesa house in Udine. Regarding the work of selective memory in the design output of Valle, Alessandro Rocca proposes an interesting interpretation referring to Freud's *Psychopathology of Everyday Life*.

See Alessandro Rocca, 'Valle ultimo. Fabbriche, uffici e frammenti di città', *Lotus Navigator*, p.8.

30   Piera Ricci Menichetti graduated in 1958 from Politecnico di Milano and became Valle's wife and a partner of Studio Valle in 1961, after having worked with Ignazio Gardella as a collaborator and university assistant in 1959–60.

31   Pietro Valle, a graduate of IUAV and Harvard Graduate School of Design, after having worked with Boris Podrecca and Frank Gehry and having taught in various American universities, founded the studio Carlini & Valle Architetti Associati in 1998 in Trieste, and became a partner of Studio Valle Architetti Associati in 2003.

32   On the work of Studio Architetti Valle after Valle's death in 2003, see *Valle architetti associati 2003–2016*, edited by Pietro Valle, with an introduction by Giovanni Corbellini, Libria, Melfi, 2016.

33   Giorgio Macola graduated from IUAV in 1969. After professional practice in Algeria and collaboration with Studio Valle from 1973 to 1976, he opened his own studio in Venice in 1976. In 1985 he began to work in Paris in association with Gino Valle and Fernando Urquijo.

34   Mario Broggi, a graduate of ETH Zurich in 1970, began working with Studio Valle in 1970. Michael Burckhardt, a graduate in 1971 of ETH Zurich, worked with Piano & Rogers from 1974 to 1976, and then founded, with Mario Broggi, the studio Broggi + Burckhardt in Milan.

35   Maria Bottero and Giacomo Scarpini (eds), 'Intervista a Gino Valle', pp.94–115.

36   Fulvio Irace, 'Intervista a Gino Valle', *Abitare*, 275, June 1989, pp.166–71. This piece was a comment on the retrospective exhibition at the Basilica Palladiana in Vicenza (17 March – 23 April 1989), conceived precisely as a selection of drawings to 'bring out this active dimension of the experimentation between the reasons of a solution, more than the icastic and summary image of the construction'.

37   Sir Patrick Abercrombie, 'Feng-Shui', in *Transactions of the Town Planning Institute*, vol.XII, 1, London, 1925.

38   Discovered by Valle in 1951, this text was first mentioned as a reference in a publication from 1965: Joseph Rykwert, 'Architettura di Gino Valle', *Domus*, 426, May 1965.

39   Pierre-Alain Croset (ed.), 'Una conversazione con Gino Valle', *Casabella*, 519, December 1985, pp.16–17.

40   Valle often associated the need for recognisability of architects with the demand of the media, thus indirectly explaining a certain distraction on the part of magazines regarding his work: 'As an architect that has always changed, and has been called eclectic, I am often overlooked because they cannot manage to classify me.' See '"Bisogna immergersi nel tempo", conversazione con Gino Valle, Udine, 29 aprile 1995', in Giovanni Corbellini, *Grande & veloce. Strumenti compositivi nei contesti contemporanei*, Officina Edizioni, Rome, 2000, p.234.

41   The essay by Francesco Tentori, 'Dieci anni d'attività dello Studio Architetti Valle', *Casabella*, 246, December 1960, was actually strongly 'suggested' by Valle himself, as demonstrated by a handwritten page from 15 November 1960, accompanied by schematic sketches made by Valle himself, conserved in the Valle archive.

42   The publication of Valle's lecture (7 April 1965) in *RIBA Journal* (May 1965) was edited by Peter Kingsland of the Editorial Office. Actually, due to Valle's difficulties in preparing a real lecture and, above all, in writing a text, Kingsland went to Udine in February for a long interview, which was to become the text of the lecture, of which the long version sent to Valle on 10 March 1965 remains. This is a very complete and significant document, due to the way Valle proposes a path of interpretation through the first 15 years of his design activity.

43   Maria Bottero and Giacomo Scarpini (eds), 'Intervista a Gino Valle', pp.94–115.

44   Our research has not allowed us to determine whether this was the AIA Gold Medal (Valle was an honorary member of AIA) or the RIBA Gold Medal, nor do we know if this form was ever submitted. The probable date, 1992, cannot be confirmed because the attached bibliography ends at 1991.

45   'The architecture of Gino Valle is a story of searching over and over again the language profoundly rooted in the thing itself, specific to place and circumstance. With each project this process, a synthesis of memory, program and technique, becomes more vast as the knowledge of each preceding project contributes to the storehouse of experience [...]. The offices for Zanussi Rex represent his first mature work, unifying language and place in a single architecture.' Document for nomination for an unidentified architecture prize, Archivio Valle, Udine, n.d.

46   'The crisis resulted in a decisive turn in the work of Valle. He began to build things which, in fact, had no place or rather "could be any place", a "non-architecture", but which also had a language clear and coherent in form and material.' Ibid.

47   'In this new-found maturity he realized works which substituted steel for stone, whose urban space did not mirror the space of the immediate past but more significantly researched the tacit traces of a cultural place overlaid by centuries of inhabitation. With each project Valle continues to sharpen his sense, his ability to scratch and dig beyond the patina of the immediate past to discover an architecture coherent in form, material and space which does not represent the place but is the place in all its qualities.' Ibid.

48   With finesse, Giovanni Corbellini has criticised the attempt of Pierre-Alain Croset, in the introductory essay of the monograph in 1989 ('L'avventura soggettiva', p.21), to call into discussion, through the investigation of four key words ('professionalism', 'eclecticism', 'regionalism',

'anti-intellectualism'), certain critical preconceptions that tended to enclose Valle's work in a cage of labels, since 'each of these categories, based on negative definitions or the recognition of a pursued marginal status, demonstrates the difficulty of classifying a production that cannot be classified'. See Giovanni Corbellini, 'Astratto e contestuale. Gino Valle in Carnia', in Elena Carlini (ed.), *Architettura in montagna. Gino Valle in Carnia*, Navado Press, Trieste, 2005, pp.13–20. See also the intelligent critical observations of Alessandro Rocca in the same catalogue: Alessandro Rocca, 'Meno forma, più concetto. 1960–65: la critica architettonica sull'opera di Gino Valle in Carnia', ibid., p.7.

49   Therefore, it is not correct to subdivide the work of Valle into separate phases, in opposition to one another. The same is true of an architect like James Stirling, in many ways comparable to Valle for his open attitude towards experimentation with different languages. Stirling himself criticised Robert Maxwell who had identified two phases of his career, and Martin Filler who had found as many as four: 'They are both wrong: there is only one phase (though our parameters are wide) and what we do now is not very different from what we have done from the start, though perhaps there are differences of scale and materials.' See James Stirling, Acceptance Speech for the Pritzker Prize (1981), published in Robert Maxwell (ed.), *James Stirling. Writings on Architecture*, Skira, Milan, 1998, pp.180–81.

50   Manfredo Tafuri, *Storia dell'architettura italiana 1944–1985*, p.212.

51   Pierluigi Nicolin, 'Il gioco delle somiglianze, Gino Valle alla Défense', *Lotus International*, 61, 1989, pp.63–8. Nicolin appears to be simultaneously fascinated by Valle, but also 'irritated' because he is not able to place him with certainty inside critical categories, thus raising questions about the future development of Valle's work: 'One wonders if a certain coherence that can be glimpsed in the latest projects will be the start of a design period based on more precise premises on the part of an architect who has so extensively and eclectically experimented in the past.'

52   Francesco Moschini, 'Gino Valle: l'avventura del collezionista', *Anfione Zeto*, 6–7, 1990–91, p.64.

53   Vittorio Gregotti, 'Gino Valle', *Da, chez, from Gino Valle*, pp.13–14. Actually, in a later passage Gregotti contradicts himself, asserting in a decidedly more correct way that 'the architectural objects of Valle are always urban objects, that immediately become protagonists of a dialectic, sensitive confrontation with the real […] or imagined city'.

54   Gillo Dorfles, *Il disegno industriale e la sua estetica*, Cappelli, Bologna, 1963; Vittorio Gregotti, *Il disegno del prodotto industriale, Italia 1860–1980*, Electa, Milan, 1982; Germano Celant (ed.), *The Italian Metamorphosis, 1943–1968*, exh. cat., Guggenheim Museum, Mondadori-Progetti museali, Rome, 1994; Annalisa Avon, 'Gino Valle. Industrial design per la casa 1956–75', *Domus*, 769, March

1995, pp.62–70; Marco Romanelli and Marta Laudani, *Design Nordest*, Editrice Abitare Segesta, Milan, 1996, pp.96–112; *100 Designs/100 Years. Innovative Designs of the 20th Century*, Rotovision, Crans-Près-Céligny, Switzerland, 1999.

55   Manfredo Tafuri, *Storia dell'architettura italiana*; Amedeo Belluzzi and Claudia Conforti, *Architettura italiana, 1944–1984*, Laterza, Rome & Bari, 1985; Giorgio Ciucci and Francesco Dal Co, *Architettura italiana del Novecento*, Electa, Milan, 1990; *Storia dell'architettura italiana. Il secondo Novecento*, edited by Francesco Dal Co, Electa, Milan, 1997. A little more attention on Valle's activity has been dedicated in recent historiographical surveys on Italian postwar architecture: Marco Biraghi and Silvia Micheli, *Storia dell'Architettura Italiana 1985–2015*, Einaudi, Turin, 2013; Carlo Melograni, 'Un cosmopolita del nord-est', in *Architetture nell'Italia della ricostruzione*; Cesare de Seta, 'Gino Valle: le nuove forme della tecnologia', in Cesare de Seta, *La civiltà architettonica in Italia dal 1945 a oggi*, Longanesi, Milan, 2017, pp.267–73.

56   Bruno Zevi, 'Astrattismo contro realismo', *L'Espresso*, 10 May 1959.

57   Reyner Banham, 'Tall Block in Trieste', *The Architectural Review*, 742, November 1958, pp.281–2; Reyner Banham, 'Studio Valle', *The Architectural Review*, 772, June 1961, p.365.

58   See Reyner Banham, 'Tornare ai tempi felici', *The Architectural Review*, 742, November 1958, p.281.

59   Rykwert, 'The Work of Studio Architetti Valle', pp.121–39.

60   Kenneth Frampton, 'Prospects for a Critical Regionalism', *Perspecta*, 20, 1983, pp.147–62.

61   Manfredo Tafuri, *Storia dell'architettura italiana 1944–1985*, p.88.

62   Alessandro Rocca, 'Meno forma, più concetto. 1960–65', in Elena Carlini (ed.), *Architettura in montagna. Gino Valle in Carnia*, Navado Press, Trieste, 2005, p.212: 'The large scale, the urban theme, the grasping of figurative echoes in relation to the context, an open-minded relationship between the "great form" and the crevices, determine the character of a new manner, for Valle, of great interest, also on a methodological level.'

63   ibid., p.212.

64   Boris Podrecca, 'Gino Valle 1923–2003, Ein Requiem'.

65   See Paul Valéry, The Course in Poetics: First Lesson (held at Collège de France on 10 December 1937), in Maria Teresa Giaveri (ed.), *La caccia magica*, Guida Editori, Napoli, 1985, p.131: 'We can only consider the work's relation to its producer, or on the other hand its relation to the one whom it affects once it is made. The action of the first and the reaction of the second can never meet. The idea each has of the work is incompatible with the other's.'

66   Concerning the possible results of a stratified analysis of a single artefact, see the recent exemplary

studies: Marco Pogacnik (ed.), *Il palazzo della Regione a Trento di Adalberto Libera e Sergio Musmeci: tra antico decoro e nuove figure strutturali*, Nicolodi, Rovereto, 2007; Franz Graf and Letizia Tedeschi (eds), *L'Istituto Marchiondi Spagliardi di Vittoriano Viganò*, Mendrisio Academy Press, Mendrisio, 2009. On a single work of Gino Valle, see Luka Skansi, *Gino Valle. Deutsche Bank Milano*, Electa, Milan, 2009.

67   One example of this type has already been approached for the exhibition 'Gino Valle in Carnia' in 2005, the first attempt at an in-depth thematic survey of a significant part of Valle's activity, focusing on a single theme like that of architecture in the mountains, inside a given chronological framework. See Elena Carlini (ed.), *Architettura in montagna. Gino Valle in Carnia*, Navado Press, Trieste, 2005.

68   Sandro Marpillero, 'A Gino Valle dedicato il primo numero di *Lotus Navigator*', *Rassegna tecnica del Friuli Venezia Giulia*, September–October 2003, pp.22–3.

69   The favourite motto of Provino Valle was 'stone is needed!', an idea he could extensively put into practice after having founded an innovative professional structure in the 1930s, since the design studio was paired with a construction firm based in Udine with a branch in Rome. See Daniela Missera and Sergio Contardo, 'Un laboratorio del professionismo italiano. Provino Valle architetto (1908–1938)', degree thesis, IUAV, academic year 1983–84. By the same authors, see the succinct article published in *Rassegna tecnica del Friuli Venezia Giulia*, 5, September–October 1986, pp.17–22.

70   Gino Valle, 'Il mestiere più bello del mondo', pp.275–90.

71   ibid.

72   Massimo Trevisan and Massimo Vedovato, 'Colloquio con Gino Valle', *Anfione Zeto*, 12, 1999, pp.81–4.

73   Anna Marcolin, 'Gino Valle: l'architettura? Ora è "vittima" dello star-system', *Realtà industriale*, 1, January 2003, pp.18–22. In the same interview, Valle stated that 'the basic problem was first of all to preserve one's dignity. And then to listen at night to Radio London, to scoff at the Germans and to conduct resistance inside the factory. That is how I survived.'

74   The dossier conserved in the Valle archive includes 15 letters from 8 October 1951 to 15 May 1952, and many were written as replies to letters from Nani explicitly mentioned, but now lost.

75   Letter of 13 November 1951, in which the problems of running the studio seemed to regard only Gino and Nani, because Provino is never mentioned.

76   Also in the letter of 13 November 1951, reference is made to a possible commission for the regional planning of Friuli, probably in the wake of the urban planning works of Provino in the immediate postwar period. Nevertheless, in this letter Valle demonstrated that he did not believe very much in the work of planning: 'When I return I will make the slaves work on thousands of maps, the way they do here, all useless in the end, but lots of work for the slaves, you make lots of maps, enormous books full of reports ... until everyone thinks the plan has already been done, and then I pull out a few ideas, I who have never read the reports, and everything blows up.'

77   On the apparent 'invisibility' of Valle's design, Annalisa Avon correctly observes: 'In the production, which we know in any case came with his consulting, the design of the product is not there, at least if by design we mean the need to make an object recognizable for its style. Washing machines, stoves, refrigerators have a guise that, though the term is not appropriate, we might call anonymous. The design, in substance, seems to lean towards its own abolition.' See Annalisa Avon, 'Gino Valle. Industrial design per la casa (1956–1975)', pp.62–70.

78   Pier Carlo Santini, 'Incontro con i protagonisti: Gino Valle', *Ottagono*, 40, March 1976, pp.76–81.

79   Gino Valle, 'Il mestiere più bello del mondo', pp.275–90. In this citation, Valle continued by comparing the architect to 'he who tries to make a Stradivarius instead of a common violin: there are always two sound boxes, but one sounds good and the other sounds bad, or less good', also criticising the 'star system' that obliges architects to want to be 'recognized' and therefore 'recognizable'.

80   Manfredo Tafuri, *Storia dell'architettura italiana 1944–1985*, p.88.

81   Significant testimony is offered by Ippolito Pizzetti in a letter dated 15 October 1995 to Gino Valle: 'But you see, you who thank heavens are not an intellectual, just as Calvino was not, by nature, in this sense you are, forgive me, provincials, and you let yourself be taken in, and admire the intellectuals [...]. Only a fool could say that they are not intelligent, it would be a contradiction in terms; but it is that we, you, Barragan, me – and I am not talking about values, for heaven's sake – are simply part of another race.' Archivio Valle, Udine.

82   Letter to Piera Ricci Menichetti, 2 December 1960, Archivio Valle, Udine.

83   Letter to Piera Ricci Menichetti, 30 January 1961, Archivio Valle, Udine. These two letters were written when Valle 'on his own' designed the Zanussi offices.

84   Many pertinent and stimulating analyses of the present and also the future of the 'craftsman' who cares about doing a job 'well for its own sake', whether he is a carpenter, a scientist in a laboratory, an orchestra conductor or an architect, can be found in the book by Richard Sennett, *The Craftsman*, Yale University Press, New Haven & London, 2008.

85   Federico Marconi worked with Valle from 1955 to 1959, before going to work in the studio of Alvar Aalto in Helsinki.

86   Federico Marconi, 'Nello studio di viale Venezia i tavoli di lavoro di Provino, Nani e Gino', in *Rassegna tecnica del Friuli Venezia Giulia*, September–October 2003, pp.23–4.

87   Donald Appleyard, who arrived in 1954, had trained at the Architectural Association School in London. He stayed in Udine until 1957, before moving to the United States, first as a collaborator of Kevin Lynch at MIT in Cambridge, where he developed the first television camera for urban planning models, and later working as a professor of Landscape Design. Valle remembered him as 'a good architect who couldn't work as an architect; after all, when you enter the world of education early it is difficult to manage to pursue both careers'. See 'Bisogna immergersi nel tempo', p.226.

88   Federico Marconi, 'Nello studio di viale Venezia'. Marconi also recalls the people who habitually spent time in the studio: the electrician Adelchi Zalateu, the painter-decorator Giovanni Nardone, the skier friends Achille Minen and Mario Mattiussi, Giuseppe Baritussio (from Carnia) who was the worksite assistant, but also the sculptor Dino Basaldella and the industrialist Fermo Solari.

89   ibid. The Carnic clientele had to do in particular with the towns of Treppo Carnico and Sutrio.

90   Francesco Tentori, 'Gratitudine per Gino Valle', talk for the day of studies on 'Gino Valle: the world in Friuli', IUAV, Venice, 19 April 2007, courtesy of Giovanni Corbellini.

91   Gino Valle, 'Il mestiere più bello del mondo', p.277.

92   Francesco Tentori, 'Gratitudine per Gino Valle'.

93   Joseph Rykwert, 'The Work of Gino Valle', *Architectural Design*, March 1964, p.112.

94   Giovanni (Nino) Tenca Montini, born in Udine in 1937, with a degree from IUAV in 1969, worked as an apprentice at Studio Valle in 1962–64, involved in particular in the definitive design of the Resistance monument and the house on Via Mercatovecchio in Udine. See Nino Tenca Montini, 'A bottega in Studio Valle', *Arti Artefatti Architetture*, Udine, 2005, pp.19–22.

95   ibid.

96   In Milan in 1977 with Mario Broggi and Michael Burckhardt, in Venice in 1980 with Giorgio Macola, in Paris in 1985 with Giorgio Macola and Fernando Urquijo.

97   Valle made many trips to the United States in this period, to develop these projects with the help of local production structures. See the letter of 29 January 1968 written from Denver to his wife Piera: 'I am working to simplify the scheme, very well then, I knew it was necessary … I work well with the company that makes the prefabricated parts. I have already simplified the structure and tomorrow I will take care of the dining hall and put it at the centre, so everything becomes blindingly simple.' Archivio Valle, Udine.

98   Alessandro Rocca, 'Lo studio a Udine', *Lotus Navigator*, p.65.

99   'Gino Valle. Dal luogo alla casa', pp.18–24.

100   ibid.

101   Interview by Ado Furlan and Alessio Princic with Gino Valle, Udine, 22 July 1996, published by the Slovenian magazine *AB*: Ado Furlan and Alessio Princic (eds), 'Gino Valle: intervju', *AB Arhitektov Bilten*, 137–138, November 1997, pp.2–13.

102   Gino Valle, 'Dal luogo alla casa'.

103   The question of the methodological affinities with the work of Scarpa is complex. Valle recorded as a clash his first meeting with Scarpa as his professor for drawing during his studies at IUAV: 'He told me that I was not even capable of holding the pencil correctly […]. But I understood that Scarpa was right, because I needed to understand the space and the light, not to make an academic drawing.' See Maria Bottero and Giacomo Scarpini (eds), 'Intervista a Gino Valle', p.91.

104   Francesco Dal Co and Mario Manieri-Elia, 'La génération de l'incertitude', *L'Architecture d'Aujourd'hui*, 181 (Italie 75), September–October 1975, p.34.

105   Valle said that when he looked back on his works of architecture, he saw them 'as a historical fact and they do not annoy me, though I would not make them like that again'. See Maria Bottero and Giacomo Scarpini (eds), 'Intervista a Gino Valle', p.94.

106   Gino Valle, 'L'architettura come pratica progettuale', pp.12–13.

107   'Sandro Marpillero intervista Gino Valle da New York', pp.62–89.

108   Alessandro Rocca, 'Meno forma, più concetto. 1960–65', p.80.

109   Maria Bottero and Giacomo Scarpini (eds), 'Intervista a Gino Valle', p.84.

110   Alessandro Rocca, 'Meno forma, più concetto. 1960–65', p.83.

111   This process of slow sedimentation reveals profound affinities with the work of Afro, one of Valle's favourite painters: 'He does not, like Michelangelo, find the figure imprisoned in the block of marble; he needs a shuddering of shadow, an interruption of the raw, empty and smooth surface, to trigger an image that emerges in his mind at the limit of definition.' See Elettra Quargnal, 'Afro', in *Quaderno 1*, Galleria d'arte moderna di Udine, 1978, p.19.

112   'On the highway between Udine and Venice I understood that speed could transform the cladding of a building into a graphic trail that remains in the eyes of passing motorists. The signal passes from the eye to the brain and completely transforms an industrial shed from a static object 400 meters long into a vibration of green colour, in the case of Dapres, or red in the case of Bergamin.' See 'Sandro Marpillero intervista Gino Valle da New York', p.69.

113   The phrases come from an interview in which Valle discusses the experiences of Pop Art, denying the relationship between his industrial sheds and this American artistic current. See Adalberto Dal Lago (ed.), 'Intervista con Gino Valle', *L'Architettura Cronache e Storia*, 4, April 1982, p.279. Another significant testimony is offered by the landscape designer Andreas Kipar, 'Il paesaggio

di Gino Valle', *Acer Magazine – Architettura del paesaggio*, December 2003, p.32.

114   Alessandro Rocca, 'Meno forma, più concetto. 1960–65', p.9.

115   Alfredo Carnelutti (1910–1984), born in Gemona, had moved to Milan at the end of the 1920s, and had worked for Edoardo Persico, for *Casabella* and his projects, but also in the advertising agency run by Persico. Besides his activity as a painter, he had also made works of applied art, in particular for the Fantoni woodworking shop in Gemona. Valle called on him to collaborate in 1956, originally for the design of refrigerators for Zanussi.

116   Nino Tenca Montini, 'A bottega in Studio Valle', pp.19–22.

117   Giovanni Vragnaz, 'Intervista a Gino Valle', pp.26–47.

118   ibid.

119   Sir Patrick Abercrombie, 'Feng-Shui', in *Transactions of the Town Planning Institute*, vol. XII, 1, London, 1925.

120   'Sandro Marpillero intervista Gino Valle da New York', p.75.

121   ibid.

122   ibid. See Valle's significant statement: 'I don't know exactly where this necessity of mine to personalize the relationships of my buildings with the geographical scale comes from. But I do know that I always start there.'

123   For Valle, architecture does not settle on the earth, but 'grows from the earth'. His idea of 'scratching' the earth to find an architecture that in a certain sense is already present at the site meets with a telling comparison in the field of painting, in this interesting remark of Braque transcribed by Jean Paulhan: 'When I begin, I feel that my painting is on the other side, only covered by a white dust, the canvas. All I have to do is dust it. I have a little brush to clear the blue, another for green or yellow: my paintbrushes. When everything has been dusted off, the painting is finished.' See Jean Paulhan, *Braque le patron*, Gallimard, Paris, 1952, p.64.

124   Joseph Rykwert, 'Due recenti edifici di Gino Valle', *Domus*, 446, January 1967.

125   Giuseppe Mazzariol, 'Gino Valle', pp.165–91.

126   Joseph Rykwert, 'Architettura di Gino Valle', p.8.

127   Alessandro Rocca, 'Meno forma, più concetto. 1960–65', p.9.

128   Giovanni Corbellini, 'Astratto e contestuale. Gino Valle in Carnia', p.13.

129   Typewritten notes, 21 June 1966: Relationship between architectural 'object' and environment, Archivio Valle, Udine. These notes were probably prepared for a series of lectures in the United States, by invitation of Esther McCoy, curator of the exhibition 'Ten Italian Architects' at the Los Angeles County Museum in February 1967, which took place at the University of California at Berkeley, the San Francisco Museum, the School of Architecture and Urban Planning of UCLA, and the Los Angeles County Museum.

130   Against the 'falsehood of discourses on environmental insertion' Valle explicitly stated that 'these discourses serve only to cover up the large guilt complex of Italian architects'. Maria Bottero and Giacomo Scarpini (eds), 'Intervista a Gino Valle', p.115.

131   Kenneth Frampton, 'Anti-tabula rasa: verso un regionalismo critico', *Casabella*, 500, March 1984, p.22.

132   Joseph Rykwert even suggests identifying the whole of Valle's output with this 'provincial' condition: 'I wish the French had not diminished the word provincial to the point of depriving it of any sense of praise: Valle's architecture is, in fact, provincial, in the literal sense, and this is precisely why it is valid.' See Joseph Rykwert, 'Gino Valle architetto'.

133   Giovanni Corbellini, 'Astratto e contestuale. Gino Valle in Carnia'.

134   Susanne K. Langer says that through the advancement of conceptual gifts an artist generally becomes 'able to seek material beyond his own personal situation, because in him there is increasingly developed the habit of seeing possible or real things already half elaborated in expressive forms, in terms of his art', and further on she specifies that no material initially has a greater or lesser probability of being used by an artist, because 'the sole condition is that the material, whatever its source, be completely reduced to artistic use, completely transformed'. See Susanne K. Langer, *Feeling and Form*, Scribners, New York, 1953.

135   Francesco Dal Co, 'Gino Valle. La necessità dell'architettura', *Lotus International*, 11, 1976, pp.172–89.

136   Matteo Vercelloni (ed.), 'Gino Valle, l'architetto che guarda', *Interni*, December 2003.

137   Franca Bizzotto and Michela Agazzi (eds), 'Gino Valle 29 marzo 1988', in *Colore Segno Progetto Spazio. Giuseppe Mazzariol e gli 'Incontri con gli artisti'*, Il Poligrafo, Padua, 2009, p.140.

138   Sandro Marpillero, 'Grattacielo a metà. Gino Valle: uffici della Banca commerciale italiana a Manhattan', and 'Post scriptum. Produzione del progetto, produzione dell'edificio', *Lotus International*, 37, 1983, pp.96–119.

139   Giovanni Corbellini, 'Astratto e contestuale. Gino Valle in Carnia', p.18.

140   Alessandro Rocca, 'Meno forma, più concetto. 1960–65', pp.19–20.

141   Paraphrasing the reflections of Gabetti and Olmo, based on a critical reinterpretation of the article on éclectisme in the *Encyclopédie* of Diderot and D'Alembert, the supposed eclecticism of Valle perhaps finds its proper definition: 'The eclectic is a philosopher who giving a swift kick to prejudice, tradition, antiquity, universal consensus and authority – in short, to everything that subjugates the throng – dares to think with his own head, tracing back to the clearest of general principles, examining them and

discussing them without admitting anything unless on the basis of his own direct experience and his own reason [...]. The eclectic is a man who gathers and sifts: enjoying what he has gathered, he will live happy, and die unknown.' See Roberto Gabetti and Carlo Olmo, 'Una eredità per l'Ottocento; l'eclettismo nell'Encyclopédie, capitolo terzo', in *Alle radici dell'architettura contemporanea*, Einaudi, Turin, 1989, pp.100–128.

142   As in the analogous 'art of the actor', the inclination to risk one's own identity of subject-architect following impulses of empathy and identification actually corresponds to the exercise of a singular art: the art of metamorphosis, which Elias Canetti recognised as the 'most specific and most enigmatic gift of the human being'. See Elias Canetti, 'La missione dello scrittore', in *La coscienza delle parole*, Adelphi, Milan, 1984 (original edition 1976).

143   'Sandro Marpillero intervista Gino Valle da New York', p.138. Valle often cited this definition as 'the best definition of architecture', not very rigorously attributing it to Louis Kahn. The true quotation of Kahn is: 'The nature of space reflects what it wants to be' (Louis I. Kahn, 'Order is', *Perspecta*, vol.3, 1955, pp.46–63. See also 'Bisogna immergersi nel tempo', p.275.

144   Alessandro Rocca, 'Meno forma, più concetto. 1960–65', p.285.

145   ibid., p.288.

146   'I always opt for something that has been made, that I can consume, experience, touch, live, rather than a communication on a piece of paper [...]. I do not feel, that is, like discussing cultural systems of reference or ideas previous to the constructed architecture: for me this alone is what counts.' See Maria Bottero and Giacomo Scarpini (eds), 'Intervista a Gino Valle'.

147   See Gino Valle, keynote address at the conference 'Razionalizzazione della produzione e gestione edilizia in rapporto al risparmio energetico'.

148   In 1965 Valle attempted to patent the prefabricated panel developed for the Cucine Zanussi factory (1963). The descriptive outline of the patent, with attached drawings, shows a simplified and 'typological' version of the real panel, without dimensional indications: to be patented were the principles of the joint, of the two different sides (one a convex curve, the other serrated), and of the method of attachment with metal bars. See correspondence with the 'Studio tecnico legale per Brevetti d'Invenzione e Marchi di Fabbrica' of the engineers Barzanò & Zanardo (Rome and Milan) from 25 June 1965 to 10 November 1966, Archivio Valle, Udine.

149   Vittorio Gregotti, 'Gino Valle', in *Da, chez, from Gino Valle*, pp.13–14.

150   See Annalisa Avon, 'Gino Valle. Industrial design per la casa (1956–1975)', p.66.

151   See Pietro Valle, 'Communicating with time', in 'Gino Valle. Progetto Fantoni', special issue of the

series *Fantoni-Blueindustry*, 7, May 2004, pp.17–18: 'The relationship between Gino Valle and Fantoni is founded upon an open and creative dialogue with time, a dialogue which accepts the unexpected and adjusts to change, integrating both into a continuous planning process based not on pre-fixed plans but rather on very precise ideas regarding the transformation process. This ongoing relationship, developed over the space of thirty years, has had a profound influence upon Fantoni, even if Valle never directly asserted his identity with the group.'

152   See Nelson Goodman, *Languages of Art: An Approach to a Theory of Symbols*, Hackett Publishing, Indianapolis, 1968.

153   Lecture at IUAV on 9 April 1994, first lesson, the 'Initiation', Archivio Valle, Udine.

154   'Sandro Marpillero intervista Gino Valle da New York', pp.62–89. Valle's reference for the term 'recycling' is the article by Pierre Schneider, 'Converting the Past. A Philosophy of Recycling, with Buster Keaton our Guide' (in *Architectural Plus*, 1974), which Marpillero had translated in 1978 for the course in Architectural Composition at IUAV: an important article, for Valle, 'that clarifies my way of working with the past of the city as a necessary fact, but also one rich in possibilities of invention'.

155   Maria Bottero and Giacomo Scarpini (eds), 'Intervista a Gino Valle', p.94.

156   Gino Valle, 'Il mestiere più bello del mondo', pp.275–90.

157   Maria Bottero and Giacomo Scarpini (eds), 'Intervista a Gino Valle', p.94.

158   Letter from Gino to Nani Valle, 3 November 1951, Archivio Valle, Udine.

159   Letter of 13 November 1951, Archivio Valle, Udine.

160   Letter of 27 October 1951, Archivio Valle, Udine.

161   Letter of 8 October 1951, Archivio Valle, Udine.

162   Maria Bottero and Giacomo Scarpini (eds), 'Intervista a Gino Valle', p.115.

163   Already in 1952 he could have stayed on at Harvard to teach City Planning, while later he received offers from his former collaborator Jack Myer to go to MIT in 1961 and in 1962 (Sloan Fellowship), and to Columbia University in 1963.

164   'It was very useful for me, because it uprooted me from the professional practice that had me blocked in the studio.' See Gino Valle, 'Il mestiere più bello del mondo', p.280.

165   Valle responded to the offer of the chairman of Harvard: 'Thank you very much, but Venice is 100 kilometres from here, and even if I will have 250 students instead of 20, I am going to see what the situation is like there.' Ibid.

166   Valle's commitment to the field of education of designers was anything but secondary, as demonstrated by his entry in the Education Working Group of ICSID (International Council of Societies of Industrial Design),

the largest international association in that field. Later he was vice-president of the Executive Board of ICSID from 1967 to 1971.

167　Gino Valle, 'L'educazione dell'industrial designer', *Edilizia Moderna*, 85, 1965. Valle took part as a delegate from Italy at the important conference in Bruges (21–24 March 1964) organised with the support of UNESCO.

168　See the document 'Topics for the discussion on architectural education' prepared by Walter Gropius as the basis for the works of the Education Committee of the 7th CIAM in Bergamo, 1949, in which we read: 'Teachers should be appointed only after sufficient practical experience of their own, both in design and building.' We would like to thank Franco Berlanda, who took part as a student in the work of this Committee, for bringing this document to our attention.

169　Following Valle's candidacy in 1971 as a lecturer, 'one of the young "*professorini*" told Samonà: "But no, Valle is a small professional, he cannot be a professor".' See Gino Valle, 'Il mestiere più bello del mondo', p.280. Valle was often very critical of the IUAV and its 'professorini' [literally: 'little professors']: 'I am talking about IUAV in Venice, where I have taught for many years. It is a department in a state of decadence, with a faculty that in most cases has never built anything: they have never designed a building, nothing. How can they teach?' Erminia della Frattina, 'Valle: ricetta Friuli per il paesaggio', *Il Sole-24 Ore nordest*, 30 April 2001, p.3.

170　Fagnoni said Valle did not address the theme of the lesson, which was 'Freedom, the foundation of teaching and university scientific research, and new methods of the architectural disciplines', and Valle defended himself in his petition to the Council (15 March 1965, Archivio Valle, Udine), saying that Fagnoni was expecting an interpretation of the theme like: 'The freedom of teaching and research that exists in the Italian university would be threatened by new methods of planning of the architectural disciplines', an interpretation that would therefore be clearly reactionary, against the of political science and sociology that were growing inside Italian universities in those years.

171　'A critical and non-dogmatic, problematic and non-normative teaching plan. Verification of the exercise of creative freedom of the students', petition to the Superior Council, 15 March 1965, Archivio Valle, Udine.

172　Valle was highly critical of the fact that this split between school and reality produced 'nominalist qualification of architects, right from the degree, as so-called researchers and professionals, where the former tend to opt for a career in teaching or criticism, simply increasing the schism with reality, while the latter are absorbed by the economic forces of reality and, for the most part, subjugated by them'. Ibid.

173　Gino Valle, 'Il mestiere più bello del mondo', p.281.

174　Lecture at IUAV on 9 April 1994, entitled 'The Initiation': 'Not an initiation to occult things, black magic, voodoo, vice or virtue. An initiation to design, architecture, to being an architect [...]. An initiation to knowledge of the world and of ourselves.' Archivio Valle, Udine.

175　Interview by Ado Furlan and Alessio Princic with Gino Valle, Udine, 22 July 1996.

176　Letter from Ippolito Pizzetti to Gino Valle on 10 January 1993, with the manuscript of an article proposed for the magazine *Folia di Acer*. Archivio Valle, Udine.

177　Lecture of 1 February 1991. Archivio Valle, Udine.

178　On the subject of never taking anything for granted and 'continuously seeking' to find a personal position, Pietro Valle offers a precious contribution: 'It was perhaps a trait of my father, which he passed on to me, and he told me not to believe even in him as a point of reference ... By the time I took the helm at Studio Valle, after my father's death, I had acquired a personal point of view, only partially influenced by his work. Maybe in this path detached from him, I have grasped his teaching about freedom of thought more than I would have had I remained at home. I don't think continuity is the most important issue in the work of the Studio.' See Roberto Gamba, 'Architetti Valle, Udine. Pragmatismo e sperimentazione. Intervista di Pietro Valle', *Costruire in laterizio*, 114, November–December 2006, p.42.

179　Lecture of 9 April 1994. Archivio Valle, Udine.

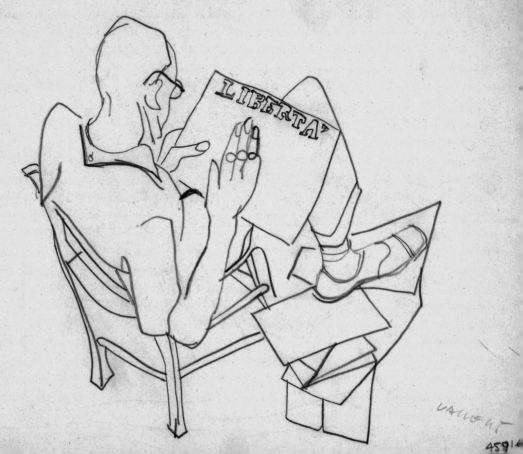

1 Formative Experiences and Early Works (1946–51)

Having graduated from scientific high school in Udine in 1942, Gino Valle enrolled at the Istituto Universitario di Architettura di Venezia (IUAV), where he took a degree in 1948. The time spent at the school was sporadic at best, due to the war and the intense design activity conducted in the studio of his father, Provino. In July 1943, after a few months at the university, Valle enlisted in the officers' training programme of the Navy at Pula, in present-day Croatia. This experience came to an end with the armistice of 8 September: captured by the Germans, he was imprisoned at Jenbach, near Innsbruck, where he remained for over 18 months.[1] He escaped the camp in April 1945, and returned to Udine on 6 May, after a difficult voyage.[2]

After the war, the completion of his studies in Venice proceeded parallel to his work in his father's studio. Provino's studio was a true workshop, in which Gino's sister Fernanda ('Nani', 1927–87) had learned the trade, and where his friend and classmate Marcello D'Olivo had also entered the profession.[3] Provino Valle, who took a degree in 1908 at the Fine Arts Academy of Venice, had held various professional positions in different Italian cities during the course of his career, also in the area of urban planning, and experimented – like many of his contemporaries – with the many stylistic trends of the time, from the historical languages of a Viennese type to the Roman 'barocchetto', all the way to the exemplary 'modernist' achievements of

the Colonia Elioterapica (1938) and the Casa della Madre e del Bambino in Udine (1938).[4] Belonging to the talented generation of Zanini, Miani and Midena, he was an outstanding exponent of professionalism in Udine in the early years of the 20th century, and he had a profound influence on the personality of his son. Proof of this is given by Gino Valle himself, in his Curriculum Vitae, prepared in 1949 in his first attempt to obtain a Fulbright scholarship to study in the United States, where he put particular emphasis on his training under his father – 'in close contact with the profession and its problems'[5] – seen as a fundamental experience in his background.

The early architectural training of the young Valle happened at the same time as a short but energetic activity as an artist, initially fuelled by the drawing exercises done in childhood with his father on their frequent walks in the mountains. Though no direct examples of his paintings have survived, the experience does not seem to have had the character of an amateur hobby. Starting in 1941 Valle's work was featured in a series of exhibitions on a local and national level, demonstrating his engagement and ambitions in this field, and offering stimuli to identify certain contents of his initial artistic and cultural interests.

His greatest success in these years was the selection of two works for the 5th Premio Bergamo in 1943, an edition with a jury containing Carlo

(*left, top*) Alpine village, 1945.

(*left, bottom*) Portrait of Provino Valle, 1945.

Carrà and Giorgio Morandi. Organised by Giuseppe Bottai and defined by Argan as the 'prize for good painting',[6] Premio Bergamo was considered the place to promote new artistic research and one of the rare cultural events of the country in which dialectical positions could emerge.[7] Participation in this competition demonstrates the maturity and level of quality achieved by Valle when he was just twenty years old.[8] A maturity that is proven above all by his contacts and acquaintances, together with D'Olivo, in Venetian artistic circles – around Vedova, Santomaso, Turcato – which shortly thereafter would give rise, through the 'Fronte Nuovo delle Arti', to an Italian reprise of the experiences of the European avant-gardes. Nevertheless, the reasons why Gino Valle brusquely interrupted his young career as an artist continue to elude us. In an interview, he recalled having concluded this experience in 1943, when '… I threw many of my drawings and paintings away, in a canal in Venice, a sort of sacrificial ritual'.[9]

The many projects assigned to him by his father in the immediate postwar period constituted the first true proving ground for the young architect

from Udine. They were commissions from different public and private clients in Friuli (Udine, various towns in Carnia, the Lignano coast) that shed light on the 'legacy' of relationships constructed by Provino during the 1920s and 1930s with local administrations and the society of Friuli, with major projects in the territory, of outstanding quantity and quality.

From these years of apprenticeship to the death of their father in 1955, Gino and Nani seem to have had plenty of room to develop projects and supervise worksites.[10] While it is not always easy to establish the contribution of each personality in the activity of the studio in these years, the evidence offered by archival sources allows us to reconstruct the specific contribution of Gino Valle, and the linguistic and design themes he addressed in these early years of his career.

One of Valle's main responsibilities, starting in the first months of 1946, seems to have been the preparation of the studio's many projects for Lignano Sabbiadoro. We do not know the context for which these projects – about 15 in all – were

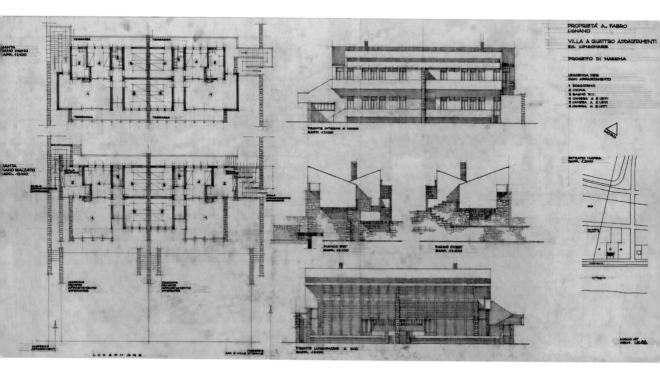

Project for the Fabro building with four apartments, Lignano, July 1947.

PROPRIETÀ BEVILACQUA MARIO
...NO

...ETTO DI MASSIMA
...A NOVE APPARTAMENTI STAGIONALI
...ERCIZIO PUBBLICO

VISTA PROSPETTICA DAL LUNGOMARE

Project for the Bevilacqua building in Lignano, July 1947.

developed. They are mostly vacation homes or apartment houses for seasonal rentals, designed for private or public clients, like the building for the Cooperativa Muratori of Udine, designed by Valle for his degree thesis, and also the only project that studio was able to build in Lignano during this period.[11]

If we closely observe these projects, we can see the particular thematic clarity of the rooting of the buildings in the earth: dry masonry walls, bases in stone or brick functioning as pedestals on which to place abstract volumes, grafts of different sizes and functions, which instead negate their own constructive material nature. This coexistence between contextual and abstract character became the recurring theme in the design exercises of Valle in these years, in absolute tune with the achievements on the Italian scene of the very early postwar period. But the interesting part of these projects does not only lie in the characterisation of the given material of the building enclosure, or the positioning of the architectural object in a

contemporary language; these projects also point to Valle's interest in exploration of the theme on a plastic and three-dimensional level.

The project for the Fabro house (1947) demonstrates how the base was composed of a series of parallel partitions that define paths, ascents, wrappers, divisions between residential cells; a two-storey volume is grafted onto the base, topped by two inverted pitches. Particular care has gone into the design of the lateral facades where the two systems meet, while the two longitudinal fronts are distinguished by two different types of treatment. In the Bevilacqua house (1947, first project), whose volume terminates with a single pitch, the facade with sunscreens becomes the characteristic feature.[12] With one or two pitches (mostly organised as an impluvium), in all these projects the roofs approach the problem of concluding the volume, more than the facade, with the objective of avoiding a serial and relatively simple planimetric arrangement in favour of a more complex design of the volumes.

Vacation housing for Cooperativa Muratori of Udine,
Lignano Sabbiadoro, 1948–49.

These projects introduce certain themes that
would accompany the first constructed work by Gino
Valle, the collective building for the Cooperativa
Muratori on the Lignano waterfront, designed in
1948 and built in the winter of 1948–49. This was a
parallelepiped on three levels, facing the sea from
its shorter side. This facade represents the place
of maximum plastic character of the building: it
was produced by the design of the roof, with two
inverted pitches, and by the particular excavation
of the end. The facade seen as a joint between the
beach and the three levels of the building, and the
entire system of vertical connections, was opened
and displayed to the outside. The result is a front with
a three-dimensional, asymmetrical character – as it
is composed of multiple planes, both vertical and
horizontal – to counter the regular, flat arrangement
of the long facades, which instead reflect the serial
sequence of the bedrooms. Certain details enhanced
the material quality of this building, like the design
of the balconies, the wooden roof, the stone walls
dividing the lot from the beach, all the way to the
design of the furnishings done by Valle and the
decorations in the common zones, for which the
architect called in several painter friends.

The project for the vacation house in Lignano was
presented by Valle for his thesis examination at IUAV
in 1948. His relationship with the school in Venice
and its renowned faculty at the time was anything
but simple and linear. He repeatedly underlined his
autonomy in both academic and linguistic terms,
displaying precocious independence with respect to

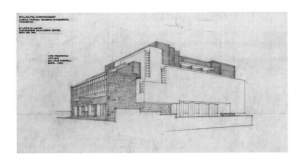

Cinema Margherita in Tarcento, 1946–48. Perspective of a design solution (May 1947).

Cinema Margherita in Tarcento, 1946–48. View of the hall.

an entire generation of figures that were involved in the national cultural debate in that period. Referring to Rogers, Samonà and Albini, rather than describing them as mentors Valle called them 'uncles', 'who in a certain sense indicated a professional path of construction which for me, personally, has always been a precedent.'[13] As we have seen, Valle's approach to architecture happened through the reality of the profession and its relationship with construction. These were the factors that led to his interest in the generation of Albini and Rogers, while he seemed to be totally detached, already in these years, regarding the theoretical and programmatic aspects of the disciplinary debate.[14]

Nevertheless, his knowledge of contemporary national and international architectural developments was far from limited. Stimulated by his father's library, which included French and German publications from the 1920s and 1930s, Valle grew up with an open, cosmopolitan attitude. Provino's magazines were used as material for discussions with his teachers Samonà and Scarpa: those pages contributed to bring into the debates at the school in Venice the 'practically unknown' Wright, Scharoun, Neutra.[15] Gino Valle took part in that atmosphere of admiration for Wright that became one of the strongest bonds of the Venetian school in the early postwar era, culminating with the visit of the American master to Venice to receive an honorary degree in 1951. It was a particularly fertile atmosphere in which teachers like Samonà, Zevi and Scarpa shared, almost on equal terms, the passion, knowledge and analysis of international works of architecture with their students.[16] Above all, it was the passion for the American master that appealed to the students from Udine: Valle, D'Olivo and above all Angelo Masieri.[17]

Observing some of his early works, we can see that Valle was not lacking in knowledge of Dutch and Scandinavian architecture, especially the work of Alvar Aalto and Willem Marinus Dudok, whose creations were shown, together with projects by Wright, Sullivan and Richardson, in the photographic exhibition 'Mostra di architettura moderna' held in Udine in 1948.[18]

(*left*) Gino Valle and Marcello D'Olivo at the worksite of Cinema Margherita in Tarcento, *c.*1948.

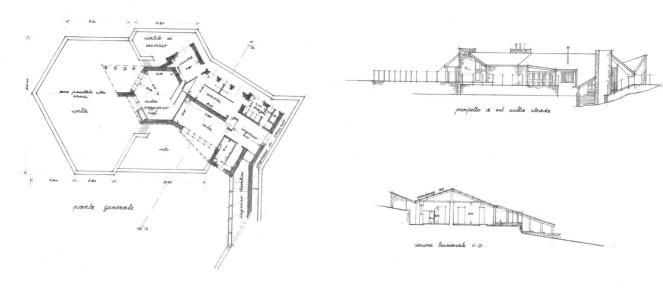

FIELIS
scuola materna
rapp. 1:200

cortile di
servizio

area parallela alla
strada

cortile

aula
soggiorno ref.

aula

ingresso

orti

pianta generale

prospetto a est sulla strada

sezione trasversale C-D

Kindergarten, Fielis, 1949–50. Project panel with ground floor plan, downhill elevation and section.

For the Margherita cinema in Tarcento, Valle came to terms with Aalto's solution for the ceiling of the auditorium of the library of Viipuri. The shape of the undulated surface that conceals the rhythm of the reinforced concrete beams was simplified with respect to its model. The hall, slightly recessed below street level, was developed and built in 1946–48, though only partially in keeping with the original design.[19] The two parallel stone partitions that form the lateral perimeters of the building were halved in height with respect to the initial project, in which they were originally supposed to function as a base for the volume of the upper theatre. In the various versions of the design for the complex we can glimpse Valle's attempt to break down the enclosure into architectural elements of different material character. He experimented with a composition of interlocked planes, of a neo-plastic nature – surfaces in stone, brick or paint finish – which, more than reflecting the experiments of the Dutch 20th-century avant-gardes, reveal affinities with the languages proposed by Dudok in the city hall of Hilversum (1923–31). Furthermore, the Margherita cinema has certain similarities to the Banca cattolica del Veneto in Tarvisio, a project from the same period by his friend Angelo Masieri (1947).

Wrightian overtones, which never descend to literal citation, can be seen in several projects developed for the Alpine areas of Friuli; first of all, the small kindergarten of Fielis (1949–50). In particular, the noteworthy features are the central importance assigned to the design of the roof, which becomes the characterising element of the volume, 'perched' on a slight slope, and the detailed planimetric arrangement that structures both the interior spaces and their relationships with the natural context in which the building is inserted. In this small-scale architecture, Valle introduces for the first time one of the themes that would stay with him throughout his career, namely the consideration of the path towards the building as a characterising element of spatial experience. Starting with the entrance steps, the movement through the kindergarten is dictated by constant changes of angles and levels. At first the visitor is guided, climbing the entrance steps, into the closed central spaces of the building; the route continues and terminates in two rooms – one with a rectangular plan, the other hexagonal – that

are entirely open to the landscape, with windows offering specific views of the But Valley.[20]

The free and open arrangement of the plan of the kindergarten reveals that Wright's lesson had already been fully absorbed by Valle. Nevertheless, we should not forget that Provino himself, already in the 1930s, had come to grips with certain Wrightian themes.[21] In this sense, it is plausible to suppose that his terrace in Lignano represented a prototype for a series of design responses that Studio Valle provided in the early postwar years to several commissions from Alpine communities, like the hotel of Forni Avoltri or the tourism complex of Monte Lussari (both in 1949).[22]

Kindergarten, Fielis, 1949–50. View of the entrance wall and the downhill facade.

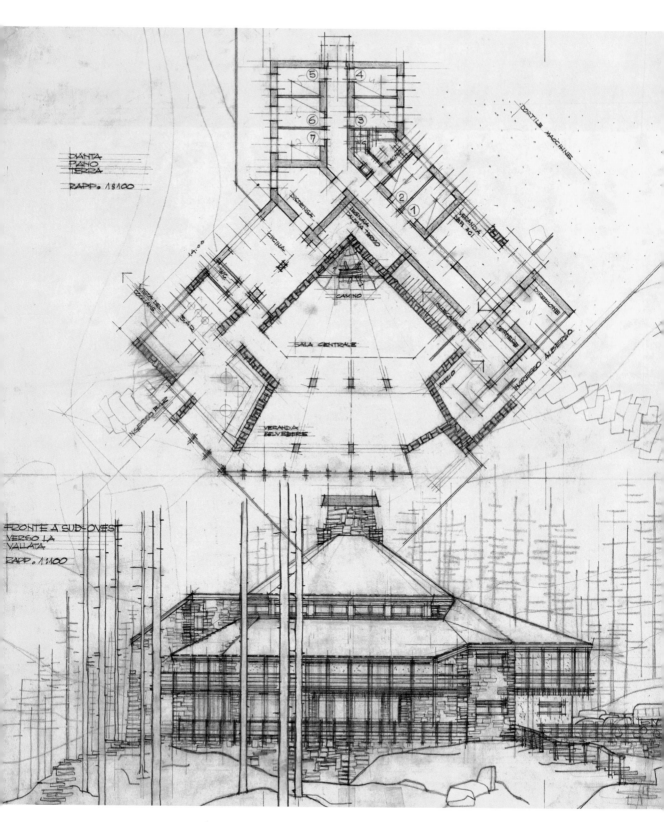

Project for a hotel at Collina di Forni Avoltri, October 1949.

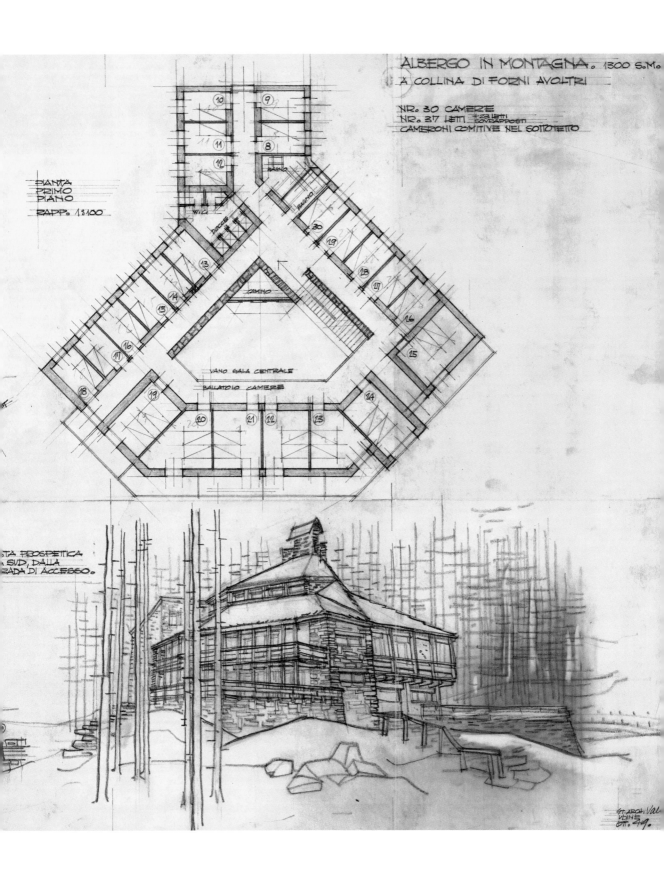

ALBERGO IN MONTAGNA. 1300 S.M.
A COLLINA DI FORNI AVOLTRI

NR. 30 CAMERE
NR. 317 LETTI 123 LETTI SOVRAPPOSTI
CAMERONI COMITIVE NEL SOTTOTETTO

PIANTA
PRIMO
PIANO
RAPP. 1:100

VANO SALA CENTRALE
BALLATOIO CAMERE

CAMINO

STA PROSPETTICA
SUD, DALLA
RADA DI ACCESSO.

Ghetti house, Codroipo, 1951. View from the street.

In 1951, still in the Carnic context, Gino and Nani Valle obtained commissions for several projects connected with the INA-Casa plan. In spite of their small size, these works reveal an approach of synthesis addressing different themes: rational layout, serial production, contextualisation in mountain towns.[23]

In all these projects, we can see Gino Valle's sensitivity to the rooting of the buildings in the territory. This theme was refined in the years to follow and was pertinent to a framework of radical rethinking of the language in Italian architectural culture after the war. The stimuli arriving from Nordic architecture and the interest in Wright shared what Giancarlo De Carlo, in one of the first essays published on the American master in Italy, defined as the pursuit of the 'unity of the landscape', i.e. the research on the identification and fusion of architectural intervention and nature.[24] In this sense, both Wright and Aalto were not seen by Valle only as linguistic sources from which to borrow, because the architect from Udine sought inspiration in their experiences to give buildings a character specifically connected to the context that hosted them – a character that manifested itself in Valle's works of this period both in the material dimension and in the physiological experience, the relationship and measure of the movements of man between constructed space and natural context.

The works of the young Valle also establish a dialogue with achievements of the same period on the Italian scene. Certain motifs of the Bisaro apartment building in Udine (1945–50) reveal awareness of the projects of Albini, Camus and Palanti for the buildings in the Fabio Filzi district in Milan (1936–38). The relationship is evident in the composition of the rear facade and the solution of the stairwell, indicated on the facade by a protruding plane featuring two continuous lateral openings. The Bisaro building also had a complicated design history, developed in five phases, with progressive simplification of the design as the date of construction approached. This evolution sheds light on the freedom granted to Valle in his father's studio. The building would also be the location of Studio Valle starting in 1952.

We should probably also add the name of Ignazio Gardella to the list of 'uncles' indicated by Valle. Besides the fact that his impluvium pitches represent a significant precedent for the volumetric experiments of the projects for Lignano, Gardella's 'Casa del Viticoltore' (1947) was cited in the small Ghetti house at Codroipo (1951, which Valle designed together with his sister Nani), in the detail of the vertical fissure corresponding to the entrance. The dialogue with Gardella, however, ends with this cut, because for the Valles this gesture not only marked the entrance to the house, but was also part of a system of strategies that constructed, in the whole, a contrast to the smooth and 'typical' constructed block: like the bending of the facade, the brick chimney, the small volume with a square plan with the terrace that protrudes from the enclosure in the corner towards the street, the roof pitches that are interrupted on the facade. These strategies set out, as Samonà indicated, to 'also grant value to those forms that are familiar to us, and are therefore sufficiently intimate to be able to assimilate them as figurative events'.[25] Figurative gestures, then, that bring out and revitalise the meaning of established forms, as can also be seen in the competition project for the Istituto tecnico in Udine (1950), marked by slightly 'expressionist' accents, and in Foghini house in San Giorgio di Nogaro (1948–52). As in his painting, then, Valle rejected the path of abstraction, and instead opted to explore the figurative dimension of the architectural language.

Competition project for the Istituto Commerciale of Udine, 1951. Panel with perspective views.

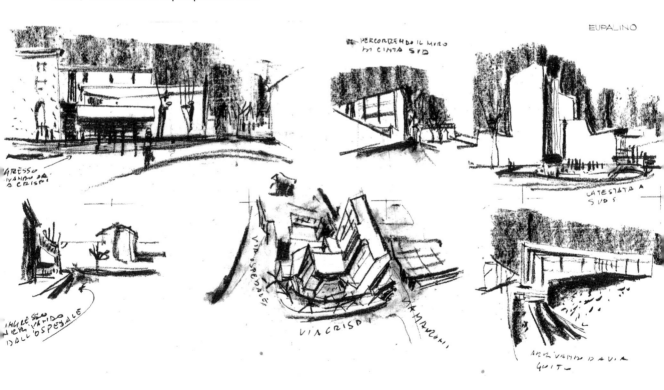

Notes

1   Curriculum Vitae of Gino Valle, 12 December 1949, Archivio Valle, Udine.

2   While imprisoned, Valle worked as a mechanical draughtsman in the factory of Ernst Heinkel in Jenbach, which produced parts for the fearful long-range V1 and V2 rockets. See Curriculum Vitae of Gino Valle, and see Dino Dardi, *Dieci profili di artisti nella regione Friuli-Venezia Giulia*, Edizioni della Galleria Il Camino, Pordenone, 1965.

3   Francesco Borrella, 'Una biografia', in Ferruccio Luppi and Paolo Nicoloso (eds), *Marcello D'Olivo: architetto*, Mazzotta, Milan, 2002, p.92.

4   For the biography of Provino Valle, see Chino Ermacora, 'Provino Valle architetto', *La Panarie*, 6, 1929, pp.355–71; Francesco Tentori, *Architettura e architetti in Friuli nel primo cinquantennio del Novecento*, Arti grafiche friulane, Udine, 1970; Marco Pozzetto (ed.), *Guida all'architettura del Novecento di Udine e provincia*, Electa, Milan, 1996.

5   Curriculum Vitae of Gino Valle.

6   Letter by Giulio Carlo Argan sent to Amedeo Pieragostini in 1989, in AA.VV., *Gli anni del premio Bergamo: arte in Italia intorno agli anni trenta*, Electa, Milan, 1993, p.16. 'Premio Bergamo', Argan writes, 'was born without the slightest political intent: that happened by reaction, because it was seen as the opposite of Premio Cremona, organized by Roberto Farinacci and supported by Ugo Ojetti. That was the prize of fascist painting, which was dreadful painting; Premio Bergamo, which had no political connotations, became the prize for good painting … As always, serious culture was considered anti-fascist, though instead it was only culture fought against by lack of culture … The winners of Premio Bergamo have remained in art history … It was a good thing that a cultured minister, Bottai, saved fascism from the nevertheless well-deserved shame of having stifled freedom of culture everywhere and in every way.'

7   On this theme, see Emilio R. Papa, 'Il premio Bergamo (1939–1942) e la politica culturale di Giuseppe Bottai', in AA.VV., *Gli anni del premio Bergamo*, pp.237–63; Sergio Bettini, 'Politica fascista delle arti', in *Museo civico di Padova*, 1939–1941, III serie, Padova, 1942, reprinted in Marco Lorandi, Fernando Rea and Chiara Tellini Perina (eds), *Il premio Bergamo 1939–1942: documenti, lettere, biografie*, Electa, Milan, 1993, pp.93–6.

8   The competition guidelines indicate that the exhibition was supposed to open on 1 September 1943. In the fourth edition, in 1942, the commission selected 192 from 1276 works submitted for the competition. See ibid., Marco Lorandi, Fernando Rea, and Chiara Tellini Perina (eds).

9   Maria Bottero and Giacomo Scarpini (eds), 'Intervista a Gino Valle', *Zodiac*, 20, December 1970, pp.82–115. Valle's activity as a painter did not completely stop in 1943, but continued, according to witnesses, for a few years after that. There is documentation of his participation in a group show in 1946, at the gallery La Margherita in Rome. See Curriculum Vitae of Gino Valle.

10   Nani Valle left the studio in December 1958.

11   Where the series of projects for private clients, which all remained on paper, are concerned, we cannot exclude the idea that their preparation had something in common with the professional activity of Provino Valle between the two wars, and particularly with the coexistence of the design studio and the construction contractor inside the company created towards the middle of the 1920s. Though the company was no longer in operation after the war, the number and characteristics of these projects (designed to a great extent on neighbouring lots) seem to respond to an attempt to 'test' the real estate market, linked to the new appeal of the zone for tourism.

12   In this four-level apartment building foundation partitions simply mark the borders of the lot and indicate the entrance to a public facility. The stairwell is positioned outside the volume and serves three apartments per floor; their entrances are located along the balconies on the facade towards the street.

13   Gino Valle, 'Il mestiere più bello del mondo', in Giorgio Ciucci (ed.), *L'architettura italiana oggi. Racconto di una generazione*, Laterza, Bari, 1989, p.277.

14   Afterwards, Valle gave his pragmatic position credit for his human and professional growth: 'It [the profession] is a sort of big craft. Only if it is seen as great craftsmanship can you abolish all the problems of relationships with history, with the avant-garde, with the masters, the fathers, the sons, etc., etc. You insert yourself, that is, in an everyday and historical flow without traumas, without problems. For me it has always been like that.' Ibid.

15   ibid. p.279; 'Casa Foghini nei ricordi di Gino Valle', interview by Enzo Volponi and Luigi Soramel, in *Annuario 1992*, Associazione Ad Undecimum, San Giorgio di Nogaro, 1992. Valle acknowledged the didactic contribution of Giuseppe Samonà only in the fact that he had taught him the 'importance of continuously changing one's mind', while the relationship with Carlo Scarpa and the mutual esteem of the two became stronger over the years, even though the initial impact with the Venetian master had been one of contrast. Valle recalled: 'He told me I didn't even know how to hold a pencil (he said that to me, and I thought I was a great painter worthy of the Premio Bergamo). However, I understood that Scarpa was right, i.e. that I had to understand space and light, not making academic design. So I simply showed up for the exam: Scarpa had understood that I had understood, and since then we have been friends', in Maria Bottero and Giacomo Scarpini (eds), 'Intervista a Gino Valle', p.84. The theme for drawing from a model chosen by Scarpa was a plaster by Donatello, the head of Niccolò da Uzzano. See Mario Pisani, 'Dialogo con Gino Valle', *Costruire in laterizio*, 40, July–August 1994, p.337.

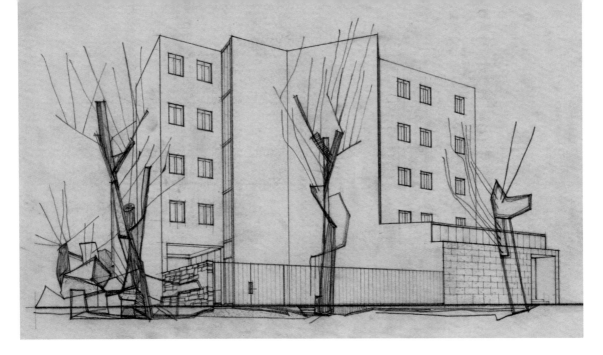

Bisaro building, Udine, 1945–50. Design variant of January 1946.

16   On the atmosphere of work in the school in these years, Samonà offered interesting remarks: 'There are moments of life we recall with particular emotion. ... Of these moments ... we intensely relive that exchange of fresh thoughts, that enthusiasm of discussing and dreaming that makes the old and the younger like brothers [...] We were like pioneers, discoverers of unknown lands, and this made us brethren in a constraining energy of collaboration, of which each of us conserves a vivid memory.' See Giuseppe Samonà, 'Ricordo di Masieri', *Metron*, 49–50, January–April 1954, p.32.

17   On the reception of the work of Wright in Venice and on the part of the students from Udine, see Francesco Tentori, 'Friuli: anni 50', in Sergio Polano and Luciano Semerani (eds), *Friuli Venezia Giulia: guida critica all'architettura contemporanea*, Arsenale, Venice, 1992, p.148; Massimo Bortolotti, 'Angelo Masieri. Architetture 1947–1952', in Massimo Bortolotti (ed.), *Angelo Masieri architetto, 1921–1952*, Edizioni Arti Grafiche Friulane, Udine, 1995, pp.33–51; Maristella Casciato, 'Wright and Italy', in Anthony Alofsin (ed.), *Frank Lloyd Wright: Europe and Beyond*, University of California Press, Los Angeles, 1999, pp.75–99.

18   The exhibition, organised by the Società Ingegneri e Architetti in Turin, contained over 800 projects and photographs of 300 architects from 16 countries. Cfr. Arturo Manzano, 'Lezione di architettura nella Loggia del Lionello', *Messagero Veneto*, 9 May 1948, p.3; 'Architetture moderne nella Loggia del Lionello', *Il Gazzettino*, 9 May 1948, p.2; Licio Damiani, 'Cultura in Friuli nel secondo dopoguerra (1945–1950)', in Massimo Bortolotti (ed.), *Angelo Masieri architetto*, pp.33–51.

19   The project underwent a complex evolution, and though it was developed in a second phase in 1957, the constructed building still represents the provisional solution.

20   On this theme see Giovanni Corbellini, 'Astratto e contestuale. Gino Valle in Carnia', in Elena Carlini (ed.), *Architetture in montagna. Gino Valle in Carnia*, Navado Press, Trieste, 2005, pp.13–20.

21   The Wrightian references for the terrace of Lignano are hypothesised by Tentori and Nicoloso in Francesco Tentori, *Architettura e architetti in Friuli*; Paolo Nicoloso, *La città inventata*.

22   Both projects are mentioned by Valle in his Curriculum Vitae.

23   The projects are well documented in Ferruccio Luppi and Paolo Nicoloso (eds), *Il Piano Fanfani in Friuli: storia e architettura dell'Ina-Casa*, Leonardo, Pasian di Prato, 2001; Ferruccio Luppi, 'I primi progetti per il territorio friulano', in Paola Di Biagi (ed.), *La grande ricostruzione: il piano Ina-Casa e l'Italia degli anni cinquanta*, Donzelli, Rome, 2001, pp.365–72. Gino Valle remembers that the INA-Casa commissions were desired and developed mostly by his sister Fernanda (Nani), who had not yet taken her degree at the time. Conversation between Luppi and Valle, 5 December 1999, in Paola Di Biagi (ed.), *La grande ricostruzione*, p.369.

24   Giancarlo De Carlo, 'L'insegnamento di Frank Lloyd Wright', *Domus*, 207, March 1946, pp.21–3.

25   Giuseppe Samonà, 'Architetture di giovani', *Casabella*, 205, April–May 1955, p.10.

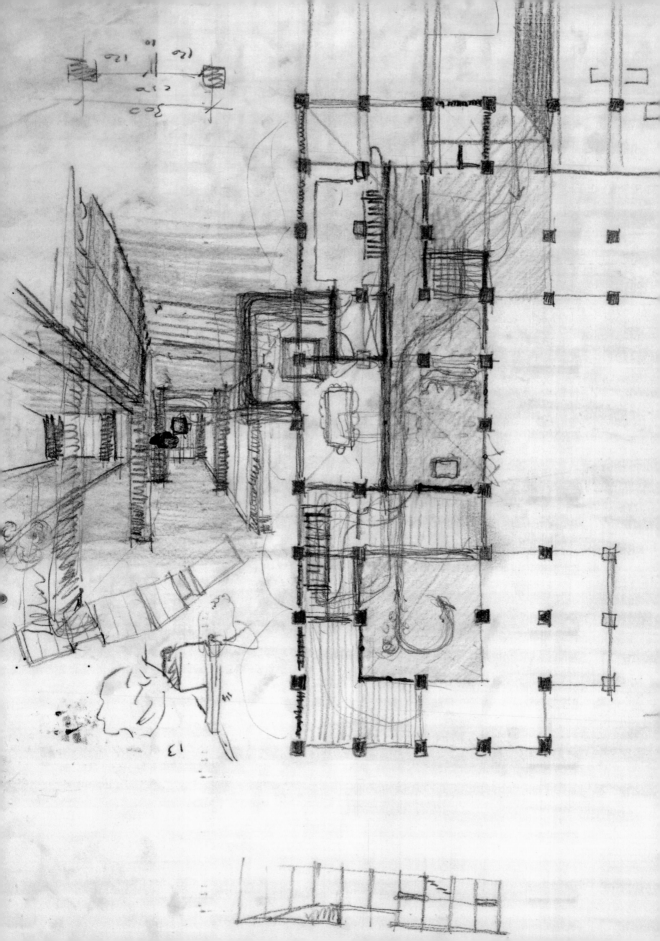

2 Return from Harvard (1951–58)

The period of time spent in the United States, from autumn 1951 to summer 1952, meant much more to Valle than just a graduate course in Urban Planning at the Harvard Graduate School of Design directed by Walter Gropius.[1] This was an authentic study trip that allowed him to greatly expand his cultural perspective. The encounters with European émigré architects, intellectuals and artists, the discovery of American avant-garde magazines and writings, the visits to the works of Wright and Sullivan were just some of the reasons why the American sojourn led to important human and professional enrichment. Valle's experience was far from isolated: in the Venetian and Udinese circles of the time, a trip overseas was seen as a cultural pilgrimage, in order to finally experience the passion for a context known exclusively through publications.[2] Architect Angelo Masieri joined Valle in 1952, to complete a tour they had dreamt about for years, which would culminate with the encounter at Taliesin with Frank Lloyd Wright.[3]

Valle was able to grasp and come to terms with a particular period in architecture and urban planning in the US, featuring the activity of Wright at Taliesin and the debates in progress at important East Coast universities. His research conducted in Boston, his profession as an architect and the many cultural activities initiated after the return from the US bear witness to the complexity and breadth of the stimuli he received; Valle continued to cultivate and update

this relationship with American circles in the years to follow.[4]

For Valle, the formation of an American cultural and expressive self-awareness, conducted in a heterogeneous way by part of US architectural culture in the framework of a general review of the features of the International Style, represented a stimulating case for comparison with the contemporary Italian debate. In this sense, besides the exploration of Wright, Valle was particularly interested in the early residential projects of Paul Rudolph, seen even before the departure for the United States on the pages of *Architectural Forum*,[5] while in the years to follow he also paid constant attention to the output of Louis Kahn. But, more in general, the themes that would soon constitute the ideological framework of the first *Perspecta* – the recognition of American vernacular architecture, the first definitions of 'regionalism' in architecture, the challenge to the legacy of the Modern masters – met with striking parallels to the reflection and production of Valle across the 1950s.[6]

His thinking on the relationship between architecture and environment, which began in Italy and was enriched in contact with the American context, was also fed by his reading of the texts of Patrick Abercrombie.[7] In particular, Valle found stimulating verification of his own design sensibilities in Abercrombie's focus on the philosophy of Feng Shui: the spiritual and practical

(*left*) Project for Villa Zanussi, Pordenone, sketch, 1958.

emphasis on the enhancement of places and sites in the Chinese tradition served the English urbanist to conceptualise the meaning of a modern kind of planning developed in total functional and aesthetic harmony between man and the environment. But for Valle this was not a romantic or folklore-steeped acceptance of oriental philosophies; it was instead a metaphor of the relations to establish between the artificialised environment and nature. His memory of the Säynätsalo City Hall by Aalto, 'discovered' from magazines 'for the first time in 1951 in Chicago', clearly conveys this meaning:

> I then understood one fundamental thing, i.e. Aalto's propensity for the non-form, which is the key for the interpretation of his architecture ... to arrive, that is, not at the form you see as the work of man, but at something that is derived from nature, that is not read as form but only as space, which you use only as space.[8]

Nevertheless, what was fully discussed by the young architect from Friuli in his studies for a Master's degree was the entire English legacy in the urban planning discipline. Valle's reinterpretation of the work of Ebenezer Howard is of particular interest – documented in the reflections organised in his papers at Harvard[9] – taking positions that contrasted with the contemporary Anglo-American debate, and particularly with the positions of Lewis Mumford, Frederick James Osborn and Erwin Gutkind, involved in those years in the historical interpretation of the work of the author of *Garden Cities of To-morrow*.[10] In those authors, Valle disagreed with the assessment of the Garden City phenomenon, which they saw as a nostalgic, anti-urban manifestation on the city, produced by a substantially static vision of society, and therefore out of step with the times. Valle's analysis instead started with strictly realistic and pragmatic considerations of the problem: the history of the Garden City should be appreciated for its value as an open laboratory, as the story of an exercise of continuous reassessment and redevelopment of its component themes. Rather than seeking a transitive relationship between ideological features,

design and implementation, or seeing the Garden Cities as the manifestation of a theory of urbanism – interpretations at the basis of the criticised positions – Valle hailed the achievement and parallel testing in reality of that experience, as if there were no definitive form of the Garden City in the mind of the author, but simply its constant refinement over time.[11] In the end, Valle saw Howard's work as a true demonstration of the potential of planning to renew itself through experience gained over time, and his project could be seen as a process towards the definition of possible forms.[12]

The knowledge gained during his studies in America in the field of urban planning led Ernesto N. Rogers to invite him to take part as a teaching assistant at the CIAM summer school in Venice, starting with the session in September 1952. Valle thus found himself inside one of the most important situations of debate, of great international impact, inside the Venetian school in the early postwar period. The summer school – under the aegis of CIAM – was strongly urged by Giuseppe Samonà and represented one of the fundamental steps of the cultural strategy through which the Sicilian director radically reorganised the Venetian school of architecture, boosting its status on a national and international level.[13] The importance of this initiative is confirmed by two parallel events that took place in Venice at the same time as the first summer school in 1952, the fourth INU conference and the first international conference of artists organised by UNESCO, to which Le Corbusier was invited: the French master also had the honour of opening the CIAM summer school, delivering his famous lecture *A propos de Venise*.[14] Valle worked as an assistant, together with his sister Nani, until the last edition in 1956, thus taking part in the educational activities, the final juries and the lectures given by outstanding figures in international architecture passing through Venice for this short but prestigious experience of the summer schools.[15]

The themes outlined above – pursuit of a rooting of architecture in the historical and natural context, the project as a continuous process of reworking of typological, constructive and formal components, the interface with Anglo-American experiences – represent the conceptual premises for the extraordinary series of projects Valle completed during the course of the 1950s in Friuli. A first-person account is provided by Valle himself, in a letter in 1960 addressed to Francesco Tentori, then a member of the research centre of *Casabella-Continuità*.[16] This is an utterly singular document in which the architect supplied a sort of list of constituent principles, accompanied by diagrams and sketches, to orient the critical interpretation of his own work, in the upcoming essay being prepared by Tentori as an initial assessment of the activity of the Udine-based studio.[17]

What emerges from the text is the author's need to underline the 'a-formal' (anti-formal), nature of his work, almost as if to defend or justify the linguistic heterogeneity that seems to emerge in the works of that period. Valle's purpose seems to be to demonstrate that his work is based on research aimed at eliminating any stylistically pre-set compositional approach, making it the result of a constant reworking of figurative elements, typologies and languages: work inserted in a continuous process in time, structured case by case on the basis of specific functional and contextual conditions.

The design techniques Valle said he used to give his works of architecture an a-formal appearance are of two types. On the one hand, work on the material aspects of the building, on the tactile and visual crafting of its constituent materials; i.e. research on expressive qualities of architecture through the 'primitive' stage of the material that expresses rooting to the context. On the other, there is the work on the structure, especially the continuous three-dimensional frameworks, seen as serial and therefore substantially anonymous components – or, in Valle's words, as 'a-formal elements by definition' – that function as generators of the architecture and somehow represent its 'skeleton'.[18]

The value of these a-formal methods – closely connected to the idea of the project as a continuing process of reworking of already tested forms, forms that never achieve definitive states – was underlined for the first time by Giuseppe Mazzariol: 'The most evident characteristic of the architectural output of Gino Valle', he wrote in an essay in 1963,[19] 'is antiformalism. ... Valle's antiformalism is first of all a fundamental part of his moral personality; he is a convinced layman.' In this sense, Mazzariol took his distance from the critical category proposed by Tentori in 1960, who had instead interpreted Valle's work as 'informal', contextualising it in the currents in painting that went under that heading in the 1950s and 1960s. Mazzariol understood the need to distinguish between 'informal' aspects of painting (against anything that could be traced back to a form, be it figurative or even purely abstract) and the research of the architect from Friuli (who attempted to get away from pre-set formal rules), to grasp the 'effort always present in Valle's architectural action, which we might simply define as an urge towards freedom, getting beyond schemes, the application of formulae to new contents to demonstrate, with open-minded intelligence, their efficiency or lack of timeliness'.[20]

The Migotto house, built on the outskirts of Udine in 1953–54, represents the first materialisation of this intention to work simultaneously on the continuous structure and the material consistency of the constructed enclosure. Twelve reinforced concrete pillars generate a three-dimensional grid that determines the volume of the object, but not the volume of the house. The two components – grid and enclosure – are clearly separated in both physical and material terms. Some walls of the house are in stucco, while others have a brick lattice. Others still are completely glazed, with steel frames: they are set back from the structure, leaving a segment of the frame free to incorporate several existing trees. Precisely at the position of this emptied sector, the access to the house and the connection to the upper level are placed, with a steel staircase facing the external space absorbed by the structure, while in the interior a second spatial grid in wood constitutes a sort of 'artificial horizon' that orients and measures the spatial experience.

The material-naturalistic and abstract dialectic between the components is not, however, expressed through the mere juxtaposition of elements: the grid does not present an image of abstract clarity,

Migotto house, southern facade, 1953.

Migotto house, 1953–54. View of the building in the completion phase.

Migotto house, 1953–54. View of the interiors (staircase and internal spatial grid).

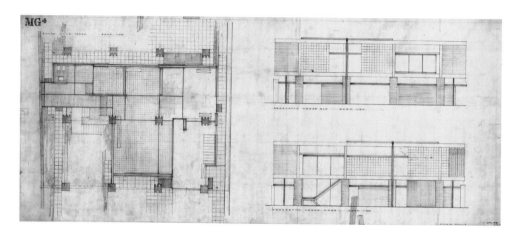

Migotto house, 1953–54. Ground floor plan and elevations (south and north).

but seems to be 'contaminated' by the presence of brick-grille screens that evoke an embroidered motif typical of the rural architecture of Friuli, and of the entire Po Valley plain. Ignazio Gardella had already used a similar perforated wall in the Dispensario Antitubercolare in Alessandria, in what was considered an example of 'heresy' with respect to rationalist orthodoxy.[21]

In the first project for the Nicoletti house in Udine (1953) – later built with different structural and compositional premises – Valle had extended the reach of the structure in four directions, changing the pace of the pillars. With respect to the previous house, this design demonstrated a desire to view the frame not as a concluded element, but as a portion of a continuous three-dimensional grid that is cut and utilised in pieces, or more precisely can expand from a single module in keeping with the desired modes and directions. Here too the structure becomes a spatial skeleton that establishes a dialogue with the cladding in the various parts of

the house in a different way: at times the walls of the house absorb the pillars, while at other times the pillars are superimposed, or even isolated. We can see an exercise of combinations, a sort of taxonomy of juxtaposition between load-bearing members and facings.

The relationship between the frame, the material expression and the spatial organisation was admirably resolved in the Quaglia house at Sutrio, from the same period (1953–54). Eight pillars – doubled with respect to the rhythm of the Migotto house – mark the perimeter of the house and support two distinct structures: four reinforced concrete beams, at the height of the impost of the slab, on which to place the first floor of the residence, and a roof with four pitches composed of a system of wooden trusses.

The constructive solution was quite unusual, but it reflected precise compositional intentions. As can be deduced from the ground floor plan, the pillars do not have any role in the design of the layout

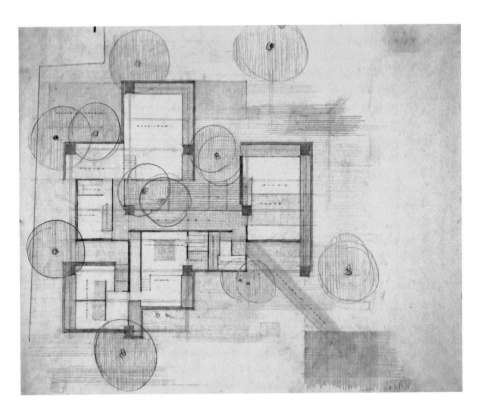

Plan of Nicoletti house, Udine, first project, 1953.

Quaglia house, 1953–54. Overall view from south.

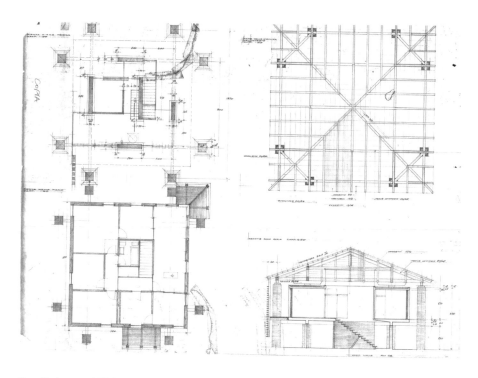

Quaglia house, 1953–54. Panel with plans of ground floor, roof, first floor,
and cross-section of the staircase.

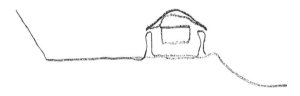

Quaglia house at Sutrio: sketch, 1953.

of the access, the path through the house, and its physical perimeters. Traces of walls, in the spirit of Mies van der Rohe, seem to be wedged into the structural cage, forming an architecture inside a spatial grid. At the same time the first floor, resting on the four crossed beams, is free for organisation in keeping with internal logic and favoured views.

Going back to the exterior, it is interesting to observe how Valle designed the facades. In a snapshot interpretation, everything that belongs to the structural system of the house is treated with material entities in dialogue with the local context: on the one hand the system of the wooden roof, on the other the pillars and load-bearing partitions in brick on the ground floor. The rest, the 'supported box', the enclosure of the dwelling, has stucco surfaces and is treated with linguistic elements extraneous to the local vocabulary. Actually, a masking of the two components was effected. The pillars and partitions were both in reinforced concrete but covered in brick, like entities that 'emerge' from the ground. Valle himself demonstrates this, stopping the cladding of the pillars at the impost of the roof. On the other hand,

the stucco walls of the house were composed of a double brick wall. The conclusive form of the roof became the primary element of figurative qualification of the building. Utterly extraneous to the typology of historic buildings in Carnia, the Quaglia house displayed a sophisticated operation of abstraction from the given context. Relationship between structure and enclosure, and figurative emphasis on the roof: among the works of this period the refined renovation of the Romanelli house (1952–53) stands out for its originality. The terrace of a historic villa in Udine was transformed by Valle into a glazed veranda to contain a space for children. The wooden pillars that support the structure of the new roof follow the pace of the lower columns but are conceived independently of the casements. This allows Valle to transform the glazing into an autonomous plastic element with respect to the remaining parts: pushed towards the outer border of the parapet and set back in the band corresponding to the roof. This project partially brings Valle closer to Scarpa, not so much for the respectful and at the same time critical approach to the existing elements, as for (above all) the solution of the ceiling of the veranda, a wooden structure that is transformed into a spatial diaphragm, a motif often seen in certain interiors of the Venetian master.

In another series of projects from the same period the joint presence of figurative and material themes with structural grids goes through new developments, further demonstrating Valle's tendency to explore the architectural form in always

Project of Villa Zanussi, Pordenone, model, 1958.

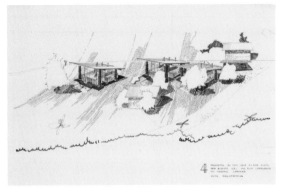

Project for three Cortolezzis houses at Treppo Carnico, 1953.

Quaglia house, 1953–54. View of the corner pillar.

different, increasingly sophisticated ways. The continuous structures vanish, leaving the pillars and roofs with the task of supplying the figurative character of the works of architecture. This series includes the project for the three Cortolezzis houses at Treppo Carnico (1953) – evoking the constructive poetics of the Pirovano shelter by Albini at Cervinia – and the project for the Zanussi villa in Pordenone (1958). In this house Valle decided to evoke the image of a large country estate formed by multiple buildings around an internal courtyard: the fast pace of the pillars and the single slope of the roofs functioned as a shared grammatical rule in a layout marked by both horizontal and vertical staggering of the residential spaces.

Francesco Tentori, in an essay dated 1960, suggested for the first time the comparison between Valle's work at the start of the 1950s and that of Louis Kahn.[22] Not only in the structural research, but also in the shared taste for regular patterns of massive pillars, in which to create plans of great spatial fluidity, can we see a parallel path in the research of the two architects, an elective affinity asserted at a distance, outside of any direct mutual knowledge of their respective works,[23] though with very different results from a figurative standpoint – an affinity that emerges with great clarity if we compare the residential projects described thus far with the plan of Kahn's project for the Adler house (1954): structure and building become inseparable terms that, besides determining the architectural language, spring from shared reflections on interior space and its relationship with the exteriors.

But it is in the Cassa di Risparmio di Latisana Bank (1954–56), one of the most famous works of this period, that Valle achieves the synthesis of the themes of his research, applied again to an urban setting.[24] A roof with a dual curvature, which Valle

Cassa di Risparmio di Latisana Bank, 1954–56. View of the corner pillar.

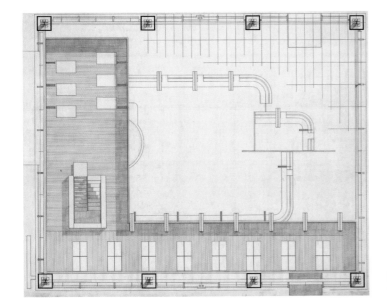

Cassa di Risparmio di Latisana Bank,
1954–56. Ground floor plan.

Gino Valle at the worksite of Cassa di Risparmio
di Latisana, April 1955.

called '*saponetta*' (soap bar), is perched on eight reinforced concrete pillars arranged in two rows, again covered in brick. The scale of the building is in relation to an urban square without any particular identities, evoking the image of an indoor market. Through a particularly refined design of the metal frames – which bend inward at the top – Valle reinforces the contrast between the heavily material character of the colonnade in brick and the sense of lightness and suspension conveyed by the metal roof. The interiors are characterised by the transparency of the enclosure and the reflections projected on the convex surface of the roof: a glass frieze runs along the entire perimeter of the building, paced by frames, confusing the interpretation of the steel posts that support the structure of the roof. Inside the bank, whose symmetry is interrupted by a balcony originally designed for offices, one thus finds oneself in direct contact with the outside, in total spatial continuity with the square.

Space is again the protagonist in the design of the structure of the Cassa di Risparmio di Udine Bank (1953–55). In this case the starting point was an 18th-century building which the bank had decided to radically transform. In particular, the ground floor and the courtyard were revised to contain offices and a large space for public services. To create a functionally and spatially unified complex, Valle decided on the ground floor to demolish long segments of the wall bordering the courtyard, while keeping its one historic, monumental side intact. The weight of the walls was supported by large steel Vierendeel trusses supported by corner pylons in reinforced concrete. These new grafts, besides redefining the image and composition of the courtyard, became places in which to organise the spatial relationships between the different levels: the steel trusses became screens between the offices and the courtyard (bringing light to the offices), while the large support pylons marked the place of excavation in

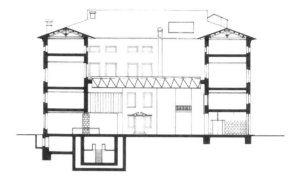

Cassa di Risparmio di Udine Bank, 1953–55. Section.

the ground to reach the underground level and the bank vault. In this case, the tectonic narrative of the structure is contradicted: the emphasis is concentrated on the corner pylons, while the Vierendeel trusses are explicitly concealed thanks to a darkening system of aluminium panels. With respect to a complete display of the structure – whose visual weight would have confused the effect desired for the public space – the architect seems to have focused on the light diffused by the particular design of the roof of the courtyard.

In fact, in the roof – published by Wachsmann in *Wendepunkt im Bauen*[25] – the grid structure reappears, with a new scale and new forms. In this case Valle proposed a solution of great technological innovation in the Italian context: a continuous spatial structure of extrados tetrahedral-octahedral parts, therefore almost invisible from the hall, based on the experimentation of Buckminster Fuller.[26] On the intrados, a series of triangular panels composed of an opalescent Perspex honeycomb forms a screen that spreads light. The diffused, rarefied light becomes the unifying force of the space, and the structure can be intuited only through a pattern of shadows, showing an autonomous shape, not coinciding with the directions of the sides of the courtyard.

Cassa di Risparmio di Udine Bank, 1953–55. View of the main hall for the public.

Notes

1   Valle's stay was made possible by a Fulbright Scholarship obtained with the support of Giuseppe Samonà and Cesare Miani.

2   In 1950 Bruno Morassutti returned to Venice with the slides he had taken during his itinerary through the works of Wright. The artist and friend Afro Basaldella had recently visited the East Coast for his first American solo show. Interview with Bruno Morassutti, in Giulio Barazzetta and Roberto Dulio (eds), *Bruno Morassuti: 1920–2008 opere e progetti*, Electa, Milan, 2009; Licio Damiani, 'Cultura in Friuli nel secondo dopoguerra (1945-1950)', in Massimo Bortolotti (ed.), *Angelo Masieri architetto, 1921–1952*, Edizioni Arti Grafiche Friulane, Udine, 1995, pp.33–51.

3   The trip is documented in photographs taken by Masieri, partially used by Carlo Lodovico Ragghianti to illustrate the essay 'Letture di Wright, 2', *Critica d'arte*, 19, July 1954, pp.355–68, and later in the illustrations of the Italian translation of Wright's autobiography, Frank Lloyd Wright, *Io e l'architettura*, Mondadori, Milan, 1955. See Massimo Bortolotti and Angelo Masieri. 'Architetture, 1947–1952', *Angelo Masieri architetto, 1921–1952*, pp.30–31. See Troy Michael Ainsworth, 'Modernism Contested: Frank Lloyd Wright in Venice and the Masieri Memorial Debate', PhD thesis, Texas Tech University, Lubbock, 2005, pp.58–60, which reconstructs in detail the voyage of Valle and Masieri.

4   At a recent conference, Francesco Tentori recalled the knowledge Valle transmitted to him on American architectural culture after his return from the United States and throughout the 1960s. See Francesco Tentori, 'Gratitudine per Gino Valle', talk during the symposium 'Gino Valle. Il mondo in Friuli', IUAV, Venice, 19 April 2007, Archivio Valle, Udine.

5   On the projects of Rudolph see 'Beach House', *Architectural Forum*, 86, April 1947, pp.92–3; 'Concrete home in Florida is one of eight prototype houses designed to solve regional building problems', *Architectural Forum*, 89, October 1948, pp.101–8 (House in Sarasota, Florida); 'House in Florida', *Architectural Forum*, 105, June 1949, pp.287–90.

6   On the themes discussed on the pages of *Perspecta* see, in particular, the essays by George Howe, 'Training for the Practice of Architecture, 3 New Directions: Paul Rudolph, Philip Johnson, Buckminster Fuller', *Perspecta*, 1, 1952; Sibyl Moholy-Nagy, 'Environment and Anonymous Architecture', *Perspecta*, 3, 1955, pp.2–7; Louis Kahn, 'Architecture is the Thoughtful Making of Spaces', Vincent Scully Jr., 'Modern Architecture: Toward a Redefinition of a Style', and Paul Rudolph, 'Regionalism in Architecture', *Perspecta*, 4, 1957.

7   Patrick Abercrombie, *The Preservation of Rural England*, Hodder and Stoughton Ltd, London, 1926; *Town & Country Planning*, T. Butterworth, London, 1933.

8   Quotations are from Maria Bottero and Giacomo Scarpini (eds), 'Intervista a Gino Valle', *Zodiac*, 20, December 1970, pp.112–14.

9   Two papers are conserved in the Valle archives – 'The creative process in urban planning' and an untitled paper on *Garden Cities of To-morrow* by Ebenezer Howard. See Letter to John M. Gaus, 22 February 1953, Archivio Valle, Udine.

10   Among the various critical essays discussed by Valle: Frederick James Osborn, *Green-Belt Cities: The British Contribution*, Faber & Faber, London, 1946; the introduction by Lewis Mumford in Ebenezer Howard, *Garden Cities of Tomorrow* (with the preface by Frederick James Osborn), Faber & Faber, London, 1945; Erwin Gutkind, *Revolution of Environment*, Kegan Paul, Trench, Trubner & Co., London, 1946.

11   'He [Howard] *invented* a machine, and the machine did work.' See Gino Valle, talk for HGSD, 1952, p.2, Archivio Valle, Udine.

12   After returning from the United States, Valle set out to encourage the translation of several texts he had discussed at Harvard. Together with Franco Berlanda and Giancarlo De Carlo he tried to promote a series of books on urbanism with the publishing house Libreria Artistica Industriale Salto, beginning precisely with the first Italian translation of *Garden Cities*. The rights to *Garden Cities* were purchased by another publisher and the initiative came to a halt. The first Italian translation of Howard's text is *L'idea della città giardino di Ebenezer Howard*, translated and annotated by Giorgio Bellavitis, Calderini, Bologna, 1962. In the list of texts proposed by Valle there were also works by Lewis Mumford (*City Development*, Harcourt, Brace and Company, New York, 1945), Pëtr Kropotkin (*Mutual Aid, a Factor of Evolution*, William Heinemann, London, 1902), Patrick Geddes (*Cities in Evolution*, Williams & Norgate, London, 1915), Frederick Osborn (*Green-Belt Cities*, Faber & Faber, London 1945), Walter Gropius (*Rebuilding our Communities*, P. Theobald, Chicago, 1945), Erwin Gutkind (*Revolution of Environment*, K. Paul, Trench, Trubner & Co., London, 1946) and unspecified texts by John Gaus, Rexford Tugwell and Mellville C. Branch. See the correspondence with Lewis Mumford and the publisher Salto conserved in Archivio Valle. Some of these texts were later inserted by Giancarlo De Carlo in the proposal of a series for the publisher Il Saggiatore, which he directed starting in 1965. For this unique account on Valle's project and the publishing activities of De Carlo and Franco Berlanda, the authors thank Francesco Samassa.

13   Ilhuyn Kim, 'Alcuni episodi della biografia intellettuale di Samonà. Dai rapporti con la scuola romana alla scuola estiva dei Ciam', in Giovanni Marras and Marco Pogacnik (eds), *Giuseppe Samonà e la scuola di architettura a Venezia*, Il Poligrafo, Padua, 2006, pp.61–92.

Veranda of Romanelli House, Udine, 1952–53.

14   Le Corbusier, 'A propos de Venise', *Giornale economico della Camera di Commercio Industria Agricoltura di Venezia*, 9, September 1952, pp.429–38.

15   Berlanda reports among the speakers and those invited to the final jury were: Max Bill, Alvar Aalto, Lucio Costa, William G. Holford, Johannes H. van der Broek, Jaap Bakema and Satou, as well as many Italians: Giulio Carlo Argan, Giovanni Astengo, Sergio Bettini, Piero Bottoni, Gino Pollini, Luigi Piccinato, Carlo Lodovico Ragghianti and Bruno Zevi. See 'Lista degli studenti e dei relatori delle scuole estive CIAM', Archivio Valle, Udine; Rossana Carullo, *Iuav. Didattica dell'architettura dal 1926 al 1963*, Poliba Press, Bari, 2009.

16   Letter to Francesco Tentori, 15 November 1960, Archivio Valle, Udine.

17   Francesco Tentori, 'Dieci anni d'attività dello Studio Architetti Valle', *Casabella*, 246, December 1960, pp.30–49.

18   Valle writes: 'The continuous structure in two or three dimensions, and in the linear dimension, is the a-formal element by definition. The form that comes from the necessary choice of the "fragment of continuous structure" to use tends to be random.' See Letter to Francesco Tentori, 15 November 1960, Archivio Valle, Udine.

19   Giuseppe Mazzariol, 'Gino Valle', *Zodiac*, 12, October 1963, pp.164–91.

20   ibid., p.166.

21   The reference to Gardella, and at the same time to rural architecture in Friuli, is explicitly acknowledged by Valle in the interview with Mario Pisani, 'Dialogo con Gino Valle', *Costruire in laterizio*, 40, July–August 1994, p.339.

22   Francesco Tentori, 'Dieci anni'. See also Francesco Tentori, 'Ordine e forma nell'opera di Louis Kahn', *Casabella*, 241, July 1960, pp.2–17.

23   On this affinity with Kahn, Valle offers significant evidence in the interview 'Sandro Marpillero intervista Gino Valle da New York', *Lotus Navigator*, monograph, Gino Valle, 1, November 2000, pp.62–89. Here he mentions the encounter in New York in 1967, after a lecture by Kahn at Columbia University, during which he identified Valle as an 'emerging young talent'.

24   The commission was actually received by the Valles in 1951, prior to Valle's departure for the United States. Valle cared deeply about this project, and he had his sister Nani send him the drawings, which he corrected and reworked starting in April 1952 to reflect different design solutions, which are all documented in Archivio Valle. An initial project was located in another position on the square, at the corner between Via Vittorio Veneto and Via Vendramin. See letters from Gino to Nani Valle, Archivio Valle, Udine.

25   Konrad Wachsmann, *Wendepunkt im Bauen*, Krausskopf Verlag, Wiesbaden, 1959, English edition; *The Turning Point of Building. Structure and Design* (translated by Thomas E. Burton), Reinhold Pub. Corp., New York, 1961.

26   The basic structural unit was composed of three tetrahedra (triangular pyramids) jointed at the vertices to form an octahedron. Valle based this on an experimental structure designed by Buckminster Fuller measuring just 3×1.2 metres, by a height of 15 centimetres, adapting the model to the *measurements* of the space to be covered (18×18 metres) with a pyramid unit having a height of 1.5 metres. See Gino Valle, 'Applicazione della struttura spaziale continua a ottaedri. La progettazione del velario di copertura del Salone della Cassa di Risparmio di Udine', *Rassegna tecnica della Regione Friuli Venezia Giulia*, 1–2, January–February 1955. In those same years Louis Kahn had also made use of a continuous spatial structure derived from the research of Fuller, for the Art Gallery of Yale University (1951–53), though this work was made in reinforced concrete, 'betraying' the lightness of Fuller's structures and their premises of assembly connected with prefabrication.

3 A Contextual Brutalism (1953–61)

Valle's taste for ongoing linguistic and compositional experimentation is confirmed by a series of buildings of the 1950s which reveal his focus on contemporary trends on the international scene. Stimulated by the developments in English architectural culture during the 1950s, Valle refined constructive typologies in direct relation to the phenomenon of the New Brutalism. Unlike the affinities with Louis Kahn and Paul Rudolph, expressed first of all at the level of compositional principles, the dialogue with the contemporary English context manifested itself in an apparently more explicit way, as a choice regarding the constructive language of the building. The relationship with the Anglo-Saxon design culture was later reinforced thanks to personal contacts: first of all through friendship with the young Joseph Rykwert, encountered in Venice during the CIAM summer school of 1952, who was the first critic to present Valle's works, in 1958, on the pages of a foreign magazine;[1] secondly, through the presence of English and American staff at the studio in Udine, in particular Donald Appleyard, who had studied at the Architectural Association in London, and John Myer, trained in the United States during the same years as Valle's stay there, who focused on the 'symbolic' dimension of the projects for the banks of Latisana and Udine.[2]

From the tower building in Trieste (1950–57) to the hospital of Portogruaro (1954–68), the Bellini double house in Udine (1956–57) to the city hall of Treppo Carnico (1956–58) and the Arti Grafiche Chiesa facility (1959–60), all the way to the Nicoletti house in Udine (1959–61) and the Zanussi offices at Porcia (1957–61), Valle developed his own constructive poetics that seems to make reference to the 'dictates' of Reyner Banham, the first critic who, in a famous essay from 1955, officialised the phenomenon of New Brutalism in England and revealed the theoretical and historical meaning of this current to international architectural culture.[3]

As Banham emphasised, the movement of the 'brick-bat flung in the public's face' was no longer a label to describe a trend that had spread in British architecture in the 1950s but had become – especially with the early works of Alison and Peter Smithson – a true manifesto of a generation. The clear display of the structural system, seen as the constructive and therefore linguistic matrix of the architectural object, and as expressive impact achieved through the renunciation of any type of cladding in favour of honesty in the use of construction materials – or, as the famous slogan of the time put it, 'as found' – constituted the premises for much of young English architecture in those years, and became the essential characteristic of the work of Valle as well, in the 1950s. Nevertheless, the 'case' of Valle should not be seen as unique on the Italian scene at the time: it is sufficient to cite certain works by

(*left*) Bellini house, Udine, 1956–57. Detail of the facade on the street.

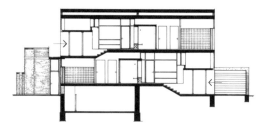

Bellini house, Udine, 1956–57. Detail of the facade on the street and towards the garden.

Mario Ridolfi and Wolfgang Frankl, Franco Albini, Vittoriano Viganò, but also several achievements in the field of industrial architecture by Marco Zanuso and Angelo Mangiarotti, to understand the importance, outside of any direct link to the English context, of the architectural pursuit of a transitive relationship between structural systems, expressive impact of materials and language. Banham himself had trouble enclosing these expressive techniques inside an exclusively English context, and also included in the Brutalist current, in his essay in 1955, the first work by Louis Kahn[4] – an indispensable reference point from the outset, for Valle, as we have seen in the previous chapter.

As Valle himself admitted, however, certain of his works from this period clearly reveal their English connection.[5] In the Bellini double house, for example, the emphasis on the display of the structure, unlike the Quaglia and Migotto houses, is reduced to the point of almost vanishing. Parallel brick walls support a floor slab and a flat roof in

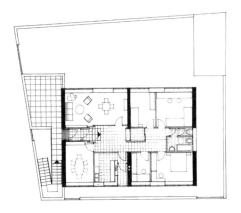

Bellini house, Udine, 1956–57. Cross-section, first and ground floor plans.

reinforced concrete, forming a simple 'box' on two levels. This system makes the internal arrangement of the two stacked apartments legible, each with its own independent entrance at the sides of the street, as well as the hierarchy of the perimeter walls of the house. If the load-bearing walls (lateral facades) are aligned flat with the horizontal elements, the non-load-bearing envelope is displayed in its function of enclosure of the interior spaces, and thus freely set back and concluded with large rectangular and horizontal windows. Due to the treatment of its details, the 'raw' display of the materials and the method of representation of its structural components, the Bellini house has a place among the most 'English' works of Valle, and though it is lacking in similar linguistic refinements, it reveals surprising affinities with the residences of the same period at Ham Common by Stirling and Gowan (1955–57).

In the Vriz complex in Trieste (1950–57)[6] these issues are taken to an urban dimension. Inserted in the nucleus of the 19th-century city, the project consists of two buildings of different types: a three-storey unit along Via San Francesco and a 14-storey residential tower set back from the street, located at the inner part of the lot. The structure and the layout of the tower determine its language. A vertical nucleus in reinforced concrete contains stairwells and lift shafts, from which the slabs project outward at the sides: a system that is statically reinforced by crosswise partitions to obtain four apartments on each floor, with a facade of approximately thirty metres. The partitions protrude beyond the line of the building to form balconies, thus enhancing the expression of the concrete skeleton with an irregular volumetric arrangement. The structural clarity is stated on the facade, and made even more explicit by the material contrast with the brick infilling walls which recalls the Bellini house facade.[7] This envelope was also studied to express the organisation of the internal spaces with the same clarity: a vertical opening divides the facades of the apartments into two asymmetrical parts, indicating the positions of the living rooms and of the kitchens inside the individual housing units.

Vriz residential and office tower in Trieste, 1950–57. Study of the southern facade, 1955.

Vriz residential and office tower in Trieste, 1950–57. Detail of the facade of the office volume towards Via San Francesco.

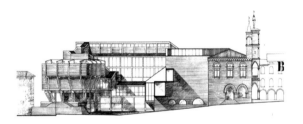

Project for the Pordenone City Hall, 1956. Longitudinal section with the new council chamber to the left.

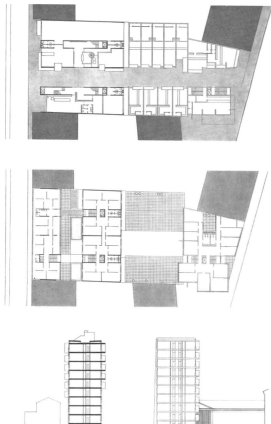

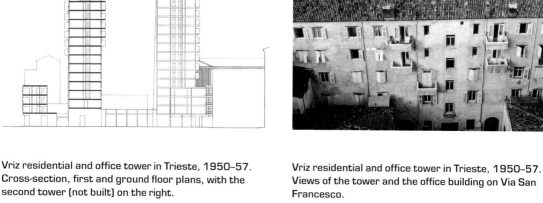

Vriz residential and office tower in Trieste, 1950–57. Cross-section, first and ground floor plans, with the second tower (not built) on the right.

Vriz residential and office tower in Trieste, 1950–57. Views of the tower and the office building on Via San Francesco.

The low volume on Via San Francesco, on the other hand, acts as an element of mediation between the new tower and the existing buildings: just three storeys high, with an overhanging structure and a continuous iron frame with a refined, technologically innovative design, the new front links with the existing 19th-century context only in its acceptance of the rule of the street alignment, while offering a strong stylistic contrast in its reference to an industrial architecture.

A facade is horizontally paced by continuous windows, slabs and sheet-metal panels containing the climate control conduits, which display their functional logic to the outside.[8] Valle was particularly satisfied with this solution because 'with its rusted iron colour' it expressed a 'commercial force, which is in the air of Trieste', and it 'gets dirty well'.[9]

In the hospital of Portogruaro (1954–68), a large-scale job commissioned to their father Provino but completed by Gino and Nani Valle, the structure with crosswise partitions was modified to suit the specific functional programme of a hospital. Another perforated beam – most probably taken from the AFL-CIO Medical Service Building (1954–56) of Louis Kahn – is placed at the height of the slab of the first floor and the roof of the building for the horizontal layout of the physical plant systems, while the vertical layout is done by means of the doubling of the load-bearing frames. Stimulated by the large scale of the project, the Valles made use of their earlier explorations and achieved greater freedom to play with the variation of the infilling walls and windows, with the overhang of terraces and ramps, with the emergence of roof elements that contribute to add character to the profile of the building when seen from a distance. The project contains interesting ideas in terms of layout, and in the organisation of the phases of expansion and growth of the structure, yet on a linguistic level it cannot match the elegance of the residential and public projects of the same period.

In 1961 Gino Valle designed the Nicoletti house.[10] On this occasion, the architect built directly on the roof of the clinic, of which he had completed just two levels of the four planned in 1953, proposing a vertical addition and a horizontal expansion towards the back garden. Paced by horizontal concrete bands that offer greater articulation to the elevations, the house looks towards the street with singular three-dimensional effects, setbacks, large openings and overhangs. With a varied section, the strong expressive impact of the overhanging volumes on the garden, the refined design of the fixed glazing in slender concrete sections, the Nicoletti house is one of Valle's most interesting works from this period.

The analysis of the works examined thus far, however, cannot be limited to consideration of the more or less direct stimuli of English New Brutalism and the search for tectonic 'honesty'. The central importance of the relationship between the architectural project and urban and natural contexts, one of Valle's main interests from the start of his career, continues to be one of the fundamental keys to understanding the projects analysed in this chapter as well. Actually, they

Portogruaro hospital, 1954–68. View of the model of the northern facade.

Portogruaro hospital, 1954–68.

reflect a change with respect to the earliest works, a variation in the area of settlement strategies.

While the work on continuous structures analysed in the previous chapter, with experimentation on systems of aggregation of elements (pillars, spatial skeletons, etc.), led to the development of open forms, the works shown here are marked instead by finite volumes, substantially open along single axes, conceived in active dialectic with the surrounding environment. On this topic, Valle described the Bellini house as a building that came from the desire to erect 'a sort of defence not exactly against but in relation to the environment'.[11] The building is closed with respect to the urban setting – Valle himself saw this in relation to a

Treppo Carnico City Hall, 1956–58. Overall view from downhill.

'pessimistic vision of the world' in that period[12] – but at the same time we can see the creation, with a new 'image' of great visual impact, of a new context, while keeping the relationship with the physical and material specifics of the place a very natural one.[13] Seen in this light, the Bellini and Nicoletti houses, or other works from this period, take form as closed 'boxes'; their language establishes a dialogue with the context, yet they also avoid any temptations of environmental or stylistic imitation.

Similar arguments apply to the Arti Grafiche Chiesa plant (1959–60) built at Tavagnacco, on the northern outskirts of Udine, a set of buildings that reprises the theme of the 'New Brutalist boxes' of the Bellini house – with crosswise load-bearing partitions and large longitudinal openings – with a new variation: the brick wall stops at the height of the first floor, while on the second floor the reinforced concrete wall extends in monolithic continuity with the roof. Again, in this case the formal force of the only apparently introspective complex acts as a counterpart to the context, laying the groundwork for the creation of a new project–environment relationship.[14] In this sense the city hall of Treppo Carnico (1956–58) takes the theme

to maximum clarity, demonstrating the complexity of Valle's design background and his ability to make different themes converge in each of the works of this period. In this work, which Tentori considers the 'most homogeneous, developed in greatest depth' of early Valle,[15] for the first time the architect rejects the logic of the building conceived as a concluded organism: though he deployed the same tectonic elements in the Bellini house[16] – the same crosswise load-bearing partitions (in stone, in this case) and double roof in reinforced concrete – the project for Treppo can be seen as the result of the assembly of multiple 'boxes' that display the various parts of the programme. The importance of the tectonic operation, in this case, is put into the background with respect to Valle's development of a composite settlement strategy: the complex plays with its volumes in order to position itself in the most appropriate possible way in the delicate environment of the small town in Carnia. The volumetric distinction of the individual parts through subtle variation of the planimetric alignments, the heights and slopes of the roofs that open and orient the section towards the valley, creates a system with clear relationships of continuity with the contours of the existing constructed landscape, though without any hint of camouflage.

On the one hand, the architectural system closes itself off with respect to the town uphill from it – Valle presented this building as 'a group of caves connected by communicating tunnels, which give you the feeling of being inside the mountain' – while on the other 'it opens towards the valley, the town and the sunshine',[17] creating a new environmental condition with its presence. In his article in *Casabella*, Tentori underlined the capacity of the city hall to take its form from the surrounding fabric, but at the same time to free itself of that fabric and reveal its status as the new social centre of a community.[18] Speaking of this contextual but not imitative attitude, and of the transformation through new architecture of a place into a specific site, Alessandro Rocca sees Valle's work as a forerunner not so much of the iconoclastic operation of the Genius Loci, as of the 'more operative concept of the site-specific' found in much modern and contemporary art.[19]

This is a very central theme to understand Valle's attitude in these years regarding morphological, urban or landscape qualities of the contexts in which he builds, especially due to the fact that his inclinations were decidedly distant from the ideological positions expressed in those same years by Ernesto Nathan Rogers on the pages of *Casabella-Continuità* regarding the relationship between modern architecture and existing environmental factors. The discussions on insertion in the landscape, on the pursuit of a vernacular language and the recovery of historical revivals even seemed like 'false discourses' to Valle, since they 'served only to cover up the big guilt complex of Italian architects who after the war were unable to avoid operating at the service of speculation'.[20] Valle even stated that he had built the tower in Trieste in explicit opposition to the Torre Velasca by BBPR, which he felt was 'a cultural fake, a way of dressing up the facts of speculation with Filarete'.[21]

In this context, it should come as no surprise that *Casabella*, in 1958, published the tower in Trieste with certain reservations, expressed in the comment of Luciano Semerani, who noticed a lack of 'greater attention to the problem of insertion in the city'.[22] Many years later, these reservations seem totally ideological, since Valle's building marked the start of a path of vertical growth that was taken forward by Semerani himself, together with Gigetta Tamaro, in the construction of the hospital of Cattinara starting in 1965. Valle himself would later recall these discussions as preconceptions, reducing them to a friendly 'dispute' with Rogers 'about the decency of bringing elephants into the city, even if they are dressed up in costume, because in any case they will always remain elephants'.[23]

Instead, the defence of the building, or, more precisely, the interest expressed by Reyner Banham in the 'New Brutalist' tower in Trieste, on the pages of *Architectural Review*,[24] seems logical, though the English critic – then personally engaged in his famous argument with Rogers

regarding neo-liberty and the supposed 'retreat from the Modern' of Italian architecture – prudently postponed his definitive verdict until the development with the shopping arcade and the second tower had been completed.[25] But what should be emphasised here is the general interest in Valle's work in this period on the part of English architectural culture. Aligned with the severe opinions of Banham regarding the neo-historicist drift of part of Italian architecture, Joseph Rykwert deemed Valle's work 'remarkable at a time when most younger Italian architects are retreating into an apparently ascetic but basically trivial historicism'.[26] This interest on the part of the English culminated in 1964 with a solo show of Valle's work at the Royal College of Art, and with the invitation of the Royal Institute of British Architects for the prestigious Annual Discourse.[27]

The ability to make new architecture establish a dialogue with existing settlements is also confirmed in several interesting competition projects. In the project for the Cassa di Risparmio di Gorizia Bank (1955), Valle breaks down the various parts of the programme into different, carefully positioned volumes to resolve a difficult corner location: set back from the street to create a plaza, the bank stands back from the tall residential volume, placed crosswise, thanks to an inner pedestrian walkway, while the stepped sections of the buildings achieve precise connection with the neighbouring structures. In the project for the city hall of Pordenone (1956) the problem of extending the old medieval town hall inside a trapezoidal block was solved through the creation of an inner plaza which isolates and enhances the existing building, while the new council hall to the south represents its 'double' with a clearly contemporary language, marked by the strong structural expressionism of the overhanging volumes.

Valle's attitude towards the context of the historic city displays a certain nonchalance, clearly expressed in the residential building on Via Marinoni in Udine (1958–60) – Valle's second and last experience with a private real estate developer. This nonchalance caused a certain embarrassment

Cassa di Risparmio di Gorizia Bank, 1955. Perspective of the corner of Via Diaz and Via Verdi.

Arti Grafiche Chiesa factory,
1959–60.

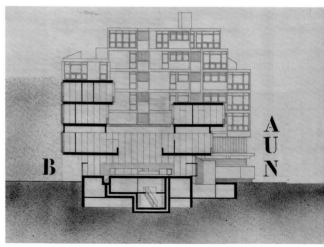

Cassa di Risparmio di Gorizia Bank, 1955.
Cross-section.

in the comments of *Casabella*,[28] which still attempted to justify the constructive solution in terms of 'mediation with the existing context'. Valle, in partnership for the occasion with Firmino Toso, had accepted the theme in all its ambiguity, proposing a major leap of scale with respect to the historical fabric, as permitted by the regulations for speculators, essentially with the aim of enriching and bringing complexity to the large constructed volume, relying on a clearly stated three-way arrangement: the two-storey base with shops and offices, with five residential levels above, topped by a penthouse in which Valle placed his own home.

Among all the works designed up to this point by Valle, this was certainly the most complex due to the particular mixture of themes and purposes. Choosing to have the masonry facade of the residential levels supported by a large overhanging perforated beam placed on the pillars of the lower levels, Valle not only returned to a structural device already developed for the hospital of Portogruaro, but also charged it with significant figurative tension: the continuity of the ribbon window on the first floor is countered by the splitting into two parts of the residential volume – one recessed, one protruding – with the consequence of concentrating the maximum expressive impact of the overhanging structure on the corner. The theme of the load-bearing masonry treated in a 'defensive' spirit in the designs for the Bellini house and the town hall of Treppo Carnico was developed in totally new terms this time: the wall is a smooth surface covered with small-scale, almost mosaic-like, ceramic tiles and perforated by groups of windows, in keeping with a mode of representation in the composition of the facade of the overlay of types of apartments, similar to the Milanese residential projects of the same period by Luigi Caccia-Dominioni.

(*right*) Building for offices and residences on Via Marinoni, Udine, 1958–60.

(*below*) Building for offices and residences on Via Marinoni, Udine. Study of the facade towards the street, 1958.

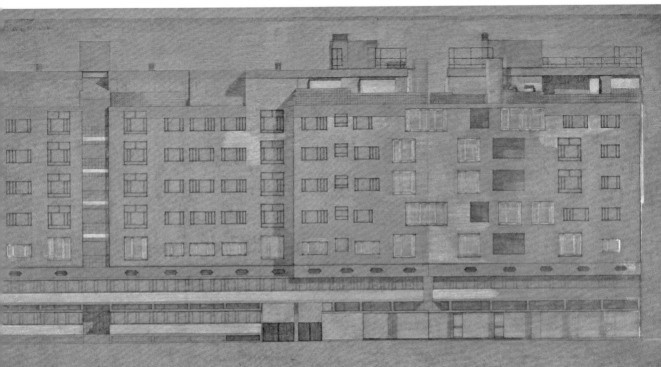

Notes

1   Joseph Rykwert, 'The Work of Studio Architetti Valle,' *Architecture and Building*, April 1958, pp.121–39.

2   Both Appleyard (in 1956) and Myer (in 1954) took part as assistants at the CIAM summer school in Venice.

3   Reyner Banham, 'The New Brutalism', *Architectural Review*, 708, December 1955, pp.355–8. For a critical discussion of the influence of the Maisons Jaoul of Le Corbusier on the formation of the 'New Brutalism', see Caroline Maniaque, *Le Corbusier et les maisons Jaoul. Projets et fabrique*, Éditions Picard, Paris, 2005, in particular Chapter 4, 'Fortune critique et destinée des maisons', pp.113–24.

4   'Only one other building conspicuously carries these qualities in the way that Hunstanton does, and that is Louis Kahn's Yale Art Center: a building which is uncompromisingly frank about its materials, which is unconceivable apart from its boldly exhibited structural method which – being a concrete space-frame – is as revolutionary and unconventional as the use of Plastic Theory in stressing Hunstanton's steel H-frames', Reyner Banham, 'The New Brutalism', p.357. Banham's position would be quite different in 1966 when, in his *The New Brutalism: Ethic or Aesthetic?* The Architectural Press, London, 1966, he included, in this aesthetic, many works by architects from different countries: for Italy, we can mention the Istituto Marchiondi in Milan by Viganò and the Madonna dei Poveri church at Baggio by Figini & Pollini.

5   'We designed a house [Bellini] which still stands, which looks rather English, I guess, because everybody says so. It is perhaps due to Appleyard.' Unpublished interview edited by Peter Kingsland (*c*.1965). See manuscript, Archivio Valle, Udine.

6   The first project for the complex dates back to 1950, before Valle's departure for the United States, and his father Provino completed the definitive design. After returning from the United States, Valle blocked the design solution developed during his absence, and set out to propose a new project. Ibid., p.8.

7   The possibility of using thick brick walls was based on the fact that the client for the tower was a brick manufacturer. Ibid., p.9.

8   The detail of the window, with the panel below in triple sheet metal containing the climate control conduits, was published in England as an example of an innovative facade for offices: John and Margaret Richards, 'Heating in Curtain Wall: Flats and Offices, Trieste, Italy', *Architect's Working Details*, 6, 1959, pp.138–9.

9   'Annual Discourse: Gino Valle', *RIBA Journal*, May 1965, p.245.

10   We have already examined the first project for the Nicoletti house. On the same lot, Valle built the expansion of the clinic, a small building in concrete and brick whose

Nicoletti house, Udine, 1959–61. View from the street; the overhanging volume is built over the existing building of the clinic, built by Studio Valle in 1951.

Nicoletti house, Udine, 1959–61. Detail of the facade on the garden.

Nicoletti house, Udine, 1959–61. First floor with the corner window on the garden.

tectonic qualities were admired by Samonà. See Giuseppe Samonà, 'Architetture di giovani', *Casabella*, 205, April–May 1955, p.10.

11   'Annual Discourse: Gino Valle', *RIBA Journal*, May 1965, p.245.

12   'These projects show the rather pessimistic, spiritual and social situation of those years. Just as the big roof and continuous frame were symbols of an early optimism.' See 'Annual Discourse: Gino Valle', ibid. On this aspect see also, Maria Bottero and Giacomo Scarpini (eds), 'Intervista a Gino Valle', *Zodiac*, 20, December 1970, p.83.

13   Again in this case, Banham's considerations on the visual meaning of the architecture of the New Brutalism seem particularly apt to examine Valle's work: 'Basically, it requires that the building should be an immediately apprehensible visual entity, and that the form grasped by the eye should be confirmed by experience of the building in use. Further, that this form should be entirely proper to the functions and materials of the building, in their entirety. Such a relationship between structure, function and form is the basic commonplace of all good building of course, the demand that this form should be apprehensible and memorable is the apical uncommon place which makes good building into great architecture.' See Reyner Banham, 'The New Brutalism', p.358.

14   For an examination of the theme of foundation architecture in the work of Valle, refer to the chapter 'Monument to the Resistance and Foundation Architecture' in this book.

15   Francesco Tentori, 'Tre opere e un progetto dello Studio Valle', *Casabella*, 226, April 1959, p.32.

16   Besides the Bellini house, the city hall of Treppo has a figurative origin in the base of the Cinema Margherita in Tarcento.

17   'Annual Discourse: Gino Valle', *RIBA Journal*, May 1965, p.245.

18   Francesco Tentori, 'Tre opere e un progetto', p.32.

19   See Alessandro Rocca, 'Meno forma più concetto', in Elena Carlini (ed.), *Architettura in montagna: Gino Valle in Carnia*, Navado Press, Trieste, 2005, pp.7–9.

20   Maria Bottero and Giacomo Scarpini (eds), 'Intervista a Gino Valle', p.115.

21   ibid.

22   Luciano Semerani, 'Una costruzione a Trieste', *Casabella*, 218, April 1958, pp.50–60. 'So I found myself in disagreement both with Zevi and with *Casabella*, which has always published my works in spite of misunderstanding them.' See Maria Bottero and Giacomo Scarpini (eds), 'Intervista a Gino Valle', p.115.

23   'L'architettura come pratica progettuale. Intervista a Gino Valle', *Casabella*, 450, September 1979, pp.12–13, 34–51.

24   Reyner Banham, 'Tall Block in Trieste', *The Architectural Review*, 742, November 1958, pp.281–2.

25   Valle later developed many variations for the second tower, until 1970, but the project remained unfinished.

26   Joseph Rykwert, 'The Work of Gino Valle', *Architectural Design*, March 1964, p.123.

27   The exhibition met with a particularly good reception on the part of the English public. See Edward Lucie-Smith, 'The Architectural Imagination', *The Times*, 21 April 1964. On the Annual Discourse, see 'Annual Discourse: Gino Valle', *RIBA Journal*, May 1965, p.245.

28   Francesco Tentori, 'Dieci anni d'attività dello Studio Architetti Valle', *Casabella*, 246, December 1960, pp.31–2.

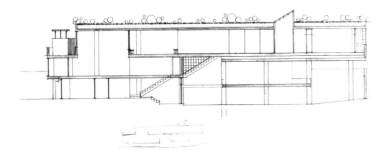

Nicoletti house, Udine, 1959–61. Longitudinal section; (*below left*) ground floor plan; and (*below right*) second floor plan.

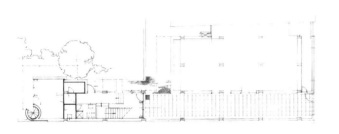

City Hall of Treppo Carnico, 1956–58

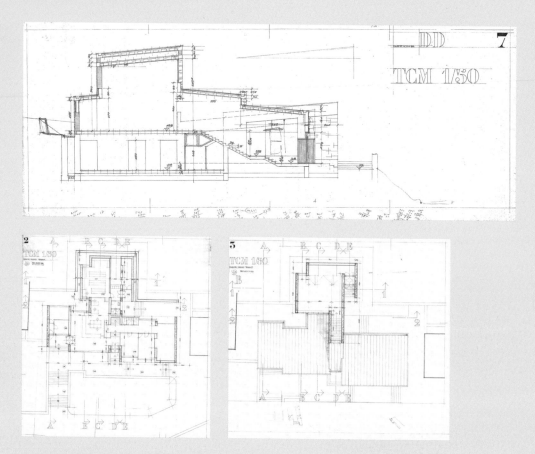

Treppo Carnico City Hall, 1956–58. Cross-section, ground and first floor plans.

The city hall lies in the centre of the town, on a slope facing south. It is set back slightly in continuity with a group of houses separated from the street by gardens and terraces, bordered by stone retaining walls. Walking up the street by these gardens, at first one sees only the lateral stone walls that contain the various volumes of the city hall. After the last garden, steps lead directly to the entrance portico and the hall for public services, while a second entrance at the centre of the facade offers direct access to the circulation staircase. From the offices one proceeds to the council chamber – of greater height – climbing a staircase that concludes with the view of the large fresco by Giuseppe Zigaina on the uphill wall. The slope of the roof accentuates the impression of being in a volume solidly anchored to the slope and open to the valley and the view of the mountains. Walking around the city hall, one discovers a small rear courtyard, terraced to contain different secondary entrances: the personnel entrance on the lower level, access to the clinic, and an external staircase for public access to the council chamber. After restoration in the 1980s, the city hall is in excellent condition and has undergone very few internal modifications.

(right) Treppo Carnico City Hall, 1956–58.

4 From the Zanussi Offices to 'non-architecture' (1957–70)

In 1956, Gino Valle began working with the industrial group Zanussi. As a product design consultant for refrigerators, he played a direct part in that which Vittorio Gregotti has defined as the 'first and most interesting process of productive rationalisation of the Italian appliance industry'.[1] This process led, in particular, to the creation in 1958 of the exemplary 'Industrial Design Unit' inside the company. The first problem approached by this unit was the coordination of size in various parts of the kitchen.[2] Soon enough, Valle found an opportunity to focus on the issues of quality of the public image of Zanussi, in relation to renewal of the company's product design, a process which had already been launched.

This initial activity as an industrial designer was therefore useful in establishing a relationship of trust with the client and obtaining a more prestigious and ambitious assignment: the design of a new office building as the face of the company along the Pontebbana, the important national route to Venice. In 1957 Valle presented a first project, 'closed and self-contained, like Caius College in Cambridge':[3] the idea of the offices as an introverted organism, isolated in front of the production facilities, betrayed a fundamentally defensive attitude, reinforced by the decision to dig a large rectangular moat in which to insert the hollow cube of the offices. In September 1959 the architect developed a second, totally different project, based on the idea of a long wall parallel to the street and entirely closed to the south, while the glass offices would open to the north, towards the factory. Once again Valle asserted a 'defensive' principle with respect to the context because the building was like a sort of dam holding back the thrust of the production facilities towards the road. Though already approved and in the final design phase, this second project was interrupted by Valle in the autumn of 1959. The interruption coincided with a moment of crisis of the studio, due to successive departures of his closest collaborators: first his sister Nani, Gino's partner since 1951 and therefore co-author of all his first projects; then Federico Marconi, who had entered the studio in 1956 with the projects for the Bellini house and the city hall of Treppo Carnico, who moved to Finland to work with Alvar Aalto after having collaborated on the second project for the Zanussi offices. Valle found himself alone in the studio, and decided to hire Alfredo Carnelutti, who had previously worked on product design for Zanussi. An anomalous figure in the field of architecture, a landscape painter who had become a draughtsman out of necessity, Carnelutti became a key personality in the studio from that moment on, responsible for the dual activity of making project renderings – with the use of a very personal figurative technique – and of preparing the

(*left*) Zanussi offices in Porcia. Valle photographed in the two-storey display space.

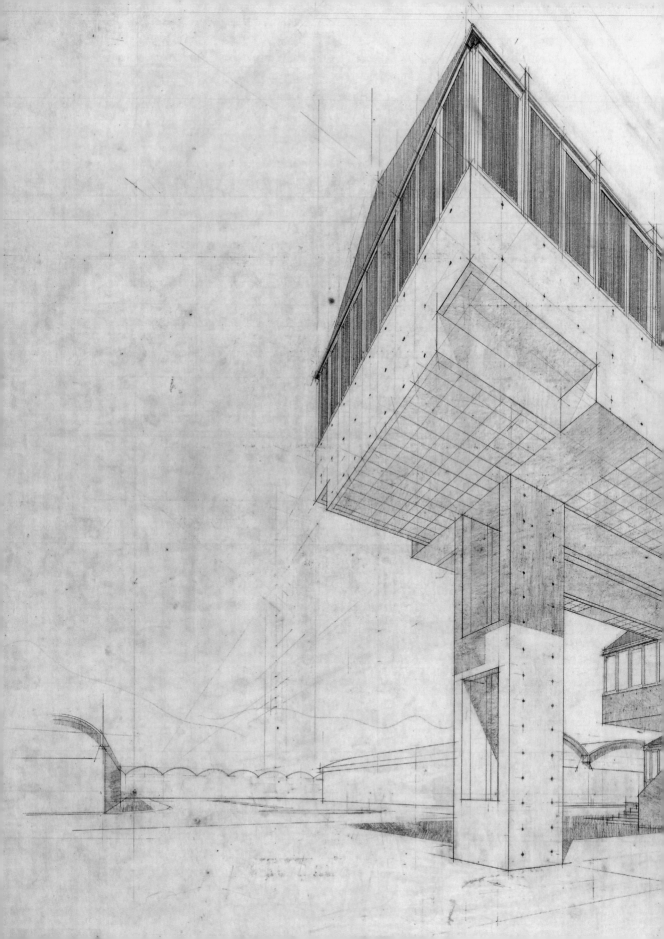

Zanussi offices in Porcia. Perspective from Pontebbana road, definitive project, 1959.

Zanussi offices in Porcia. Plan and front of a version of the first project, 1957.

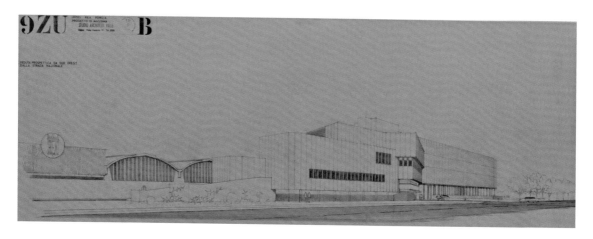

Zanussi offices in Porcia. Project B, September 1959.

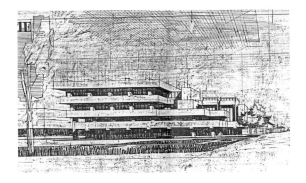

Project for the city hall of Jesolo. Perspective
from the square, 1962.

working drawings. At this point Valle thus decided
to completely revise the spatial theme of the wall
closed to the south and the offices open to the
north, and quickly reached the definitive solution,
presented in December 1959. This third and final
project was based on an extraordinary arrangement
of the section, conceived as a series of descending
levels – 'like stacked sheds' – on a structure of paired
crosswise partitions. This particular structure also
made it possible to contain the staircases and to
extend them outward, as overhangs on the facade:[4]
in this reference to the theme of the 'structure
shaped by circulation' already explored in the
design for the hospital of Portogruaro, Valle again
displayed meaningful affinities to the constructive
thinking of Louis Kahn, though the formal results
were completely different. Through the projection
onto the facade of the structural rhythm of the
building, but also the clear differentiation between
'heavy' load-bearing structure and 'light' supported
elements, Valle significantly enhanced the formal
complexity of the building envelope. Where the
'defensive' spirit of the two previous projects was
expressed in archaic images of reference like the
walls and gates of a settlement, now Valle seemed
to make reference to the 'heroic' spirit of great
works of engineering, through this architecture of
accentuated overhangs that prompted new visual
associations, like the back of a stadium or the stands
of a glass amphitheatre facing the landscape of the
production plants.

This heroic spirit was recognised, although
with some perplexity, by Reyner Banham on the
pages of *Architectural Review*,[5] immediately after
completion of the building in 1961: insisting on the
substantial 'quality of structural bravura' of the
building, Banham praised the Zanussi offices as
'a striking addition to the small roster of original
factory-designs produced by European architects'.
Thanks to this positive critical reception, confirmed
later by many other publications, the Zanussi
offices marked a very important moment for Valle's
architectural production: more than any earlier
project, this work displayed the fact that its maker
had reached maturity – at the young age of 38 –
and it was, therefore, the work that brought Valle
international visibility.

The Zanussi offices, emerging from a
programme of industrial architecture, embodied
surprising qualities of tectonic refinement, which
emerge in particular in the interface between the
'heavy' load-bearing structure in exposed concrete,
paced by the design of the vertically grouped metal
formwork, and the 'light' supported structure of
the continuous ribbon windows. This tectonic
refinement is perhaps also due to the fact that
Valle was alone in the studio, at that moment
of interruption in autumn 1959: the obligation
to design everything 'on his own', down to the
constructive details on a scale of 1:1 of the window
frames, facings and formwork for the pouring
of the concrete, became, in a particular sense,
an exceptional stimulus for Valle to express the
sum of everything he had learned in his previous
design experiences. It is nevertheless curious
to observe how Valle, in his reference to earlier
projects to rationally explain the genealogy of the
Zanussi offices, never once mentions, in his written
elucidations, one very significant work: the school
of Sutrio, designed in 1957 but built in 1961–62, after
the completion of the Zanussi offices.

Observing the school, we seem to see the
Zanussi offices moved into a mountain context.
Actually, the project foreshadowed the main
constructive themes of the offices: the linear layout
– already evident in the second project in 1958 –
the 'shifted' section with a structure of crosswise

School in Sutrio, 1957–62.

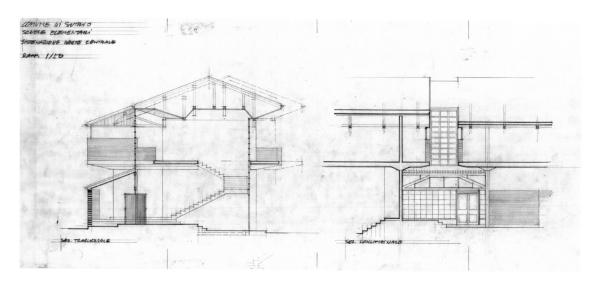

School in Sutrio, 1957–62. Cross-section, detail of longitudinal section at the entrance.

load-bearing partitions, the dialectic of 'heavy' and 'light' parts.[6] But the school is also surprising for another reason. It contains the characteristic features of previous buildings constructed by Valle in rural contexts: the brick lattice of the Migotto house, the lateral stone walls of the city hall of Treppo Carnico, the wooden roof that reminds us of the monolith of the bank of Latisana.

The mixture of these elements inside a work still having a strongly neo-Brutalist tone seems decidedly mannerist: a characteristic that can also explain why Valle later 'repressed' the memory of the school of Sutrio. Mannerism, then, as a threat: and this is precisely what Valle experienced after reaching maturity with the Zanussi offices. Commissioned in 1962 to design the city hall of Jesolo, Valle set out to use the same constructive grammar, but this thinking soon led to a profound crisis:

> I was convinced that I had understood everything and I tried to settle down, i.e. to acquire that famous consistency critics accused me of lacking. After one year I realized that the Zanussi offices were not the beginning, but the conclusion of a discourse. I understood that I had nothing in hand, I knew nothing, and I had to start over again, from scratch.[7]

To break this stalemate of summer 1962, Valle developed two different lines of research. The first, which found its most advanced expression in the hot springs of Arta (1960–64), which we will discuss in the next chapter, was based on autobiographical memory. Though he later acknowledged the hot springs complex of Arta as 'a more mature discourse', Valle was also aware of the limits of this nostalgic approach in the renewal of his research. So he initiated a second, very different line of investigation, a sort of formal purgatory, even interpreted by the architect as a 'reaction to the nostalgic approach of Arta':[8] an investigation aimed at achieving a 'non-architecture', which Valle ideally conceived as an 'almost invisible' object, free of any communicative value.

Standard warehouse of Zanussi-Rex, 1963 (warehouses built in Bergamo, Milan, Padua, Perugia, Rome). Overall view with the two-storey office volume in the foreground.

The opportunity for research was offered by programmes of industrial buildings, for which Valle began to consider the problem of the reproducibility of architecture for the first time. Valle wanted to take a decisive step beyond what had happened in the crisis after the Zanussi offices: the impossibility of repeating a design experience, with its uniqueness in terms of place and time.

In the architect's imagination, the Zanussi offices had grown like a living being, designed in every part, as is also confirmed by certain coloured elevations that even evoke the storybook figure of an immense green 'crocodile'. As opposed to this way of designing, Valle set out to construct buildings without time or place, whose ease of reproduction would indicate their belonging to industrial production cycles. The idea was not so much to transfer the methods of product design into the field of construction, but to propose a new production process for industrial buildings, based on the assembly of prefabricated pieces, to permit modifications and continuous expansion required by productive organisation. So at first Valle's projects concentrated on the constructive definition of infill panels. In the Sipre production plant for pre-stressed reinforced concrete parts, built in 1962–63, a panel with a height of seven metres produced by that same factory was deployed with a flexible joint that permitted angles of 90, 45 or 135 degrees: the idea was to obtain a universal system to respond to the various situations and various functional parts of the building, which were unified by this continuous 'skin'.

In the Ceramiche Scala factory in Pordenone, Valle chose instead to assemble the prefabricated panels with joints formed by a quarter tube in PVC to allow light to enter. The most interesting experimentation was conducted in the Zanussi kitchen factory (1963–64), where the constructive choices were associated for the first time with an 'expressive' quality: through the use of a very narrow and tall prefabricated panel, with a concave form, installed by alternating front and back sides to form a 'chained' wall, Valle managed to create the motif of a colonnade, representing the structural rhythm of the building.

That same year, in 1963, Zanussi developed a plan of regional and zone affiliates for the warehousing and distribution of products. This plan offered Valle the opportunity, for the first time, for concrete experimentation on reproducibility of one of his works of architecture: when the entirely prefabricated construction system had been defined, the individual warehouses could be built in keeping with simple rules of assembly of the various components, adapting to the different settlement contexts, from the industrial outskirts to the open countryside or urban suburbs. Valle, nevertheless, did not limit his efforts to solving a problem of rationalisation in construction; he also focused on the question of architectural expression in the buildings, which he wanted to be 'as anonymous as possible (programmed invisibility) to achieve a visibility and personalization not connected with neon signs, but with a presence through contrast'.[9] This form of absolute neutrality, which Valle called 'non-architecture', became paradoxically the most refined sign of the quality achieved by the company.

Production plant for Zanussi stoves, Porcia, 1963–64.

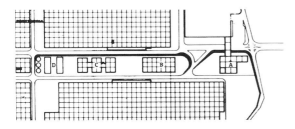

Zanussi Equipped Axis, 1966–70. Siteplan: (a) East gatehouse and staff offices; (b) Dining hall; (c) Diad offices; (d) Central heating plant.

The Zanussi 'standard warehouse', though included by Valle in the category of 'non-architecture', turned out to be rich in innovative constructive solutions that were continuously taken up and refined in successive industrial projects: a metal structure on a square grid of 12 × 12 metres, facades divided into a lower part made with concrete panels, forming a base against impact, and an upper part in light insulating Luxaflex panels. This division of the facade between 'heavy' and 'light' elements returned to the theme of the 'neo-Brutalist boxes' which Valle had already used in the Bellini house, in the city hall of Treppo Carnico and in the Arti Grafiche Chiesa factory (1959–60). With respect to these earlier projects, the two-part division of the facade of the Zanussi 'standard warehouse' seemed even more radical because the different materials were not deployed in keeping with the idea of an organic composition, but were simply juxtaposed, without joints or elements of 'mediation'. The dominant factor at this point was the assembly of heterogeneous parts, leading Valle to seek expressive effects ideally connected with two of his favourite poetic procedures: the 'ready-made' of Duchamp – which stimulated the reuse of ordinary construction elements in decidedly irregular ways in different contexts – and the '*cadavre exquis*' of the Surrealists, that made the most incongruous and at times monstrous encounters and combinations arise, for example, between concrete and Luxaflex in the standard Zanussi warehouse.

In 1964 Zanussi offered Valle another chance for new experimentation: this time the task was to

Zanussi Equipped Axis, 1966–70. Dining hall building, view of the access ramp (*top*) and detail of the stairs and the metal structure (*bottom*).

build an 'equipped axis' of service buildings inside the enclosure of the plant at Porcia, starting with the principle that a system of buildings could be generated by the same constructive grammar.

Here again, the construction parts to be assembled were extraordinarily reduced and simplified: a crossed beam metal structure on a square grid, that repeated and further rationalised that of the standard warehouses; prefabricated slabs; pre-stressed infill panels in concrete, mounted horizontally for the first time; and metal window frames. The first building, constructed in 1966, was a dining hall for 2,000 seats: the system of entrances, staircases and ramps projecting outside the facade formed a characteristic motif that made the building's connection to the ground expressive. In the Diad offices, built in 1967, the plan was divided into three rectangular units connected by a module for staircases and restrooms, while the expression on the facade was enhanced by the presence of aluminium sunscreen panels. Completed in 1969, the personnel offices, finally,

formed the eastern end of the equipped axis, together with the reception: a large canopy marked the new entrance to the enclosure of the factory at this point, replacing the 'factory door' function that had previously been assigned to the office building constructed in 1961.

The Zanussi standard warehouse and the 'equipped axis' thus permitted Valle to explore the possibility of using the same constructive language, based on an extreme formal reduction, in buildings with different scales and functions. During this exploration the initial resolution to achieve an 'architectural expression as anonymous as possible' was nevertheless partially contradicted by the emergence of elements that resulted in granting the 'industrial container' its own character, specifically linked to its function: it is in these exceptional elements – the ramps and staircases of the dining hall, the sunscreen panels of the Diad offices, the large canopy of the reception – that the expressive quality of the architecture now seemed to be concentrated.

Zanussi offices in Porcia, detail of the southern facade with the big window towards the entrance and the showroom.

Zanussi offices in Porcia, detail of the entrance portal with the cantilevered staircase.

Notes

1   Vittorio Gregotti, *Il disegno del prodotto industriale, Italia 1860–1980*, Electa, Milan, 1982.

2   Valle's first intervention at Rex, in 1956, was to 'remove' style and 'formal quality' from the first refrigerators produced, with the elimination of the rounded form and the simplification of the form of the handle. See Annalisa Avon, 'Gino Valle. Industrial design per la casa (1956–1975)', *Domus*, 769, March 1995, pp.62–70.

3   Maria Bottero and Giacomo Scarpini (eds), 'Intervista a Gino Valle', *Zodiac*, 20, December 1970, pp.82–115.

4   In the development of this latter solution, Valle later recognised the influence exerted by the memory of two buildings made in the same period: the expansion of the offices of the Loro & Parisini factory in Milan by Luigi Caccia-Dominioni (*Continuità*, 217, December 1957, pp.42–7) and the Nations building at the Milan Fair by Cesare Pea, recalled for the particular solution of the staircases protruding from the facade. See Gino Valle, 'Il mestiere più bello del mondo', in Giorgio Ciucci (ed.), *L'architettura italiana oggi. Racconto di una generazione*, Laterza, Bari, 1989, pp.275–90.

5   Reyner Banham mentions the Zanussi offices for the first time in 1961 in a short editorial note ('Studio Valle', *The Architectural Review*, 772, June 1961), which drew on the article by Francesco Tentori in *Casabella* on the ten years of activity of Studio Architetti Valle (F. Tentori, 'Dieci

anni d'attività dello Studio Architetti Valle', *Casabella*, 246, December 1960, pp.30–49), expressing doubts that the published project 'could appear as a design seriously intended for construction, rather than a fourth-year student project'. After the completion of construction in 1961, Valle sent some photographs of the building to Banham, who had to adjust his view: 'Since *World* [the editorial section curated by Banham] went so far as to doubt that the project was seriously intended for building, it is only proper now to make the *amende honorable* and draw attention to the fact that the Rex factory at Pordenone has now been completed. What is more, comparison of this photograph with the drawings of the original project by Studio Valle will show that it has been built substantially as they designed it.' See Reyner Banham, 'Rex', *The Architectural Review*, 779, January 1962, p.4.

6   These characteristics of the school of Sutrio were perhaps influenced by the reference to the building of Caccia-Dominioni, mentioned above, and already published in 1957 in the pages of *Casabella*.

7   Maria Bottero and Giacomo Scarpini (eds), 'Intervista a Gino Valle', pp.62–70.

8   'Annual Discourse: Gino Valle', *RIBA Journal*, May 1965, p.245.

9   Maria Bottero and Giacomo Scarpini (ed.), 'Intervista a Gino Valle', pp.62–70.

Zanussi Offices

Porcia, 1957–61

For those speeding past on the Pontebbana road, the entrance to Pordenone from Venice, the view of the building looks like a long, high wall, paced by its load-bearing structure, forming a strong contrast with the sequence of houses and sheds on both sides of the road. Around the building a moat contains the parking facilities, creating a space of mediation with respect to the street that accentuates the visual perception of a type of dam solidly anchored to the ground. The interruption of the support structure forms a large gateway offering a glimpse of the world of the factory. After crossing this threshold, one discovers the intriguing section of terraces that evokes the image of stacked sheds, or of industrial greenhouses from which to observe the 'spectacle' of production. This section allows each level of the offices – facing north – to make use of zenithal lighting. The corner staircase leads to the entrance lobby, where the gaze is drawn by the intense light that crosses the large glazing to the south of the two-storey display space: in this space it is possible to read the layout of the building, revealed first of all by the staircases built directly into the load-bearing structure of double pillars.

The experience of the visit is transformed at each level: rising from the ground floor, an initial staircase measures the depth of the showroom space, along which visitors can walk thanks to a gallery on the first floor, all the way to the staircase leading to the second floor. The experience then becomes more intimate, like the passages inside the walls of castles, and one has the sensation of the overhang: emerging beyond the facade line outlined by the lower levels, the path ascends until it reaches the corridor on the second floor, in a shifted position.

Through this differentiation of paths depending on the levels, but also in the clear orientation of the building towards the light of the north, it is possible for visitors to immediately sense where they are and where they are going.

The outer image of the building has changed little over more than fifty years. Even inside the offices, the original character of Valle's architecture has been maintained, marked by the sober elegance of the materials – composite floors with brass seam covers, exposed concrete pillars and staircases with wooden-edged casings, suspended ceilings with mineral fibre panels, metal partitions with transoms in glass and wood – and the discretion of the furnishings, some of which are the original pieces.

On the other hand, the context of the industrial closure, for which the building was once the only entrance, has changed extensively. With the strong growth of Zanussi and the creation of the so-called 'equipped axis' that includes a new reception and a series of structures for offices and services, the office building has lost the meaning of a gateway to the factory, because since then this entrance has been used only by managers who work in the building.

Zanussi offices in Porcia, 1957–61. Southern facade towards the Pontebbana road.

Zanussi offices in Porcia. Perspective of the final project, December 1959.

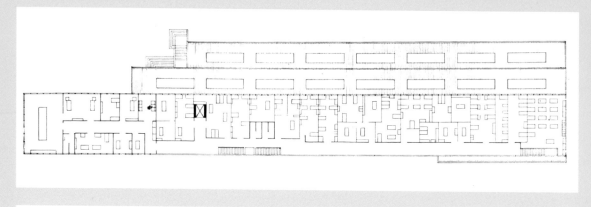

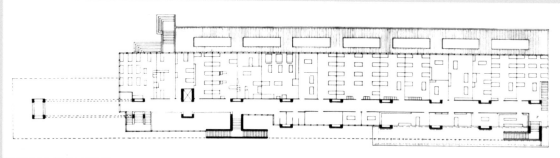

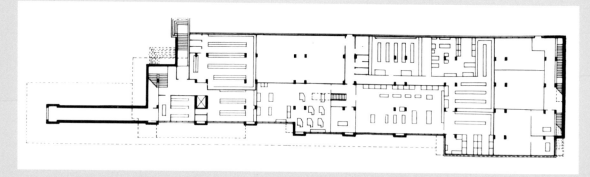

Zanussi offices in Porcia. Plans of second, first, ground and basement levels.

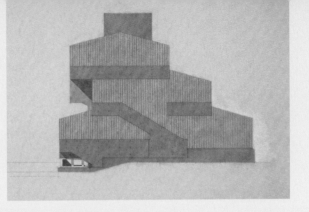

(*left and right*) Zanussi offices in Porcia, 1957–61. Short facades towards west and east.

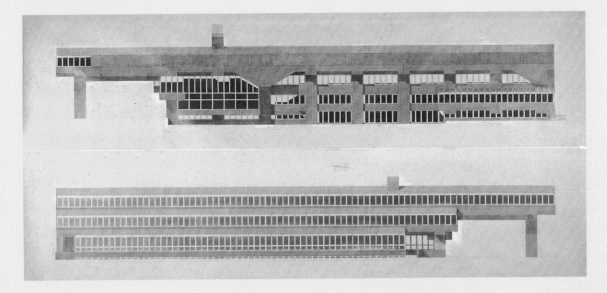

Zanussi offices in Porcia. Southern facade towards the street. Northern facade towards the sheds.

View of the terraced northern facade towards the sheds.

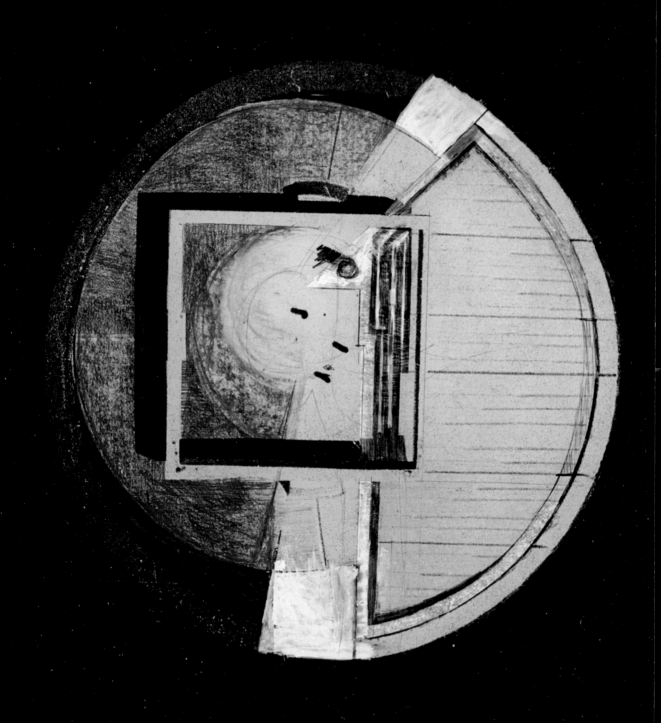

5 Monument to the Resistance and Foundation Architecture (1959–67)

Parallel to the design of the Zanussi offices, the competition for the Monument to the Resistance of Udine allowed Valle, in February 1959, to begin a totally different project, to which Federico Marconi again made a significant contribution in the reference to the naturalistic themes of Aalto. The task was to intervene in a peripheral zone of the city in ongoing expansion, at the centre of a roundabout. For Valle this was also a place charged with childhood memories: it was the square he crossed every day to go to school, a place marked by the imposing bulk of the Tempio Ossario, built from 1925 to 1942 by his father Provino.[1]

'To profoundly characterize' this place, according to Valle, would be a way of getting beyond the limitations of a figurative and representative approach to the monument: while reference to the epic imagery of the Resistance would have brought to mind the historical fact itself, Valle preferred to try to 'stimulate future men to relive the generating motives of the historical fact in themselves'. These motives, more than ideological or political, were first of all 'anthropological' in Valle's view, recognisable with great clarity in the phrase of Piero Calamandrei which Valle had engraved in the heart of the monument:

> When I ponder this mysterious and miraculous movement of the people, [...] who in a sudden

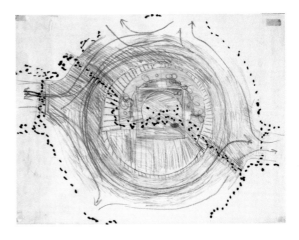

Monument to the Resistance of Udine, sketch by Valle with studies of pedestrian routes, 1959.

illumination felt that the time had come to head for the hills, to grip a rifle, to gather in the mountains to fight against terror, I am reminded of certain inexplicable rhythms of cosmic life [...]. The time had come to resist; the time had come to be men: to die like men in order to live like men.

Valle's insistence on the construction of a 'place' was also related to the 'rhythms of cosmic life': the Chinese philosophy of Feng Shui was

(*left*) Competition project for the Monument to the Resistance of Udine, 1959. Coloured pencils on heliographic copy (drawing: Alfredo Carnelutti).

Monument to the Resistance, sketch of one
of the first project versions.

Monument to the Resistance, (*above*) panel of a project
variant with the 'pergola' structure in reinforced
concrete, extending in a linear configuration towards
the facade of the adjacent ossuary, (*below*) section of
the 'pergola' (detail), 1959.

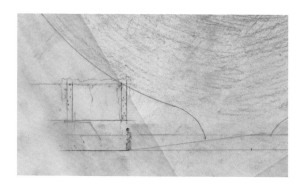

fully represented here for the first time in the
conception of the monument as an authentic
microcosm, enclosed in the conclusive form of
the large circle of the traffic roundabout. Already
in the first sketches, the monument was split into
two parts, one of earth and one of water, while
later the elements of air – the sky framed by the
large suspended square – and of fire, represented
by the iron sculpture by Dino Basaldella, also
emerged. Linking back to the formal potential
of the continuous structure, already explored in
many earlier projects, Valle introduced in one of
the early design solutions a pergola-like structure,
interrupted by an irregular rhythm of crosswise
elements, by only partially random perimeter
cuts, and by an opening in the spatial grid at the
position of a tree, which according to the sketch
would emerge from a pool of water with a vague
form. The red thread of Valle's reasoning was the
spatial itinerary: from the small section to the
side of the page we may surmise that the system
of walls in reinforced concrete (slightly over two
metres in height), perched on voluminous plinths,
constituted a sort of heavy and irregular coffering,
whose background was obviously the sky.[2]

In the successive projects the break of the
circle was no longer based only on symbolism:
there was also a functional motivation that led
Valle to establish a pedestrian crossing in the
square, a path whose tracing was associated with
the memory of the 'black sign of the streetcar
on the white plaza on a snowy day'. For Valle,
the architecture of the monument did not
therefore have to mark the place of memory, but
to construct it through profound shaping of the
ground: excavated to make the water run along
a large hollow, the ground had to evoke, on the
other hand, the arid vegetation of the scrubland
emblematic of the Resistance. As in the Zanussi
offices, the mature compositional knowledge

applied by Valle to the Monument to the Resistance took the form of a mixture of multiple formal and constructive themes previously explored: it even seems as if the exclusively symbolic programme of the monument acted as a profound stimulus to investigate the associative possibilities of these individual themes. The large concrete square thus harks back to the central space of the Cassa di Risparmio of Udine, though the sky it frames appears real, no longer simply metaphorical. The supports again emerge from the ground as the representation of a 'heap of earth', but their position at the centre of the beam brings out the strong tension of the structural overhang. Two other themes were explored for the first time: the foundation of architecture on a path of crossing, and the use of 'complex traces' to determine the geometry of the plan. Subtle asymmetries and slippages can in fact be recognised in the position of the square and the non-concentric circles. Valle experimented, in this work, with what would later become one of his most characteristic compositional procedures: the use of geometry to regulate, a posteriori, a figure 'found' and 'obtained' in the free gesture of the hand that draws. But while Valle sought a geometric rule to contain and specify the figure born of an intuition, the geometry of reference was far from any ideal of purity or mathematical rigour, so much so that he reached the point of speaking of 'geometric blasphemy' regarding his 'complex alignments'.

The compositional tension established between the 'square enclosure' suspended in the air and the figure of the circle contributes to qualify the symbolic heart of the monument as a place of commemoration and ceremony. Through the choice of the square, Valle also seemed to be experimenting, however – perhaps unconsciously – with an ideal continuity with the abstraction of exemplary monuments designed by Italian rationalist architects, particularly the monument of the Ardeatine Caves Memorial[3] in Rome by Mario Fiorentino (1944–47) – described by Manfredo Tafuri as an 'impenetrable suspended boulder, bearing mute witness to the place of the massacre'[4] – or the Palazzo dell'Acqua e della

Monument to the Resistance, the cantilevered structure over the fountain.

Unveiling of the Monument to the Resistance, 1969.

Arta Terme, perspective view of the complex from the opposite bank of the But River.

Project for the production plant in Denver, Colorado, 1966–68. Perspective from downhill.

Luce at EUR by the group led by Ignazio Gardella (1939), in which the square internal space opened simultaneously onto water and sky.

Valle's project had a long, troubled genesis, with many variations,[5] and it took ten years to complete the monument, which was presented on 25 April 1969. One substantial change had to do with the measurements and position in height of the 'square enclosure' suspended in the air. In the competition project of 1959, the large square was suspended just 1.3 metres above the level of the plaza: a standing observer would not have been able to see the other side of the plaza beyond the square, that had a height of a full four metres, and to enter the monument it would have been necessary to descend below the suspended enclosure, following the deep hollow in the central part of the plaza.[6] In April 1962, Valle altered the characteristics of the enclosure, reducing the height from four metres to 3.1, and raising it to a level of 2.1 metres above the plaza. In this way, the perspectives from the various avenues converging on the plaza were no longer blocked by the enclosure. This effect of visual encumbrance caused by the monument at the centre of the plaza was used by the opponents of the project to try to further postpone its construction.

Faced with this controversy, in 1963 Valle had a mock-up in actual size made with scaffolding pipes and jute canvas of the large suspended quad to assess its insertion in the space of the plaza. This initiative turned out to be decisive both on a political level and on an architectural level, leading to further study and simplification of the relations between the quad, the sculpture by Basaldella[7] and the landscaping features of the project.

The Monument to the Resistance of Udine is perhaps the project in which Valle most intensely expressed the idea of 'foundation' of architecture. For two reasons: the first programmatic, leading Valle to bring out the symbolic meaning of the monument in the construction of a microcosm; the second contextual, producing the meaningful transformation of a traffic rotary into a genuine place, to be entered and in which to spend time. In other contexts, Valle instead firmly linked the foundation idea of architecture to that of the relationship with the landscape or the environment. Regarding the Zanussi offices, Valle stated that

> the environment to which one must refer is that of the geographical scale, i.e. the plain, the mountains, the street. The building asserts itself as defence from the street and the chaos of the suburb, and as openness towards the factories and the geographical landscape. We might say that the building rejects the immediate surroundings to connect itself with the natural, geographical environment.[8]

Discussing this relationship of the architecture with the landscape 'geographically perceived', Francesco Tentori correctly observed that 'the open landscape seems to free the architectural image and enhance it'.[9] In effect, this liberation of the image is manifested in the abundance of visual associations found in the Zanussi offices: the 'walled city', the 'dam', the 'stadium', all images of a strong architecture capable of asserting itself in the plains landscape and therefore of expressing the idea of 'foundation' on a geographical scale. In the way in which the buildings take possession of the site, a strong analogy can be seen between the Zanussi offices and the school of Sutrio, which also forms a sort of dam at the foot of the town, open to the mountains on the other side of the valley. But already in previous projects Valle had addressed the image of strong architecture in relation to the openness of the landscape, as, for example, the Portogruaro hospital, which effectively stands out in the open countryside, like 'one of those castles that once studded the Friuli plains at the edge of the lagoon'.[10] In the project for the Arti Grafiche Chiesa plant in Udine (1959–60) the compact planimetric solution again bears witness to Valle's focus on the act of foundation of architecture in the landscape. In the midst of fields at the time of its construction, the factory seemed to evoke the compact presence of a country cemetery, enclosed by high walls, structured in keeping with a clear distinction between production facilities, with vaulted roofing, and the service buildings on the street, in concrete and brick.

Production plant in Denver, Colorado, 1966–68. Photomontage of the model with the landscape of the Rocky Mountains, seen from the position of the parking area, offering access to the facilities.

Nevertheless, it is in the project for the spa of Arta (1960–64), mentioned in the previous chapter with respect to the resolution of the creative crisis of 1962 following the project for the city hall of Jesolo, that the theme of foundation of architecture in the landscape reaches full maturity. On a site between the mountains and the river, accessed by means of a bridge, the setting had a profound influence on the design choices: Valle began, in fact, in 1960, with the idea of building a covered bridge – in keeping with the image of the Palladian bridge at Bassano del Grappa – leading to a platform from which the structures of the spa branched off into the landscape like the fingers of a hand, to achieve a dynamic layout of the various elements of the programme. After the rejection of this idea

on the part of the client, Valle started again with a new image, springing from the memory of a Renaissance castle on the road from Florence to Bologna that had struck him 'for its unity and the complexity of its right angles'.[11] This image was used to define the new footprint of the spa, conceived as a compact bridgehead with a plan organised around a central courtyard. Valle said that the castle also corresponded to a 'storybook reference', 'because as a child I spent all my summers in Arta':[12] as in the project for the Monument to the Resistance of Udine, the foundation of the architecture was therefore deeply connected to the autobiographical memory of the experience of a place from childhood.

Maria Bottero has proposed a meaningful analysis of the 'subtle play of memory' in the spa at

Arta, a memory that 'extends and continues beyond the boundaries of personal experience', giving the complex a 'vaguely 19th-century flavour, variously of a barracks or a hospital, a rest home or a hotel, the result of a traditional typological approach'.[13] But while it is true that a Viennese world of forms can be seen evoked in the design of the interiors, in the sizing and arrangement of the windows and the mouldings of the facades, the strong figurative presence of the roofs – which responds to the discovery of the complex from above, from the main road – seems to directly link back to the architecture of Frank Lloyd Wright. Once again, however, with a storybook reference: it is the legendary Orient filtered through the gaze of Wright that Valle wants to call forth, especially in the pagoda roof that

stands out over the reception hall to form the most characteristic landmark when seen from a distance, like the bell tower of a Zen monastery. Inside, the space of the reception hall seems to be powerfully shaped by the complex load-bearing structure of the three stacked roofs that allow light to filter from above: four hollow pillars in reinforced concrete, treated as a sculpture,[14] with a cruciform plan that is modified at each level to support the perimeter beam of the roof with an overhang. The structural theme, already explored in the Monument to the Resistance and the Cassa di Risparmio in Udine, is therefore repeated at each level, as in a complex game of nesting dolls: the great square of concrete that cuts out the sky, supported by pillars that have 'grown from the earth'.

Production plant in Denver, Colorado, 1966–68. Perspective view of the facilities from the street.

Valle photographed by Fulvio Roiter in front of the hot springs complex in Arta Terme, 1964.

Though Valle's determination to 'adhere to the landscape in its geographical scale' seemed to be strongly motivated by autobiographical memory, it also returned in projects far from his Friuli homeland. The design for a production plant in Denver developed during his first visit to the site in January 1966: a sloping plot, far from the city, open to a beautiful view of the Rocky Mountains. Valle suggested placing the plant on the lower part of the terrain, parallel to the level contours, while the land uphill was shaped in steps, to contain the parking areas: those entering thus discover the factory from above, scanning the orientation of the mountains over the horizon of the roof, and penetrating the building through a 'tube' that frames the landscape. Once again, the idea of 'foundation' in the landscape relies on the image of a strong work of architecture – the 'walled city' or fortress – with a 'defensive' front towards the valley, while from inside the central layout spine, conceived as a spyglass aimed at the mountains, terminates in the large panoramic terraces of the common areas protruding from the building's enclosing walls.

Notes

1   Valle remembers that his father often took him to construction sites, and that in 1931, when he was eight years old, he went up on the dome, 'attracted by this enormous white egg, not yet clad in copper, with a metal ladder along the meridian that led to the lantern'. See Giovanni Vragnaz (ed.), 'Monumento alla Resistenza a Udine. Intervista a Gino Valle', *Piranesi*, 9–10, Autumn 1999, vol.7, pp.6–27.

2   If we consider the hypothetical path of the visitor, the monument would be reached, after leaving street level, by descending the excavation in the terrain. This idea of a change of section was maintained until the definitive project. The exterior view of the complex – a solid perimeter, with a frontal view of the concrete planes – was reversed upon reaching the centre of the monumental area: the planes would then be perceived as a series of blades. The weight of the system experienced from the outside would be transformed, according to this idea, into a suspended skeleton, and visitors would find themselves immersed in a path where the structure took on a substantially figurative value. Everything was enhanced by the cutting of lights and shadows, and by the ivy that spread over the structure.

3   Speaking of the suspended quad of the Monument to the Resistance, Valle said that it should seem to be 'wrested from the earth, made with course foundation concrete, and raised to frame the sky', also saying that for this reason, in a certain sense it was 'the inversion of the Ardeatine Caves Memorial in Rome, a very beautiful project, where there is the lateral opening for light, and the sky cannot be seen'. See ibid.

4   Manfredo Tafuri, *Storia dell'architettura italiana 1944–1985*, Einaudi, Turin, 1986.

5   The complex evolution of the design of the work is reconstructed by Francesco Tentori in the essay 'Il Monumento alla Resistenza', *La Panarie*, 3, December 1968, pp.58–64.

6   Tentori acutely interpreted this downward movement of the square as a strategy to 'accentuate the sense of the shrine, the chapel that encourages meditation', ibid., p. 59.

7   In a recent essay Paolo Campiglio has reconstructed the reasons for the changes in the plastic form and position of the sculpture of Dino Basaldella inside the monument, analysing in particular a remarkable variation in the third project of December 1963, which was higher than the sanctuary and became very visible from the outside. The abandonment of this project was interpreted by Tentori (ibid., p.62) as a decision of Valle alone, while Campiglio hypothesises that this decision was also connected with the political clients (who preferred an interpretation of the Resistance as a concluded, circumscribed episode), as well as the greater coherence between the architectural and sculptural ideas. See Paolo Campiglio, 'Dino monumentale: dal "far grande" alle sculture ambientali', in *Dino Basaldella*, exh. cat. MUSMA, the Museum of Contemporary Sculpture of Matera, Edizioni della Cometa, Rome, 2009, pp.24–37.

8   Pierre-Alain Croset (ed.), 'Una conversazione con Gino Valle', *Casabella*, 519, December 1985, pp.16–17.

9   Francesco Tentori, 'Dieci anni d'attività dello Studio Architetti Valle', *Casabella*, 246, December 1960, pp.30–49.

10   ibid.

11   'Annual Discourse: Gino Valle', in *RIBA Journal*, May 1965.

12   Maria Bottero and Giacomo Scarpini (eds), 'Intervista a Gino Valle', *Zodiac*, 20, December 1970, pp.82–115.

13   Maria Bottero, 'Un edificio termale nelle Alpi carniche', *Zodiac*, 14, April 1965, pp.128–45.

14   Regarding the relationship between structural solution and formal research, Giovanni Corbellini has proposed an interesting comparison between the Quaglia house at Sutrio and the spa of Arta, speaking of 'a shared reference to compositional techniques of a neo-plastic type: more like Mondrian, two-dimensional, at Sutrio, and linked instead to the sculptural experimentation of Vantongerloo at Arta'. See Giovanni Corbellini, 'Astratto e contestuale. Gino Valle in Carnia', in Elena Carlini (ed.), *Architettura in montagna, Gino Valle in Carnia*, Navado Press, Trieste, 2005, p.19.

Monument to the Resistance

Udine, 1959–69

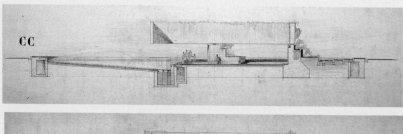

CC

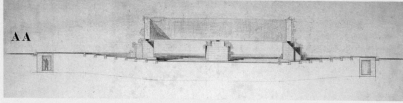

AA

Sections, competition panels, 1959.

The monument is located at the centre of Piazza XXVI Luglio, a roundabout along the ring road, surrounded by banal construction dominated by the monumental presence of the Tempio Ossario. For those arriving by car from Viale Venezia, the monument marks the entrance to the historic centre: the first glimpse is that of the large concrete square that crosses the horizon, while upon approaching one notices the transparency that has been maintained at street level. For pedestrians, on the other hand, the monument is an island in which to linger during the path of crossing of the plaza. One enters the place of memory following a fissure that divides the large circle into two parts. While on one side it is possible to listen to the water that flows in a large fountain, on the other one enters the central space of the memorial, from which it is possible to perceive the configuration of the monument as a microcosm: the sky framed by the large concrete square, the flowing water, patches of cultivated earth from which the three load-bearing pillars emerge, along with the solidified fire of the iron statue by Dino Basaldella. Two flights of steps lead to a recessed platform, in contact with the water: from this level one sees the basin as a large stone amphitheatre, while the sound of the water evokes the atmosphere of a small garden, protected from the traffic.

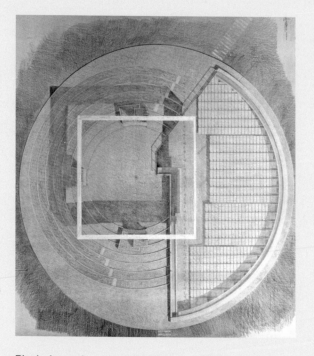

Planivolumetric, competition panels, 1959.

View of the internal space of the quadrangle with the staircase leading to the platform recessed at water level.

View of the monument in the plaza with the Tempio Ossario in the background.

Spa in Arta

1960–64

Perspective of the spa complex from the opposite bank of the But River.

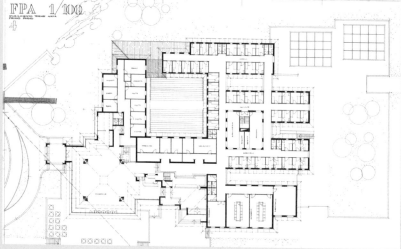

Ground floor plan.

The building is located on a narrow lot at the foot of the mountain, along the But River that descends from the Carnic Alps. Arriving from the state highway, one discovers the building from above, isolated on the other side of the river, and placed diagonally with respect to the valley: the varied profile of the roofs and the pale walls stands out against the dark backdrop of the forest. The path of approach across the bridge is oriented towards the pointed roof of the Kursaal, which forms a clear sign for the entrance to the building. The visitor passes diagonally beneath a low pavilion and enters the large space of the Kursaal, lit from above and from large windows offering a view of the mountains. On the western side, the Kursaal opens to a large outdoor terrace organised around the spring. From this corner space, access is provided to the other zones for the public: going up some steps, one reaches the orthogonal wings that intersect to form the inner courtyard, and then extend like wings with the volumes of the baths; at a slightly lower level, the cafe opens towards the outdoor terrace. Descending further, the visitor reaches the lower floor, at ground level, where the general services are organised around the central courtyard, which has its own vehicle accessway.

View of the entrance hall.

Model of the three structural rings of the roof. The four cross-shaped pillars are placed at the inner vertices of the load-bearing structural square and support the beams and the three levels of the roof.

The structural system of the roof of the entrance 'pagoda': view from below.

6 A First Synthesis (1961–78)

As we have seen in previous chapters, Valle's research after the construction of the Zanussi offices (1957–61) developed along two main lines. In the first, Valle focused on a process of autobiographical memory to firmly anchor his works of architecture in the context, and to concentrate on the figurative value of architectural language, referencing precise formal elements existing at the project site. In the second line of research, explored in a certain sense as a reaction to the first, instead the architect attempted to erase any autobiographical content, to achieve the greatest possible expressive 'neutrality'. Pursued in parallel, the two lines could sometimes cross: this happened, for example, in the project for the theatre of Udine, which offered Valle an opportunity to intervene on a particularly difficult site in the historic centre.

Already, from 1956 to 1958, Valle had developed several planimetric schemes for the insertion of a large theatre inside the monumental complex formed by the 14th-century church of San Francesco and the old neoclassical hospital built in the 1800s to replace the Franciscan convent annexed to the church.[1]

Later, in 1961 Valle won first prize in the national competition, organised by the City of Udine, with an interesting project that decisively rejected any solution of continuity with the symmetrical structure of the hospital: shifting the theatre as close as possible to the church, Valle proposed limiting demolition and concentrating the project

in place of a single courtyard in the old hospital. A strong spatial tension was created between the structures of the stage and the apse of the church, which made the new public building appear as the church's 'double'.

After having won the competition, Valle had to rework the project based on a new programme of the municipal administration, which had decided to sell the eastern part of the block along Via Morpurgo as an area for office facilities, thus obtaining income to devote to the creation of the theatre. This changed the relations among the parts: the theatre was moved south, towards Via Crispi, outside the neoclassical enclosure, while the eastern half of the hospital was demolished and replaced by a new building for private offices. In the definitive project, from 1963, the theatre thus appeared as an isolated object to the south of the area. The solid facades, clad with prefabricated panels mounted vertically on a continuous concrete base, gave the theatre an image of severity and closure that seemed to directly reflect the spirit of the projects of 'non-architecture', though the extreme reduction of the language was enhanced by the use of white Carrara marble built into the prefabricated panels.

The theatre project for Udine was never built and therefore not entirely resolved in terms of the critical relationship of the existing architecture of the historic city. However, in 1963, on Via Mercatovecchio, again in Udine, Valle instead had

(*left*) Commercial and residential building on Via Marinelli, Udine, 1970–71. View of the corner opening.

Project for the theatre of Udine, 1957–64. Study sketch of the facades on Piazza Venerio, first project, 1961.

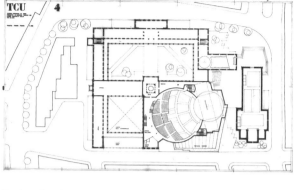

Project for the theatre of Udine, 1957–64. Siteplan at the level of the cavea of the first project, 1961.

the possibility of making an intervention that revealed an extraordinary sensitivity and refinement when addressing this same theme. Faced with the problem of replacing a corner building on a narrow lot, Valle again employed memory as a design tool, as he had in an exemplary way for the design of the spa in Arta. While at Arta the reference was still an autobiographical fact, here, the recollection took on a less personal dimension, connected with the collective memory of a 'medieval Udine with wooden houses' which Valle had already evoked in 1961 in a competition project for the Banca Cattolica on Piazza Bertrando in Udine.[2] The use of memory in the genesis of the project on Via Mercatovecchio was clearly explained by Valle himself:

> I had the problem of building next to a facade in stone and frescoed stucco. ... The iron facade I have built applies the same language, and in a certain sense I have simply changed the material. But then the same facade could be juxtaposed with the representation of Venice in the paintings of Carpaccio and Canaletto, where we see houses in wood. So I obtained an iron facade that represents a wooden facade. On the other hand, if you go back to closely observe the Renaissance facade from which I started, you realize that it too reminds us of the wooden houses that were there before. This game of allusions interests me, because in the end simply by changing material

I found myself recovering this sort of 'collective memory' of the facades that were there in the past, that constituted the city and were gradually replaced.[3]

Valle did not in any way want to apply an imitative approach. Instead, he wished to represent, through the use of a new, specifically modern material, the process of historical transformation of the typology of the merchant-class house in Udine. More than ten years after Rogers' appeals for dialogue between modern architecture and 'existing environmental factors', the house on Via Mercatovecchio seemed like a particularly apt example of insertion in the context of the historical city: it thus took a position of continuity with an important thread of Italian architectural research at the start of the 1950s, which Manfredo Tafuri had identified with examples such as the INA building in Parma by Albini, the building on Via Borgonuovo in Milan by BBPR, and the Commodities Exchange of Pistoia by Michelucci.[4] The choice of building a facade entirely in iron seemed new for Valle, who until then had only made partial use of metal structures to achieve an image of lightness and modernity – for example, in the infill panels of the bank in Latisana and the street-front facade of the low volume in front of the tower in Trieste. But this choice may have been influenced by the contemporary experience of Albini for the building of La Rinascente in Rome, completed in 1961, to which Valle also seemed to refer in the treatment of the cornice with openings to offer a view of the sky.

Again, in this house, Valle returned to familiar themes like the ground attachment of the pillars protected by stone partitions (an abstract version of the 'heap of earth' pillar, resembling the one used in the Monument to the Resistance), or the structural differentiation between the mezzanine level, enclosed between two sturdy architraves, and the lower levels with more detailed mouldings.

Though it was later deemed by Valle himself as 'too complicated', the red building on Via Mercatovecchio marked the start of a new phase of research characterised by the focus on the capacity of new architecture to evoke a previously existing one. Applying different means from those involved in the contextual architecture of the 1950s, Valle returned to the discourse on the representation of a temporal experience in architecture: through the design's reference to precise images of architecture present in the place, he set out to give his buildings a particular quality that would make them seem 'as if they had always existed there', without in any case ever overlooking the need to establish a rigorous critical distance with respect to the existing architecture.

In the project for the Manzano house – a house with two apartments built in 1965–66 on the outskirts of Udine – the reference to an existing architecture was no longer based on a real presence, as in the building on Via Mercatovecchio: the initial image, this time, was instead the product of fiction, leading Valle to suggest not one precise building, but a generic house – a 'true house' in the traditional sense of the term – with a large overhanging roof that was supposed to evoke both Central European architecture and that of Frank Lloyd Wright. Starting with this image, Valle intervened with great creative freedom: he removed one corner of the volume to bring the entrance to the centre of the house, created a small roof garden, shaped the terrain with excavation and terraces on multiple levels, using a system of ramps to make a true 'architectural promenade' around the house. Unlike the building on Via Mercatovecchio,

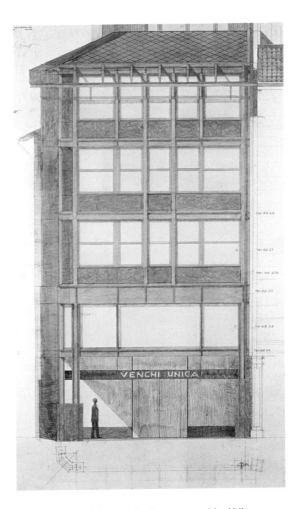

Commercial building on Via Mercatovecchio, Udine, facade study, 1963.

Manzano house in Udine, 1965–66. Entrance facade.

139

Manzano house in Udine, roof plan, 1965.

Manzano house in Udine, 1965–66. View of the facade towards the fields, with the kitchen terrace on the ground floor and the two-storey window of the studio.

the red colour was used this time to attenuate the discontinuity of the materials and to intensify the perception of the house as a single compact mass subjected to a brutal gesture of breakage. While Valle seemed to return to the spa at Arta in the design of a light moulding in the concrete walls, inserting floor-marker bands and making the first floor protrude slightly, the surfaces generated by the gesture of breakage instead reveal a sculptural treatment of the concrete: the vertical cuts, the setbacks, the protrusion of the octagonal drum of the staircase make this gesture more dramatic.

In parallel, Valle designed Chiesa house, with Piera Ricci Menichetti, that has profound similarities to the Manzano house in terms of design strategy. Here, Valle was faced with the problem of expanding and restructuring an existing building proceeding through a dual operation: adding a volume without openings towards the street to produce the image of a house closed off from the outside and joining the new volume to the existing ones by means of a large pitched roof that encloses, with a C-shaped plan, the living room taken as the centre of the composition. The architectural quality of this project therefore shows how Valle was able to exploit even an initially modest opportunity in order to conduct very meaningful conceptual experimentation. As in the Manzano house, Valle

performs gestures of 'fracture' in the spaces under the large roof, introducing diagonal cuts to make an 'architectural promenade' across the roofs, and a succession of terraces. The theme of the insertion in existing urban contexts was again addressed in the project for a residential tower on Lake Shore Drive in Chicago, in 1967, commissioned by Unimark International. On a very narrow, long lot, not unlike the 'Gothic lots' of Europe, Valle – in collaboration with Piera Ricci Menichetti – concentrated on the spatial quality of the apartments, which exploited the orientation towards the lake by means of a section of stepped levels. On the upper floors, above the rooftops of the surrounding buildings, the section was modified to host descending terraces that seemed like the transcription, on an urban scale, of the expressionist motif of the 'fracture' of the form applied in the Manzano and Chiesa houses. Valle thus obtained a highly original overall image, based on a strong and decisive volumetric arrangement of the various parts. The impossibility of excavation in the rock produced the unusual solution of an above-ground parking facility shaped as an enormous closed structure, nine storeys high, hollowed out by circular access ramps, adding very expressive character to the ground seam of the tower. Starting with the subdivision of the facade into three spans, Valle introduced not only

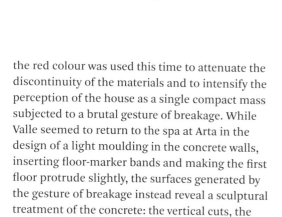

variations in the width and height of the apartments – of which many are duplexes – but also slight shifts of the elevation, to suggest great freedom in the assembly of the individual residences. Instead of the traditional image of a modernist high-rise block based on vertical repetition of floors that are all identical in size and layout (as in the nearby residential towers by Mies van der Rohe on Lake Shore Drive), in this tower Valle expressed a principle of montage and overlapping of individual 'houses' very different from each other, a principle made possible by the use of a deep beam structure that permitted not only overhangs, but also movements of shifting both in depth and height.

All these projects illustrate how Valle was able, in a short time span, from 1961 to 1967, to gradually refine his own design sensibilities regarding the insertion of new architecture in the context of the historical city. During the same years in which he was exploring this fertile line of research, Valle continued to come to grips with that of 'non-architecture', but it was not until the project for the city hall of Casarsa della Delizia, begun in 1966 with Piera Ricci Menichetti, that he was able to make a true synthesis that would lead to a new cycle of research.

The interpretation of the site – at the edge of the ancient centre and near the railway station – led to an initial setting idea: the new city hall had to be conceived not as a large representative object, but as a sort of gate located on a pedestrian walkway on axis with the station. This idea linked back to the theme of the foundation of a public place on a path of crossing, which Valle had already approached with particularly positive results in the Monument to the Resistance at Udine. Not an object, then, but a place to be crossed, conceived as a composition of three elements that interpret the various functions of the programme: the two volumes of the offices on one side of the path, and the taller volume of the council chamber on the other. Unlike what had happened in the city hall of Treppo Carnico – where the volumetric division of the building corresponded to a functional separation – at Casarsa Valle rejected any mediation with the traditional edification of the town, introducing deliberately extraneous architectural forms: three elements derived from the research on 'non-architecture', three 'industrialized boxes' with a square plan (14.40 × 14.40 metres) in which every trace of monumentality was eliminated.

In the equipped axis of Zanussi at Porcia, Valle had experimented with the possibility of concentrating the expressive quality of architecture in just a few elements that stood out against the

Chiesa house in Udine, 1963–66. The covered terrace on the first floor and the diagonal staircase rising across the pitches of the roof.

Chiesa house in Udine, 1963–66. View from the street, with the covered terrace on the first floor.

Residential tower on Lake Shore Drive, Chicago, 1966.
Perspective view from the lake.

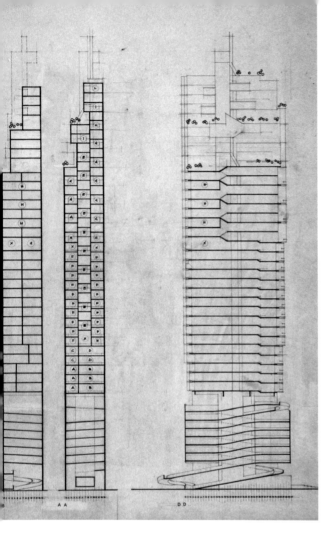

Residential tower on Lake Shore Drive, Chicago, 1966.
Cross-sections and longitudinal section.

Headquarters of the newspaper *Il Messaggero Veneto*,
Udine, 1967–68. Nocturnal view from the street.

backdrop of the absolute neutrality of the buildings. At Casarsa he returned to this principle, taking it to an extreme: all the necessary representative value of the public building was gathered in its attachment to the ground and in the entrances of the three 'non-architectures'. Valle thus managed to separate the volumes from the piazza and the surrounding buildings, through two different operations: on the one hand, fencing off the offices with a base and a moat, generating an ascending entry path, therefore 'ritualised' like the access to a secular temple; on the other, by raising the council chamber to create a sheltered plaza, obtaining greater height and, as a result, an accentuated presence of the volume in the profile of the town.

A synthesis of two lines of research, the city hall of Casarsa is also a work of singular complexity, due to the range of themes and projects to which it is connected. First of all, Valle returned to the question of the 'diagonal cut' in the outlining of the plans, developed this time on three different levels: at the level of the entrances and internal routes of relation between the various elements; at the level of the structural grid, also placed diagonally to free up the corners; and at the level of the overall composition of the three squared elements, which were not aligned but diagonally staggered.

Built in 1972–74, the Casarsa City Hall also incorporated constructive solutions developed in the building for the editorial staff and print facility of *Messaggero Veneto* – constructed on the outskirts of Udine in 1967–68 – where Valle again concentrated his attention on the diagonal path of access and the shaping of the terrain with a large recessed parking facility. The entrance solution – a sort of 'tube' with a rectangular section that penetrates the facade – was directly reprised at Casarsa in the external steps for access to the council chamber. The facades of the city hall, on the other hand, referenced the theme of the heavy–light dichotomy previously explored, in particular, in the standard warehouse for Zanussi, with vertical panels and frames in aluminium that convey the visual impression of simply resting on the reinforced concrete base.

While in the design of the city hall of Casarsa Valle experimented for the first time with the

possibility of obtaining a complex whole based
on the combination of multiple building parts,
it was in the context of the historical city that
he found the opportunity to apply his acquired
experience with the greatest creative intensity.
This opportunity was prompt, because already in
1966 Valle had directly re-employed compositional
features from Casarsa in a project for the Palazzo
delle Associazioni Culturali on Via Manin in Udine,
near the historic city gate: in the first solution,
two square volumes were placed on the street in a
shifted position – freeing up the view of the tower
– while on the back a triangular volume permitted
diagonal crossing of the lot. In a subsequent
version the crossing was directly entrusted to a
shopping arcade not unlike a 19th-century urban
passage. Refining and developing the project until
1974, Valle ended up assigning greater importance
to this theme of the passage: the 19th-century
building, slated for demolition in the first version,
was now diagonally cut by the passage, becoming
a triangular prism with the conservation of only
the facade and the roof. Commenting on this
project, Valle stated that 'the overall intervention,
in its brutality, determines a hierarchy of image
and use among the parts, and permits their
interpretation and crossing, through the diagonal
passage'.[5] This character of brutality revealed a
very different attitude from the one Valle had
displayed in the building on Via Mercatovecchio:
the brutality seemed necessary in order to create a
tension between the new building and the existing
features of the place, translating into a 'strong'
gesture of insertion corresponding to the radical
functional change of the area. In this sense, for
Valle the project on Via Manin displayed a striking
resemblance to the settlement principle proposed
during those same years by Vittorio Gregotti in his
design for La Rinascente in Turin (1969), also based
on the idea of diagonal crossing of a large urban
block.

   At the same time as the development of the
project for Via Manin, Valle built another work in
the historical centre of Udine in 1970–71 – the INA
building on Via Marinelli, in collaboration with
Piera Ricci Menichetti – which expresses the same

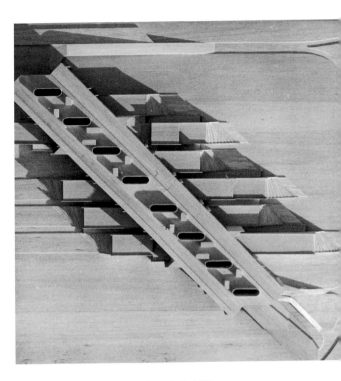

Competition project for the hospital of Mirano,
1967. Model.

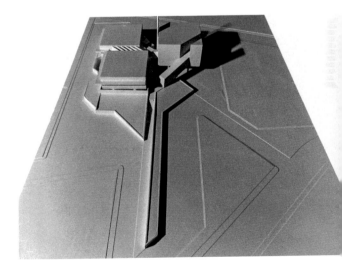

City hall of Casarsa della Delizia,
1966–74. Model.

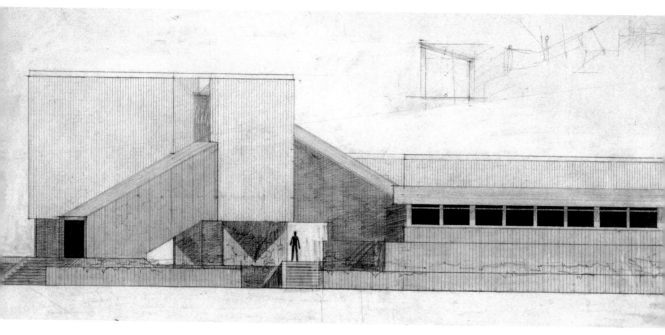

City Hall of Casarsa della Delizia, rear facade.

change of attitude with respect to the earlier project on Via Mercatovecchio. The description supplied by the architect himself bears clear witness to the passage from a conception of the new as an evocation of what already exists to a principle of dialectical tension to be established between the two terms: 'I made a cut, as if with a circular saw, between the two old lateral houses, a new concrete facade with holes and that's all, cut like a piece of cheese with wider and narrower parts, three storeys high. On a street with a width of five metres it takes on the value of an enormous gash.'[6]

The project, in fact, was based on a 'poetics of tension' that appears with particular relevance in the empty hinge created between the two buildings. By means of the 'painterly' treatment of the old restored house – red, like the Manzano house – Valle attempted to accentuate the material contrast between the two buildings, while at the same time seeking a relationship in the projected overhang of the wall of the new part towards the old building, almost to the point of touching it. All the force of

the project is concentrated in this simultaneous proximity and maximum opposition between 'old' and 'new', without in any case excluding certain refinements in the tectonic definition of the building, which can be seen, for example, in the treatment of the concrete surface with horizontal floor-marker bands – as at the spa of Arta and the Manzano house – in the top with a tall parapet in painted tubing – a 'naval' touch, as in the building on Via Marinoni – and in the ventilation pipes that sprout horizontally from the facade on the courtyard, as a rather surreal presence.

This 'poetics of tension' behind the INA building was later reprised by Valle in a series of projects for the Palazzo della Regione and the judicial offices on the site of the earlier project for the municipal theatre of Udine, over a period of nearly 15 years. After approval in 1964 of the definitive project for the theatre, the eastern part of the old hospital was demolished, but already in 1967 a new ministerial restriction,[7] corresponding to this demolished part, greatly reduced the allowable volume of

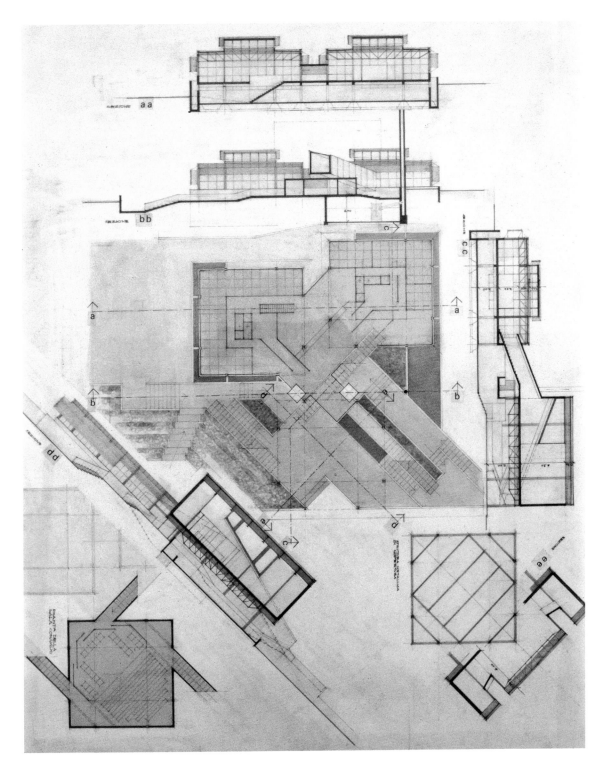

City hall of Casarsa della Delizia, panel of first project, 1966–68.

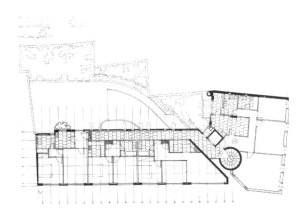

INA building on Via Marinelli, Udine, 1970–71;
(*top*) standard plan; (*bottom*) courtyard facade.

the construction. To find a way out, the regional government asked Valle, in 1968, to work on a new overall arrangement of the area, also incorporating the land to the south that had previously been earmarked for the theatre. In 1971, Valle presented a first draft, in which the new building was positioned in continuity with, and partially interpenetrating, the old construction. In the second project, in 1972, Valle replaced this principle of interpenetration to establish a precise tension between the two buildings, organised as very close parallel volumes. In yet another version of the project, in 1975, Valle moved forward with the research on the establishment of meaningful tensions between the new and existing buildings. In the large excavated ditch, this time Valle inserted a single linear volume, in a rotated position which tended to make the new object more autonomous, eliminating any geometric continuity with the neoclassical structure of the old hospital. Unique in many ways, this project displayed a high degree of complexity that already foreshadowed later projects by Valle in the 1980s, especially in its use of a 'complex geometry' to establish spatial tension among heterogeneous elements. The experiences gained in this project could, in any case, be directly reused by Valle in the competition project for the judicial offices, in 1978, still in that same area: partially due to a programme requiring less floor space, the rotation of the new volume appeared this time contained inside an enclosure that retraced the position occupied by the demolished part of the hospital. Therefore, this was a solution offering greater respect for historical memory, but also in a certain sense more subtle, in linguistic terms, in its use of the tools of suggestion and allusion.

In a very synthetic way, this project managed to represent the entire history of the area and its transformations. The lacerations caused by the demolition were not concealed, while the new building asserted itself as a double of the one demolished, though only in an allusive way: in this sense, it did not make the slightest attempt to smooth over the contradictions that emerged during the long, complex process of transformation of the area, and left meaningful testimony as its legacy, yet, unfortunately, designed and never built.

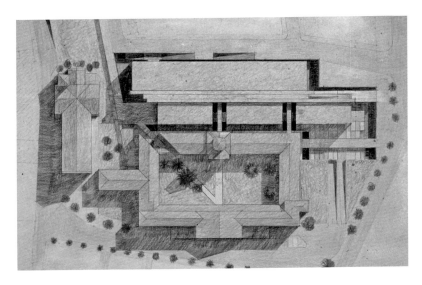

Palazzo della Regione in Udine, 1969–75. Second project, 1972. Siteplan.

Palazzo della Regione in Udine, 1969–75. Second project, 1972.
Perspective from Piazza Venerio.

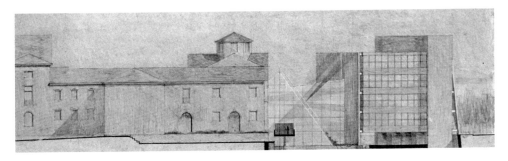

Palazzo della Regione in Udine, 1969–75. Third project, 1975. Northern facade with
the renovated former monastery to the left.

Notes

1   These planimetric schemes had to do with the possibility of utilising the entire block, with the insertion of the theatre at the centre, the conservation of the west wing of the hospital, demolition of the east wing and the creation of new volumes along Via Morpurgo to the east, and along Via Crispi to the south, outside the enclosure of the hospital, for municipal and private offices. The guidelines of the national competition in 1961 had to instead take the protected status of the former hospital into account, due to the ministerial decree of 10 December 1959, against which the City of Udine filed an appeal on 20 October 1961, following the results of the competition.

2   The regional competition for the Banca Cattolica headquarters addressed the same site as the competition in 1958 for the centre of Udine. Valle took second place with an interesting proposal, where this time the large block was organised in 'houses' of different heights, joined by a continuous portico and by the two-storey volume of the hall of the bank.

3   Pierre-Alain Croset (ed.), 'Una conversazione con Gino Valle', *Casabella*, 519, December 1985, pp.16–17.

4   Manfredo Tafuri, *Storia dell'architettura italiana 1944–1985*, Einaudi, Turin, 1986.

5   From the project description, quoted in Francesco Dal Co, 'Gino Valle. La necessità dell'architettura', *Lotus International*, 11, 1976, p.186.

6   Maria Bottero and Giacomo Scarpini (ed.), 'Intervista a Gino Valle', *Zodiac*, 20, December 1970, pp.82–115.

7   These later projects by Valle were connected with a range of ministerial rulings and appeals on the part of the municipal government, following the demolition of the east wing along Via Morpurgo, because many years were required for the precise stipulations for replacement of the demolished wing. The ministerial ruling of 23 October 1967 called for reconstruction of the original volumes, with stylistic restrictions regarding the pitches of the roofs. After the city government's appeal, a new ministerial ruling of 26 July 1971 proposed less restrictive parameters, with the possibility of construction along Via Morpurgo with less 'philological' accuracy.

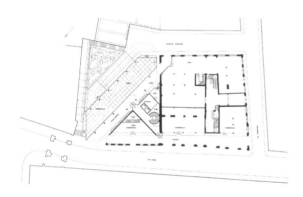

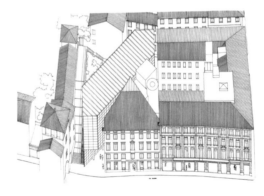

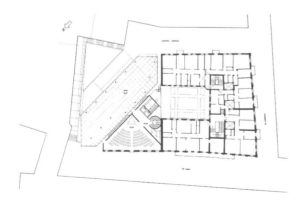

Palazzo delle Associazioni Culturali on Via Manin, Udine, second project, 1971–74; (*top left*) ground floor; (*bottom left*) standard floor; (*top right*) isometric.

CR71 IOE

vista da porta manin

Palazzo delle Associazioni Culturali on Via Manin, Udine, second project, 1971–74.
Perspective view from Porta Manin, pencil on transparent film.

Commercial Building, Via Mercatovecchio

Udine, 1963–65

Front on Via Mercatovecchio.

View of the corner solution.

The building is located in the old commercial centre of Udine and reflects the morphological features of the other buildings on Via Mercatovecchio. On the ground floor the portico offers access to a store with a mezzanine organised around a central void, while from the lateral street one enters the lift/stairwell leading to the upper levels: three floors of offices and an attic organised as a studio apartment with a large terrace. The staircase is double on the ground floor to offer separate access to the store mezzanine. The building is iron-framed with exposed rustproofing, in which marble infill panels and window/door frames are inserted.

View from Via Mercatovecchio.

City Hall of Casarsa della Delizia

1966–74

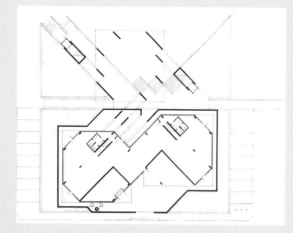

Ground floor plan.

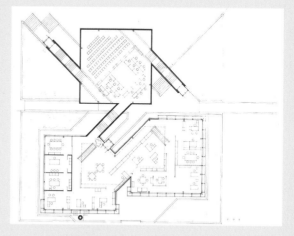

First floor plan.

From the station the street descends towards the city hall. Three buildings are situated on a platform covered by vegetation and crossed by a pedestrian passage: to the left, the low volumes of the offices, and to the right the taller volume of the council chamber. Going up the ramp on the platform, one notes the different ground seam of the buildings: while the offices on two levels emerge from an excavation, the council chamber seems to be raised atop a high portico. Entry to the offices is along an enclosure wall that bends 45 degrees to form a bridge placed over a 'moat'. Climbing several steps, one enters the central part, for the public, lit by zenithal skylights. The perimeter offices are lit by a ribbon window protected on the outside by sunscreens on the south and west sides. Two diagonal staircases connect the level of the offices to the semi-basement used for storage and files, directly accessed from a small service court that communicates with the

lateral street. Access to the council chamber is provided by diagonal staircases: two connected to the outer platform for public entry, and a third in direct relation to the chamber for the meetings of the city government and the office of the mayor.

Visitors pass from the narrow, shadowy space of the steps-tunnel to the large, luminous volume of the chamber. Light enters through large triangular openings placed above the public staircases: the two glazings face each other, but with an opposite slope, creating an asymmetrical division of the light. This particular descent of light grazes the walls and, combined with the diagonal orientation of the roof structure and the arrangement of the furnishings, triggers a perceptible effect of optical deformation of the parallelepiped: the right angles are attenuated and the walls seem to curve, conveying the impression of being in a space with an elliptical plan.

View of the complex with the access ramp to the council chamber in the foreground and the volume of the offices in the background.

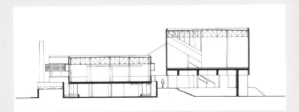

Cross-section.

Council chamber with furnishings from the Multipli Ufficio line by Fantoni, designed by Gino Valle and Herbert Ohl.

7 Large Building Complexes (1967–82)

In parallel with the design process for the city hall of Casarsa, the project for the central offices of La Rinascente in Milan offered Valle the opportunity to explore, from 1967 to 1971, new issues connected with design on a large scale. Tomás Maldonado – who had been appointed to oversee the image of the department stores of the La Rinascente group, after long experience as Rector of the Hochschule für Gestaltung in Ulm, from 1954 to 1967 – directly called on Valle for this job, to be done in collaboration with the German architect Herbert Ohl, also emerging from the methodological experience of Ulm. Maldonado's desire to apply the neo-positivist design methodology on all scales for La Rinascente – from graphics to signage to the architectural object – obliged Valle to accept this tandem organisation of the design work, in which every choice had to be 'objectively' driven by reasons which were primarily functional.

Located on a large plot of land in the suburbs of Milan, at the foot of Monte Stella, the office complex was conceived in this initial phase as a large object free of relations with its immediate context. Valle seemed to dispense with the reuse of formal and functional solutions already tested in previous projects: on the one hand he accepted the role of cooperation in the discussion of the layout variants and the organisation of the workspaces, yet on the other he conducted radically new structural and formal experimentation, achieving solutions derived from the geometry of the circle and the octagon that seemed to link back to the spirit of the 'megastructures' favoured in the 1960s in England, Germany and Japan – with the rise of immense hollow pillars to contain security stairs and climate control systems.

In 1969 this neo-positivist conception of design – shaped around the processes and methods of industrial design – entered a crisis due to an 'external' factor: the reduction of the available land area and the simultaneous insertion of the Lampugnano underground station in the immediate vicinity. Nevertheless, this crisis offered Valle a firm possibility of taking back control of the project, through the intelligent proposal of a car park for the underground station, financed by La Rinascente in exchange for permission to open a large shopping centre. The proposal allowed Valle to overturn the relationship with his client and to return the focus to design concerns that had previously been left at the margins: first of all, the desire to define the relationship between the large complex and the site, expressed not only in the alignment with the River Olona, but also in landscaping the large mass with stepped terraces and gardens, in order to create a dialogue with Monte Stella. The desire to open the complex more towards the direction of Monte Stella resulted in generating a new figure (phase 7, 1969–70), with two parallelepipeds cut diagonally to form a sequence of terraces.

(*left*) Administrative Centre, Pordenone, 1972–82. View of the east-west pedestrian axis.

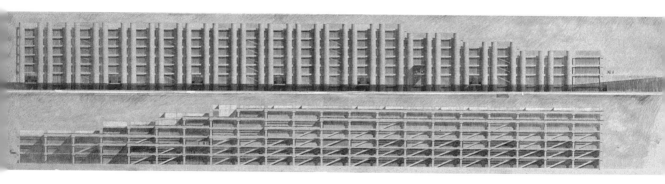

Project for the headquarters of La Rinascente, 1967–72. Project phase 7, 1970. Facades of the offices and the parking facility.

Project for the headquarters of La Rinascente, 1967–72. Project phase 4, with a polygonal scheme and a squared structural grid.

Project for the headquarters of La Rinascente, 1967–72. Project phase 8 (final), 1970–71. Perspective view.

In a rather forced interpretation of this project Joseph Rykwert[1] proposed recognition of certain metaphorical elements of military architecture: while to the north the terraced excavation of the terrain could make the building seem like 'a castle sunken in the open landscape', the internal street between the two volumes could be seen as a moat that divides the 'walled city' of the high volume from the 'faubourg' of the low volume, in keeping with a relationship of subordination underlined by the access over a bridge spanning that moat.

But while Rykwert correctly identified one of the main qualities of this project in its suggestion of 'such a rich fabric of associations through the use of extremely simple elements', in the final versions many of these associative qualities of the image vanished, as did the diagonal cuts, leading to an overall simplification of the linear arrangement, with a long blank wall for services to the south and stepped offices to the north. This apparent formal depletion was nevertheless partially evened out by the greater precision of the constructed image, conceived by Valle as a prefabricated structure displayed by the doubling of pillars and beams and the setback of the facades, though this use of prefabricated parts seemed to further accentuate a 'non-finished' appearance of the building.

Though perhaps disappointing in its final form, the project for La Rinascente nevertheless represented, for Valle, a significant field of experimentation, and it became a certain point of reference for subsequent projects. Of all the themes explored, one in particular deserves critical investigation, because Valle returned to it later in other large-scale projects: excavation and 'landscape' modelling of the land to organise parking areas. More successfully than in the La Rinascente offices, the design of the parking area in the project for the plant in Denver (1966–68) had been conceived as a work of Land Art. In later projects, Valle confirmed the effort to offer precise visual or topographical references, turning to radial figures to focus the flow of visitors towards the entrances: a good example is the parking area in front of the historic centre of Pordenone, where the tree-lined streets were arranged like spokes to orient the routes on the axis of the city hall.[2]

The project for the stadium of Udine also seems singular for the way in which Valle refused to think of the large object as an autonomous entity. On the one hand, the figurative weight of the object was forcefully attenuated by the landscaping of the site. On the other, the traditional ring of the stands no longer appeared as a regular ellipse, but as the sum and juxtaposition of individual units of 800 spectators: Valle's design work therefore focused on the architectural and constructive definition of a module that would permit great flexibility of use and construction in phases, for a capacity from 16,000 to 32,000 persons. This solution, though clearly influenced by the stadium already built for the Montreal Expo in 1967,[3] foreshadowed the one proposed by Renzo Piano in 1990 for the construction of the stadium of Bari.

Also in urban contexts, Valle approached the problem of the large parking facility as an opportunity to reshape the ground: in the project for Piazza Primo Maggio in Udine (1970–72) he connected this theme to establishing a new access to the castle on the hill, obtaining an interesting solution of topographical continuity between Piazza Castello and Piazza Primo Maggio through the creation of an 'artificial hill' beneath which underground parking places and streets were organised. A greater focus on the urban structure,

Project for residences in the Moretti area along Viale Venezia, Udine, 1973–76. Model.

on the other hand, can be seen in a significant large-scale project for the Moretti area in Udine (1973–76), facing Piazza XXVI Luglio, where Valle had already built the Monument to the Resistance. To enhance this important area Valle decided to use a very strong setting gesture, in the form of a large terraced linear building, on axis with the centre of the piazza and the bisector between Viale Venezia and the Tempio Ossario, taking advantage of large areas of public greenery. But it was with the project for the administrative centre in Pordenone (1972–82) – the only one of the projects discussed thus far in this chapter to be built – that Valle finally managed to achieve greater complexity and a more precise relationship with

Administrative Centre, Pordenone, 1972–82. Collage drawing, 4 February 1973. Overlay on an aerial photograph of an initial pencil sketch and a second sketch made with oil paints.

the context in a large-scale settlement. The design work for Pordenone began in 1972 with a review of the proposals of the Master Plan for an area located in a strategic position between the railway line and the historic centre. Previously occupied by the Valdevit property and the Galvani factory, this area had undergone extensive alteration of its original topography, including the channelling of the Codafora canal and the filling and levelling of the sides of the small valley. Since it called for the creation of a street network to cross the zone, the original proposal threatened to destroy the morphological and topographical identity of the area. Opposed to these plans, Valle at first proposed a variation for the streets and the reorganisation of the administrative centre as a terminal rather than as a zone to be crossed. Once this variation to the plan had been approved, Valle then concentrated on developing the planimetric solution. In the first sketches the priority assigned to the definition of a series of setting rules was clearly legible: the excavation of the terrain for parking facilities and the clear separation of vehicle and pedestrian traffic on two different levels, the reconstruction of the green valley behind the historic centre, the organisation of a network of routes and relations between the station and the city centre. The form of the place was then measured with constructed

'pieces' arranged on highly diversified figures and dynamic tracings, reminiscent of certain compositional procedures of Alvar Aalto. The decisive step was represented in a fascinating collage drawing, in which the final figure emerged: two long volumes that appeared rotated by 45 degrees, while a curved facade defined the edge towards the canal.

In this work Valle applied a very open and free process of formal development, calling into play the high quantity (about 200,000 cubic metres of offices), established by the Master Plan, to achieve unexpected solutions. Nevertheless, it is important to observe that Valle returned to the most characteristic themes of the city hall of Casarsa in the definitive solution: the pedestrian crossing serving as the 'foundation' of the public place, the 45-degree rotations (also in this case, the 'pieces' themselves rotate with respect to the others), with the moat establishing a 'sacralising' distance from the context. But unlike Casarsa, the project in Pordenone no longer followed the previous logic of arranging encoded 'pieces' in a new figure: therefore, this was a key project, not just for the new way of establishing relations between a complex of buildings and its context, but also for the fact that it offered Valle an opportunity to experiment with a new constructive language, which will be analysed in a following chapter.

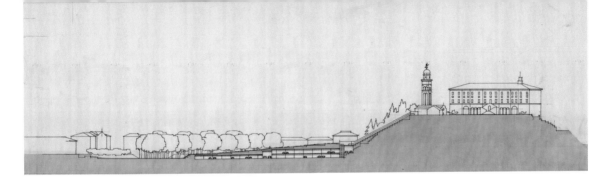

Project for Piazza Primo Maggio in Udine, 1970–72. Section.

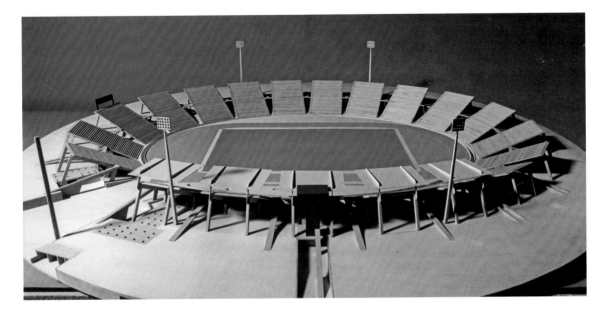

Competition project for Udine stadium, 1971. Model.

Notes

1   Joseph Rykwert, 'Alle porte di Milano', *Domus*, 486, May 1970, pp.3–7.

2   This parking facility was much admired by the landscape designer Andreas Kipar, who from then on always carried with him a photograph of the facility to show his students 'the efficacy of a skilful landscape design', without knowing that it was by Valle. See Andreas Kipar, 'Il paesaggio di Gino Valle', *ACER Magazine – Architettura del paesaggio*, December 2003, p.32.

3   Newspaper clippings with photographs of the Montreal stadium are found in the folder of drawings of the stadium of Udine, clearly demonstrating that this was an explicit reference for Valle. The tender-competition procedure, in which Valle participated with the firm Cisa Udine S.p.A., required a detailed definitive design. The construction solution developed by Valle was significantly different from the Canadian model on which it was initially based, deploying a structure of large prefabricated reinforced concrete trestles. The similarities between Valle's project and the stadium in Montreal did not go unobserved. After the publication of the bidding results on 17 December 1971, the Tobia Clocchiati company of Udine, excluded from the process for not having submitted a certificate of registration in the national construction association, lodged a complaint demanding that the competition be nullified, precisely because the project by Valle, ranked third, seemed to them to be a 'slavish copy of the stadium built for the Montreal Exposition, therefore lacking in any creative contribution, unless ... it is not decided to grant the commission to the designer of Montreal, in place of the designer from Udine'.

Administrative Centre

Pordenone, 1972–82

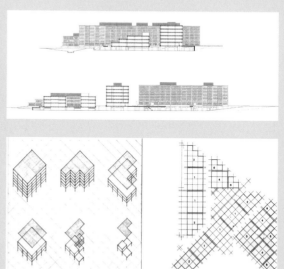

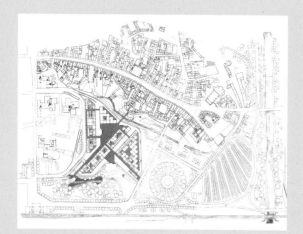

Siteplan.

Schematic plan with six types of buildings. Sections.

Arriving from Venice, one encounters the clear structure of the ancient centre of Pordenone, built on a moraine. From the porticoes of Corso Vittorio Emanuele – the backbone of the urban structure – deep plots branch out to reach gardens and terraces against a small valley containing fragments of the historic walls. This valley clearly borders the morphological structure of the old centre and forms a backdrop for the side streets that penetrate into the plots. The presence of the new administrative centre can be glimpsed on the other side of the valley, reached from the centre at a single point at the end of Vicolo delle Mura which marks the emerging tip of the urban fabric: at this point, a bridge makes it possible to cross the canal, and to traverse the new edification as far as the Valdevit Park and the railway station. In the central plaza this axis of east–west pedestrian crossing intersects

a north–south axis that connects the tree-lined circle of Viale Gorizia to Via Mazzini. A portico accompanies the pedestrian routes along the two linear volumes.

Cars and public transport circulate at the lower level, excavated in the terrain, and organised as a parking facility under the buildings. Access to the offices is through the blocks for staircases and lifts, directly from the parking lots or from the pedestrian level. All the buildings are based on a structural module of 8.4 × 8.4 metres: the linear volumes have a depth of 25.2 metres and are organised with closed offices reached by means of a double corridor around the central service zone, and with open-plan offices; the two triangular buildings that connect the system to the context instead feature great flexibility for the internal layout of the various types of offices.

Panel with the elevation, the cross-section and the plan of the base module of the volume aligned with the walkway.

Administrative centre, Pordenone, 1972–82. Detail of the building facing the small valley.

View of the pedestrian plaza.

Administrative centre, Pordenone, 1972–82.

8 Industrial Objects and Pictorial Gestures: Towards an Architecture of Pure Relationships (1972–96)

For many of the projects discussed in the previous chapter, Valle had studied the possibility of using prefabricated components in reinforced concrete. This choice of construction did not correspond to an ideological tenet, but simply to the interest in reducing his architectural vocabulary, relying on a few ordinary elements directly selected from the 'production catalogue' and deployed in very different buildings and contexts. In this sense, it should come as no surprise if certain constructive solutions seem to migrate from one project to another, as in the case of the double beams and columns seen in the last project for La Rinascente, which are literally replicated in the project in 1971 for the Palazzo della Regione in Udine. In the equipped axis of Zanussi, and later in the city hall of Casarsa, Valle had indicated the possibility of getting out of the 'formal purgatory' he had imposed on himself with 'non-architecture' and the so-called 'programmed invisibility', concentrating the expressive quality of the architecture in just a few elements that stood out against the absolute neutrality supplied by industrialised components. Likewise, in his projects in the 1970s Valle seemed to call upon the linguistic 'neutrality' inherent in prefabricated constructions to make clearly oversized features stand out, making them take on great expressive force. It is therefore possible to speak of a new constructive poetics that took

concrete form for the first time in the Zanussi electronics centre, completed in 1973. Valle accentuated the 'machinist' expression of the building through the exhibitionism of the large ventilation pipes in the middle of the facade, thus introducing a 'shift' to prevent the use of prefabricated parts from generating an excessively banal image.

The same constructive poetics was asserted with even greater force in the project for the Fantoni offices and service centre in Osoppo (1972–75). As an industrial company, Fantoni offered Valle another chance to establish an ongoing relationship of design work, extending from the overall organisation on an urban scale, starting in 1961 with the Master Plan for the entire Osoppo-Rivoli industrial zone, to the design of the new production facilities, as well as a relationship of consulting for the design of furniture – which Valle developed with Herbert Ohl,[1] before calling in his Milanese partners Mario Broggi and Michael Burckhardt. This design experience was exceptional due to the fact that it would last over twenty years, giving Valle the possibility of gradually constructing what Alessandro Rocca has called 'a true industrial campus'.[2] For the design of the offices, located in a central position with respect to the factories, Valle returned to the linear layout principle already applied to the

(*left*) Fantoni industrial complex, Osoppo, 1972–96. View of the volume of the offices and the MDF plant.

Warehouse and showroom Geatti in Terenzano, 1973–74. View from the street.

Warehouse and showroom Geatti in Terenzano, 1973–74. View of the showroom with the ramp leading to the underground garage.

Zanussi offices and those of La Rinascente. The 'backbone' of circulation, however, connected three 'containers' built this time with prefabricated parts and was conceived as a tube that contained all the physical plant systems in its lower part, while the upper part housed the circulation corridor, placed at an intermediate level between the lower floor and the mezzanine of the 'containers'.

In revealing remarks that accompanied the publication of the Fantoni offices in *Casabella*[3] in 1979, Valle associated the building with the memory of the Hera temples at Paestum. A classical character of the construction can indeed be seen in the absolutely systematic regularity of the prefabricated parts, but also in the relationship of the buildings with the landscape of the Tagliamento Valley open to the mountains. This pursuit of 'order' and 'regularity' seems nevertheless to be challenged by the gigantic entrance canopy, which is the result of a gesture of overturning of the large roof of the three volumes.

After the collapse of the structures caused by the earthquake of 1976, Valle fastened the pillars together by means of metal tie-rods that made this image of a 'montage' of prefabricated construction components even more evident. Achieving a subtle balance between assertion of a constructive order and the action of expressionist 'gestures', with the Fantoni offices Valle produced the most mature and significant work among those involved in his pursuit of new architectural expression using prefabricated parts.

In his reference to the temples of Paestum for the design of the Fantoni offices, Valle was not interested so much in the architectural form as in the strong relationship established between the architecture and the landscape. The personal memory of such a relationship therefore acted as a stimulus to define the settlement presence of the new architecture, similar to what had already happened for the Zanussi offices – designed in relation to the memory of a dam – or the spa at Arta – related to the memory of a castle.[4]

In the standard warehouses of Zanussi, Valle had instead focused on forceful reduction of the presence of the architecture in the landscape, through an intentional 'neutrality' of form and maximum indifference to the settlement context along busy traffic arteries. About ten years later, Valle approached the theme of the large industrial container facing the road in very different terms, explored in three projects for the Dapres facility in Portogruaro (1973–74), the warehouse and showroom of Geatti in Terenzano (1973–74), and the Bergamin Distribution Centre in Portogruaro (1978–80). The 'conversation with the landscape' seemed to be pursued and even enhanced at this point: 'The problem was how to control a situation facing the highway in the landscape of the place, a very interesting landscape that

Zanussi electric accounting centre, Pordenone, 1971–73.

had the light of the sea on one side, mountains on the other, and therefore frequent changes in the weather, the colour of the territory, the colour of the sky.'[5] Valle reacted to this 'colour of the territory' by suggesting an architecture that no longer evoked a castle or a temple, but was reduced to the 'abstract' form of a large coloured object: the blue of Geatti, the green of Dapres, the red of Bergamin seemed like pure patches of colour in the landscape. Valle's vision of the landscape was that of a painter, just as the desire to follow the cue of a 'colouring sensation' seemed painterly. Francesco Dal Co proposes analysing these buildings in terms of information theory, focusing in particular on their advertising function, reflected in the large letters directly inscribed on the facade panels. The advertising impact of the buildings, in fact, was conceived for 'very rapid viewing times', starting with the perception in motion on the road, which led to a 'synthetic and almost schematic character' of the building. Regarding the Dapres facility, Dal Co specified, in his analysis: 'The main volume of the factory ... is identified with a pure sign: the communication ... is no longer based on the schematic and elegant composition of an extraneous event in a conclusive volume determined by its own specific functional requirements, but on the identification of the entire project with a gesture.'[6] In a certain sense, this was a more radical version of what Valle had proposed for the first time in the Zanussi standard warehouses, where the upper part in light Luxaflex panels expressed the full continuity of the surface of the cladding, in clear opposition to the classic expression of industrial buildings based on a clear tectonic distinction between structure and cladding. He therefore eliminated any element that could permit identification of the real scale, producing an immediate and unified impression of the large object.[7]

Painterly gestures and elementary volumes were also used by Valle in a series of later projects inside the enclosure of the Fantoni plant: he spread dark blue uniformly over the old factory, reused the same infill panels of Dapres for the new one, with a dark grey colour, while he moved away from the

Dapres factory, Portogruaro, 1973–74.

usual orthogonal geometric figures in two other production facilities, designed in 1985–86, for which he proposed, for the first time, the sections of an equilateral triangle and a Gothic arch.[8] He also improved the entrance zone with the expansion of the reception (1995–96) marked by the sculptural presence of an anemometric tower, and with the elliptical volume of the auditorium and showroom space (1996) that emerges from the wall of the factory.[9]

In the design for the IBM Distribution Centre in Basiano, 1980–83, Gino Valle further refined the colouring and graphic treatment of the 'skin' of the building: the design of the cladding – an alternation of white and grey horizontal lines – made direct reference to the company logo. This graphic choice, nevertheless, was not only aimed at making the cladding into an advertising tool: the horizontal aluminium panel with a height of thirty centimetres was also used as a unit of measure and proportion for all the fronts and sections. The continuous skin was therefore designed as a tool to control the heterogeneity of the volumes, keeping them at just

three heights, marked in the three cases by bands of three, four or five white panels.[10] The stripes were not deployed by Valle simply as a chromatic artifice. This choice was also associated with the memory of the chromatic motif of the Tuscan Romanesque and the cathedral of Siena, in particular, in which the moulding is represented in the striped design of the facades.

The IBM Distribution Centre represented a particularly successful result of the research on the external image of large 'coloured containers', but also reflected the experience of the Fantoni offices in Osoppo, directly taken up in the balcony, staggered in height, offering access to the two levels of offices, arranged like the teeth of a comb around small courtyards that gave the working environment the character of concentrated, intimate space. The portal-like closure of the courtyards, nevertheless, took on a particular meaning in the relationship between the building and the landscape. Not just one portal, but an entire succession marks the depth of the different vertical planes, from the gate of the reception on the street to that of the shipping and receiving dock, and the series of portals enclosing the courtyards of the offices. The gate functions as a diaphragm in two directions: from the inside it frames the landscape and the nearby town, while from the outside, and from a distance, with the help of the stripes that confuse the depth of the successive planes, it creates the effect of a long continuous wall perceived as a monumental facade on the street and towards the town.

These lines of research developed by Valle in the field of industrial constructions brought significant results not only in terms of the relationship between architecture and landscape, but also at a strictly constructive level: studying the various possibilities for combining 'serial' prefabricated parts to obtain extreme reduction of the constructive language, Valle gradually found that he was able to transfer this research into other fields as well, not just industrial facilities.

Already in 1976, he therefore began to develop, in collaboration with Giorgio Macola, a system of prefabricated schools for the Valdadige company, following the approval of new regulations for

the construction of schools[11] that had triggered a massive programme of construction across the whole country. Valle was prepared for this development, since he had already proposed, in 1974, the use of a prefabricated constructive system in a project for the Istituto tecnico professionale of Pordenone. In this project we can already see the fundamental elements that were later applied and developed in the Valdadige schools: the structure with a rectangular grid, the layout of the peripheral classrooms around a central two-storey atrium, the external cladding in horizontal panels of reinforced concrete. The choice in 1974 of a prefabricated solution also corresponded to the breakdown of the programme into multiple, self-sufficient units capable of growing to meet the requirements of the various functional parts. The final result of the 'growth' could be recognised as the sum of 'containers' arranged on the terrain.

A similar combinatory logic was then applied to the system of the Valdadige prefabricated schools, though with greater functional and quantitative flexibility. Each school was like the result of the arrangement along a pedestrian axis, and depending

Bergamin Distribution Centre and warehouses, Portogruaro, 1978–80.

(*left*) IBM Italia Distribution Centre, Basiano, 1980–83; (*right*) detail of the western facade with the expansion joint between the various volumes. The cladding is in aluminium panels with a height of thirty centimetres.

IBM Italia Distribution Centre, Basiano, 1980–83. Perspective from the reception towards the entrance of the complex.

on a great variety of layout schemes, of four types of 'containers' for homogeneous activities: teaching, gymnasium, dining and central heating plant. The entire system, in its typological definition and constructive grammar, was based on a generative logic that left large margins of flexibility in the definition of the individual projects, which could vary in the choice of the various 'containers' and in their 'assembly' around the pedestrian axis of connection.

As had already happened in the Zanussi standard warehouses, Valle experimented with the reproducibility of architecture in the Valdadige schools.[12] But while in the earlier project the intention had been to make the object almost invisible in the visual chaos of the urban periphery, in the latter Valle instead used colour to accentuate the artificial, abstract and therefore extraneous character of the buildings, positioned for the most part at the edge of small residential zones. The 'conversation with the environment' was thus reduced to its 'zero degree' in the absence of any trace of mediation with respect to local formal elements. The extremely schematic relations established between school and urban context,

nevertheless, represented a clear limitation of the system, which perhaps explains why Valle never considered the schools to be among his favourite works. Perhaps personal intervention was also too reduced, which Valle needed in order to get beyond the mere assertion of a standardised construction catalogue. In certain spaces in the schools it was, however, possible to observe the effects of some leeway of this kind, as was clearly underlined by Joseph Rykwert: 'The schools ... also provide a sort of collective space that is almost neutral. But the term "almost" is essential here. The short pauses prompted by elements like the handrails, the use of bright and complementary colours, transform these very simple volumes into clear, vital spaces.'[13]

In another critique, Germano Celant considered the Valdadige schools as a work 'balanced between sculpture and architecture',[14] suggesting a comparison between Valle's architecture and certain significant experiences of contemporary art. In the same years, Valle worked in direct contact with some of the finest contemporary artists as the exhibit designer for the Venice Biennale from 1974 to 1976. This undoubtedly stimulated him to delve deeper into formal themes with which he had avowed

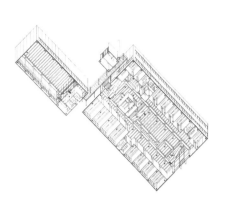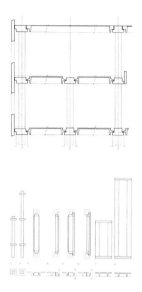

Valdadige prefabricated schools, 1974–84: (*left*) axonometric from below; (*centre*) typology of prefabricated parts; (*right*) school interior.

Valdadige prefabricated schools, 1974–84: (*left*) School of Chirignago, view of the entrance and the glazing towards the hall; (*below left*) School of San Quirino.

affinities: in particular, with Minimal Art, oriented towards maximum reduction of linguistic means.

In the work of the Minimal artists, this reduction was associated with a constant reference to the 'phenomenology of perception' of Merleau-Ponty: the artists' interest in the use of simple forms was therefore very distant from any reference to neo-Platonic geometric purism, and instead reflected the desire to shift the focus of the observer away from fixed contemplation of the object, towards the mobile experience of relationships established between the object and the space. As the sculptor Robert Morris put it: 'Simplicity of shape does not necessarily equate with simplicity of experience. Unitary forms do not reduce relationships. They order them.'[15] What Valle attempted in the Valdadige schools can therefore be interpreted in the light of this observation by Morris: the simplicity of the forms obtained by the assembly of the 'prefabricated pieces', very limited in number, did not represent a formal quality of the object itself, but simply the condition to intensify the relationships established between the various buildings. Valle stated in the project description that 'the assembly of the containers already organises an environment, transforming the school from a building into a portion of urban fabric'. This was clearly a metaphorical statement, since the number of pieces and the variety of the aggregative schemes were actually too limited to be able to generate something even vaguely urban. The comparison with Minimal Art, nevertheless, remains significant with respect to another theme addressed by Valle's architecture: the one we have already examined of the placement of the building on a path of crossing, as seen in the Monument to the Resistance and the city hall of Casarsa. As in the sculpture of Robert Morris – or even more in the landscape installations of Robert Smithson – it is the experience of the path that achieves the 'value' of the work: there no longer exists any autonomous aesthetic quality, enclosed in the object, while the quality of the perceptive experience can arise only inside the system of relationships established between the object and space. The administrative centre of Pordenone also seems to be based on a path of crossing: but

Kursaal of Arta Terme, 1975–78. View of the entrance facade.

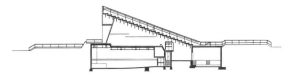

Kursaal of Arta Terme, 1975–78. Longitudinal section.

while Casarsa was still a project on the scale of an individual building, in Pordenone Valle effectively was able, for the first time, to create a 'portion of urban fabric' with a central plaza, a portico and two axes of crossing. The complexity of the relationships is not concentrated, however, only in the order established between the single 'pieces': it is a complexity that extends to all the relations between the new centre and the urban fabric.

These relations are therefore much richer and more varied than those established between the Valdadige schools and their settlement context: in the latter, Valle focused only on linking the system of the school to the already existing urban routes. Instead, in Pordenone the outline of the plan, and then the design of the individual 'pieces', seems to be 'found' on the project site itself. Valle therefore appears to have followed a process of deduction to obtain the design, while in the Valdadige schools the generative grammar of the architecture existed prior to its fixed anchoring in the physical reality of a place.

Other affinities with the works of Minimal Art can be seen in a group of three projects done from 1973 to 1981: the Kursaal of Arta Terme and the city halls of Sutrio and Fontanafredda.

City hall of Fontanafredda, 1973–81. View of the main facade from the plaza-podium.

At Arta, on an open plot behind the town, Valle translated the theme of the path directly into the form of the building, which literally became an architecture of routes: a monumental flight of steps oriented towards the amphitheatre of the mountains – almost a mountain version of Casa Malaparte by Libera – connected to the ground by means of a rich, perhaps excessive, system of parallel routes (staircases, bridges, ramps, terraces). In a certain sense, Valle reinterpreted the model of the box closed by solid lateral walls, as in the Bellini house or the city hall of Treppo Carnico. But he did so by enhancing the arrangement of the section of the building, with rooms on different visually connected levels, applying a prismatic shape that reinforced the sculptural presence and opacity of the object, open only on the facade towards the town. This 'poetics of the box' is also visible in the city hall of Sutrio, where again Valle heightened the discontinuity between the reinforced concrete enclosure and the well-recessed wooden window frames. The building, however, rejects any form of dialogue with the surrounding buildings: it turns a blind wall to the lateral piazza,

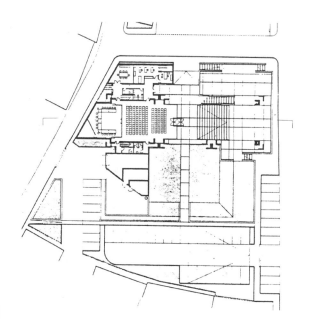

City hall of Fontanafredda, 1973–81. Ground floor plan.

and its setback from the street forces access across a bridge. This effect of distance – both physical and figurative – from the urban context corresponded to Valle's intention to favour the relationship with the geographical scale of the valley, which becomes evident only when one enters the building, discovering the mountain landscape through the large full-height glazing.

In the city hall of Fontanafredda Valle created three juxtaposed volumes, no longer a single object with minimalist overtones, achieving greater complexity of the relationships between the various parts of the building and between the building and its context. In structural terms the building was conceived as a juxtaposition of three tables that shelter three other smaller tables that support the level of the offices: also deployed for seismic reasons, this structure proposed a minimalist version of the game of 'Russian dolls' but in a warped – or ambiguous – way, due to the structural need to anchor the external structure to the internal structure at the first floor. Around the building, placed crosswise to the main street, the terrain was shaped to host the parking area and a small recessed inner garden, while the technical

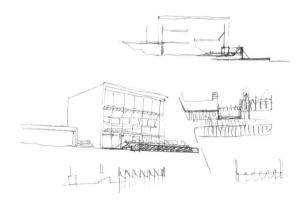

City hall of Sutrio, 1975–78. Study sketches indicating the section with staggered levels and the scheme of the wooden screen of the eastern facade: the lower level contains the council chamber, the upper contains offices and the registry office.

City hall of Sutrio, 1975–78. View of the eastern facade.

Installation of the exhibition by Ugo Mulas for Venice Biennale at the Magazzini del sale, 1974.

large opening that therefore added drama to the longitudinal penetration of the building. Designing this exception with great precision, Valle seemed to bear witness, however, to a very different mood than the one that drove him to experiment with an 'aesthetic of repetition' in the Valdadige schools, and perhaps even close to the structural heroism manifested in the Zanussi offices: like the Zanussi offices, the city hall of Fontanafredda seems like a hyper-designed work, with a refined treatment of the concrete surface and a series of variations along the facade that challenge the principle of essentiality on which the building is based. In this work, but also in the city hall of Sutrio – where we can observe subtle asymmetries in the design of the frames and tenuous floor markers in the concrete surface – Valle demonstrated that the desire to put the accent on the relations between the object and the settlement context did not necessarily have to exclude care for the specifically tectonic quality of the building itself.

If the city halls of Sutrio and Fontanafredda represent the highest degree of maturity of Valle's 'minimalist' research, stimulated by certain affinities with parallel experiences in the visual arts, other projects on very different scales demonstrate the lasting action of these affinities. On a large scale, for example, in the project for a Brionvega plant at Agrate (1978), in collaboration with Mario Broggi and Michael Burckhardt, Valle proposed shaping the entire terrain like a work of Land Art: elementary gestures like raising a wall or making a minimum base of just three steps therefore seemed sufficient to achieve a very different image from that of traditional industrial

volumes were naturalistically treated as mineral boulders that had 'grown' from the earth, covered by vegetation.[16]

This treatment of the ground also corresponded to the logic of the routes: while the axis of crossing of the lot descends and passes under the building – which therefore seems like a bridge spanning the axis – arriving at the recessed parking area, the path of access to the offices is developed longitudinally on a ramp starting from a plaza-podium placed at the corner of the two streets. Demonstrating great compositional ability, Valle used the dynamism of the diagonal design of the ramp to add movement to the whole facade on the plaza, clearly indicating it as the main facade: by subtracting external pillars, he introduced a strong structural exception translated into a single

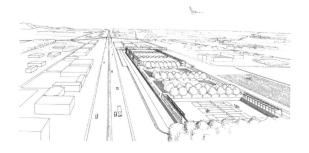

Project for the Brionvega plant at Agrate, 1978. View of the circulation spine along the courtyards and overall perspective of the complex.

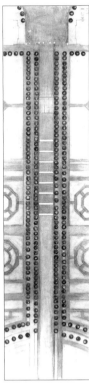

Competition project for the Monument to the Partisans and Victims of the Massacre at Piazza della Loggia in Brescia, 1975.

Tomb of Pier Paolo Pasolini, cemetery of Casarsa della Delizia, 1977.

architecture, making a forceful imprint on the landscape of the Po Valley plains.

On a small scale, Valle reduced the architectural action to a minimum to grant formal identity to the tomb of Pier Paolo Pasolini, made in 1977 by request of the mother of the Friulian poet: a laurel tree cast its shade on the sole commemorative sign, a thin square sheet of marble, while another long, narrow marble block made a line in the gravel of the avenue of the cemetery. The experience of walking seems to be virtually interrupted by this 'nearly invisible' presence of the stone, simply resting on the gravel, as in a work by Carl André. The interruption enacts the commemorative function of the architecture, as already happened for the Monument to the Partisans and the Victims of the Massacre of Piazza della Loggia in

Brescia, in 1975, created for the access avenue of the Vantiniano cemetery: 'a square of marble and eight strips that cut the route of access, one for each of the victims, so that funeral processions will commemorate them with a slight pause produced when crossing each piece'.[17] A monument lying on the ground, conceived more for tactile than for visual perception,[18] the tomb of Pasolini suggested comparison – for Richard A. Etlin – with the tomb of Maria Christina by Canova: in both, the visitor is taken 'to the threshold of death' to better measure the metaphysical distance, the abyss that separates him from the world of the dead. And while in the tomb by Canova this was represented 'in the halting of the procession before the shadowy portal', in the 'minimal' monument of Valle 'the same effect is produced by the line

Bergamin sales centre, Latisana, 1994–95.

that stops at a short distance from the square sign. While the metaphysical space between these two pieces of stone cannot be crossed, the smaller size of the sign sheltered by the laurel tree humanizes the monument in such a way as to offer deep communion with the dead Pasolini.'[19]

After examining these beautiful places of memory invented by Valle, abstract and conceptual as well, we have to discuss one last series of projects to conclude this chapter dedicated to the research on industrialised architecture. It is a series of projects for the Bergamin company, mentioned above in reference to the 'volume of pure red colour' of the Distribution Centre of Portogruaro (1978–80) along the Venice–Trieste motorway. Valle worked

for almost twenty years with this small family firm that had expanded over the years to become the most important sales network in the Veneto for furniture and entire kitchens.[20] But unlike Fantoni, for which Valle worked for more than twenty years in a single site that became a true 'industrial campus' over the years, the projects for Bergamin were scattered in various small towns of the Veneto and Friuli.[21] Valle did not apply a standardised construction system, but made very free use, adapting it to different situations, of cladding in red sheet metal panels – first with vertical strips, and later with horizontal segments – with the name of the company written in large letters. While in the first project for the Distribution Centre in Portogruaro (1978–80) the compositional game was still based on an aesthetic borrowed from Minimal Art, in later projects Valle bent and deformed the cladding to achieve greater volumetric complexity. In the sales centre of Istrana (1995–96), Valle added character to the building with a forceful, almost brutal, gesture, making a full-height opening in the facade that spread like a large wing to welcome visitors. Valle applied a similar gesture of deformation of the volume to add quality to another industrial project done in that same period: the Eco Refrigerazione facility at Pocenia (1995–96), where the deformation of the corner to create a striking pointed crown marks the entrance to the plant.

Deformations and exceptions also appear in the most mature of all the projects in this series: the Bergamin offices, built in 1988–91 at Portogruaro

on the same site as the Distribution Centre. Valle improved the entire site with a landscape intervention of quality, done with great sensitivity by Ippolito Pizzetti. First of all, the employee parking area, located between the existing central warehouse and the new service centre, was divided in a series of 'green rooms' enclosed by rows of hornbeams, making the cars disappear. Second, the four square courtyards around which the offices were organised were made into gardens. The regular pattern of the square courts, also conceived by Valle for possible future growth in two directions,[22] seems to be broken in the first entrance court, deformed and irregular at the position of the access on the diagonal that cuts across the enclosure of the offices, and also marked by the presence of the cylinder of the training room.

Eco Refrigerazione plant, Pocenia, 1995–96. End of building with entrance to the offices.

Notes

1   By 1974, the '45°' furniture series (G. Valle with H. Ohl) had already been included in the permanent collection of MoMA New York.

2   The initial nucleus of Fantoni had only two buildings, from 1963, designed by the architect Lucci. The growth of the complex was linked to the partial modification of the production activities, 'since the production of furniture, especially for offices, had gradually spread into the dense fabric of small and medium businesses in Friuli, while the production of MDF (Medium Density Fibreboard) panels gradually took on a central role, a field in which the company had reached a position of worldwide leadership'. See Alessandro Rocca, 'Valle ultimo. Fabbriche, uffici e frammenti di città', *Lotus Navigator*, monograph, Gino Valle, 1, November 2000, pp.4–23. On the growth process, see the interesting observations of Pietro Valle: 'The relationship between Gino Valle and Fantoni is founded upon an open and creative dialogue with time, a dialogue which accepts the unexpected and adjusts to change, integrating both into a continuous planning process based not on pre-fixed plans but rather on very precise ideas regarding the transformation process'. Pietro Valle, 'Communicating with Time', 'Gino Valle. Progetto Fantoni', special issue of the series *Fantoni-Blueindustry*, 7, May 2004, pp.17–18.

3   Gino Valle, 'Progetto realizzato', in Giovanni Testi (ed.), *Polis, quaderni di architettura e urbanistica*, 22, Marsilio, Venice, 1980, p.240.

4   Valle, in an interview in 2000 with Sandro Marpillero, returned to the question of the relations between the Fantoni offices and the geographical context, saying that the orientation parallel to the valley was chosen precisely to avoid blocking the Tagliamento River: 'I don't exactly know where the need to personalize the relationships of my buildings with the geographical scale comes from. But I do know it is always where I start.' See 'Sandro Marpillero intervista Gino Valle da New York', *Lotus Navigator*, monograph, Gino Valle, 1, November 2000, pp.62–89.

5   Adalberto Dal Lago (ed.), 'Intervista con Gino Valle', *L'Architettura Cronache e Storia*, 318, April 1982, p.279.

6   Francesco Dal Co, 'Gino Valle. La necessità dell'architettura', *Lotus International*, 11, 1976, pp.172–89.

7   Alessandro Rocca also acutely observes the architectural role played by the large logos printed on the walls, as well as the role of the colour and texture of the cladding to make the volumes lose any reference of scale, becoming 'pure wrappers, big boxes resting on the ground', in which the monochromatic facings in bright hues 'completely conceal the structure, and dematerialize the building in planes and volumes of pure color'. See Alessandro Rocca, 'Valle ultimo', pp.4–23.

8   ibid. Again it is Rocca who analyses the role played by the 'pure forms' of this production plant, with respect to the linear design of the offices: 'The ogival housing imposes itself as an absolute form, a signal of great visual impact that arrests, with its brightness and precision, the long course of the production chain of the panels. On the other side of the facility, a response comes from the two glowing metal pitches that cross like two pieces of paper to form a perfect triangle, for the roof of the wood warehouses.'

9   After the death of Gino Valle, the 'Fantoni Campus' continued to grow with interventions designed by Studio Valle, under the direction of Pietro Valle. Particularly interesting are the renovation of the company restaurant in the service centre (2015), and the huge Plaxil 8 MDF plant (2017), 300 metres long and 28 metres large, with the west side over 50 metres, the largest press in Europe for the production of MDF boards, entirely clad with prefab concrete panels.

10   The introduction of an exception in the regular alternation of grey and white bands was also chosen by Valle for an expressive reason: 'The initial idea was that it should all be striped, and I said to myself: at the 1st level I remove one stripe, at the 2nd I remove two, at the 3rd I remove three, and it becomes a work of architecture. Otherwise it was just a box.' See Giovanni Vragnaz, 'Intervista a Gino Valle', *Piranesi*, January 1991, pp.26–47.

11   From 1976 to 1986, 39 projects were built by the Valdadige company: 18 middle schools, 16 elementary schools, one technical institute, two community centres, two gymnasiums.

12   D. M. (Ministerial Decree) 18-12-1975, 'Updated technical standards for school buildings, including minimum indices of educational, constructive and urban functioning, to be complied with in the implementation of works of scholastic construction'.

13   Joseph Rykwert, 'Gino Valle architetto', in *Gino Valle. Architetto 1950–1978*, exh. cat. Padiglione d'arte contemporanea in Milano, Edizioni PAC & Idea Editions, Milan, 1979, pp.6–7.

14   Germano Celant, 'Al limite dell'avventura', in *Gino Valle. Architetto 1950–1978*, exh. cat., Padiglione d'arte contemporanea in Milano, Edizioni PAC & Idea Editions, Milan, 1979.

15   Robert Morris, 'Notes on Sculpture I', *Artforum*, February 1966.

16   This clarity in the relationship between the large longitudinal building and the lower volumes treated as 'mineral boulders' was unfortunately compromised in 1990–95 by an addition, designed by Valle himself, of a new two-storey volume, in clear contrast with the minimal qualities of the existing buildings.

17   From the project description. Valle looked back on this project in an interesting interview in 1999 on the Monument to the Resistance of Udine, saying that 'the

monument I like the most is the project for the victims of Piazza della Loggia in Brescia', because he considered it 'more mature, more intense, though a bit sinister' with respect to the monument in Udine. See Giovanni Vragnaz, 'Monumento alla Resistenza a Udine. Intervista a Gino Valle', *Piranesi*, 9–10, Autumn 1999, p.27.

18   ibid. Valle had a very 'beautiful and intense' memory of the burial: 'the urn was brought from the crematory, the tree arrived from outside the wall, lifted by a crane, and Pasolini's friends, on their knees, positioned the stone and the ground around it with their bare hands'.

19   Richard A. Etlin, 'The Geometry of Death', *Progressive Architecture*, 5, May 1982, pp.134–7. Leonardo Benevolo (in *L'architettura nel nuovo millennio*, Laterza, Bari, 2006, p.51) also greatly admired these commemorative projects: 'the most moving, of greatest composure, ever designed in modern Italy, without concessions of any kind'.

20   At the beginning Bergamin was a small company of brothers who produced vats, basins and tubs, which gradually became an industrial structure. The firm used its

storage facilities scattered through the Veneto provinces first to sell the appliances of Zanussi, then expanding to the sale of entire kitchens, thanks to a dense network of small artisan producers that, 'interpreting the materials and methods of industrial production with the flexibility of the craftsman, guaranteed Bergamin an extremely elastic, economical network'. See Alessandro Rocca, 'Valle ultimo', p. 17.

21   An in-depth analysis of the design strategies applied by Valle in the projects for Bergamin is provided by Giovanni Corbellini, 'L'architettura è ciò che il non luogo si aspetta. Gli edifici Bergamin di Gino Valle', *Architettura/ Intersezioni*, 8, October 2000.

22   For this organism of square courtyards, Valle returned to solutions already applied in the second project for the Bicocca in Milan (1987–88): the research laboratories had been proposed in low buildings with a courtyard organisation and an L-shaped arrangement that Valle developed with the patio house of Mies van der Rohe in mind. See Giovanni Vragnaz, 'Intervista a Gino Valle', p.43.

Fantoni industrial complex, Osoppo, MDF plant (the 'cathedral'), 1985–90.

Fantoni Industrial Complex

Osoppo, 1972–96

The production plants of Fantoni Arredamenti are located in the industrial zone of Rivoli at Osoppo, in the flood plains that open out from the Tagliamento Valley. The industrial lots are oriented on a north–south axis, parallel to the Pontebbana railway and the Udine–Tarvisio highway. One reaches the Fantoni complex along a road placed at 45 degrees, with parking facilities along the way. Conceived for 800 factory workers and 120 other employees, the service centre is located halfway between the existing plant and the new factories of the expansion, made later, with a continuous wall from which the elliptical volume of the auditorium emerges. From the street one discovers an intriguing diagonal view of the three volumes in sequence against the backdrop of the mountains: the offices, the showroom and the dining hall are differentiated in terms of the length of the buildings, but seem to be closely connected by the image of a giant discontinuous colonnade produced by the use of tall prefabricated parts. One then passes along the raised garden in front of the southern facade of the offices and reaches the gate: two ramps lead to the entrances placed on two levels – for the office personnel and visitors on the upper level, and for the factory workers on the lower level.

The entrance portico is created by an interruption in the solid wall of the layout spine and the corresponding turn to the west of the large roof of the containers, below which stands the gatehouse, expanded in 1995 and marked by the sculptural presence of the anemometric tower. One enters the lobby that opens with a full-height glazing to the garden between the offices and the showroom. From here a corridor extends, halfway up between the lower level and the mezzanine of the offices and showroom. The restrooms and the mezzanine appear as white 'boxes' inserted in the large volume. The offices have an open plan, with the exception of the meeting rooms placed in glass cages. Proceeding along the corridor towards the north, one passes a bridge over the crosswise connection tunnel, reaching the dining hall after a slight ascent. The factory staff enters at the lower level through the crosswise tunnel that connects, from east to west, the complex of the services to the two factories. The dressing rooms are located below the dining hall, while below the north–south circulation spine there are spaces for the archives and the air conditioning systems. The various routes at the lower level converge towards the southern end of the dining hall, where the crosswise tunnel opens upward, lit by a large sloping window. From there, ramps lead to the upper levels of the dining hall and the corridor for access to the offices. The roof of the connection tunnel functions as a ramp to move from the dining hall to an outdoor zone equipped for free time, located between the service centre and the new factory to the east. The entire outdoor space between the two buildings is treated as a linear terraced garden, open to the mountains to the north.

The industrial complex has undergone many transformations over time, with the addition of new factory facilities designed by Valle as very expressive volumes: in particular, the 'Plaxil 5' production facility for MDF panels is conceived as a 'cathedral', with a pointed arch section, and the two 'huts' for the storage of wood chips are shaped as elementary prismatic volumes, with the section of an equilateral triangle.

Offices and service centre, 1972–74. After the earthquake in 1976,
the structure was reinforced with a bracing system.

Interventions by Gino Valle (1972–2001)

1. Offices and service centre (1972–74)
2. Rebuilding of sheds (1977–78)
3. Workshops (1977)
4. Tank and silos (1977)
5. Plaxil 5 MDF plant, the 'Cathedral' (1985)
6. The 'Huts' (1985 and 1984)
7. MDF storage (1987)
8. Glue plant (1990)
9. Plaxil 6 MDF plant (1994)
10. Entrance and reception (1972, enlargement 1996)
11. Fantoni Research Centre (in collaboration with Broggi + Burckhardt, 1995–96)
12. MDF storage (1997)
13. Finishing line (1999–2000)
14. Plaxil 7 MDF plant (2001)

Interventions by Studio Valle (2015–17)

15. Company restaurant (renovation 2015)
16. Plaxil 8 MDF plant (2017)
17. Sigmat rack connection (2017)
18. Boiler (2017)

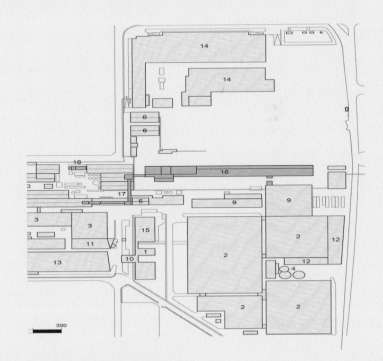

Siteplan of the industrial campus.

Fantoni industrial complex, Osoppo, 1972–96.

Mezzanine plan (top):
1. Offices
2. Showroom
3. Void of the dining hall

Ground floor plan (bottom):
1. Access ramp to offices
2. Access ramp to plant
3. Security
4. Circulation and services spine
5. Gardens
6. Offices
7. Showroom
8. Dining hall

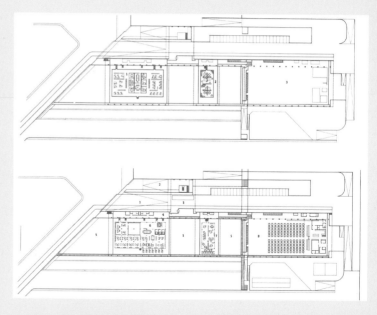

Offices and service centre.

Interior view of the offices, facing
one of the gardens.

The bracing added after the earthquake of 1976: outside the glazing on
the southern ends, inside on the northern ends.

Auditorium and display space, 1996.

Entrance to the complex, 1972 (refurbished 1995–96) with the finishing plant
to the left and the MDF plant in the background.

Bergamin Offices

Portogruaro, 1988–91

View of the complex from the street.

The Bergamin complex stands out in the countryside along the Postumia state highway, between Venice and Trieste, thanks to the characteristic red colour of the sheet-metal facing. After passing through the enclosure, along the access route one encounters the staff parking area, configured as a sequence of 'green rooms' enclosed by tall hornbeam hedges, and the service centre on the right, reached by means of an awning of metal tubes and glass, rotated 45 degrees with respect to the building. Here one enters an open courtyard whose irregular form is marked by the presence of the cylinder of the training room and the orientation of the left wall, slightly rotated with respect to the orthogonal layout of the building. In the entrance lobby the gaze is immediately attracted by the bright light coming from the square courtyard on the left, followed by the organisation of the offices in L-shaped volumes around four concatenated square courtyards. The courts stand out for their landscaping, with two colours of stones – red or black – and four types of tree (cork, strawberry tree, hawthorn, pomegranate). The perimeter walls are perforated at the base to offer a view of the countryside, contributing to give the working environment the character of a cosy, 'domestic' space.

View of the building at the entrance, western facade.

Axonometric.

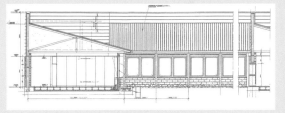

Cross-section detail of one of the internal courtyards, featuring gardens by landscape designer Ippolito Pizzetti.

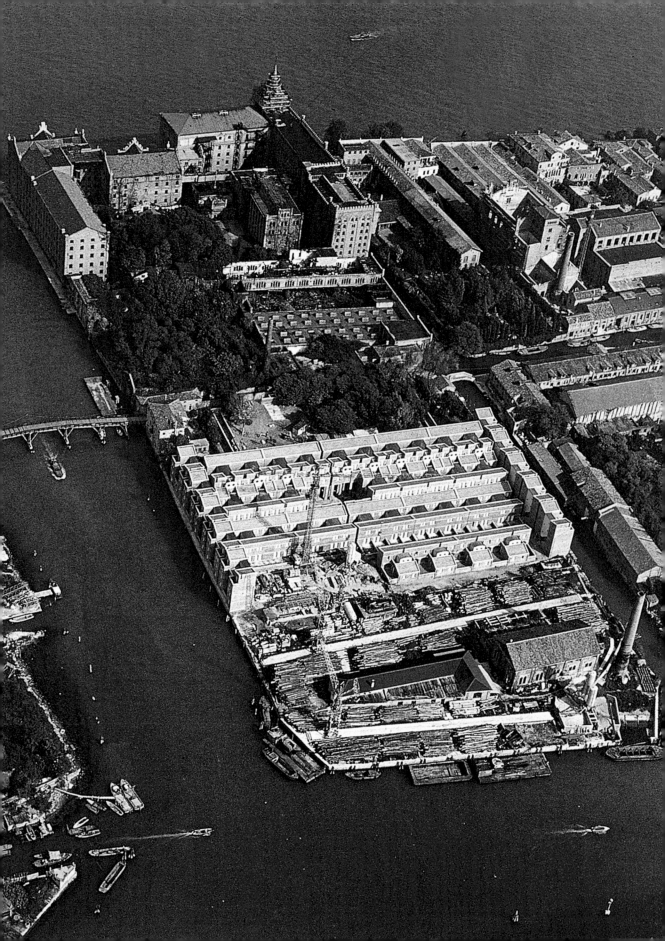

9 Low-cost Housing (1975–95)

After the very early projects at the start of the 1950s within the INA-Casa programme, Valle had no other opportunities to design low-cost housing projects before 1975. In all the other private residential projects until that date, each design was approached by Valle in a spirit of lively experimentalism, in terms of both typology and language. The single or double houses all seem to be different from each other, while in an urban context the apartment buildings reflect very different ways of making modern architecture establish a dialogue with historic centres. In all these projects the theme of residence was therefore never associated by Valle with principles of typological repetition and constructive rationalisation, principles required to guarantee extreme limitation of construction costs in the field of social housing, and had instead been successfully applied by Valle in his projects of industrial architecture.

So it was not until 1975 that Valle received his first commission for a low-cost housing project on the outskirts of Udine, in the Peep-est Master Plan designed by Renzo Agosto, Emilio Mattioni and Gianugo Polesello in 1970–71. Valle was called in to work on the completion and saturation of the existing zone, built from 1956 to 1971 by the 'Istituto autonomo case popolari' (IACP) of Udine, with 'a wing of 180 meters for one hundred units' that would conclude the existing courtyard. The large size of the project offered an opportunity to make an architectural landmark for the entire district.

Valle's design work, done in collaboration with Giorgio Macola parallel to the design of the Valdadige schools, began with a critique of the typology of the other linear buildings already constructed in keeping with the rules imposed by the planivolumetric (underground garage, open ground level, six floors of apartments with a depth of twelve metres), with staircases offering access to two apartments per floor:

> I had seen the neighbouring wings, at the staircase and elevator landing, and all the human ants who emerged from the door to go to take the bus in that no man's land formed by the streets and green areas of these developments. We felt that we had to do something about this passage from the compressed private dimension, that of the elevator, to the public void.[1]

Concentrating on the theme of the path of access to the house, Valle proposed referencing a layout scheme developed by Peter and Alison Smithson at the start of the 1950s, in open debate with the Unité d'habitation of Le Corbusier, and based on the idea that the access to the houses should happen through true 'streets in the air' for every three levels, not closed like the corridors of the Unité but open to the landscape. This principle was directly reprised in the section of the building, while later the three towers for the stairwells

(*left*) Low-cost housing complex at Giudecca, 1980–86. Aerial view.

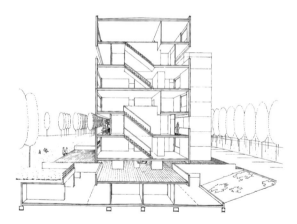

Building for 100 IACP housing units, Udine, 1976–79. Perspective section.

Alison and Peter Smithson, residential project at Golden Lane, London, sketch, 1952.

and lifts were shifted to outside the volume to completely free up the ground level.

This project was an important experience for Valle, above all because it allowed him to come to terms for the first time, freely and without preconceptions, with the very rigid rules of social housing:[2] while the layout solution, seen in the section, was effectively innovative in the Italian context, the 100 units were subject to a strict rule of forceful typological reduction, with just two types of duplex apartments and a single type of mini-apartment. This typological repetition corresponded to extreme rationalisation of construction, directly based on the research developed for the system of the Valdadige schools. Prefabrication, nevertheless, was limited to the concrete facade panels, while the tunnel structure was poured into place. As in the schools, colour was used to add character to the various parts of the building: red for the zones of passage, green for the zones of residence. Thus, seen from a distance, the large 'wing' looks like a coloured dam, figuratively detached from the indeterminate environment of the quarter, in a dialogue with the geographical scale of the landscape.[3] A second opportunity to work on low-cost housing arose after the earthquake of 1976, following a donation made by Confindustria for reconstruction in Friuli, on a zone at the edge of the severely damaged historic centre

of Santo Stefano di Buia. From the interpretation of the site, crossed by a road leading to the neoclassical cemetery, Valle obtained the fundamental principles of arrangement of the small settlement of 42 units: three rows of attached houses placed parallel to the axis of symmetry of the cemetery, with a square plaza located at the point of encounter between this orthogonal grid and the road crossing the zone. In conceptual terms this plaza was made by subtracting some of the houses from the two upper rows, creating an excavated space for parking and transforming the existing street into a bridge. Valle's focus on the quality of the paths of access to the lodging emerged again in the design of the section of the duplex homes, to obtain a true portico on the ground floor: a decidedly 'urban' solution, seldom seen in row housing, with the portico that seems like a 'balcony brought down to the ground', along which the concrete chimneys are aligned to evoke the image of a giant colonnade.

As in the IACP building in Udine, major rationalisation made it necessary to limit the range to three types of houses, differentiated by their structural spans: 7.2 metres for type A, 3.6 metres for types B and C. The lesson of 'minimalism' seen in the city halls of Sutrio and Fontanafredda and the Kursaal of Arta is here again at work in Buia, where the extreme linguistic reduction of the elements

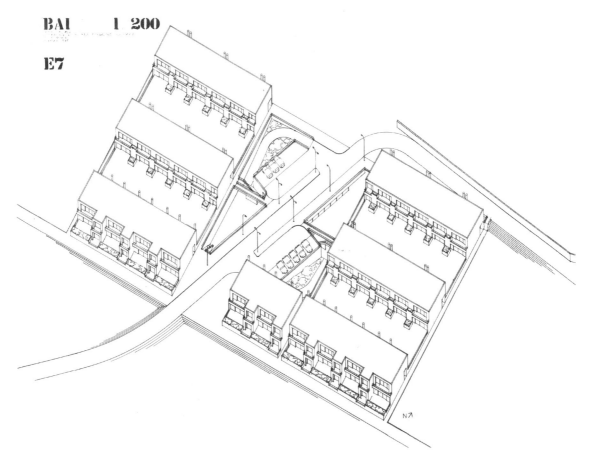

BAI   1 200

E7

Low-cost housing complex in Santo Stefano di Buia, 1977–79. Axonometric of the complex and view of the development from south.

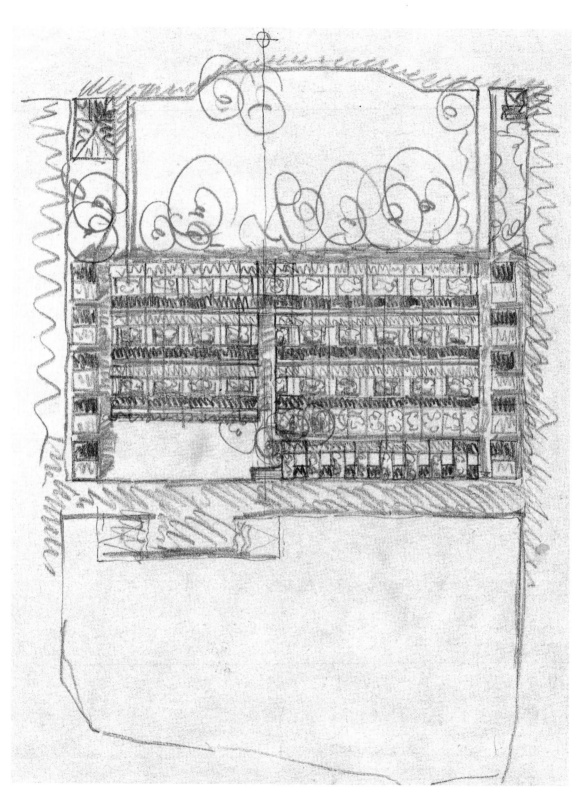

Low-cost housing complex at Giudecca, 1980. Sketch of the 'residential carpet'.

deployed was asserted by Valle not to achieve some 'elementary' formal character, but to generate meaningful variations in the combination of the elements. As in the previous building in Udine, he used colour to underscore the sculptural image of the houses immersed in the landscape: while three tones of green, from pale to dark, add shading to the presence of the three rows of houses against the backdrop of the forest, the lateral walls are coloured in a 'rosewood' tone to bring out the gesture of the cut in the continuous, abstract grid of the homes.

Starting with a long linear volume, and continuing in a small, newly created settlement, Gino Valle's research in the field of low-cost housing developed along a path of increasing complexity, culminating in the project for a residential complex on the island of Giudecca in Venice.[4] When Valle received the commission in May 1980, he had vivid memories of his years as a student in Venice: the sight of Molino Stucky from the Zattere:

> a strange castle on the water, against the light in the evening, with the open lagoon behind it, without definition if not for the *bricole* [the traditional oak poles used to indicate the navigation channels inside the lagoon]. Beyond the Stucky complex there was nothing: then Sacca

Fisola was formed, and I remember that when I returned from America in 1952 they were building it. The result was a piece of the outskirts of Mestre, cut out and set down there on the lagoon.[5]

Valle's state of mind when he began his design seemed to depend on this dual identity of memory: the recollection of Molino Stucky with the fairy tale tones of a 'strange castle on the water' – the same type of memory evoked by Valle in the design of the spa at Arta – and that of the shock of the new – Sacca Fisola as an abstract implant in the 'infinite' lagoon landscape. Based on this double memory, Valle developed the project by patiently constructing a singular tension between design tools linked to the dimension of memory – thus calling on a language rich in allusions to the edification present at the place – and tools linked to the dimension of abstraction, like typological rationalisation and an orthogonal layout grid.

Starting with a respectful interpretation of the specific characteristics of the area, Valle identified the principles of intervention in the conservation of Calle dei Lavranieri, which crosses the island, and of the existing garden against the old cement factory that occupied the area, and in the proposal of a form of compact construction,

View of the portico towards Calle dei Lavranieri.

View of the towers facing the canal of Sacca Fisola.

clearly concluded, organised in crosswise bands, in tune with the settlement principle of the whole island. In morphological terms, the new complex therefore had to appear as a compact, conclusive masonry mass, making it establish a dialogue with the other 'finished parts' of the island marked by the industrial architecture: the gigantic bulk of Molino Stucky to the north and the shipyard of the Trevisan area to the south. This respectful attitude was also motivated by the forceful physical presence of the old cement factory: for Valle, the project had to metaphorically mean 'transforming this pile of bricks that was the cement factory into another pile of bricks, i.e. from the ground there arose this new organism, this new Golem'.[6]

Already in the first sketches, the structuring of the complex in three parts was clearly outlined, each a response to its own particular setting: along the two lateral canals, a continuous curtain of four-storey 'towers' consolidates the banks in a symmetrical way; in the central part, the 'mat' of houses descends by the use of terracing from four storeys to two, allowing each occupant a view of the lagoon over the rooftops; to the south, finally, a row of two-storey houses is aligned with a new canal that forms the border between the new residential complex and the southern part of the island.

Rejecting the abstraction of typological solutions and the aggregative schemes proposed by regulations on low-cost housing, Valle therefore set out to base his project on three specific principles of residence in such a particular place: individual access to the single homes (rejection of stair-blocks); vertical organisation of the apartment around a small courtyard – a reminder of the spatial qualities of the 'introverted' plan of the Nicoletti house in Udine;[7] and visual openness towards the lagoon for the upper levels, to compensate for the relative closure of the rooms facing the courtyard. The consideration of the quality of the paths of access already seen in the projects for the IACP building in Udine and the development at Buia led this time to the definition of a dense network of paths, organised in keeping with a clear hierarchy of outdoor spaces that evoke the typically Venetian spatial qualities of the *calle* (street), the *sotoportègo* (portico), the *campiello* (small square) and the *campazzo* (large square).

From the house to the urban 'fabric': this particular structure of the 'residential mat', so pertinent in the Venetian context, had already been explored by Valle in a singular project from 1978, the 'Teo system' proposed in response to a competition for a range of standard designs for the 'Istituto autonomo case popolari' of the Lombardy Region, and developed together with the Valdadige company with which he had made the prefabricated schools in Friuli. In this proposal, Valle defined 'mat' as a 'continuous fabric of edification that makes it possible to maintain a direct dialogue between the apartment and the terrain, with an overall density that is significantly higher than that of the row house solution'.[8] Several years later, Valle remarked on 'the grand illusion of the pursuit of a system that could do everything: the grouping of rooms and the grouping of houses, meaning the project and the type of production for all the typologies, in all places and all times'.[9] The compositional and combinatory logic deployed in this abstract, universalist project, nevertheless, turned out to be very useful for Valle to propose compact edification on the Giudecca site: the typical sloping section of the design can in this sense be interpreted as the result of the deformation that had to necessarily be applied to the abstract settlement model as it entered into direct contact with the form and history of this particular place.

The project development provides a clear lesson in the way Valle was able to play with the rules imposed by low-cost housing regulations.[10] Valle based the grid of the entire project on a module of 165 × 165 centimetres that made it possible to obtain the two types of rooms required (nine square metres corresponding to four modules, 14 square metres corresponding to six modules). To achieve the desired mat building he did not simply repeat a basic type, however, but introduced a single exception, setting aside a space of transition with the width of one module between one row of houses and the next: this space of expansion could be used by one row or the other, depending on the level, leading to an original 'interlocking section' that noticeably enhanced the grouping of the individual homes. After having defined the layout of the residence and therefore the fabric of the central part, Valle decided to remove four houses to obtain a small central square, repeating the gesture of 'subtraction' already applied in the project at Buia. The same module was also used to make the plans of the row houses along the new canal, and the 'towers' at the edges.

After beginning as three distinct parts, the project therefore matured in the gradual definition of the plan of the housing, not so much as a cell to be repeated, but as a common denominator capable of generating a complex system of differences.

A common denominator: the theme returns of the 'generative grammar' we have already seen at work in projects for building complexes produced by starting with strong reduction of the linguistic means. While at Buia the variation in the grouping of types was sufficient to differentiate the three successive rows, in Pordenone a combinatory logic was applied to produce, starting with elementary volumes, four different buildings arranged in the plan to form a small 'piece of city'. At Giudecca, Valle specifically experimented with the variation of the basic element in keeping with its position in the system, therefore refusing to make an architectural expression based on the aesthetic of repetition. From the plans of the published project[11] a rigid spirit in the composition seemed to spread, due to the strong graphic presence of the modular grid

Competition project for residences in the Fregnan area, island of Sacca Fisola,
Venice, 1984. Perspective view from the lagoon.

and the thick blackened walls. In reality, in the
constructed work, the rigid conceptual framework
of the project – the module, the type, the grid, the
repetition, all indispensable tools of compositional
rationalism – is instead attenuated, and one realises
that this compositional rigour was a design tool
required in order to generate a controlled system of
differences.

In the experience of the route through the
complex, in fact, one realises that the orthogonal
character of the layout system is not the rigid,
neutral order of a chequerboard: the freedom to
choose different itineraries, the continuous variation
of the spatial and lighting conditions encountered
along the way, the differentiation of the entrances in
the successive rows of dwellings (balcony walkway,
portico, narrow alley or flanked by gardens), all
transform the walk into a rich, complex urban
experience marked by exceptions and differences.
Walking through this dense mat building one has
sensations close to that 'queer air of sociability,
of cousinship and family life' that in Venice so
intensely strikes the narrator of *The Aspern Papers* by
Henry James: 'without streets and vehicles ... with

its little winding ways where people crowd together,
where voices sound as in the corridors of a house,
where the human step circulates as if it skirted the
angles of furniture and shoes never wear out, the
place has the character of an immense collective
apartment'.[12]

This uniquely 'sociable' character of Valle's
architecture, with its ability to instil a deep sense of
identification with the characteristics of the place in
its inhabitants, marks a decisive improvement with
respect to the previous low-cost housing projects.
At Giudecca, the slow work of evolution and deeper
development of the compositional materials makes
it possible to banish any schematic character from
the architecture, instead bringing to light figurative
elements that evoke historic architecture, at times
with surprising results.[13]

This appeal to the visual memory of the
architecture of Giudecca was thus used by Valle as
a preferred means of getting beyond that feeling
of 'extraneousness' that the emergence of the new
threatened to cause.[14] For Valle, this was not an
operation of formal cosmesis: brick, the typical
material of the industrial construction of the island

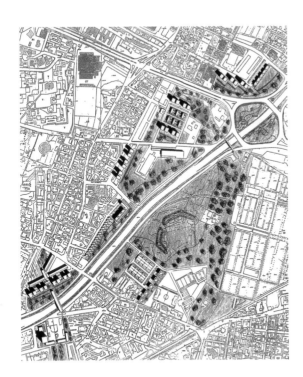

Siteplan of the guideline plan for the Barca-Casteldebole area in Bologna, 1990–95.

and the existing cement factory, was used not as a facing material, but to erect true masonry walls, a choice that permitted extraordinary control in the construction phase, directly relying on the measure of the individual brick. The particular tectonic quality of the brick masonry was then enhanced with other qualities, derived indirectly from careful observation of the constructive characteristics of individual buildings produced by two local traditions: on the one hand, the industrial construction of the island of Giudecca, evoked in the continuous surface – underlined by concrete belt courses – of the masonry and the precise definition of the repetitive rhythms of the facades; on the other, the 'minor' edification on the lagoon, with the contrasts between materials and chromatic games of the stucco, the frames and shutters in wood, the external chimneys: all qualifying elements of the individual dwelling, conceived to be perceived from up close, in a familiar rapport with the architecture that takes on 'a sense of softness or Venetian reflection of the light'.[15] The expressive richness of the architecture built by Valle at Giudecca also comes from this subtle blend of elements that simultaneously address both traditions.

The low-cost housing complex at Giudecca met with widespread critical acclaim at the end of the 1980s, as can be seen in many publications,[16] and it is comparable in terms of importance to the positive reaction of critics to the Zanussi offices at the start of the 1960s. Nevertheless, this international attention did not have direct effects on the public clientele, and Valle found few other opportunities to design low-cost housing facilities.

In 1984, when construction had just begun at Giudecca, Valle was invited to submit a project for a complex of 80 low-cost housing units on the island of Sacca Fisola in Venice, which allowed him to directly utilise the design expertise developed in the Giudecca project. Facing each other across the banks of the Lavranieri canal, the two buildings display clear methodological and linguistic continuity, aptly described by Marco De Michelis:

> Here too, the canal front is occupied by a series of tower buildings, which filter the passage to the linear edification behind them. [...] Thus the decisive gesture with which the long linear building and the two shorter ones behind it reformulate the perimeter of the disorderly settlement of Sacca Fisola is dialogically connected to the edges of the island and the architectural episode on the other side of the canal, through the repetition of two structurally equal but differently interpreted figures.[17]

Valle's project made no attempt to construct a 'piece of city' with reference to the settlement structures of Venice, but simply tried to shed light on a particular and even paradoxical condition of Sacca Fisola,

measuring it and confirming it, where the abstract settlement model based on alternation of linear buildings and green spaces breaks down when it reaches the edge of the water.

Nevertheless, the positive conditions in Venice which had made it possible to control the project on all scales, from the design of the urban arrangement to the typological, linguistic and constructive choices, never arose again. This is demonstrated by Valle's last project in the field of low-cost housing, developed from 1990 to 1995 for a consortium of seven cooperatives in Bologna, in a suburban area (Barca-Casteldebole) along the motorway connecting Bologna and Casalecchio. This was an important opportunity for urban renewal, which had to start with urban design and then reach the scale of the individual building. Valle proposed unifying the seven different segments with a linear park and a residential complex formed by buildings at single points, creating a filter between the surrounding suburbia and the new park that functioned as a green barrier with respect to the motorway. The Detail Plan, besides indicating the settlement schemes of the various parts, included a very detailed range of plans and facades, organised for four types (tower building, row house with patio, linear volumes with staircase points, urban cross-plan villas), and certain particulars of construction for the installation of the brick masonry with prefabricated concrete framework. In spite of the appeal of the residential solutions proposed, the constructed result was unfortunately disappointing, due to the lack of possibility offered to Valle to personally control the definitive design, which was done directly by the technical divisions of the individual cooperatives.

Notes

1 Gino Valle, 'Sei posizioni. Progetti di edilizia economica', contribution to the course for technicians for building design in residential cooperatives and service structures, Pomezia, 15–16 June 1983: see Manuscript, Archivio Valle, Udine.

2 ibid. On his apparently nonchalant way of 'playing' with rules, Valle said: 'I cannot manage to read the regulations, I read them and immediately forget them, for me they are like those things written in tiny letters on the back of insurance policies: if you read them you don't buy the insurance. In any case, we have been able to demonstrate that our project was more practical, per linear metre of length, than the types designed by the IACP technical division for linear buildings with staircase points.'

3   The visual effects in the perception from a distance, in this sense, have certain similarities to the strong semantic reduction of the architectural object that Valle had applied in the large coloured warehouses for Dapres and Bergamin, arranged along the highways of the Friuli plains.

4   A very detailed reconstruction of the development of the project for Giudecca is found in Pierre-Alain Croset, 'Sul progetto di Gino Valle alla Giudecca' [in Italian and English], *Lotus International*, 51, March 1986, pp.109–14.

5   Gino Valle, 'Sei posizioni. Progetti di edilizia economica', p.6,

6   Lecture by Gino Valle at Ca' Foscari on 29 March 1988, in Franca Bizzotto and Michela Agazzi (eds), *Colore Segno Progetto Spazio. Giuseppe Mazzariol e gli 'Incontri con gli artisti'*, Il Poligrafo, Padua, 2009, p.141.

7   Regarding this type of 'introverted house', Valle said it was a spatial condition that had always appealed to him: 'These houses look inward, i.e. from one window of your house, or from multiple windows of it, you can see other windows also belonging to your house. I think this is a very interesting thing, which I have always tried to achieve, and maybe it is a thing that comes from my childhood memories: I had a house full of little courtyards, so I looked inside my own house.' See ibid., p.148.

8   Gino Valle, project description, published in *Casabella*, 439, September 1978, and later in the book *Regione Lombardia: Repertorio progetti tipo*, Be-Ma Editrice, Milan, 1978.

9   Gino Valle, talk at the conference 'Razionalizzazione della produzione e gestione edilizia in rapporto al risparmio energetico', Abano, 23 February 1980, published in Atti del convegno, Consorzio regionale IACP, Regione Veneto, 1980, pp.11–18.

10   Valle acknowledged that it would not be possible to 'play' with the rigid regulations on low-cost housing had he not had valid collaborators capable of checking on the compliance of the project, and in particular he pointed to the decisive role played by Giorgio Macola: 'So I never even read the rules for the low-cost housing. Luckily there was Giorgio Macola, my excellent collaborator, who instead had a passion for those rules, and we found this *modus* ... You need someone to check. If I didn't have people in the studio who check on costs, square meters, etc., I'd be out of a job. Afterwards, having completed the project, I say: "You see? My instinct was correct." Because my instinct is pretty good.' See 'Gino Valle, 29 March 1988', ibid., p.142.

11   The project at Giudecca was published for the first time in 1982 on the cover and inside issue no. 478

of *Casabella* (March 1982, with critical commentary by Giacomo Polin), at the start of Vittorio Gregotti's period as editor of the Milan-based magazine.

12   Henry James, *The Aspern Papers*, Dover, Mineola, NY, 2001.

13   For example, projecting the barrel section of the stairwell onto the outer row of terraces, and perforating this screen with two circles to obtain a high parapet that separates the distant view from the closer view, Valle generates the somewhat disquieting figure of a 'Venetian mask' that gives the architecture an anthropomorphic character, as well as echoing the 'eyes' of the destroyed cement plant.

14   With great perception, Giuseppe Mazzariol recognised, in the project by Valle at Giudecca, the ability to interpret the 'long term' of Venetian architecture. In particular, he saw the 'masks' of Valle's buildings not just as the memory of the 'eyes' of the cement factory, but also as ways of evoking other Venetian themes: 'the Gothic double windows, first the mullioned windows of Byzantine matronea ... and then the great masks of Ca' Pesaro, of Longhena, of the Baroque, and there are those signs that reappear today in very timely terms, and have this age-old memory. So then, this is making Venice by adding to Venice.' See 'Gino Valle, 29 March 1988', pp.151–2.

15   Gino Valle in ibid., p.146: 'Inside this grid elements of domestic interpretation have been introduced, which are, for example, this pale green on this stucco, and these pink and beige colours you see on the stucco panels. And then the ones you see around the doors are reprised features, but not an imitation of Venice, i.e. one finds familiar pieces that in my view convey an unconscious sense of reassurance, which means recognizing a colour, recognizing a material. And it is very important because if those things were not there, it would really be a mountain of bricks, it would be too hard.'

16   Among the most important international magazines: *Arquitectura y vivienda* (8, September 1986), *Casabella* (528, October 1986), *Abitare* (248, October 1986), *L'Architecture d'Aujourd'hui* (248, December 1986), *Domus* (678, December 1986), *Werk, Bauen + Wohnen* (3, March 1987), *Lotus International* (51, March 1987), *Bauwelt* (30, August 1987), *Baumeister* (9, September 1987), *Process: architecture* (75, 1987), *GA Houses* (23, 1988), *Progressive Architecture* (2, February 1988), *A+U* (215, August 1988).

17   Marco De Michelis, 'Nuovi progetti alla Giudecca', *Lotus International*, 51, March 1986, pp.79–94. Instead of this interesting project by Valle, the client preferred the design by Cappai and Mainardis with Valeriano Pastor, which was subsequently built (1985–90).

Building for 100 IACP Housing Units

Udine, 1975–79

View of the southwestern facade, towards the green space.

The building closes off an existing residential courtyard. From a distance it stands out, due to its large size, resembling a colourful 'dam' marked by the alternation of residential floors in green and circulation levels in red. The ground floor is a continuous portico that forms a transparent filter between the green area of the courtyard and the street. The portico is accessed by means of bridges that span the recessed area of the parking facilities and cellars. The upper levels are reached via three staircase-lift shafts, coloured red and placed along the street outside the building: the six residential levels are divided into two groups of three, with access from their respective central levels at the second and fifth floors. Emerging from the lift, one takes a bridge that leads to the open circulation level. The path to the door of the apartment is accompanied by a panoramic view of the landscape. Each level provides access, on the two sides, to eleven groups of four apartments – two above and two below – while the mini-apartments are placed in the middle parts. Management and maintenance issues led IACP to separate the three sectors of the circulation levels with grilles, unfortunately eliminating the possibility of varying the paths of access to the apartments.

View of the northeastern facade on Via Riccardo di Giusto.

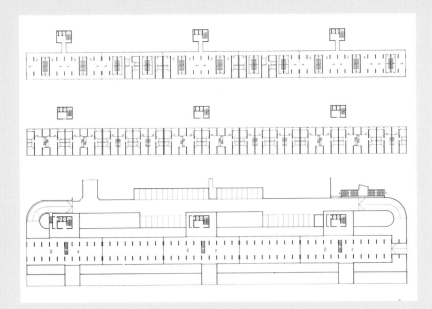

(*above*) Plans of the second floor (circulation balcony, entrances to the apartments at the first and third floors, mini-apartments), the first floor (22 housing units) and the ground floor (portico with partitions); (*right*) axonometric of standard apartments with access from the balcony.

Low-cost Housing Complex at Giudecca

Venice, 1980–86

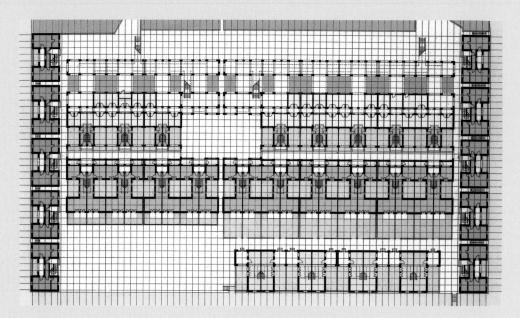

Ground floor plan.

The first impression of the complex, arriving from Sacca Fisola or from Giudecca, is the deep affinity of its image with the characteristic industrial edification on the island: rather than a row of five detached houses, along the canal one perceives a single masonry mass, vertically paced by the setback of the terraces. These setbacks bring out the lateral volumes, causing a surprising effect of visual chaining from one tower to the next: this illusion of coupling of the lateral volumes is further reinforced by the motif of the interrupted tympanum formed by the slope of the roofs.

After the view of the towers, one enters Calle dei Lavranieri. Here the path of access to the individual dwellings begins, during which the physical presence of the walls gradually increases, reinforcing the sensation of intimacy at the same time. The walls guide the steps and frame the view of the architecture, nearly always oblique, or only partial in the rare situations of frontal perception: the entrance sequence thus prepares for the gradual discovery of the high wall of the first row of houses, visible in its full length only when approached almost to the point of being able to touch it. At this point the path can continue in three different directions, depending on the destination: one takes the staircase leading to the balcony of the entrances to the apartments of the first row; one skirts the wall to enter the bordering street along which the entrances to the 'towers' are placed; or one follows the portico leading to the central square, in order to continue into the built 'fabric'.

The 'familiar' character of the public space of circulation triggers its perception as a single,

View of the towers facing the canal of Sacca Fisola.

continuous and articulated antechamber of
the dwellings, while the dynamic of the path of
penetration proceeds in terms of a regression of
light, passing from the brightness of the canal to the
shade of the houses.

Inside the apartments, the path continues with an
opposite dynamic: the higher the ascent, the greater
the intensity of the lighting. The spatial richness
of the house is underlined by the strong contrast
between the introversion of the plan on the lower
levels, with rooms facing a small courtyard, and the
openness of the view of the lagoon on the upper
level. The variations of the lighting conditions, the
height and form of the ceilings, the arrangement of
the terraces, are so clear that they overshadow the
rule of repetition that is the basis of the design of
the plans.

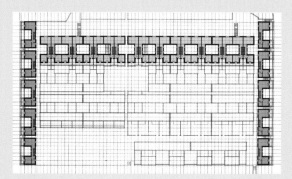

Fourth floor plan.

Low-cost housing complex at Giudecca, Venice, 1980–86.

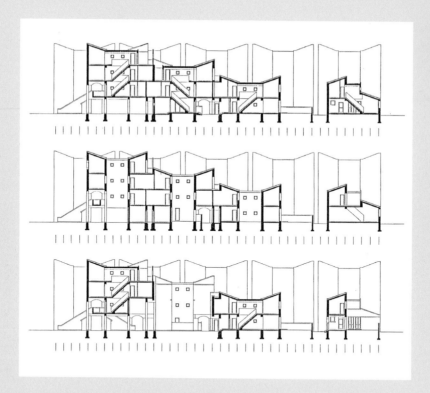

Cross-sections.

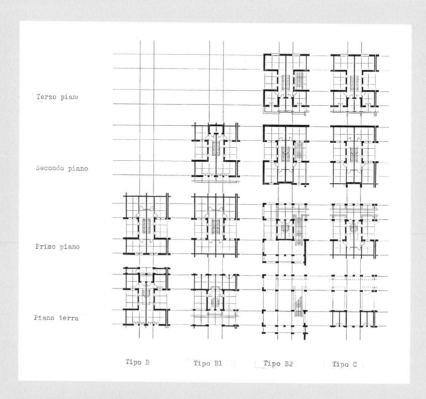

Terzo piano

Secondo piano

Primo piano

Piano terra

Tipo B   Tipo B1   Tipo B2   Tipo C

Plans of the apartment types.

View of the 'carpet' sloping towards the lagoon, with Molino Stucky in the background.

View from a terrace towards the towers and the lagoon.

10 Reusing, Restoring, Restructuring: Architecture as Brand (1977–99)

During the same period as the development of the three low-cost housing projects for Udine, Buia and Venice, Valle worked on a series of projects for Banca Commerciale Italiana regarding the restructuring and expansion of existing buildings, thereby promoting a new brand image of architecture, without a priori financial limitations.

At the time of the opening in Milan of a studio in partnership with the Swiss architects Mario Broggi and Michael Burckhardt, the first project covered a series of renovations of the whole block of the bank's headquarters in Milan, especially the radical transformation of Palazzo Besana (1977–81) for the 'stock market and investment' division on the very central Piazza Belgioioso. Built at the end of the 1700s, the building had undergone a slow process of functional and formal modification. More than twenty years after the renovation of the headquarters of the Cassa di Risparmio di Udine, Valle had a chance to approach the theme of the internal metamorphosis of a historic building: this time the functional programme was to insert highly specialised and equipped offices inside the old building, from which to conserve not only the facades, but also the rooms facing the piazza on the ground floor and first floor. All the other internal parts were completely rebuilt, in keeping with a U-shaped arrangement that reinterpreted the original plan of the historic *palazzo*.

Valle created a strong dialectical tension between the old parts that had simply been restored and the new ones, relying on a very limited range of industrialised elements to give the new offices a character of rigour and modern efficiency. He experimented with innovative solutions in the facades of the inner courtyard, using metal grilled screens, usually applied to make suspended ceilings, at a slight distance from the coloured concrete walls, thus obtaining an interesting effect of filtered light.

Against the backdrop of this neutral tone of the whole, the most exceptional place in the building stands out: the large boardroom on the ground floor, on axis with the entrance, lit from above by two glazings that put the space into visual contact with the courtyard, transformed into a raised garden. Completely different problems were involved in the design for the new offices in New York of Banca Commerciale Italiana (1981–86). In a well-documented essay on the project development, Sandro Marpillero explained how the choice of moving the New York facility into a significant building in lower Manhattan, just south of Wall Street, meant the assertion on the part of the Italian bank of a 'clear position with respect to the real estate dynamics of Manhattan. Instead of adding another anonymous tower to the city's skyline ... the prestige of the Italian bank would

(*left*) Banca Commerciale Italiana, One William Street, New York, 1981–86.

Banca Commerciale Italiana, One William Street, New York, 1981–86. Axonometric from below.

depend on a relationship with the metropolitan tradition of New York.'[1] The object of this relationship was an 11-storey building constructed in 1907 with a design by Francis M. Kimball, with a steel structure and stone cladding attached, with a construction system based on the experiences of the Chicago School, previously the home of the historic and illustrious financial institution, Lehman Brothers.

Valle had already come to terms with the theme of an addition to an existing building in the projects in the historic centre of Udine. In these earlier projects the relationship between the existing and the new had been expressed by establishing a strong dialectical tension, while in New York Valle chose to construct 'a positive but also critical double'.[2] The formal development of this 'double' followed two parallel lines: at the level of the plan, Valle called complex geometric rules into play to 'regulate' the tracing of the addition, in such a way as to unite old and new parts inside the asymmetrical polygon of the lot; at the level of the facade, Valle came directly to grips with the classical order of Kimball's composition, to the point of obtaining an elegant modern version with a minimalist look[3] of the rustication and ornamental decorations of the original building.

Valle skilfully reproduced the compositional rhythm of Kimball's building, repeating the distance between the openings of the old facades on the new ones, and granting importance in the plans to the generating role of the bisectors used as shifted parallel axes, and to the arrangement in tension of the workspaces around a central egg-shaped hall. In the building on Via Mercatovecchio in Udine, Valle had already directly experimented with the design of a new facade in a relationship of dialogue with an existing work of architecture: the necessary critical distance from the model was asserted through the choice of the iron construction system, and the new facade appeared as the representation of the traditional stone and stucco facade in a new material. In New York, this theme of allusion and representation was instead approached by Valle without changing the material, this time obtaining a facade conceived as a sort of graphic representation of the moulding of the building, through the use of various hues of stone for the shaded surfaces. Though he used stone of unusual thickness, with monolithic blocks for the jambs of the windows and in the corners, Valle deployed this stone in such a radically different way with respect to the existing building as to make it seem like another material. He exploited 'the extraordinary capacity of stone to change appearance depending on the light, especially polished black granite that becomes a mirror when

Banca Commerciale Italiana, New York, 1981–86, the addition and the historic building seen from Stone Street.

there is sunshine. So the moulding is represented alternately as positive or negative, playing with the colours and the reflections.'[4]

Marpillero interpreted the choice of keeping 'constructive faith' with the existing model in relation to the character as a 'precious exception' that the Italian bank assumed in the context of commercial architecture in Manhattan.[5] This characteristic of preciousness is further emphasised by the crowning of the building with an aviary, a tower five storeys high, forming a delicate sign of recognition in the skyline: a beacon that captures and reflects sunlight when the building is observed from the relative shadow of the street. Kenneth Frampton criticised this 'tower of air and light' for its excessive formal autonomy and dematerialisation, which in his view caused an apparent loss of volumetric unity.[6] Though this

critique has its merits, we should nevertheless acknowledge the sculptural qualities of this metal skeleton: the 'critical distance' needed to avoid making respect for the past translate into pure imitation is thus manifested in the materials of the constructive tradition of Kimball's building itself, a tradition to which Valle's project pays sensitive, refined homage.

The Banca Commerciale Italiana building in New York had important consequences in the development of Valle's work after the second half of the 1980s. On the one hand, it confirmed his vivid focus on the urban context in which to intervene, already expressed with particular clarity in the low-cost housing complex at Giudecca: in New York, Valle found himself in a certain sense in the particular position of someone who has to learn the language of his 'host' to be able to

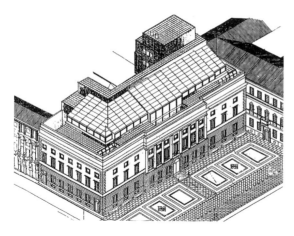

Restoration of Palazzo Besana, Milan, 1977–81.
Axonometric from Piazza Belgiojoso.

Restoration of Palazzo Besana, Milan, 1977–81.
View of the front on the courtyard.

pay him tribute, reprising certain construction materials and traditions to produce a 'sense of belonging' of the architecture. On the other, Valle's renewed interest in the qualification of the image connected to the representational value of architecture, already evident in his previous projects for banks, marked an apparent shift of focus onto the tectonic qualities belonging to the architectural object 'in itself'. With respect to the terse and intentionally 'abstract' language of the 'minimalist' projects of the 1970s, used by Valle to shift the attention of the observer from visual perception of the architectural object to tactile experience of the relationships between building and context, it was now possible to observe greater refinement in the design and deployment of materials. Immediately after the completion of the building in New York, Valle built three small buildings[7] in rural contexts or small towns, which confirm his renewed focus on the representational value of architecture. The Cassa Rurale ed Artigiana of Azzano Decimo (1987–89) is the most interesting one, offering a serene relationship with the urban context – with the need to add quality to the corner of a square in an area of expansion – and a refined way of calling into play the classical rules of architecture: besides the tripartite plan, like that of a basilica, noteworthy features include the vertical composition of the elevations, rigorously cut in two with clear separation between the brick base and the upper part in white stucco, enhanced by bands of Piasentina stone.[8] Valle introduced subtle interruptions of symmetry in this 'classical' layout, especially in the end towards the square – where the curved treatment of the corner and the deformation of the entrance canopy stand out – but also in the raised 'parvis' that extends the plan of the building outward and seems to be eroded by a tree-lined plot with a curved shape – almost a tribute to the organic forms used by Alvar Aalto. Francesco Moschini has correctly pointed to a Loos-like character of this small building by Valle,[9] but this character could also be the result of the influence of certain works by Álvaro Siza, in particular the 'Loosian' Avellino Duarte house at Ovar (1981–85), conceived during those same years as 'minimalist' interpretations of 'classical' compositions. Valle himself indicated another reference, mentioning 'the banks of Sullivan, which are of the same type as mine, popular, rural. They are very beautiful, not monuments but a representation of those who thought of them and the time in which they were made, and they will continue to have their weight in the future.'[10] These small banks by Sullivan, which Valle had visited during his first trip to America in 1952, were made 'in the despairingly solid banality of the American inland',[11] and represent the high point of the last phase of the career of the American master (1909–20). Besides the similarity to the 'popular and rural' context of the projects, these extraordinary buildings by Sullivan also deserve attention due to a very particular relationship between the Cartesian rigour of the volumetric arrangement and the tectonic richness of the masonry texture. It is interesting, for example, to compare the Cassa Rurale of Azzano Decimo with the People's Savings Bank in Cedar Rapids, Iowa (1909–11), the most important of these small banks by Sullivan, acclaimed at the time of its construction as 'the most interesting event that has taken place in American architecture today':[12] subtle linguistic affinities emerge in the shared base in brick paced by horizontal bands – in stone in Valle's building, and with a different pattern of the bricks in that of Sullivan; in the basilica layout; but also in the sequence of vertical windows with a tight rhythm, resting on a continuous sill.

It is interesting that Valle, commenting on these works, stated that they are 'not monuments', when actually the sacral, almost tomb-like character of the building by Sullivan seems quite clear. Nevertheless, we can interpret this intriguing statement by Valle in terms of a positive integration of the architecture in the context of a small rural town: in spite of the reference to courtly and sacred images, these are buildings that manage to express an almost 'domestic' and 'everyday' value in their identity as public buildings, and are therefore without arrogance, without the forced effect of 'off-scale' elements.

During the same years, Valle explored the theme of metamorphosis and 'recycling' of an existing building of limited architectural quality but of great importance for its position in the historic city,[13] confirming his renewed interest in the representational value of architecture. The only project to be built was the transformation of the Alitalia tower in the EUR district in Rome as the headquarters of IBM Italia (1986–93). It demonstrates that the theme of 'recycling' of obsolete architecture was a theme of maximum importance for Valle.[14] The programme of interventions was quickly outlined by IBM after the purchase of the building in 1985. On a technical level it was necessary to revise all the building-plant system, to adapt the building constructed in 1964–66 to new standards of energy saving and fire security, but also to remove a layer of asbestos from all the metal structures. On an architectural level, IBM wanted a new, strong, recognisable image that would make a clean break

Cassa Rurale ed Artigiana in Azzano Decimo, 1987–89. View of the entrance facade and the plaza in front of it.

Alitalia tower at EUR prior
to renovation.

Alitalia-IBM tower: the change of the skin
of the building.

with the dated language of the existing tower, while exploiting the prestigious location of the building at the end of the axis of Via Pastore. To describe his project, done with the collaboration of the Roman architect Carlo Costantini, Valle used an organic metaphor: 'The problem was to intervene in a building while conserving only its skeleton: it was necessary to introduce flesh and blood to give it a new life.'[15] The first design operation had to do with the replacement of the old facade – a banal polygonal curtain wall – with a new continuously curved 'skin' formed by alternating strips of glass and white aluminium, repeating the motif – taken from the company's logo – already used at the Distribution Centre in Basiano. Valle explained the choice of materials with a 'pictorial' rationale:

> The whole building is an object that works with light: in certain photographs, from particular angles, you can see the sky that crosses the building. The 'trick' lies in the fact that the facade is not entirely made of glass but of bands of glass and opaque white strips, so the reflected clouds pass from one pane to the next, while the white in the middle becomes a void, a hole.[16]

From a distance it can be seen that Valle applied 'pictorial' devices and light materials to create the illusion of architecture made of only air and light, in the close-up view he underlined the weight of the architecture, with a travertine base that by contrast might seem curiously 'archaic'. The problem Valle faced was to correct a particularly inept connection to the ground, where a slender, excessively low portico made the tower look as if it was crushed into the ground. In its place, Valle proposed a series of parallel walls clad in travertine,[17] evoking the image of an archaeological dig. The strong, almost surreal contrast between the rugged travertine of the base and the smooth aluminium and glass surfaces of the facade seems to respond to a desire to create a temporal fiction: after its metamorphosis, the tower at EUR no longer looks like a single, homogeneous building, but like the result of slow temporal stratification.

IBM Tower, Eur, Rome, 1986–93. View of the base of the building with the partitions covered in tuff.

IBM Tower, Eur, Rome, 1986–93. View from
Via dell'Architettura.

Valle himself did not hesitate to acknowledge the
'scenic design' elements in the project, saying
that it was 'all theatre, but a theatre that creates a
magical atmosphere'.[18]

The possibility of improving buildings of little
architectural value through the metamorphosis
of the 'skin' had already been explored by Valle
in various projects for the Bergamin company,
illustrated in a previous chapter of this book.
During the same period, Valle did another
'repackaging' project at a very prestigious site,
on Avenue Victor-Hugo in Paris, to give new life
to a building of Société Générale reconstructed
in the 1960s. As in the IBM tower at EUR, the
project (1993–99, with Giorgio Macola and
Fernando Urquijo) concerned the exterior
image of the building, as well as the complete
internal reorganisation, including substantial
modifications of the load-bearing structure, and

The building on Avenue Victor-Hugo in Paris
prior to renovation.

an interesting excavation of the rear courtyard, with a sequence of walls and terraces that create a spatial relationship with the neighbouring garden of the Angola Embassy. The remaking of the facade, on the other hand, seems very distant from the 'painterly' abstraction of the Roman tower: Valle decided, in fact, to come to terms with the compositional principles of the facades of the Paris of Haussmann, still a vivid presence in this luxurious district of the capital, embracing a design attitude of allusion and representation of historic architecture already successfully applied for the New York facility of Banca Commerciale Italiana. The new facade, in a certain sense, had to erase the negative effects of extraneousness to the urban context produced by the reconstruction project in the 1960s, with its flat, prefabricated facade with concrete cornices, returning on the one hand to the compositional principles of three-part subdivision (two-storey base, four-storey elevation, top with mansard roof) of the historic buildings on Avenue Victor-Hugo, and on the other to the subdivision of the long front into three different lots, evoking the original Haussmannian arrangement. Another important question was the need to restore the thickness and rhythm of the facade: unlike the

project in New York where the moulding of the facade was represented by a 'graphic' play on the use of different hues of stone to design the shaded surfaces, in Paris Valle decided to stage a refined three-dimensional composition of semi-columns and horizontal bands, with results that are not lacking, however, in a certain ambiguity.[19] New York, Rome, Paris: three interventions on existing buildings, approached by Valle starting with an idea of temporal fiction, but also using principles of 'scenic design' already seen at work in previous projects, especially the transformation of Palazzo Besana in Milan. Regarding the tower at EUR, Valle said it was 'all theatre'. His interest in theatrical techniques found further room for experiment in two projects for the Pasolini cinema-theatre in Cervignano (1995–96) and the reconstruction of Teatro La Fenice in Venice (1997). At Cervignano, Valle designed a measured project, respectful of the original building, the Cinema Nuovo built by Ermes Midena in the 1950s, maintaining the original composition of the facade and demolishing just one span of the hall to insert the fly tower and the dressing rooms, while the space inside the hall seems uniquely 'dynamic', enlivened by the red colour of the seats and the black facing panels sloped to match the angle of the balcony. The project for the reconstruction of Teatro La Fenice, after the fire in 1997, is instead an interesting demonstration of the contemporary ambiguities of the reconstruction of historic buildings, where Valle subtly proposes subverting the ideology of reconstruction 'as it was, where it was' required in the competition guidelines.[20] Decisively rejecting the idea of a complete reconstruction, he opted to stage the 'drama' of a reconstruction that, since it could not be 'true', had to necessarily be displayed as fiction, in his view: Valle spoke explicitly in the project description of the 'collage of the most representative parts of the antique theatre, reconstructed as a document', creating a clear gap between the zone of the 'as it was' – the proscenium arch, the proscenium with its boxes, the reconstructed royal box – and the rest of the hall treated in a 'minor tone' so that

Cinema-Teatro Pasolini in Cervignano del Friuli, 1995–96. Facade towards the plaza.

Cinema-Teatro Pasolini in Cervignano del Friuli, 1995–96. View of the hall: the hall is wrapped by inclined sound-absorbing panels; the interspaces contain the lighting and air conditioning systems.

it would clearly be seen as a 'reconstruction', using a refined red brocade that uniformly clads the structure of the boxes to 'evoke' the original splendour, in contrast with the gold colour of the new seating. With respect to the projects of Gae Aulenti and Aldo Rossi,[21] Valle's design was the only one that approached the theme of reconstruction in innovative terms: a project that was both visionary and concrete, capable of creating a poetic tension between conservation and renewal, which can be aptly compared to the similar project for the reconstruction of the Gran Teatre de Liceu in Barcelona by Ignasi de Solà-Morales, Xavier Fabré and Lluís Dilmé (1994–99).

Project for addition to the Kulissengebäude of the Staatstheater of Stuttgart, 1986. Perspective from the street with the new Staatsgalerie by James Stirling on the left.

Notes

1 Sandro Marpillero, 'Grattacielo a metà. Gino Valle: uffici della Banca commerciale italiana a Manhattan', *Lotus International*, 37, 1983, p.96.

2 ibid.

3 Kenneth Frampton has proposed associating the 'minimalism' of Valle's project with the constructive ethic of 'less is more' of Mies van der Rohe: 'We might say that we are close to the conception of the "almost nothing" as perhaps not even Mies could have imagined, given the fact that the strong tectonic presence of this work is simply the result of the alternation between joints and surfaces.' See Kenneth Frampton, 'Gino Valle, Edificio per uffici, New York', *Domus*, 683, May 1987, p.29.

4 Pierre-Alain Croset (ed.), 'Una conversazione con Gino Valle', *Casabella*, 519, December 1985, pp.16–17.

5 Sandro Marpillero, 'Grattacielo a metà', p.98.

6 'This super-articulation is perhaps most evident in the cylindrical "aviary" that tops the corner cylinder ... Valle's initial sketches suggested a closer fusion between the stone cylinder and that of steel, an intuition that has somehow been lost in the final constructed work, partly due to the excessive setback of the glass at the level of each floor, and partly due to the not sufficiently visible connection between the pinnacle of the cage and the corner tower.' Kenneth Frampton, 'Gino Valle, Edificio per uffici', p.29.

7 These are two small banks (Cassa Rurale ed Artigiana) in Schio (1982–87) and in Azzano Decimo (1987–89), and the Elea dining hall at Burolo (1985–88) on a bucolic site at the foot of the Serra d'Ivrea.

8 Luciano Testa has proposed a suggestive interpretation of this facade, insisting on the marked horizontal character of the building, underlined by the six string courses of which just one, between bricks and stucco, effectively had the function of indicating the internal structure, while the others had an 'ornamental'

function: 'A repetitive addition that reprised with elegance by the cornice pleonastically emphasises the horizontality of the building, and when juxtaposed with the rusticated/smooth opposition references the technology of the masonry work.' See Luciano Testa, 'I materiali dell'opera: le pietre dell'oblio', *Anfione Zeto*, 6–7, 1990–91, pp.92–9.

9 Francesco Moschini states that 'what brings Adolf Loos into the picture is not the assonance of the formal elements, nor the reference to the tomb and the monument ... but instead the character of commentary on the tradition that is found in the work of the Viennese architect and that in the building in Azzano Decimo institutes different and more reflective relations with the context'. See Francesco Moschini, 'Gino Valle: l'avventura del collezionista', *Anfione Zeto*, 6–7, 1990–91, p.72.

10 Margherita Petranzan (ed.), 'L'opera in memoria. Intervista dialogo Valle–Petranzan', in 'Gino Valle. Casse rurali e artigiane: Azzano Decimo (Pn)-Monte Magré-Schio (Vi)', monograph, *Anfione Zeto*, 6–7, 1990–91, p.49.

11 'This, in any case, is the comeback of Sullivan: the quality he achieves is very high. The extraordinary charm of his small, precious buildings in the despairing solid banality of the American inland also undoubtedly lies – beyond the anticipations of Kahn visible in the People's Savings Bank – in the ambiguous anachronism conveyed to us by their contradictory appeal.' See Mario Manieri Elia, *Louis Henry Sullivan 1856–1924*, Electa, Milan, 1995, p.159.

12 Montgomery Schuyler, 'The People's Savings Bank of Cedar Rapids, Iowa', *Architectural Record*, 31, January 1912, pp.45–56, cited in Manieri Elia, *Louis Henry Sullivan*, p.154.

13 See also two interesting competition projects in 1986 for the expansion of the Casino Winkler in Salzburg, and for a new façade in Stuttgart for the Kulissengebäude (set design workshop) built in the 1960s next to the state theatre designed by Max Littmann in 1910–12, in an urban

(*right*) Reconstruction of Teatro La Fenice in Venice, 1997. Longitudinal section: note the opening that separates the proscenium ('as it was') from the hall clad in red brocade.

context made even more appealing by the obligatory face-off with the new state gallery by James Stirling.

14   Regarding this project, Valle said he was convinced that 'architecture has always evolved by recycling constructed things. It is clear that if I had the chance to design a new tower in Rome, it would be conceived in a totally different way: a tower completely in stone, for example, very heavy, solidly anchored to the ground. The need to recycle the existing tower, for reasons of both urbanism and economy, dictated the formal choices, but also those regarding construction, structure and materials.' From a conversation between Gino Valle and Pierre-Alain Croset in Udine, 28 February 1995: Pierre-Alain Croset, 'Gino Valle. Trasformazione della torre IBM a Roma', *Casabella*, 622, April 1995, pp.59–60.

15   ibid.

16   Massimo Trevisan and Massimo Vedovato, 'Colloquio con Gino Valle', *Anfione Zeto*, 12, 1999, p.82.

17   Davide Ruzzon has acutely analysed the way Valle attached the travertine sheets to a metal frame, playing with the deep seams to create a 'graphic game' that would suggest classical rustication: 'The large seam thus created erases an important ambiguity: it prevents its shadow from being the result of the presence of the strip that usually separates two juxtaposed sheets. Given the size of the seam, the sheets can only be separated and hung. This gesture leads to a second gesture: the vertical joints of the sheets are not installed with staggering, simulating the solid stone blocks used for construction in ancient times. The sheets are placed so that the joints are vertically aligned. The external facing thus informs us of its impossibility to bear weights.' Davide Ruzzon, 'I materiali', *Anfione Zeto*, 12, 1999, p.64.

18   Massimo Trevisan and Massimo Vedovato, 'Colloquio', p.82.

19   See the following critical commentary by Carlo Magnani: 'The principle of the facing accepts the need to come to terms with the ambiguity of a possible character of urban decoration; it does not accept totalizing simplifications, but patiently regains a composite order of pilasters, half columns and string courses ... seeking, instead, a sober elegance between the unity of the overall compositional order and asymmetries completed by the lateral supports of the figure on the streetfront, reminders of other episodes in Paris at the start of the century.' Carlo Magnani, 'Costruire sul costruito: riflessioni sul rapporto tra recupero e trasformazione', *Costruire sul costruito. Sei architetture di Giorgio Macola*, Il Poligrafo, Padova, 2007, p.11. The results of the more structural and less 'image-oriented' operations, on the other hand, are much more convincing, and regarded the organisation of the interior spaces and the layout system, in particular by shifting the entrance lobby, which became a luminous, large covered passage between the street and the patio-garden to the rear.

20   As part of a wider design group (with Giorgio Macola, Mario Valle Engineering, set designer Ezio Frigerio and the technical staff of the contractor, Carena), to respond to the difficult conditions set by the competition, Valle devoted maximum attention to the architectural expression of the historic theatre.

21   In an interesting comparative analysis of the projects of Valle, Gae Aulenti and Aldo Rossi, Sebastiano Brandolini has clearly shown that Valle's project was the only one capable of implying 'the possibility that the new Fenice could be better than the one that burned down', having rejected the ideology of 'philological reconstruction' to attempt to safeguard the atmosphere of the place, rather than its value as an 'established image'. Sebastiano Brandolini, 'Tre ipotesi per le ceneri della Fenice', *Lotus International*, 103, December 1999, pp.40–46.

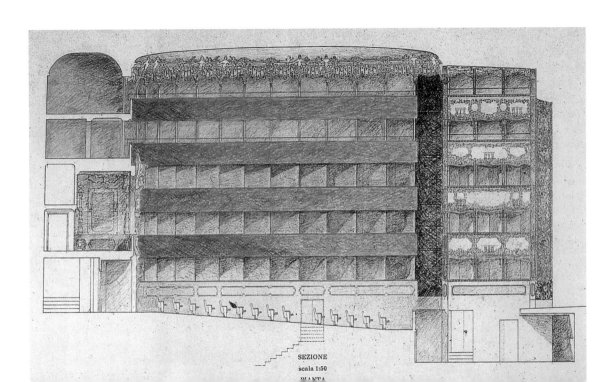

SEZIONE
scala 1:50

Headquarters of Banca Commerciale Italiana

New York, 1981–86

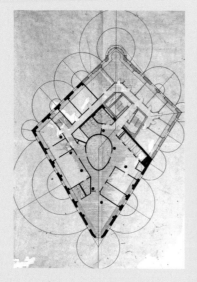

(*far left*) Standard floor plan.

(*left*) Cover of *The New Yorker* (1 February 1982) with insertion of the front of the BCI tower.

The building stands on a small plot between One William, South William and Stone Street, in historic downtown Manhattan. It is composed of two parts: the historic building by Kimball, which has simply been renovated, and the new addition. The best view of the new part of the complex is to be had by entering South William Street from Broad Street and heading north. From the narrow, shady space of the street one discovers the emerging facade along Mill Lane – bright with light from the south – and the new tower at the corner of Stone Street topped by the metal framework that gleams in the sunlight. Arriving from the north, on the other hand, one finds the characteristic corner tower of the building by Kimball and notices the subtle relationship between the old and new parts: the reference to the three vertically stacked parts – two-storey base, six-storey central part, two-storey top – the continuity of the rustication in the stone facing, the repetition of the size and groupings of the windows with respect to the rhythm of the existing facades.

The public entrance is located at the foot of the tower in the restructured part: from the circular corner lobby one enters the old restored hall, faced in travertine with a golden-coffered ceiling of painted tiles. The staff entrance is from South William Street, at the position of a group of four renovated lifts. The base of the new tower at the corner of Stone Street and Mill Lane contains the entrance to the platform lift offering access to the underground car park.

The internal arrangement of the floors calls for perimeter offices organised around a central nucleus that includes the staircases, the lift landing, the restroom grouping, and a central space with an egg-shaped plan used as a meeting room or waiting area. The roof at the twelfth floor, accessed through a two-storey dining room, is organised as a 'promenade' inside the technical volume enclosed by a grille: from the existing turret one enters a roof garden that concludes with the steel framework, also accessed from the eleventh floor.

The addition and the historic building seen from Stone Street.

The new building at the corner of Mill Lane and Stone Street.

Detail of the cladding of the new building (left) in continuity with the existing building.

Offices of Société Générale

Avenue Victor-Hugo, Paris, 1993–99

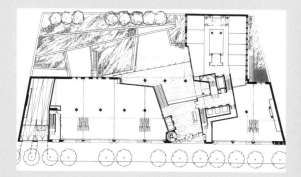

Ground floor plan.

View of the courtyard, below street level, from the
corner of the retaining wall.

The new facility for the offices of Société Générale
is in the heart of Paris, 200 metres from the Arc de
Triomphe. On Avenue Victor-Hugo, the building
asserts its character with a monumental facade in
'Paris stone', which reinterprets the rhythm of the
openings of the original building from the 1960s,
while on the inside the structures have undergone
substantial modifications. The new facade is based
on a 'classical' three-way subdivision: a base with
stores, two storeys high, a segment of four floors
of offices marked by a rapid sequence of half-
columns and cornices, a typically Parisian top with
a cylindrical-section roof, set back and clad in zinc.
A large two-storey opening clearly indicates the
entrance to the building. From the lobby visitors
discover the patio in the back, below street level,
through a large window. This recessed patio, faced
by the cafe, is enclosed by inclined stone walls that
support a raised garden, reinforcing the intimate,
almost domestic, character of the place. The height
and transparency of the entrance lobby offer a
glimpse from the street of the presence at the back
not only of the recessed patio, but also of the garden
behind the Angolan Embassy, with the foliage of the
trees emerging over the stone wall. On the upper
levels the offices are organised along the perimeter
walls, with a double circulation corridor and a
single slightly rotated stairwell with three lifts. The
offices along Avenue Victor-Hugo are based on a
module size of 190 centimetres, corresponding to
the existing facade, while those facing the courtyard
have a smaller module of 142.5 centimetres.

View of the courtyard facade.

Front on Avenue Victor-Hugo.

11 Constructing 'pieces of city' (1983-2003)

The projects for the low-cost housing development on Giudecca and the headquarters of Banca Commerciale Italiana in New York revealed Valle's renewed focus, at the beginning of the 1980s, on the insertion of new architecture in urban contexts. During those same years, as we saw in the previous chapter, Valle's concern with representational values of architecture led to intense experimentation with extremely diversified linguistic approaches, calling into play the tools of allusion, memory and analogy to enrich the dialogue with existing urban factors. In parallel to the development of the projects for Venice and New York, Valle had two other prestigious opportunities to demonstrate his fertile willingness to absorb the figurative and structural echoes of complex urban contexts in his architecture: for a school in Berlin, and for a large office complex in Paris, in the Défense district.

In 1983, Valle was invited to take part in a competition organised by the Internationale Bauausstellung (IBA), to design a large elementary school in an empty area near Mehringplatz, Berlin. The competition was part of a programme outlined by Josef Paul Kleihues, director of the IBA, of 'critical reconstruction' of the historic urban structure in one of the most devastated areas of Berlin. One particular emblem of this destruction was Lindenstrasse, originally an urban street converging on the circular plaza of Belle-Alliance-Platz – the focal point of the Baroque trident composition of Südliche Friedrichstadt – which had become a sort of high-speed boulevard after the war, while a small, artificial hill constructed with rubble left by the war represented the only characteristic feature of the plot. Built in 1989–91 in collaboration with Mario Broggi and Michael Burckhardt, the Galilei school on block 606 was one of the few non-residential projects – together with the Jewish Museum designed by Daniel Libeskind – organised by the IBA in this part of the city, which would include residential buildings by Peter Eisenman, Rem Koolhaas, Raimund Abraham, John Hejduk, Herman Hertzberger, Rob Krier and Hans Kollhoff.

Valle's project began with the decision to concentrate the construction on the western part of the area, in order to conserve the small hill on the eastern part. As he had previously done in the Giudecca project, Valle combined conceptual tools of typological rigour and urban memory to generate a planimetric solution, based on the principle of the urban schools of the Wilhelmine era: a small facade on the street from which to access the large built units in the courtyard, arranged as parallel wings of classrooms around two tree-lined courts, while the central part contained an underground gymnasium and collective services. The border

(*left*) Restructuring of the Édouard VII block on Boulevard des Capucines, Paris, 1995–99.
View of one of the inner courtyards.

Elementary School, Berlin, 1983–87, axonometric.

between the constructed parts and the open spaces was precisely defined by replicating an old division line of the land parcels that cut across the area on a diagonal, following the bisector of the corner of Friedrichstrasse and the original Lindenstrasse. This diagonal crossing the area is countered by the access sequence of the school, which constitutes an axis of connection between the two streets: from Friedrichstrasse one enters a small glass tunnel with steps leading to the large entrance hall, where the path continues on a higher level as far as Lindenstrasse, following the slope of the small hill. As in the Giudecca project, the use of a sober repertoire of forms, reduced to a few elements capable of generating a very Berlin-like 'rhythmical essentiality',[1] does not produce excessive rigidity in the repetition, but instead appears to be softened by the emergence of local exceptions, like the portico on the street to the north, or the slight bend in the facade of the main volume to indicate the entrance towards the courtyard.

In Paris, in the modernist Défense district, Valle had to come to grips, instead, with the problems of insertion of large office buildings inside urban fabric, directly returning to a series of themes already explored in the project for the administrative centre in Pordenone. Initially, the client, IBM, hired Valle[2] to design the offices of a new European headquarters inside a building already in an advanced design phase. Faced with the poor architectural quality of the project, Valle suggested to the real estate developer of the operation[3] that the project should be restarted from scratch, replacing the envisioned large 'object' with a system of buildings capable of granting architectural measure to the large scale of the work. Through this proposal, Valle also wanted to react to the difficulty of the urban context: 'La Défense is a chaotic place where you find a series of objects of all kinds ... My first reaction was to do the precise opposite, i.e. to construct a true city piece, recognisable for those walking in this place, conceived as a system of buildings, with true Parisian houses and two ends, approached in my original idea as two castles.'[4]

Elementary School, Berlin, 1983–87, aerial view.

The challenge of building a true 'city piece' at La Défense went well beyond the improvement of an existing design. On the one hand, his gesture seemed to be clearly defensive, with the metaphor of two castles protecting an urban fragment and enclosing it within its haughty isolation. On the other, Valle seemed to indicate the possibility of establishing a precise system of defined rules that would guide the future transformation of the Défense district. So, pessimism and optimism seemed to coexist in the design, not without ambiguity. Valle did not want to choose between two extreme positions – acceptance or denial of the context – and instead tried to shift the terrain of the discussion:

I can do nothing against chaos, and I do not attempt to organize or reassemble the objects of the Défense. I simply try to make the construction have roots. And now that the project is in the construction phase, I see it grow like a sort of Golem that emerges from the ground, that has relations with the real ground, with what lies below it.[5]

IBM office complex and hotel at La Défense, Paris, 1984–88. Perspective from the Esplanade.

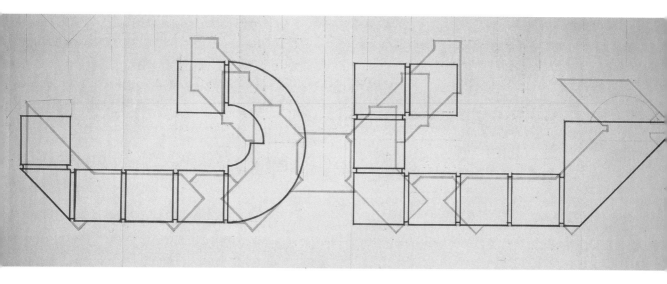

IBM office complex and hotel at La Défense, Paris, 1984–88. Planimetric sketch of the project by Valle (in red) overlaid on the profile of the previous project of SARI (in yellow).

Though it seems paradoxical to speak of 'real ground' in the case of the 'artificial land' of the Défense, this was not simply nostalgia for the constructive rules of the traditional city, because what interested Valle was first of all to be able to 'artificially' reconstruct fragments of a typically urban experience: to walk along porticoes, to pass from one square to another, to perceive the play of light on a stone facade.

Constructing a small 'city piece', the Défense project has significant methodological similarities to the one for the administrative centre of Pordenone, but there are also profound differences. While in Pordenone the regularity – as a condition to generate urban complexity – was manifested as the interpretation of a basic module in different constructed segments, excluding any possible exceptions, in Paris the exceptions open and close the repetitive system of constructed blocks, in the form of the ends – the 'castles' – that undergo a complex process of sculptural shaping. This work on form is manifested in the motifs of swelling of volumes, of crossed entrance arches, the corner turret, or the interruptions and expansions of the cornice: as demonstrated by the varied sequence of

design sketches, these exceptions arise at first as the product of an expressionistic gesture, a formal excess, a break with the rule, and only later do they find a precise formal configuration through the development of a complex geometry.

This particular compositional procedure had already been explored by Valle in previous projects, especially at Giudecca, where figurative motifs like the Venetian carnival 'masks' in front of the terraces were not the result of an a priori desire for image, but emerged almost by chance, found rather than sought, during the slow development of the design. Valle also focused on the use of allusion to historic architecture: it is a Paris more imaginary than real, filtered by memory, to which Valle made reference during the complex task of elaboration of the form. This indirect reference could therefore be freely associated with other memories of favourite works of architecture, from Sullivan to Plečnik, Fabiani to Perret, connected to a 'modernist' tradition of the office building, which Roberto Gabetti has aptly identified in the recognition of a given 'novecentista' tone of the architecture of Valle at La Défense.[6] Faced with the 'majestically urban tone' applied by Valle, Gabetti states his profound admiration, but also his difficulty in describing in precise terms – not only with 'wide metaphors' – an architecture that is so rich in intertwined historical references.[7]

Pierluigi Nicolin wrote an in-depth critical essay in 1989, published in *Lotus International*,[8] on the paradoxical character of Valle's contextualism, bent on evoking the distant architecture of the centre of Paris instead of the immediate context of La Défense, concluding with an interesting question: 'if this project at La Défense is not just a concession to that imperceptible colonization of the present on the part of the "nostalgic manner", but instead rests on more solid foundations, a question arises: what would Gino Valle have proposed on a real boulevard?' The answer was provided a few years later by Valle himself, in two projects developed in parallel in Paris from 1993 to 1998, both for the same private client, Société Générale: the first for the renovation of the building on Avenue Victor-Hugo, discussed in the previous chapter, and the second for the reconstruction of the Édouard VII block and the Olympia theatre on Boulevard des Capucines.

Office building and hotel at La Défense, Paris, 1984–88. View of the ends of the two buildings.

Regarding the first project, we have already shown how the use of 'theatrical' devices and the allusion to a temporal fiction produced a partial character of 'historical fake' and arbitrary language due to the absence of a direct relationship between the new facade and a real building of reference. These problematic aspects are also found in the second project, based on a very different and much more complex strategy of urban transformation. Valle, again working with Macola and Urquijo,[9] was asked to completely reconstruct an entire block in a position of great prestige, where only the outer facades would be conserved, and also to make an underground parking facility in the core of the block for 500 cars and 15 buses. Therefore, this was a project that epitomised the urban strategy known in Paris as '*façadisme*',[10] whose consequences for the conservation of urban heritage have been clearly described by the historian François Loyer: 'It is no longer the monument as such that is protected, but the wrapper of an urban void seen as an inalienable collective asset. While the public space calls for the conservation of the orders and their arrangement, at least in terms of appearance, the private space authorizes a renewal, free of the constraints of the existing building'.[11] Facadism actually conceals a practice with a long tradition in Paris, reactivated after 1989 following the revision of the Master Plan that lowered the floor area ratios: simply by preserving the outer enclosure of a building or a block, it was possible to construct a floor area equal to the existing one, avoiding the new constraints.[12] The Édouard VII block is the result of a complex process of historical stratification that gradually transformed it into a true 'miniature city',[13] containing two historic theatres (Théâtre Édouard VII and the Olympia, Paris's most famous music hall) and an extraordinary private street that penetrates into the heart of the block to increase the linear extension of the facades, in response to the need to host the many rooms of a luxury hotel: Rue Édouard VII, built in 1912 based on a project by Paul-Henri Nénot,[14] which connects Boulevard des Capucines to Rue Caumartin across the octagonal Place Édouard VII. On the level of urban morphology it was necessary to re-create a system of connections and internal crossings to make the whole block permeable, and the solution proposed by Valle featured a sequence of three new 'courts' connected by four new 'passages'. The final solution is a sort of compromise between two extreme positions, the first oriented towards reconstructing a fast-paced fabric of small internal courtyards, the second aimed at creating a single large central void faced by the reconstructed Olympia, obtained following a long, patient operation of excavation clearly represented in a singular sketch by Valle: a collage of the plan of the internal street and the new courtyards with 'four photocopies of the irascible dog drawn by Keith Haring'[15] used to metaphorically devour the heart

Édouard VII block during restructuring.

of the block. At the level of linguistic choices, on
the other hand, Valle called on an architectural
language that rewrites the Beaux-Arts language of
Nénot in a 'minimalist' key, with a refined vertical
arrangement in three parts, underlined by slim
cornices, the use of three types of facing stone
and the gradual reduction in size of the openings,
while a detailed system of terraces and walkways
adds character to the upper levels.

One problematic aspect of the project had to
do with safeguarding heritage, because apart from
the facades on Rue Édouard VII and the square of
the same name, only a few significant architectural
fragments (lobbies, staircases, interiors) were
conserved and restored, leading to a 'caricature
of the envisioned protection and enhancement'.[16]
The intervention in the theatre space of the
Olympia[17] is decidedly more convincing in terms
of historic conservation. As a listed interior it was
reconstructed 'as it was' with balcony, red seats
and black walls, but not 'where it was':[18] the new
position, set back by about thirty metres inside
the area and with a new orientation parallel to Rue
Caumartin, made it possible not only to improve
the stage – expanded and with better access – but
also to make the function of the theatre compatible
with the presence of the underground car park and
access ramps.

In the three projects for Paris, Valle approached,
in different terms, the relationship between
conservation and transformation of the historic
city, with results that can trigger not a few
'objections regarding the ambiguity between
true, plausible and false'.[19] Of the three works, the
Édouard VII block represents the most complex
and most mature experience, and in a certain
sense the least 'theatrical', due to the interior
conservation of the facades in the Beaux-Arts style
on which was based the 'new' architecture, with

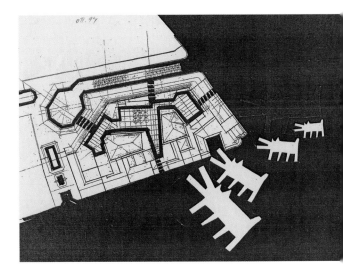

Edouard VII block, collage of the planimetric sketch of
the internal streets of the block with the barking dogs
by Keith Haring, 1999.

subtle play on resemblance and difference, not
unlike what happened in New York in the critical
juxtaposition of the historic facade by Kimball
and the 'critical double' proposed by Valle. It is
also possible to interpret this experience within
a long tradition of interventions of 'critical
reconstruction' of blocks in historic centres
destroyed by war, earthquake or fire, a tradition
also familiar to Valle because he had worked,
from 1980 to 1986, on a series of projects[20] for the
reconstruction of several towns in Friuli destroyed
by the earthquake of 1976. This tradition also
includes the exemplary project by Álvaro Siza,
greatly admired by Valle, for the reconstruction of
the Chiado area in Lisbon (1988–95), marked by an
attitude of great respect and wisdom regarding the
traditional values of the city, translated into a very
rigorous and therefore 'almost invisible' project.[21]

Notes

1   See Rita Cappezzuto, 'La ricostruzione urbana
come scuola. Valle, Broggi, Burckhardt: intervento in
Friedrichstrasse a Berlino', *Lotus International*, 74, November
1992, pp.37–8: 'The precise geometry of the plan corresponds
to the linguistic rigor entrusted to a few elements, in
which we can sense the echo of the architecture of Berlin
of the 1920s and 1930s. The flat, linear fronts, the squared
and regularly paced windows, the single-pitch roofs, the
traditional stucco coating all the exterior masonry with
the exception of the stone base on Friedrichstrasse, which
repeats in the retaining walls and the enclosure of the
garden: thanks to these choices the compositional image
achieves clarity and takes on expressive force without having
to resort to spectacular gestures.'

2   See, ibid., pp.37–8.

3   SARI (Société d'Aménagement Régional Industriel)
was the largest real estate developer for office buildings in
France at the time and had also built many towers in the
Défense district from 1980 to 1989.

4   Pierre-Alain Croset, 'Una conversazione con Gino
Valle', *Casabella*, 519, December 1985, pp.16–17.

5   ibid.

6   Roberto Gabetti, 'Alla Défense c'è Gino Valle', *Atti e
rassegna tecnica della Società Ingegneri e Architetti in Torino*,
11–12, November–December 1990, pp.373–92, reprinted in
Anfione Zeto, 6–7, 1990–91, pp.89–91. In the Parisian project,
Gabetti sees Valle 'directly pick up a Mediterranean
discourse, perhaps also a "*novecento*" discourse, oriented
towards the United States of America', with a certain focus
on the theme of the 'monumental': 'He addresses the
theme of the monumental, keeping it to a minimum, but
without sacrificing that tone that makes "city"; he seems to
remember an Italian tradition he never lived, proposing it
precisely here, to a foreign city.'

7   ibid. Gabetti also mentioned a connection with the
architecture of Otto Wagner, 'not just for certain evident
signs – the black gables of the buildings – but also for that
vitality – vivacity – that great master knew how to give to
the theme of the monumental; where a "modern" building
meant being "organized" in the spaces and functions,
"orderly" in the structures and facades; where a "public"
building meant the convinced force of the administration'.

8   Pierluigi Nicolin, 'Il gioco delle somiglianze, Gino
Valle alla Défense', *Lotus International*, 61, 1989, pp.63–8:
'The apparent contextualism of the project at La Défense is
utterly conceptual, since the evoked boulevard architecture
is contextualized "*in absentia,*" given the fact that the
Parisian boulevards are a few kilometres away, and do
not have porticos.' The essay by Nicolin, though precisely
associating Valle's research with similar experimentation
of Stirling and Ungers, as well as Siza and Eisenman,
nevertheless seems to lack prudence in its interpretation

of the Parisian project as proof of a 'second manner' of
Valle. The statement that 'the Parisian project, for the first
time, puts Gino Valle on the terrain of ideology and the
architectural manifesto' also seems very tendentious and
ungrounded.

9   The progress of this commission actually went
through a much more complex itinerary, because at first
Société Générale had assigned the project, in 1989, to the
Parisian architect Anthony Béchu, a specialist in '*façadisme*'
and major real estate operations involving historical
constraints. After an interruption of three years, in 1993 the
client combined Béchu with the trio Valle-Macola-Urquijo,
encountered in the past for other projects, in particular at
La Défense, to bring greater prestige to a very complex and
avowedly speculative real estate operation.

10   The so-called '*façadisme*' ('facadism' in English)
is defined by the International Council on Monuments
and Sites (ICOMOS) as intervention on historic buildings
'gutted in their interiors or … the entire structure other
than the facade is demolished to allow for a new modern
building to be erected behind it, beside it and above it'.

11   François Loyer, 'Le patrimoine. Évolution et enjeux
du Plu de Paris', *Monumental*, 14 (Le façadisme), September
1996, pp.147–66. Loyer cites among the first prestigious
projects of 'façadisme' in modern Paris the headquarters of
Société Générale on Boulevard Haussmann, which behind
the conserved historic facades was completely gutted and
reconstructed in 1905 with a metal structure.

12   In the case of the Édouard VII block the difference
was estimable, because in the case of demolition-
reconstruction without conserving the external facades the
permitted area would have been much less.

13   A precise reconstruction of the complex story of
the block, together with in-depth critique of the project,
is offered by Marc Bédarida, 'La città simulata, tra
restituzione e finzione', *Lotus International*, 103, December
1999, pp.6–11.

14   Paul-Henri Nénot, winner in 1927 of the
competition for the Palace of Nations and as such a
historic enemy of Le Corbusier, demonstrates great
mastery of the compositional knowledge of his academic
background in this operation.

15   This extraordinary sketch with Haring's famous
'barking dog' also seems to hint at a zoomorphic form
in the figure of the four concatenated courtyards. Sketch
and quotation from Valle published in: 'Sandro Marpillero
intervista Gino Valle da New York', *Lotus Navigator*,
monograph, Gino Valle, 1, November 2000, p.88.

16   Marc Bédarida, 'La città simulata', p.8: 'A more than
debatable solution, this selective choice of conserving
certain elements *in situ*, moving others and destroying the
rest, formed the basis for the compromise that permitted
restitution of part of the particular characteristics of the
site.'

(*right*) **Restructuring of the Édouard VII block on
Boulevard des Capucines, Paris, 1995–99. View
of the inner courtyard facade.**

17   The Olympia theatre was opened in 1893 and
entirely reconstructed in the 1930s. It was listed in the
Inventory of Cultural Assets in 1993 at the time of the
centennial of its founding.

18   Regarding this reconstruction in another position,
Valle says he remembered the Japanese Shinto temples of
Ise 'where every twenty years a new building is constructed
next to the previous one, which is then demolished ...
I have restored the cycle of transformations of the site,
regenerating its meaning and moving the elements to
promote a new quality of the spaces'.

19   Alessandro Rocca, 'Valle ultimo. Fabbriche, uffici
e frammenti di città', *Lotus Navigator*, monograph, Gino
Valle, 1, 2000, p.21.

20   These projects of true 'identical reconstruction' or
'allusive reconstruction' were based on the visual memory
of the inhabitants – as in the most significant case, a large
block in Gemona designed on the basis of the memories of
Alfredo Carnelutti and a few period postcards.

21   Faced with criticism of his design attitude,
deemed 'too conservative' by many observers, Siza
responded that it was imposed by the particular urban
context of the Baixa Pombaliana, born as a regular part
of the city after the earthquake of 1755, and subject to
interpretation as 'a single prefabricated building ... based
on very precise drawings in terms of the sizes of the
facades, the modules, the rhythms, etc. ... Therefore it is
difficult to take advantage of a fire to be able to reinsert
a building with the language of the 19th century, but to
insert a contemporary building, with its own formal and
fashionable tics, in such a uniform context is an absurd
idea.' See Antonio Angelillo, 'Il piano di ricostruzione del
Chiado. Conversazione con Álvaro Siza', *Casabella*, 628,
November 1995, p.28. On the Chiado project, see also the
essay by Gonçalo Byrne, 'Lisbona: una città vulnerabile.
Il Chiado di Alvaro Siza', *Lotus International*, 64, 1990,
pp.33–7.

Building for Offices and a Hotel at La Défense

Paris, 1984–88

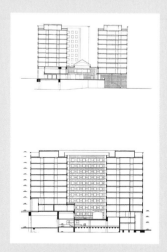

Cross-sections.

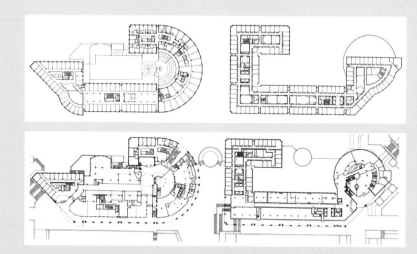

(*top*) Standard floor plan; (*bottom*) ground floor plan.

The complex formed by two buildings is located on the lower part of the Esplanade that forms the central axis of the Défense district. It borders the south front of a tree-lined avenue that constitutes the only truly urban space of the neighbourhood. Already, from a distance, one clearly perceives the subdivision of the complex into multiple 'houses' whose rhythm evokes that of a Parisian 'boulevard', while the masonry stands out for the two colours of the stone: the top in polished porphyry that reflects the sky. Walking along the Esplanade towards the centre of Paris, from a distance one discovers the end of the office building, bent at 45 degrees, with a large opening formed by two crossed arches. Approaching, the portico with shops leads along the offices. At a small plaza placed between the volume of the offices and the round facade of the hotel, the space is compressed to encourage the observer to turn the corner and descend to the lower plaza, with a shift in level of three floors. From the lower plaza the complex can be seen at its most imposing, with the rear of the offices facing a raised courtyard.

The large arched openings in the end of the office building and the opposite end towards Paris clearly mark the main entrances. Inside the hall of the office facility, one finds a large space organised on three visually connected levels: looking down, the entrance atrium at the level of the underground street can be seen, along with the overhang of the oval auditorium supported by pairs of pillars. The vertical access routes extend around the triangular void and are divided in terms of users: a reserved cylindrical lift between the hall and the lobby of the lower entrance, staircases and escalators along a wall in pink stone offering access to the dining hall on the lower level, and to the mezzanine of the conference rooms on the upper level. All the offices are closed and accessed by means of a double corridor, with a central band containing staircases, lifts, restrooms and small meeting rooms. Walking down the long corridors, one clearly perceives the passage from one block to the next, marked by the possibility of looking outward through the double glass that encloses the ventilation shafts.

The IBM building seen from the Esplanade towards La Défense.

Detail of the portico at the corner of the IBM offices.

Édouard VII block and Reconstruction of the Olympia Theatre

Paris, 1995–99

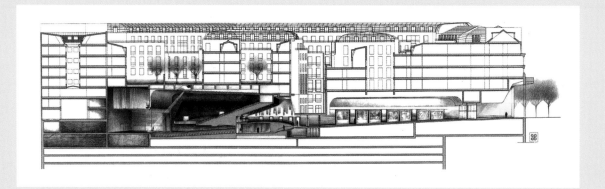

Longitudinal section of the Olympia theatre.

The block is located in the historic centre of Paris, along the Grands Boulevards, near La Madeleine, Opéra Garnier and Place Vendôme. The renovation project addressed a complex programme of almost 70,000 square metres of area, including offices, shops, apartments, a hotel, the relocation and reconstruction of the Olympia theatre, as well as an underground parking facility for 500 cars and 15 buses. The block is crossed by Rue Édouard VII, which leads into the octagonal Place Édouard VII and then continues, bending towards Rue Caumartin. This historic crossing, along which the fine neoclassical facades from the early 20th century have been completely restored, is now enhanced by another pedestrian route through new courtyards connected by covered 'passages'.

Penetrating the block, one finds a true 'miniature city' that offers a range of different perspectives and spatial experiences. While the route along Rue Édouard VII evokes the character of a classic Parisian 19th-century street – with a rigorously repetitive order of the facades, marked by the portals of two-storey windows and continuous balconies – the crosswise and longitudinal paths through the new courtyards offer a less linear and more secret experience, marked by sudden compressions and expansions of the urban space.

Access to the Olympia theatre is also organised as an urban itinerary. From Boulevard des Capucines a large opening, three storeys high, encourages entry to a long covered 'passage' that descends on a slight slope as far as the foyer, introduced by a short compression due to the presence at the upper level of the 'Passage Caumartin'. The two-storey foyer leads to the access ways for the hall of the Olympia, reconstructed exactly as it was, with the characteristic red colour of the seats and the facings: walking down a large flight of steps one reaches the main seating area, while the balconies are reached by ascending steps at the sides of the hall.

Access to the underground parking area for 15 buses is provided by a ramp from Boulevard des Capucines: at level -6, a circular plaza under Place Édouard VII permits movement of the buses and offers the possibility of parking four trucks directly beside the stage. The five garage levels are deeper still (from -9 to -19), with their own access ramp descending along the edge of the lot, at the meeting point of Rue Édouard VII and Rue Caumartin.

View of the inner courtyard.

View of Rue Édouard VII.

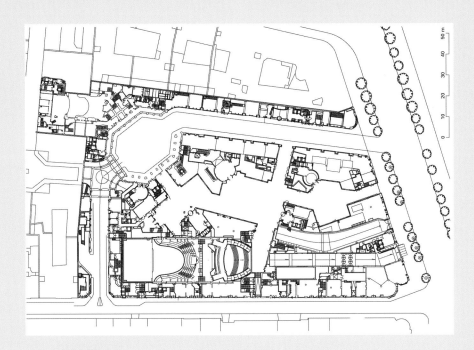

Plan of the complex.

12 Urban Design and Public Buildings (1984–2003)

In parallel to the development of the project for La Défense in Paris, in 1984 Valle began to work in the city of Padua on the creation of a new courthouse. This was an opportunity to apply both architecture and urban planning to improve a large area of the city previously occupied by a railyard and partially abandoned industrial facilities, between the Fair to the east, the railroad to the north and Via Niccolò Tommaseo to the south. Valle developed a 'guideline plan' that could function as a variant of the Master Plan, within which to place the new courthouse. In a peripheral context seen by Valle as 'chaotic and unrecognisable', his idea was to organise a new structure of blocks that could form the urban backdrop for the large public facility, in relation to the only monument of any interest: the Tempio della Pace, a World War I memorial built in 1920–34. The orientation of the Tempio della Pace, rotated with respect to Via Niccolò Tommaseo, became the axis of the new urban design proposed by Valle, with a 'boulevard' traced on the longitudinal axis of the temple and the new blocks parallel to it. To include the large volume required by the programme in this urban composition, Valle decided to break up the courthouse into two parts: the central semi-cylindrical nucleus, five storeys high, with the straight side facing the railway, and a lower perimeter volume, just three storeys, paced by a sequence of 'houses' and following the street boundaries, with a bevelled corner to form a

triangular entrance plaza at the intersection of Via Niccolò Tommaseo and Via Goldoni. After having already outlined this planimetric device at the end of 1984, Valle developed many variations to sharpen the formal expression of the facades, studying in particular the relationship of scale between the almost 'domestic' character of the 'houses' of the low perimeter volume and the 'monumental' presence of the semi-cylindrical body.[1] One particular problem was that of the entrance, which imposed a frontal view of the semi-cylinder starting from the small plaza. Valle's research on this theme is well documented by a fine sequence of sketches based precisely on this frontal perspective. Valle realised that it was necessary to introduce an element of mediation and transition between the plaza and the monumental rounded volume: a circular courtyard, offering a pleasant threshold of transition between the public space of the plaza and the interior of the building, reprises 'on a surprising "intimate" scale the circular geometries that marked the entire complex'.[2]

Finally completed in 1993,[3] the courthouse of Padua demonstrates Valle's ability to insert a 'large form' inside an overall urban design, with a quality of scale decisively sustained by the refined treatment of the stone cladding, both in the choice of two colours for the stone and in the arrangement of the slabs with deep, slender joints that suggest a motif of 'rustication'. The complex definitive development

(*left*) New courthouse of Brescia, 1986–2004. View towards the historic centre, with the cathedral and the castle.

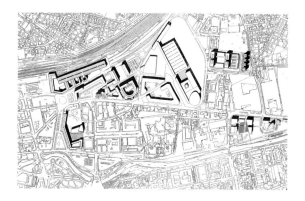

Guideline plan for the urban reorganisation of
the territory between the Fair, the railroad and Via
Antonio Grassi in Padua, 1990–95.

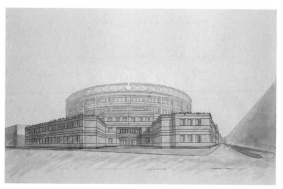

Courthouse of Padua, 1984–90. Perspective of
a project variant.

of the architectural expression was influenced
not just by Valle's parallel work on the project at
La Défense, but also by his deep interest in the
contemporary work of James Stirling, especially for
the Staatsgalerie of Stuttgart[4] opened in 1984.

So, the Padua courthouse represents further
proof of Valle's interest, in the 1980s, in the
relationship between architecture and urban
design, as already emphasised in the previous
chapters regarding the projects for Pordenone,
Venice, Paris and Berlin. Though developed during
the same years, the projects for the complex at
La Défense and for Padua applied very different
methodological tools: in Paris, the idea of building
a 'city piece' was manifested above all in the
transformation of a 'large object' into a 'system
of buildings' and in the choice of an architectural
language capable of evoking a more fabulous
than real 'Parisian tradition', while in Padua the
construction of a large public building had to take
on the value of an act of foundation capable of
orienting all the future development of a part of
the city. In the late 1980s, Valle was commissioned
to propose realistic images and concrete scenarios
of transformation for abandoned industrial areas,
zones beside railways and the interspaces of the
urban periphery in medium-sized Italian cities
like Vicenza, Ivrea, Florence, Parma and Bergamo.
This activity, approached more 'as an architect'

than 'as an urban planner', was influenced by new
ways of thinking about planning processes which
Bernardo Secchi and Giuseppe Campos Venuti had
proposed in those years as characteristics of an
'urbanism of the third generation':[5] in a cycle of
urban transformation no longer based on growth
but on internal renewal of the existing city, new
tools were applied to focus on the need to associate
planning hypotheses with a more precise definition
of the morphology and architectural image of
the types of intervention envisioned. Though his
analysis stopped at the year 1985, and therefore did
not cover the significant case of the courthouse in
Padua, in the second part of his *History of Italian
Architecture 1944–1985*, Manfredo Tafuri clearly
revealed that the most recent work of Valle, and in
particular the projects for Venice, New York and
Paris, should be interpreted in the context of the
progressive rise in European design culture of a
thread of research that focused on the 'concepts
of place, context, modification, re-knitting and
relation between intervention and the surrounding
conditions, of (typological and morphological)
continuity'.[6] He therefore recognised, in these latest
works by Valle, a 'new manner of great interest,
also from a methodological standpoint', marked
by particular interests in 'the large scale, urban
issues, the inclusion of figurative echoes in relation
to the context, an open-minded relationship

Courthouse of Padua, 1984–90, plan and view of the southern facade of the
building at the position of the entrance from Via Tommaseo.

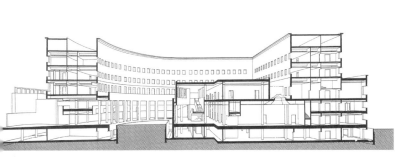

Longitudinal perspective section
of the entrance.

Southern facade: detail of the
entrance, courtyard.

PROGETTO BICOCCA   GINO VALLE

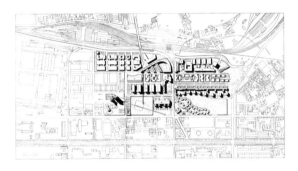

Competition project for the Bicocca area, overall plan, second phase, 1988.

between "large form" and open seams'.[7] Without discerning unitary positions in the Italian debate on the relationship between architecture and planning, Tafuri nevertheless identified a specific contribution of Valle with respect to the large scale, to be seen in relation to the work of Vittorio Gregotti, which appeared to be 'among the few equipped to respond to the problems raised by the new emerging themes of cities and territories in transformation'.[8]

In spite of these shared interests regarding urban design and the relations between architecture and urbanism, in 1985, Valle and Gregotti[9] found themselves in direct competition in the international consultation for a 'multifunctional and integrated technological centre' in the Bicocca area in Milan[10] organised by Pirelli for the regeneration of over seventy hectares of land occupied by production facilities. The competition, set up and supervised by Bernardo Secchi, in two phases, involved the invitation in September 1985 of twelve international and eight Italian designers,[11] making this one of the most important competitions held in Italy in the second half of the 20th century. In March 1986 the jury,[12] chaired by Leopoldo Pirelli, announced the winners of the first phase: three Italian projects, respectively by Gabetti and Isola, Gregotti Associati, and Gino Valle.

The project submitted by Gino Valle appealed to the jury for its 'great compositional elegance, the clarity of the overall arrangement … the flexibility

and realism'.[13] Faced with the very elaborate conceptual-analytical formulation of the project by Gregotti and the intense poetic invention unleashed by the ideas of Gabetti and Isola, Valle's proposal might even appear to be too realistic and 'prudent' with the statement that

this project of the Bicocca conserves its character as a piece of the city that has already narrated a mutation and requires no other revolutions, but simply adjustments that can be proposed in time and space through individual places on a precise scale, immediately identifiable and manageable, making it already a concrete thing that does not imply indeterminate expectations, sketched out futures.[14]

Interested only in 'making things' – the real things of architecture – Valle based his project on maintaining the intervention inside its land limits, urging the necessity of restoring the physical isolation of the Bicocca with respect to the context: 'What needs to be done is to give the Bicocca back its wall', Valle continues in the project statement, 'which can continue to narrate, without metaphors, the history of what is there, what already exists, and what will soon be there.' The guiding idea of the project, the new 'wall' of which Valle spoke, was a dense park of 860 × 165 metres, along the entire strip that divides the Bicocca from the urban frontage on the other side of Viale Sarca. The park, designed by Ippolito Pizzetti, was not conceived as an 'urban garden' but as a 'forest' in which the trees could 'grow freely, in keeping with their natural rhythms: for those who frequent the technological city of our nearest future', Pizzetti continues in the statement, 'alongside the rhythm of work, the alternation of day and night, the presence of the continuous biological clock that is contained inside the trees, the time of always, which we hope can last, in the trees, for centuries'.[15] Thanks to this astute move, Valle was able to approach the theme of urban 're-knitting' in unorthodox terms.

The second phase of the competition came two years later, on the basis of a more precise

(*left*) Competition project for the Bicocca area, axonometric, second phase, 1988.

functional outline dictated by the variation of the Master Plan approved in May 1987, although large spaces were still set aside for requirements of flexibility over time, for the market and for the technical implementation, which Pirelli considered necessary to ensure concrete feasibility of the project.[16] In the reworking of the project Valle clearly specified the architectural image. Going beyond the generic quality of the previous design, he established clear relationships between the settlement principle and the typological definition of the individual works of architecture entrusted with the character of the places of the project. This wealth and variety of architectural solutions deployed in the Bicocca area harked back to many of the formal themes explored by Valle in the most recent years, so much so that the project can be interpreted as a true anthology of 'architectural pieces' assembled to form a unique urban 'composition'.

Although he did not win the competition, Valle soon had other opportunities to demonstrate his mastery of urban design and his ability to create a meaningful dialogue between different 'architectural fragments'. The first such chance was the international competition for a museum complex on the site of the former Imperial Stables in Vienna,[17] in 1987. Here Valle made the strategy of functional subdivision applied in the Bicocca project more radical, setting up a true 'collection' of building types behind the long palace of Fischer von Erlach that functions as a monumental facade of the complex beside the Ring, on axis with the Hofburg. The architectural design of the individual fragments reflected precise relationships with the various elements of the context, making the montage of all the fragments reveal the complicated historical stratification of the area.

Shortly before this, in 1986, Valle was invited to Brescia to design the new courthouse in that city, which marked the beginning of a complex project, perhaps the longest and most troubled of his career. As in Vienna, Valle had to come to terms with a site of great historical importance, the Spalti San Marco in the southeastern quadrant of the circle of the old Venetian walls. After the demolition of the fortifications at the end of the 19th century, this site had never lost its status as a border of the historical city, hosting the new municipal slaughterhouse in correspondence with the positioning of a series of public facilities along the planned 'Ring' of Brescia. The design challenge of reconciling the very large gross floor area of over 50,000 square metres with a site packed with existing historical features was brilliantly met by Valle[18] through the proposal to build a true 'city part' instead of a mere 'office complex'. In the projects for Pordenone and La Défense, Valle had already broken up the very large built volume required by the programme by organising it in

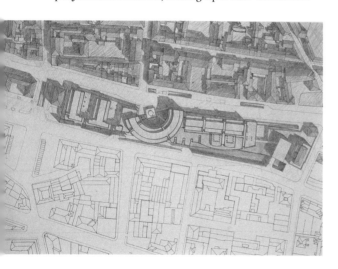

Courthouse of Brescia, first project on the Spalti San Marco, 1986.

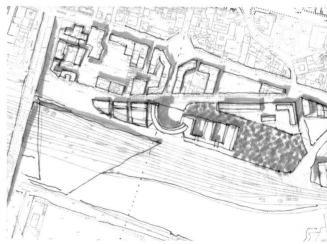

Courthouse of Brescia, second project on the area of the former produce market along the railroad, 1996.

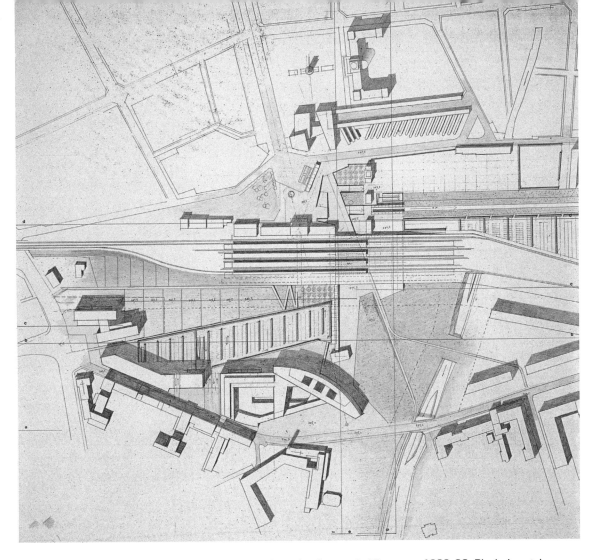

Area plan and urban project for the areas of the 'southern development' of Bergamo, 1988–96. Planivolumetric.

different constructed parts, to create a complexity of relations similar to that of typical urban formations. In Brescia, however, he introduced an important new feature: while in the earlier projects the 'system of buildings' was based on a principle of repetition and regularity, the 'urban complexity' of the system was expressed this time in the architectural heterogeneity of individual 'houses', corresponding to clear differentiation of the functional parts and to precise contextual relationships.

Seen by Valle as a metaphor for all design activity,[19] the work of 'excavation' seemed to be emphasised in Brescia: a complex architecture of walls, ditches, ramps, bases, irregularly cut out and covered in stone, contributes to evoke the image of fragments of an ancient city on which the new 'city piece' would grow. The materials used – Botticino marble and brick – were also intended to evoke a typical local tradition of construction, though without any imitation or nostalgia.

After a complicated process to obtain approval and funds for the project, the work began in 1990 with demolition and excavation for the foundations, but was soon interrupted due to the discovery of archaeological remains. In 1992 the

Ministry of Culture blocked any suggestion of resuming the work, listing it as a heritage site.[20] At this point it was very important for the city government to quickly find another area on which to build the courthouse, so as to avoid losing the state funds already set aside for the project.[21] The new area was selected by Bernardo Secchi in 1996, at the time of the development of the new Master Plan of Brescia: the site of the former fruit and vegetable market on Via Gambara, close to the railway, which had the advantages of proximity to the historic centre and the station, as well as certain similarities to the previous project area, due to its long, narrow form.[22] Valle had to explore the concrete possibility, in a series of sketches, of 'recycling' his previous design, a necessary condition so as not to lose funding.[23] Valle skilfully overturned the original figure in a specular way: using the central semicircle as a pivot for the composition, concluding the urban axis of Via Ferramola leading towards the historic centre, Valle placed the linear volume of the courthouse in the narrowest part to the west of the site, while he shifted the parallel wings of the three crosswise blocks against a high wall to the east, aligning them with a new pedestrian axis parallel to the railway. After approval of the definitive project in October 1998 by the Board of Public Works, ensuring the continuation of state financing, Valle had to work for almost four more years on the preparation of the final project, to respond to demands for modifications and additions formulated by the various judiciary departments. After having obtained additional funding to cover the expenses of an increase of over 8,000 square metres of floor space, the City of Brescia finally submitted the definitive project in 2002; construction was very fast, and by January 2004 the finished building was delivered to the City. Nevertheless, five more years passed before the Ministry of Justice financed and realised the complementary works required to make the courthouse fully operative in July 2009.

It took 23 years to complete a work the city of Brescia had been expecting for over fifty years: a very long time period, covering the terms of seven mayors and 16 Ministers of Justice, but also a timespan in which it was possible to verify the 'long term' efficacy of Valle's architectural ideas based on the principle of representing the process of historical stratification specific to the site in a complex volumetric figure. On the new site at Via Gambara, it therefore seemed difficult, a priori, for the same volumetric figure, though overturned in a specular way, to maintain its urban meaning. Yet in the view of the constructed work of architecture, above all if one knows nothing about the complex history of the project, the building actually communicates a sense of belonging to the place with great force, of its condition at the borderline between the historic centre and the neighbourhoods of postwar expansion to the south of the railway. The principle of suggestion of the historical walls, embodied by the base in Botticino marble erected on the southern front to form the blind ends of the office 'wings', paradoxically takes on a value of greater truth on this site than on the original site of the Spalti San Marco, because on the overall scale of the city today the large void of the railway takes on the function of separation between the centre and the outskirts once performed by the Venetian walls. The increased volume, on the other hand, turned out to be more problematic, because the added height has decisively reinforced the contrast of scale with the historic fabric, not just in the 'houses' of the offices, but also in the semicircle that has perhaps become excessively monumental, looming as many as three levels above the other parts of the complex.[24]

In Brescia, as in Padua, the project of large public building was therefore approached by Valle in apparently anti-monument terms, or more precisely in pursuit of a relative alleviation of the impact of monumental forms – the semi-cylinder in Padua, the large rotated hemicycle in Brescia – through the construction of an 'urban fabric' of 'houses' for the offices. Valle used the same design strategy in a subsequent project for a judicial facility – the competition project for the International Tribunal for the Law of the Sea in Hamburg (1990) – although in this case the character of the site was closer to landscape than to urban settlement, inside the park of the Elbe riverfront on the western outskirts of the

Project for the International Tribunal of the Law of the Sea, Hamburg, 1990; (*top*) perspective view of the internal street; (*bottom*) sections.

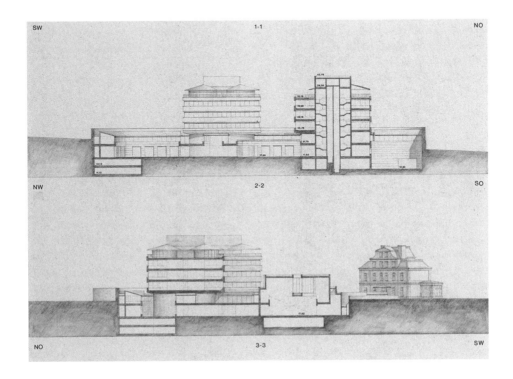

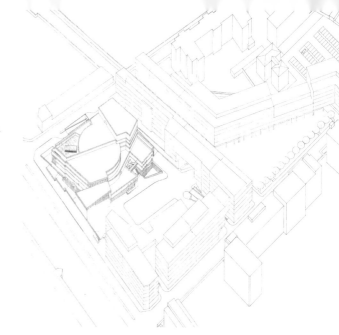

Municipal Theatre, Vicenza, 1985–2007, axonometric of the whole complex according to the detail plan by Valle, never implemented: the recessed plaza against the theatre is enclosed in the project, by the frontage of offices.

city. Valle proposed enhancement of the prestigious site, marked also by the presence of a fine neoclassical villa, with a composition of three 'urban villas' rotated to offer the best views of the river.

Starting in 1992 in Bergamo, Valle approached a particularly complex situation, proposing an extension beyond the barrier of the railway of the north–south axis that connects Porta San Giacomo to Porta Nuova and terminates at the station, together with the urban design of a large area along the land abandoned by the railway yard. Before working in Brescia, Bernardo Secchi had worked in Bergamo, from 1993 to 1995, for the preparation of the new Master Plan, when he invited Valle to refine his design hypotheses inside a 'guideline plan' entitled 'Il Nuovo Sentierone'[25] that called for resizing of the gross floor areas permitted in the previous Master Plan, and creation of a new 'centre' straddling the area of the station. A new courthouse had to be inserted in the urban design, a facility of large size, though slightly smaller than the one in Brescia, prompting Valle to again propose a configuration of the building as a small 'city piece' with volumes of variable form and size, arranged in a complex figure.[26]

We began this chapter with the urban consulting activity of Valle in the city of Padua, which led to the preparation of a 'guideline plan' inside which the new courthouse, completed in 1993, was inserted. In 1994 Valle developed a new 'guideline plan' that expanded the initial hypotheses along the entire urban axis of Via Niccolò Tommaseo, to the point of including new blocks in the western end towards the railroad station, as well as a proposal for the redesign of the area of the Fair facility to the east of Via Goldoni.

Continuing eastward, the plan defined the settlement rules of the new university centre located between Via Venezia, extending the axis of Via Niccolò Tommaseo, and the promenade along the Piovego River. As had already happened with the courthouse, Valle developed the architectural design of the four new buildings of the campus inside an overall urban design based on recognition of two different orientations: while the perimeters of the four buildings extend the axes of existing streets outward, on the inside they surround a square plaza positioned parallel to the river. Therefore, this was

a very interesting opportunity for Valle to make all the buildings that formed a unified public space. The individual buildings were then given a precise image and typological organisation, to respond to highly varied functional specifications. The presence of two grids in the project – the urban grid and the 'landscape' grid of the river – rotated by 15 degrees with respect to each other, was skilfully used by Valle to significantly enhance the architectural expression of the first building to be constructed, the Department of Psychology 2, completed in 1998: in keeping with the compositional procedure behind the urban figure, Valle skilfully eroded the volume of the building, especially on the southern side facing the plaza, where a two-storey portico is cut into the corner, while the facade is set back above the fourth floor, at the position of the library on the two upper levels of the building. To reinforce the perception of the volume as the result of excavation, Valle decided to paint the base black, making the upper levels seem to float over the ground when seen from a distance. On the north side towards Via Venezia, the sculptural treatment of the volume takes the form of crossed double fire staircases, a clear tribute to the Palazzo delle Poste by Libera[27] on Via Marmorata in Rome (1933–34). The two buildings that complete the front along Via Venezia present slight variations of the same language, rigorously organised with a base, an elevation and a top: while the Linguistics Centre at the eastern end resembles the Department of Psychology 2 due to the fenestration and the same double staircases at the centre of the facade, the Convention Centre in the middle has more differentiation, with the high windowless base that contains the auditorium with seating for 500 persons. In its appearance as a volume horizontally split into two parts, the Convention Centre conveys the stacking of the functions, with the three upper floors of offices hung with tie-rods from the roof structure, suspended over the large void of the hall. The Students' Centre concludes the south side of the plaza with a volume composed of two buildings enhanced by different variations of height, orientation and openings, and by the presence of a high portico that offers a view from the plaza towards the Piovego River.

During the years of work in Padua, Valle was asked to intervene with the same design method in the city of Vicenza, though in a less intensive context. In 1985 he developed a series of Detail Plans for the renewal of the so-called 'west shoulder', directly up against the historical centre, with the aim of reconnecting a very heterogeneous urban fabric composed of jagged blocks and abandoned industrial areas. Though this work of urban design led to few concrete results due to lack of political resolve and poor programming, it was very positive for Valle, as it gave him the opportunity to design the new civic theatre which the city of Vicenza had been lacking for over forty years following the destruction in World War II of Teatro Eretenio and Teatro Verdi.[28] The new theatre was included in the Detail Plan 6 ('Gresele'), at the intersection of Viale Mazzini and Via dei Cairoli, in a context of prestige due to the presence of a well-preserved portion of the historic fortifications. To reduce the visual impact of the new structure, and in particular the impact of the fly tower, establishing a harmonious relationship with the historic walls, Valle proposed a recessed internal plaza beside the theatre in the core

of an urban block open towards Viale Mazzini. Valle thus confirmed his 'anti-monumental' approach, also seen in the projects for the courthouses of Padua and Brescia, assigning the architecture of the large public building a role of 'accompaniment' and 'civil dialogue' with the urban fabric and the existing historical features. An initial rough project, presented in 1989, established the layout principles of the theatre organism, which remained the same in the constructed building: a hall with an ovoid plan in a single sloped space, a fly tower placed on the side furthest from Viale Mazzini, a foyer facing the view of the Scaligere historic walls, and a long volume on Via dei Cairoli with dressing rooms for the artists. Once the overall organisation had been defined, Valle conducted patient research on the form, leading to significant changes in the volumetric arrangement, attenuating the usually disproportionate relationship between the theatre hall and the stage.[29] The building now seems like a single skilfully sculpted mass, with alternating straight and curved cuts that gently absorb the height differences. This image of a sculpted block is underlined by the particular cladding in brick and white Vicenza stone, evoking the physical character of the nearby fortifications, but without imitating them.

Municipal Theatre, Vicenza, 1985–2007, view of the building from Via Bonollo through the arch of the Scaligeri historic Walls.

Notes

1   For a precise analysis of the building and the project history see Marco De Michelis, 'Gino Valle. Nuovo palazzo di Giustizia di Padova', *Domus*, 785, September 1996, pp.30–36.

2   ibid., p.36. The author continues with an evocative description of the final planimetric figure: 'the low volume was divided into two asymmetrical jaws of a clamp that opened at the position of the entrance on the bisector of the corner'.

3   Construction began in 1986 and was completed only in 1993, after two interruptions in 1988–89 and 1991–92. Two more years were required, nevertheless, to complete the furnishings and the interiors, finally allowing the facility to open in 1995.

4   More evident than in the built solution, many intermediate sketches reveal Valle's interest in specific compositional solutions as applied by Stirling in the Staatsgalerie, Stuttgart, in particular, the use of overhanging cornices and segmented arches in the low volume. The drum was also treated in all the intermediate variations in a way similar to Stirling's solution, with stone cladding up to the top; only in the final version did Valle decide to introduce an upper band of white concrete and a slender cornice, a solution that clearly distances itself from the language used by Stirling.

5   Bernardo Secchi asserts that in the plans of the third generation 'the urbanist is led to address the conditions of his project in terms of modifications of existing situations or interstitial spaces with a character of strong specificity in themselves or at their margins'. See 'Piani della terza generazione', *Casabella*, 516, September 1985, reprinted in Bernardo Secchi, *Un progetto per l'urbanistica*, Piccola Biblioteca Einaudi, Turin, 1989, pp.112–16.

6   Manfredo Tafuri, *Storia dell'architettura italiana 1944–1985*, Piccola Biblioteca Einaudi, Turin, 1986, p.208. Tafuri continued by stating that these were 'themes very similar to those at the center of attention of the "plans of the third generation". The scale of the analysis and the proposals may vary – though not always – and above all the testing of the hypotheses is translated into self-testing, as is logical for any architecture.'

7   ibid., p.212.

8   ibid., p.210.

9   The relations between Gregotti and Valle, for over thirty years, were always marked by the highest mutual esteem. After having met him at the CIAM summer school in Venice in 1952, Gregotti supported Valle's work in his writings and activities, first in Rogers' *Casabella* (1953–63), then as editor of *Edilizia Moderna* (1963–67) and *Casabella* (1982–96), but also as director of the Venice Biennale in 1976, when he invited Valle to design exhibitions of art and architecture, and as the director of architecture exhibitions at the Padiglione di Arte Contemporanea in Milan, when he organised the retrospective exhibition 'Gino Valle architetto 1950–1978' (16 May – 30 June 1979).

10   The competition is fully documented in Bernardo Secchi (ed.), *Progetto Bicocca. Concorso internazionale di progettazione urbanistica e architettonica ideato e realizzato per iniziativa dalle industrie Pirelli*, exh. cat., Triennale di Milano (14 June – 28 September 1986), Electa, Milan, 1986.

11   The foreign designers, one from each country, were Tadao Ando, Mario Botta, Henri Ciriani, Frank O. Gehry, Joaquim Guedes, Herman Hertzberger, Richard Meier, Rafael Moneo, Gustav Peichl, Justo Solsona, James Stirling and Oswald Mathias Ungers, while the Italians, apart from Gregotti and Valle, were Gae Aulenti, Carlo Aymonino, Giancarlo De Carlo, Roberto Gabetti and Aimaro Isola, Renzo Piano and Aldo Rossi.

12   The jury, which met from 23 to 27 March 1986, was composed of representatives of Industrie Pirelli SPA (besides Leopoldo Pirelli, the CEO Gavino Manca), of the upper ranks of local administrations (the mayor of Milan, Carlo Tognoli; the president of the Province of Milan, Ezio Riva; the president of the Lombardy Region, Giuseppe Guzzetti), Italian experts in the field of socio-economic research (Mario Monti, then a professor of Political Economics at Bocconi University; Giuseppe Dematteis, professor of Geography at Turin Polytechnic; Giuseppe De Rita, director of Censis), an urbanist (Bernardo Secchi) and two of the most influential postwar architectural historians (Reyner Banham and Manfredo Tafuri).

13   Bernardo Secchi, Report of the Jury, *Progetto Bicocca*, p.305.

14   Gino Valle, Project Description, ibid., p.271.

15   Ippolito Pizzetti, Project Description, ibid., p.273.

16   This can effectively be seen in Bicocca today, which displays modifications, though not substantial ones, with respect to what was prescribed in 1987 in the winning project by Gregotti Associati: over time more than 20,000 square metres of cooperative housing were added in an area initially set aside for open space, and the triangular plot of Via Cozzi, which was to host a convention centre, was converted in 1996, by initiative of the city, into a space for a new theatre, Teatro degli Arcimboldi. For a reconstruction of the complex history of the project, see Vittorio Gregotti and A. Cagnardi (eds), *Progetto Bicocca, 1985–1998*, Skira, Milan, 1999.

17   On the results of this important international competition, considered 'scandalous' and 'provincial', see Dietmar Steiner, 'Un valzer viennese', *Casabella*, 544, March 1988, pp.18–27.

18   Though very critical of the administration's choice of this location, Leonardo Benevolo recognised that 'the contrast between the program and the limitations of the site has been resolved by the performance of the designer, who has managed to achieve a positive balance between sacrifices and achievements'. See Leonardo Benevolo, 'Brescia: prospettive di politica urbana', *Casabella*, 548, July–August 1988, p.21.

19   Regarding the project at La Défense, Valle significantly stated that 'when I begin a project I start

(*right*) Competition project for a museum complex in the area of the Imperial Stables, Vienna, 1987.

to scratch around the place. And with experience, I have learned more and more how to have a nose for scratching, like a dog that finds truffles. I scratch until I find something, as if I were extracting it from the ground.' See Pierre-Alain Croset, 'Una conversazione con Gino Valle', *Casabella*, 519, December 1985, pp.16–17.

20   After this listing the area was set aside, in keeping with a proposal of Italia Nostra, as an archaeological park named for the Memorial of the Twin Towers Attack in Manhattan.

21   If the work was not built, the city would have had to reimburse the funds already invested, including interest, and would also have lost the grant funding, leading to a loss of municipal funds of about 28 billion lire (approx. 14 million euros). See *Corriere della Sera*, 22 April 1993.

22   The new area was larger than the original zone (over 31,000 square metres as opposed to the previous 14,000), but it was necessary to purchase from the rail system about 12,000 square metres, most of which contained abandoned railway tracks.

23   It was not enough to find a new area; it also had to be demonstrated that the new project was really a 'partial and not substantial variant' of the definitive design already approved for state financing, with at most 25 per cent of variation.

24   In the project description for the variant, Valle defended the choice of the added levels, which he felt reinforced the urban presence of the building: 'The central semicircle, in its concave form, absorbs the arrival of the city; the structure of the streets and the plaza is absorbed by the mass of the courthouse, almost a lengthening, made stronger and more perceptible by the augmented height of the building.' See Gino Valle, Technical Description, Archivio Valle, Udine. In the original project the 'houses' had four floors and the semicircle had six, while in the constructed work they had five and eight respectively. Valle probably realised that the raising of the hemicycle by two floors could be harmful for the proportional relationships between the parts, and this might explain the decision to increase the brick cladding by just one level, so as to maintain the two-floor difference with the lower parts, and to absorb the second raised level inside the high

white cornice. In this regard, Valle's choice of using the same windows on this upper level seems debatable, since it would probably have been more correct to alter the measurements of the windows, making this upper level 'vanish' more into the top of the building.

25   The new Master Plan of Bergamo, prepared by Bernardo Secchi with Vittorio Gandolfi, was effectively a 'third generation' plan, after those of Muzio-Marini in 1951–56 and Astengo-Dodi in 1965–69.

26   This project was later reworked from 1996 to 1998 as a preliminary architectural design but was then abandoned due to the objection of judges and lawyers of Bergamo to the suggestion of relocating the judicial offices out of the urban centre.

27   See 'Sandro Marpillero intervista Gino Valle da New York', *Lotus Navigator*, monograph, Gino Valle, 1, November 2000, p.72: 'I could tell you that I have made ... a citation of the central post office of Libera in Rome!' Actually, in the famous building by Libera the motif of the crossed diagonals was purely sculptural, due to the presence of a single staircase. Crossed ramps, on the other hand, can be seen inside the Palazzo dei Congressi at EUR, also by Libera (1937–42).

28   For a detailed reconstruction of the 36 reconstruction projects that were never built, see Antonio Di Lorenzo, *L'altalena dei sogni: il teatro mai realizzato a Vicenza*, Ergon, Vicenza, 1998. The last project before Valle's was the definitive design by Ignazio Gardella for the new Teatro Verdi at Campo Marzo (1979–80), eleven years after the invitational competition with the participation of Franco Albini and Carlo Scarpa: the project was published in *Lotus International*, 25, 1980, pp.92–102, with an introduction by Giulio Carlo Argan.

29   Valle received the commission for the definitive project in 2000. In 2001 the city approved financing of 26 million euros obtained by selling the Centrale del Latte of Vicenza, and work could finally begin in January 2002. After work was blocked for six months as the result of the bankruptcy of the contractor, construction resumed in the summer of 2005 with another company, and was completed on 9 November 2007. The theatre opened on 10 December 2007.

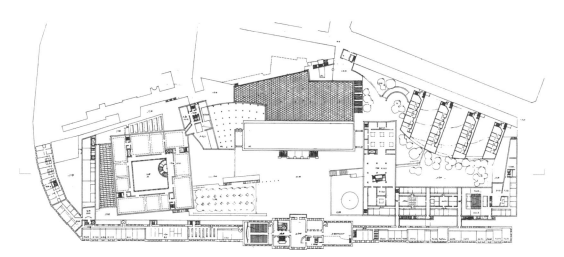

Courthouse of Brescia

1986–2004

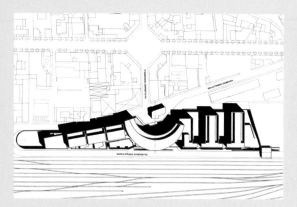

Planivolumetric drawing.

The building stands on a narrow lot between the historic centre and the railway. The very complex functional programme required the organisation of spaces with very different sizes and spatial characteristics, leading to the conception of the new complex as a set of buildings related to each other and communicating, to form a 'citadel of justice'. The offices are organised in three separate parts: at the centre, a hemicycle borders the entrance plaza and contains the offices of the court of appeals and the public prosecutors; to the west, along Via Gambara, the linear volume of the tribunal extends, with the two large spaces of the court of assizes; to the east, parallel wings of three crosswise volumes placed against a high wall host the offices of the magistrates' court, the public prosecutor's office and the judiciary offices. The building is vertically structured with three different materials: the base is clad in Botticino marble and faces the railway to form a high protective wall; the middle part of the elevation is in exposed brick; and the top is in concrete, coloured white, concluding in a slender cornice.

For those arriving on the north–south axis of Via San Martino della Battaglia and Via Ferramola the large hemicycle clearly concludes the urban perspective, masking with its height of eight storeys the emerging presence of the towers of the business district to the south of the railway. For those arriving from the south, crossing the railway on the Kennedy overpass, the overall view of the large complex is dominated by the defensive image of the stone wall that vividly conveys the idea of the edge of the historic centre, clearly visible beyond the building due to the landmarks of the castle and the dome of the cathedral. Walking down Via Gambara, on the other hand, one clearly perceives the way the long front is rhythmically paced to form the image of three 'houses' in dialogue with the residential fabric of the zone. From the central plaza one enters the two-storey lobby leading to the public circulation routes. The various functions are vertically organised according to the degree of public traffic and depending on needs of privacy and security: archives and reserved parking on the basement levels, hearing rooms in the base, offices on the upper floors, with those receiving more visitors on the first levels, such as the records office and the civil court, and those requiring greater privacy, such as the court of appeals and the public prosecutor's offices, on the upper levels.

View of the building towards the historic centre.

View of the building towards the railway.

New University Campus

Padua, 1991–2014

Siteplan of the university campus, with the volume of the Psychology Department, upper left.

The new university complex is located between the important artery of Viale Venezia and the Piovego River. The four new buildings are aligned towards the outer part of the area with the axes of the existing streets, and form a perimeter for the campus, while on the inside they border a pedestrian plaza whose square form is slightly rotated to make it parallel to the river. A large underground garage is placed below the plaza, with access ramps parallel to Viale Venezia. All the buildings were designed by Studio Valle: the Department of Psychology 2 building was completed in 1998, while the three other buildings (the Convention Centre, the Linguistics Centre and the Students' Centre) have been revised, completed and built by Studio Valle Architetti Associati since the death of Gino Valle in 2003 (completion, 2014).

Arriving from Viale Venezia, the main building for Psychology 2 can be seen from a distance as a compact solid, in which the composition of the various forms of openings reveals the stacking of the functional parts: administrative offices on the first two levels, the teaching facilities with 16 lecture halls on the second, third and fourth floors, for a total of 1,440 persons, the library on the fifth and sixth floors, with a capacity of 160, and technical spaces on the upper level, faced with aluminium panels. The southern facade towards the plaza has greater volumetric variety: the base is hollowed at the corner to form a two-storey portico that shelters the main entrances; the third floor with the lecture halls is bent slightly in the central part, while the upper volume containing the library is forcefully set back to create a large terrace. From the portico, one enters a large two-storey lobby, with separate entrances for the two functional parts: to the left, one enters the administrative area, with the students' secretariat at ground level and offices on the first floor connected by an open staircase; to the right, one reaches three elevators with staircases placed behind them, leading to the levels above. The staircases are doubled towards the outside, forming four straight ramps and joined by fire exit stairs. The two innermost ramps are separated from the outside by a glass wall, so that besides offering an evacuation route, they can also be used to reach the lecture halls or the library. On the facade towards Viale Venezia the security stairs are incorporated in the volume and match the black paint finish of the base, forming the image of a large excavation that makes the pale mass of the building seem to float in the air.

The library has a U-shaped layout around a central nucleus, with shelving and offices at the centre and two reading rooms, two storeys high, along the east and west facades, lit by vertical windows. On the two sides of the mezzanine, with a structure suspended from the ceiling, two sectors provide space for storage and reference of periodicals, facing the two-storey space of the reading room and connected to it by two open staircases.

View of the Psychology 2 building from the plaza.

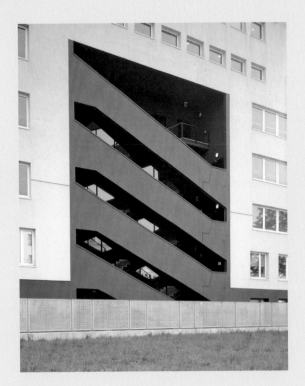

The emergency staircase on the northern facade
of the Psychology 2 building.

Theatre of Vicenza

2000–2007

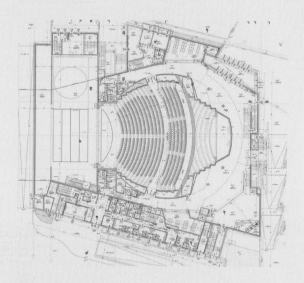

Plan at the level of entrance from the plaza and of the cavea of the large hall.

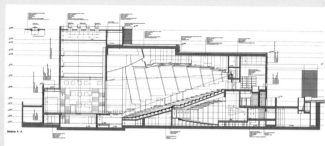

Longitudinal section with the interlock of the two theatre spaces (908 and 400 seats).

The theatre is located along the Scaligere historic walls, on the axis of Viale Mazzini, where a Detail Plan (also prepared by Gino Valle) inserts it in a set of linear buildings organised around an internal plaza recessed about 1.5 metres below street level.

Since the death of Gino Valle in 2003, the theatre project has been revised, completed and built by Studio Valle Architetti Associati.

Seen from a distance the building appears as a compact and shaped volume, with a terraced profile sloping from the corner of Via Cairoli and Via Torino – with the presence of the fly tower – to the corner between Viale Mazzini and the internal plaza, marked by a large portal parallel to the Viale that indicates the public entrance. The particular cladding of the building, exposed brick alternating with bands of white stone, reinterprets the material layering of the nearby historic walls with a different design. Arriving from the historic centre of the city, the most revealing perception of the building happens when one has passed the fortified walls, crossing the arch of Via Bonollo: it becomes clear that the facade on the avenue retreats diagonally, while a large ramp encourages descent towards the plaza by way of the large portal. Besides providing useful space for people to gather before entering the theatre, the portal frames an interesting diagonal view of the Scaligere walls for those arriving from the underground parking facility and from the internal plaza.

Entering the theatre, visitors encounter a large, well-lit foyer, organised on three levels, which wraps

View from Viale Mazzini.

View of the foyer on three levels, from the level of entry from the plaza (-1.5 metres) to that of the upper foyer (+3.2 metres).

The large hall with 908 seats.

the circular volume containing the two performance spaces, stacked and oriented in opposite directions. From the entrance level of the foyer (-1.53 metres), with its two lateral cloakrooms, visitors directly access the large hall (908 seats), a single sloping space, or ascend to a circular balcony (+3.23 metres) from which to enter the space from above. At the position of the corner of Viale Mazzini and Via Cairoli, the cafe area is raised to a height halfway between the entrance level and the circular balcony. The lower theatre space (400 seats) at the level of -5.10 metres, again a single sloping hall, has an independent entrance from the ramp along Viale Mazzini, and is connected with the level of the main entrance; it has its own foyer with cloakroom, permitting simultaneous or independent use of the two halls. While the foyer and the circulation spaces have an image of great simplicity thanks to the use of white plaster and pale wood, the large theatre space features a contrast between the red colour of the seats and the black enclosure, punctuated by the design of the panels that conceal the indirect lighting system in their open joints.

The area set aside for the performers is located in the lateral wing along Via Cairoli, with its own entrance offering direct access to the dressing rooms and the two-storey rehearsal rooms lit by recessed courtyards. The stage offers great flexibility of use thanks to the presence, along with the fly tower, of a large lateral stage, a pit for an orchestra of up to eighty members, and a storeroom for the sets placed behind the stage, with direct vehicle access.

View from the plaza-parking area.

13 Complex Volumes and Blocks: Office Buildings (1985–2003)

As we have seen in the previous chapters, the office complex at La Défense (1984–88) marked an important moment of transition in Gino Valle's work, coinciding with unprecedented intensification and diversification of his design activity, reflecting the achievement of creative maturity. The complexity of the project came above all from the fact that it represented a crossroads between several design themes – new or already explored – for which Valle attempted to formulate a synthesis for the first time: in particular, he associated his recurring interest in the figurative quality of architectural language – manifested in an exemplary way in the projects for New York and Giudecca – with the principle expressed in the Pordenone project of creating a system of buildings to generate urban complexity. This synthesis of design, however, had taken on ambiguous tones in the relationship between the new architecture – intended to evoke 'real Parisian houses' – and the immediate context of La Défense, which Valle appeared to challenge. For this reason, we can interpret the project at La Défense as an 'imperfect attempt', more interesting for its methodological value as an 'open process of research' than for the results achieved. Though 'imperfect', it was a decisive project to begin the period of large public buildings imagined as 'city pieces', discussed in the previous chapter, but also a fine series of projects

for office complexes, all developed between 1985 – when the Parisian worksite had just begun – and 1990.

The first project concerned the expansion of the Olivetti headquarters in Ivrea, undertaken in 1985–88. Unlike the project conditions encountered at La Défense, Valle was faced with a highly stimulating and positive context: a plot strategically positioned along the main avenue entering the city, at the foot of a hill, with the strong architectural presence of the office complex designed at the start of the 1960s by Bernasconi, Fiocchi and Nizzoli. Although he saw this building as having an evident 'off-scale' character, Valle did not avoid dialogue with it, and even proposed basing his own project on an idea of completing the existing situation:

> At Ivrea I have taken the same pieces from Paris and arranged them in a curve pointed at the existing star-shaped building, which I have thus managed to make realer than it is now, a bit as if it were a monument. Since the blocks are arranged along a curve, the gap between two blocks becomes a hinge, a sort of skeletal joint.[1]

Valle thus obtained a dynamic figure that evoked, in his view, the tail of a comet,[2] bringing a new quality to the existing context by assigning an orientation, a scale and a stable attachment to the ground.

(*left*) Headquarters of Deutsche Bank Italia, Milan, 1997–2005. View of the plaza and the base of the building from Via Pirelli.

Olivetti offices, Ivrea, 1984–86. Detail of the entrance block with shift of the facade.

The linear system applied in Pordenone and at La Défense was then used in Ivrea with extraordinary freedom, yet at the same time with great precision as required by the relationship with the existing building and the hilly landscape.[3] Also in the language of the facades, Valle demonstrated evident maturity by achieving a simpler expression, free of the temptations of 'preciosity' that accompanied the use of stone in the project for La Défense: featuring an alternation of lengthwise windows and bands of brick masonry supported by slender, round steel pillars and string courses in concrete, the facades seemed this time to suggest the civil architecture of Alvar Aalto – in particular, the National Pensions Institute in Helsinki (1952–57).

For Valle, the apparent return to an 'Aaltian' language did not imply a regression to the expression of tectonic truth that he had explored in the short period of 'neo-Brutalist' building (1953–61). Valle

instead demonstrated great freedom and openness in his linguistic choices, profoundly in tune with his temporal conception of architecture that permitted formal themes and linguistic elements to be resuscitated in keeping with the dictates of the circumstances and context of a new project. In New York Valle had applied the choice of building in stone as an option dictated by the context, and at Ivrea the choice of an 'Aaltian' language admirably addressed the need to establish a dialogue with a building from the 1960s and to obtain a more 'humble' expression of the facade, to refine the relationship with the landscape and the vegetation. Valle was highly critical, in fact, of the stone facings and anodised aluminium of the existing building, which 'do not work in this hillside setting, because they convey the image of an urban work of architecture taken into the country'.[4] He therefore chose exposed brick for the facades, and fair-face concrete for the base, cut by deep lines to evoke 'a "countrified order" that assigns great weight to the wall as an outgrowth of the ground'.[5] The choice of bringing the load-bearing structure outside the frames, on the other hand, had both constructive and expressive purposes. In constructive terms, the very close pillars make the structure concretely function as a continuous load-bearing wall, facilitating the worksite because the slabs can be poured directly over the pillars, with a beam of the same thickness as the slab, without any need to use a parapet beam.[6] At the level of tectonic expression, this ribbon window takes on a three-dimensional value and a depth that Valle associated with the memory of the cast-iron facades of industrial lofts in New York: 'The window loses its dimension as pure surface to become construction, with a chiaroscuro effect that reveals its material weight.'[7] To further rationalise the worksite, Valle used a single prefabricated piece of the same length as the spacing of the pillars, to make both the rib and the parapet, with two support flanges on the sides of the pillars: with this prefabricated part mounted on the edge of the slab, it was possible to proceed quickly with the brick facing, placed directly on the rib.

Though in this case it was a facing with a thickness of 13 centimetres, Valle used alternated sides and ends of the bricks to suggest a full load-bearing wall. The image of a mass of masonry horizontally paced by prefabricated concrete strips is shared by the Olivetti offices and the houses at Giudecca, which represented its transcription into a service industry facility. As in the office complex at La Défense, Valle introduced subtle variations in the repetitive order of the single blocks, especially slight swellings and overhangs to mark exceptional features in the ends and the entrance block.

In the later projects for office complexes, Valle returned to two of the basic principles of the Olivetti offices: the arrangement of the individual blocks along a curve, and the continuous facade with small columns and deep ribbon windows. In the competition project for the fifth SNAM office building[8] at San Donato Milanese (1985), the curve became a semicircle, leading to the deformation of the individual block in a trapezium with a double hinge. It was therefore the open

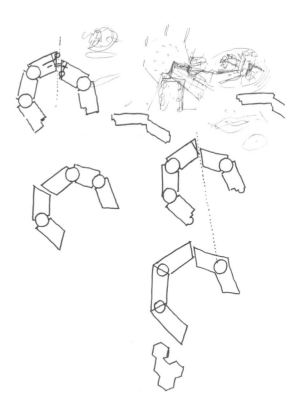

Competition project for the new SNAM offices, San Donato Milanese, 1985. Studies of grouping of office modules.

character of the landscape that made Valle sense the need to evoke the strong image of a work of foundation architecture, and this was confirmed in the subsequent project for the Alisarda offices in Olbia (1987–88), on a site of great landscape beauty bordering on the airport. Recycling the planimetric figure already proposed at San Donato (a heptagon lacking two terminal segments), Valle arranged the office blocks around an arid hill with a rock at the centre, obtaining a very different architectural image. In the last version of the project, the building was shifted along the road leading to the airport, on the north side of the lot, with a decidedly introverted layout in which a curved wall, forming a shield against the wind, contained the corridor leading to the offices arranged like a comb around courtyards open to the central hill. This solution,

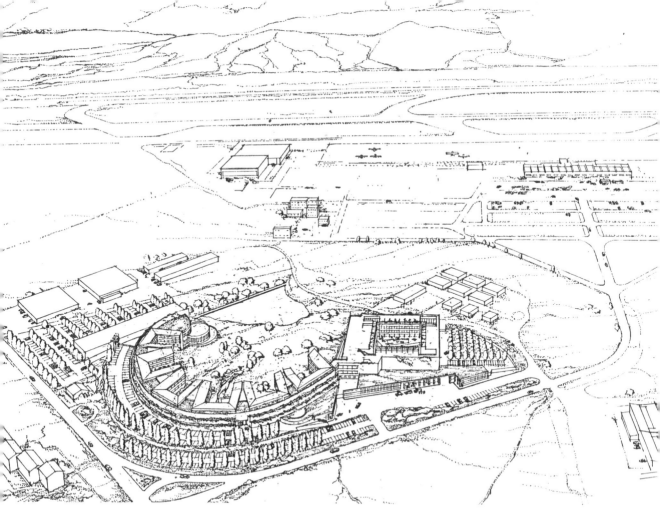

Project for Alisarda offices, Olbia, 1987–88. Perspective view of the complex.

besides permitting better occupation of the land and correct exposure of the offices towards the south, was also interesting because it proposed, for the first time, the curved development of the linear layout principle of the offices through an opaque 'backbone' that characterised the series of projects for the Zanussi offices, for La Rinascente, Fantoni and the IBM Distribution Centre. In order not to make the large curved wall seem like that of a fortification, Valle shaped it with terraces covered with typical Mediterranean vegetation, making it become 'a landscape piece, a representation of the hill',[9] with a landscape image reinforced by the terraced and tree-lined parking areas, again placed along the curve of the street.

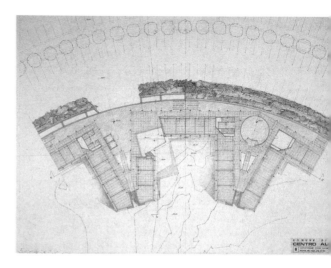

Project for Alisarda offices, Olbia, 1987–88.
Standard floor plan.

The Legacy of the Olivetti Offices

The facade of the Olivetti offices was thus taken by Valle as a sort of prototype,[10] ready to adapt to the different forms of the office blocks, but also to different materials. In the choices regarding the language of construction, and in those related to the rules of urban composition, at the end of the 1980s, research on office complexes intersected with the development of large public buildings. Valle literally reiterated the facade of the Olivetti offices in the first project for the courthouse of Brescia (1988), though in this case the choice of brick seemed to refer to the presence of existing industrial buildings in the area. In Olbia, on the other hand, Valle changed the material for the Alisarda offices, proposing sand-coloured stucco for the two upper levels and Sardinian sandstone cladding for the terraced wall, to accentuate the image of an artificial hill invaded by vegetation. In the competition project for the Mercedes offices in Frankfurt (1989), the same facade – clad this time with white aluminium panels – was used for the first time in the cylindrical form of three towers, with 15 floors of offices raised with a mushroom structure over a glass base, with the aim of constructing an urban front that would be 'continuous but punctiform, to allow the sunlight to reach the residences'.[11]

In other projects for large office complexes that were never built, Valle further diversified his compositional techniques, not hesitating to mix the different expressive languages of the facades, as well as different layout footprints and geometric figures. In the project for the addition to the IBM offices at Segrate (1992), on the other hand, Valle abandoned a compositional technique of assembly of differentiated blocks and proposed a very closed, compact settlement figure, on an open site of great prestige, between the IBM offices by Marco Zanuso and the Mondadori building by Niemeyer, both built in 1968–75. Instead of placing the addition near the existing complex, Valle proposed placing the new facility on the most distant part of the site, connecting it to the existing central plaza with a

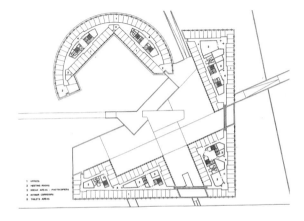

Project for addition to the IBM offices, Segrate, 1992. Standard floor plan.

Competition project for the new Bayer offices at Portello, Milan, 1989–90. Perspective view of the courtyard.

Competition project for the new offices and garage of Mercedes, Frankfurt, 1989. Perspective.

sheltered pedestrian axis that passed in front of a large auditorium placed halfway along the path. The new figure with a semi-open courtyard was based on the elementary form of the large square of Zanuso's building, a form Valle subjected to various operations of splitting and subtraction: the excavation of a square plaza rotated by 20 degrees; the breaking of the southwest corner and insertion of a semicircular volume with a square courtyard, also rotated by 45 degrees; cuts with a height of five storeys in the eastern and northern facades, to open the view from the plaza towards the countryside. The outcome of these morphological transformations was a complex, detailed volume – three rectilinear bodies and one curved body connected by the base of the raised inner plaza – no longer the result of the assembly of individual volumes, but of the overlay of two different orientations inside a large form.

The Lafarge Headquarters in Avignon

After this long and varied series of projects that were never built, Valle completed an interesting work for the headquarters of Lafarge Plâtres in the Agropole industrial park to the southeast of Avignon (1995–2000), following an international competition, in collaboration with the French architect Daniel Fanzutti. The four-hectare plot was still marked by previous agricultural activity, with the presence, in particular, of a large orchard and a row of tall plane trees beside a canal. Drawing on the organisational principles of the agricultural landscape, with rows of trees, hedges and walls for protection from the wind, Valle decided to base the project on the opposition between two landscape grids rotated by 45 degrees with respect to each other, and on the division of the lot into two large squares corresponding to the separate functions of the research laboratories – in the part near the street – and the administrative offices – in the part near the canal, better shielded from the street noise. Resembling the plan of the Bergamin offices (1988–91), he organised the parking areas in 'green rooms' enclosed by low concrete walls, accompanied by rows of almond trees and shrubs to

make the cars vanish when viewed from the street. The two buildings were oriented in the same east–west arrangement, both with a height of just three storeys, but with a different volumetric configuration: the research laboratories as a monolith of forty × fifty metres, the administration building as a long double volume diagonally cutting the border between the two squares. Valle also decided to use a range of materials that would emphasise the products – above all cement and plaster – of the Lafarge group: concrete poured in place for the ground seam of the complex (the low walls of the parking areas, the outdoor routes, the bases of the buildings), with a 'brut' texture that incorporated local ochre-coloured stones, and prefabricated concrete panels for the cladding of the buildings, with the use of white and grey concrete. The outstanding landscape quality of the project is particularly evident in the view from a distance, which seems to be structured by a succession of parallel horizontal planes: first, the walls in ochre-colour concrete, then the rows of almond trees, over whose foliage only one level emerges of the profile of the large white monolith of the laboratories and the long line of the office building, with the row of plane trees, finally, in the background, closing the horizon and marking the presence of the canal. The main path of entry along an existing row of trees penetrates the building diagonally, generating a covered full-height passage that reveals the internal organisation of the building.

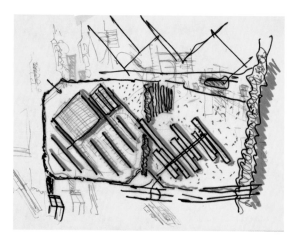

New Lafarge offices and laboratories, Avignon, 1995–2000. Planimetric study.

New Lafarge offices and laboratories, Avignon, 1995–2000. Administration building, southern facade.

Entrance portico.

The facades, on the other hand, are conceived as the latest evolution of the 'wall with windows in line' of the Olivetti offices, with a clear difference between the northern and southern facades. While in the previous office complexes Valle had always clad the parapet with different materials (bricks, stone, aluminium panels), in the Lafarge offices he preferred to leave the precast concrete panel visible, making it the sign representing the company.

The Deutsche Bank Headquarters at Milan-Bicocca

The last major office complex designed and built by Gino Valle was the Deutsche Bank Italia headquarters in the Bicocca district in Milan (1997–2005). It is interesting not only for its architectural qualities, but also for the complexity of the design process[12] and for the fact that it offered Valle an opportunity to return to Bicocca after the negative outcome of the competition[13] in 1988. The area selected in the zone designed by Gregotti Associati was at the southern tip of the directional axis. Originally, Pirelli Real Estate intended to build eight seven-storey towers with porticoes envisioned by the plan, which would then be put up for sale. Following consultations with some of the architects involved in the design of the towers stipulated by the plan (Gae Aulenti, Vittorio Gregotti, Gino Valle), the German group chose Gino Valle to develop a preliminary project. The complex functional programme called for the positioning in a single building of multiple activities of the bank scattered in various facilities in Italy, with spatial requirements (33,000 square metres) that went beyond the size indicated in Gregotti's plan. Valle's initial choice, dating back to January 1997, was to form a single edifice to clearly conclude the Bicocca area to the south. Besides the functional reasons outlined above, this solution went back to Valle's intentions expressed in the competition project of 1985, which saw the 'walling up' of the Bicocca as the most legitimate way to conserve its integrity with respect to the chaotic urban context. In keeping with these initial ideas, the side of the building facing

the new zone would become a 'Lombard courtyard' system, with the creation of a significant public space between the three towers by Gregotti (under construction) of the original eight, and the new building, which maintained the height set by the plan of 32.3 metres and the continuous portico along the entire perimeter. In this sense, the first sketches for the Deutsche Bank already clearly showed the intention to work on two separate complexes: on the one hand, the front of the offices, seven storeys high, that exploited the freedom of rotation of linear volumes already tested by Valle in the many previous projects for large office complexes; on the other, a low volume, with autonomous architectural logic and functions, would contain the entrance, the foyer and the dealing room – a large single-span space required by the programme for the investment banking office. Following these initial sketches, Valle's idea of including the view of the only significant landscape element came into play: the 'hill of the cherry trees', the artificial slope obtained with excavation material, representing a concrete green presence on the western side of the lot. Later, to compensate for the loss of office area caused by the opening towards the hill, Valle proposed a third design solution that modified the footprint from a C-shaped plan to an E, with the formation of a true plaza wrapped by the offices and oriented towards the green zone. To further reinforce the visual plaza–hill relationship, the western wing was reduced as much as possible, with only the two upper levels extended in an overhang to form an architectural figure which Valle called a 'nose'.

Valle's other concern was the treatment of the south side, towards Via Figini, which had become the wall concluding the complex. Presented with the need to interrupt the continuity of the long front of the construction, Valle broke up the 'E' of the plan around its middle bar and rotated the volume towards the southwest. With this gesture, the facade towards the outside of the Bicocca was divided into two segments, interrupting uniformity and generating different views and compositions of overlapping of the windows. The complex geometry of the definitive volumetric set-up is the result of mediation between Gregotti's plan and autonomous

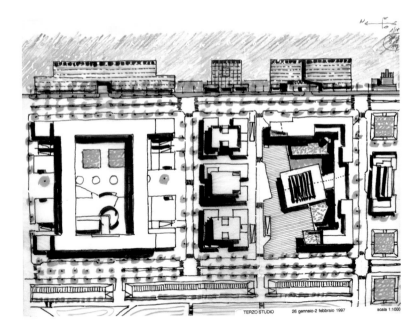

Headquarters of Deutsche Bank Italia, planivolumetric studies, third version (2 February 1997).

settlement principles, whose reasoning is clearly revealed in the visual and physical path around the building. As one gradually approaches the plaza, the building starts to open and to change face, losing the character of a closed mass and transforming into a welcoming place that embraces a public space, the spatial nucleus of the complex. The ground floor of the building, along the whole perimeter, is clad in shiny black marble ('absolute black') with particular reflecting effects, while the rest of the building is clad in grey Repen stone. The material chosen by Valle to function as a base responds in an intentionally ambiguous way, maintaining a solid chromatic character but lightening its surface, making it almost totally reflective, and thus contradicting its role as a base.[14] What is supposed to anchor the building to the ground becomes light, and completely alters the visual approach to the object: the entire context is reflected in the material and the effects gradually multiply as the vantage point changes. The 'absolute black' also clads the entire low volume towards the plaza, in keeping with the principle of linguistic differentiation of the various volumes of the complex. Other expedients contribute to generate these effects of lightening the

mass, like the overhang of the volume towards the plaza and the bevelling of the base that suggests the porticos envisioned in the initial project. Also, the choice of Repen stone, which Valle had already used for the offices in Paris, enhances the volumetric expression of the building thanks to its property of absorbing natural light and forming an irregular chromatic pattern in relation to the different exposures of the facades.

It is important to observe how Valle used aligned and not staggered rectangular slabs in the stone facing to give force to the expression of a single large sculpted monolithic mass. This cladding therefore represents the last development of Valle's thinking on stone facing with the use of thin sheets, which began with the office complex at La Défense,[15] where deep seams evoked the design of a framework of pillars, capitals and beams. In the facade of the courthouse of Padua, Valle continued to use staggered joints 'as if the stone bore a load',[16] but he abandoned any suggestion of a 'classic' moulding to express greater abstraction of the masonry surface. The next step was the travertine base of the IBM tower in Rome, where for the first time he used non-staggered sheets. This evolution towards

(*overleaf*) Aerial view of Bicocca with the Deutsche Bank building in the foreground, 2009.

greater abstraction and simplification did not only have to do with the cladding of the facade of the Deutsche Bank, but also with the arrangement of the windows, different depending on the side: point by point on the facades towards the city, continuous on the facades towards the plaza. In the building at Bicocca, the windows in line have definitively lost the slender circular columns that characterised the expression in all the projects derived from the Olivetti offices: the difference between the two facade types now has to do only with the treatment of the cladding, with the insertion of recessed aluminium frames between the windows in place of the stone, creating the effect of continuous ribbon windows.

In the headquarters of Deutsche Bank, Valle thus developed the highest synthesis of a series of themes explored not only in the large office complexes starting in the mid-1980s, but also in the public buildings conceived as 'city parts' discussed in the previous chapter. He combined research on the possibilities of bending and shaping linear volumes to form complex urban figures with research on the more 'sculptural' treatment of the volume.[17] Alessandro Rocca has aptly pointed out that Valle, to some extent, had to build the context on his own, with an architecture that would challenge the classic typology of the 'office building' in the overall form of the structure and in the dematerialisation of its facades, although this idea of the building resurfaces 'in the way the building seeks and obtains the urban form of maximum resistance, tracing new and lasting hierarchies and becoming neighbourhood and landscape, stabilising element and architectural value as a guarantee for a still unstable, provisional urban setting'.[18] The apparent linguistic austerity of the building is suited to Valle's desire to make a work of architecture of great civil value last in time, connected to the tradition of the great urban architectures, of institutions or service industries, that characterised European cities of the early 1700s, and found continuity in the Italian and German experiences of the 20th century. It is sufficient to mention, for example, the Palazzo delle Poste in Naples by Giuseppe Vaccaro (1928–1936), specifically referenced by Valle in the treatment of the cladding with large aligned, non-staggered sheets, or the volumetric articulation and composition of the facades of the IG Farben Building (1928–30) by Hans Poelzig: works of architecture that do not represent actual sources, but are examples of projects and types that can be ascribed to a long 'modernist' tradition of the office building,[19] to which we can also add not only the Deutsche Bank facility, but all of Valle's later work.

Notes

1   Pierre-Alain Croset (ed.), 'Una conversazione con Gino Valle', *Casabella*, 519, December 1985, p.17.

2   'The offices were later renamed "Valle's comet", confirming the ironic character of my anecdote. The base, instead, in the image became a sort of "ship" in motion that emerges from the tangential line of the blocks, reinforcing the dynamic movement of the curve.' See Gino Valle, 'Alcune osservazioni sugli ultimi progetti', *Casabella*, 563, December 1989, p.15.

3   The first rough project was based on six modules, while only five modules were developed in the final project, slightly larger in size. For a complete description of the design process, see Daniele Boltri, Giovanni Maggia, Enrico Papa and Pier Paride Vidari, *Architetture olivettiane a Ivrea*, Fondazione Adriano Olivetti, Gangemi Editore, Rome, 1998, pp.130–40.

4   Gino Valle, 'Alcune osservazioni sugli ultimi progetti', p.16.

5   ibid.

6   After the pouring of the slabs the pillars are connected to the slab by simple joints rather than interlocks, thus limiting the forces of torsion because the attachment has only the height of the slab. The advantages of this construction, besides the speed and simplicity, are that the frames are deeply set back (45 centimetres) and therefore protected from water and sunlight, leaving plenty of space to insert the blinds.

7   Gino Valle, 'Alcune osservazioni sugli ultimi progetti', p.16.

8   The 'city of methane' was envisioned by Enrico Mattei at the end of the 1950s, at the gates of Milan in an area then occupied only by rice and corn fields, in keeping

with an idea of a 'company town' that would integrate, in a single location, managers, clerks and workers of ENI. The competition was won by the project by R. Gabetti and A. Isola, with G. Drocco, and the Quinto Palazzo was built in 1988–92.

9   Gino Valle, 'Alcune osservazioni sugli ultimi progetti', p.17.

10   In the lecture of 29 March 1988 at Università Ca' Foscari in Venice, already mentioned regarding the Giudecca project, for the first time Valle made the comparison between the facades at La Défense and those of Ivrea, insisting on the shared load-bearing character of the facade: the facades of the IBM building in Paris are 'a wall with window holes' while those of the Olivetti offices are 'a wall with windows in line, a bit like Aalto', and thus 'very different because the pillars remain outside the window'. See Gino Valle, 'Gino Valle. 29 marzo 1988', in Franca Bizzotto and Michela Agazzi (eds), *Colore Segno Progetto Spazio. Giuseppe Mazzariol e gli 'Incontri con gli artisti'*, Il Poligrafo, Padua, 2009, p.156.

11   Gino Valle, 'Alcune osservazioni sugli ultimi progetti', p.22.

12   A very detailed reconstruction of the whole design process is contained in Luka Skansi, *Gino Valle. Deutsche Bank Milano*, Electa, Milan, 2009.

13   Valle was very critical of the winning project by Gregotti Associati, as he stated in an interview on the day of the announcement of the competition results (Enrico Regazzoni, 'La disfida di Bicocca', *Europeo*, 30, 22 July 1988, pp.104–7): 'The defeat in itself does not bother me, I have a pretty thick skin. My staff can tell you: I did not go into a rage when I found out I had lost, but when I saw the winning project: an ugly project.' Furthermore, Valle acknowledged that he belonged to the same culture of urban design, saying: 'It is precisely in the light of this culture, so often described by Vittorio, which I have always practised, that I can say that my project is much more "Gregottian" than his.'

14   Already in the Department of Psychology 2 of the University of Padua, Valle had tested the effects of dematerialisation of the base with the use of black, while in the earlier projects he had instead preferred to reinforce the sense of heaviness of the base, profoundly rooted to the ground, making use of deep seams to suggest the idea of a modern 'rustication': this was particularly evident in the Olivetti offices (with a concrete base) and the IBM tower at EUR in Rome (with travertine cladding). The base of the Deutsche Bank headquarters has been described very perceptively by Alessandro Rocca as 'a vice versa rustication that removes weight and holds the entire volume in suspension'. See Alessandro Rocca, 'Due architetture a Milano, in presa diretta con la città', in Nico Ventura (ed.), *Da, chez, from Gino Valle*, exh. cat. MusArc, Ferrara, 2005, pp.21–5.

15   'In the project at La Défense in Paris, in the columns, between the stones, you see the light, in that spreading stone that does not intend to be heavy, you see the light filter through; it is a stone with a thickness of four centimetres, but it is used as a facing material, as if it was light.' See Massimo Trevisan and Massimo Vedovato, 'Colloquio con Gino Valle', *Anfione Zeto*, 12, 1999, pp.81–4.

16   Davide Ruzzon, 'La sottile evidenza della leggerezza. Dialogo con Gino Valle', *Anfione Zeto*, 12, 1999, p.56.

17   Regarding this, Alessandro Rocca has written: 'At Bicocca the starting point is the gigantic monolith that Valle shapes, sculpts, excavates and shifts like a sculptor, or a set designer, neo-Expressionist.' See Alessandro Rocca, 'Due architetture a Milano', p.24.

18   ibid.

19   Other architects admired by Valle and mentioned by him, although privately, were Sullivan, Plečnik, Fabiani, Perret, but also Behrens and Fahrenkamp. Roberto Gabetti was the first to identify a certain 'fully Italian *Novecentista*' tone in the later work of Valle, prior to the offices at La Défense (Roberto Gabetti, 'Alla Défense c'è Gino Valle', *Atti e rassegna tecnica della Società Ingegneri e Architetti in Torino*, 11–12, November–December 1990, pp.373–92, reprinted in *Anfione Zeto*, 6–7, 1990–91, pp.89–91), after the Olivetti offices which in his view went against the 'internationalist' tradition of Ivrea: 'Here, with Valle, we are at the opposite pole: the tone is utterly Italian, so Italian as to remind us of our *Novecento*.' See Roberto Gabetti, 'Un tono tutto italiano', *Casabella*, 563, December 1989, pp.4–5.

Olivetti Offices

Ivrea, 1985–88

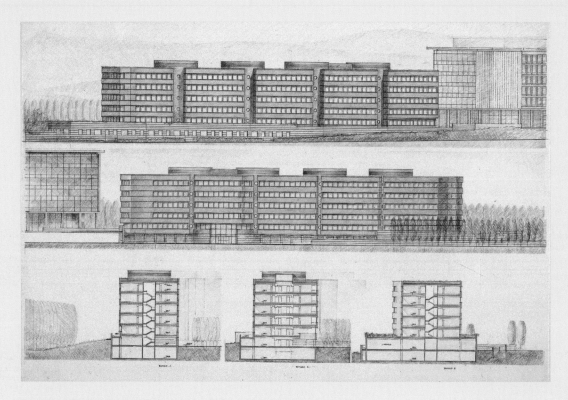

Facades on the street and towards the hill, and cross-sections.

Entering Ivrea from the motorway, one discovers the new offices along the main avenue of access to the city. The five blocks form a curve that moves away from the street to connect to the existing 1960s office building. Joined by a powerful cylindrical hinge, the blocks appear firmly anchored to the ground by a concrete base that contains the dining hall and suggests a bastion cultivated as a garden. Access to the building is through the terraced parking area placed at the foot of the hill, while a passage along the outer wall connects the dining hall to the existing building. Seen from the parking area, the new complex borders an oblong plaza that terminates at the base of the existing building. The entrance is marked by an outcropping of the facade of the second block, below which curved full-height glazing encourages visitors first to enter the large hall and then to proceed to the smaller lobby with lifts. The closed offices are accessed from a double corridor with a central service strip, while in the ends of the building large corner offices form a characteristic swelling protrusion of the facade. Passing from one block to another, one notes the gap open to the outside, revealing the rotation of the planimetric figure.

View of the end of the building from the parking area, with the corner of the dining hall in the foreground.

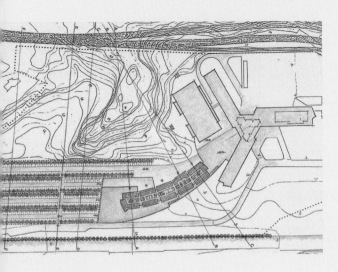

Siteplan.

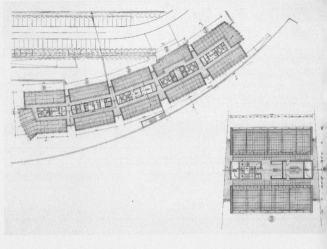

Standard floor plan with indication of the base module of the volume of the offices.

Deutsche Bank Italia Headquarters at Bicocca

Milan, 1997–2005

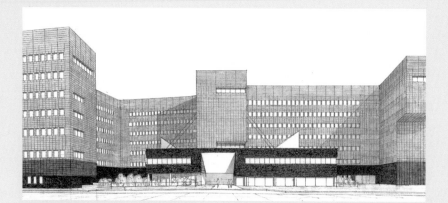

Perspective view of the building from the plaza towards the entrance.

The building is located on the southern border of the Bicocca district created through the conversion of an industrial zone of Pirelli. It completes a block already partially built, with three towers on the northern side designed by Gregotti Associati, the firm in charge of the entire urban plan for the Bicocca area. The building reacts to this particular context by proposing a rich, detailed perceptive experience that varies vividly depending on the vantage point. For those arriving from the centre of Milan, the building seems like a compact mass of masonry, seven storeys high, closing off the three sides of the block towards the streets, and thus marking not the start of the Bicocca district but its end: the sole exception in the continuity of the constructed frontage, the southern facade is split in two, with the western part slightly rotated and set back. For those arriving from the centre of the Bicocca zone, on the other hand, the volume appears more complex, bending with an E-shaped figure around a large pedestrian plaza. This plaza concludes the pedestrian axis that crosses the district lengthwise. A lower volume, two storeys high and clad in polished black marble, clearly marks the entrance to the building and is slightly rotated,

underlining the orientation of the plaza towards the adjacent 'hill of the cherry trees' which is the only significant landscape feature of the site. The western wing of the offices is emptied at the base by a cut with a height of four storeys, further opening the plaza in the direction of the hill.

Entry is through a two-storey lobby lit by continuous glazing on the plaza and a large skylight placed on the eastern facade: from the lobby, it is possible to reach the first floor directly – which contains the dealing room required by the functional programme, a large, single-span space – or to descend on a large staircase to the lower level, containing the dining hall that faces a recessed court. The offices on the upper levels are reached by means of four blocks of staircases and elevators, two of which have an independent entrance atrium from the plaza.

All the facades are clad in polished black marble for the base, and in grey Repen stone for the levels above. Walking along the building, one experiences surprising effects from the reflections that tend to erase the sense of weight of the base: the entire context is reflected in the marble, and those effects multiply as one gradually shifts the vantage point.

Ground floor plan of the block.

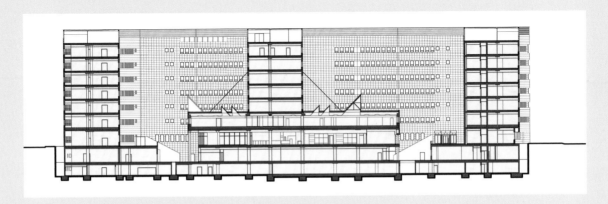

Cross-section through the low volume of the entrance hall and the dealing room.

View of the complex that opens with the plaza towards the hill, and detail of the base in shiny black marble.

View from the plaza of the entrance volume, with the recessed level and the glazings of the dining hall.

View of the staircase of the hall leading to the basement.

View of the building and the plaza from Via Pirelli.

14 The Architect of Major Urban Transformations (1991–2003)

In the previous chapters, we have seen how Valle's research on the theme of large public buildings intertwined in the 1980s and 1990s with renewed interest in large-scale urban design. This was particularly true in the case of large public buildings in Padua (courthouse and university) and Vicenza (theatre), designed in relation to the formulation of urban 'guide plans' as elements capable of granting a lasting identity to a new part of the city. The theme of the large scale had been approached in the Bicocca project as well, no longer in relation to a public programme, but in the context of an operation based on the private initiative of an industrial company interested in real estate: the conversion of an 'urban void' left behind by abandonment of production activities. This project, in many ways part of the 'foundation' of new design attitudes and methods, began in the 1980s, during a moment of extensive transformation of procedures of decision-making and planning, which marked the beginning in Milan and many other Italian cities of a new period of 'negotiated urbanism' in which private enterprise took on an increasingly frequent role as the motor of urban change. This led to forms of greater flexibility, even to the 'instability' of urban planning faced by the pressures of private interests, which Valle was able to skilfully use in the case of the Deutsche Bank headquarters, managing to vary Gregotti's rigid urban scheme to obtain a volumetrically complex architectural organism.

Confirming the renewed role of private enterprise in processes of urban transformation, in the last ten years of his career Valle was commissioned by the owners of areas to design and implement two large-scale urban interventions in Milan (Portello) and Rome (Bufalotta), projects that share the factor of a large shopping mall seen as the motor of urban development. The theme of large retail architecture was not totally new to Valle, since he had already approached it in projects that were never built: for La Rinascente in Milan, from 1967 to 1971, as well as the series of projects for the retail facilities of Bergamin. What was new was the possibility of positive consideration of the shopping centre as a lever of urban design: Valle demonstrated, as in few other cases in Europe, that it was possible to 'make culture in spite of the limitations of the client',[1] overcoming prejudices regarding an apparent 'vulgarity' in the design theme.

In both cases, Valle was commissioned to focus on the overall urban design as well as the architectural design of the shopping centre, whose construction (in both cities) began before Valle's death in 2003, when all the fundamental design decisions had already been made. The two projects may be interpreted in parallel, though the urban contexts were profoundly different from each other:

(*left*) Shopping cluster at Portello, Milan, 2001–2005. View of the plaza under the sail and the portico with the shops.

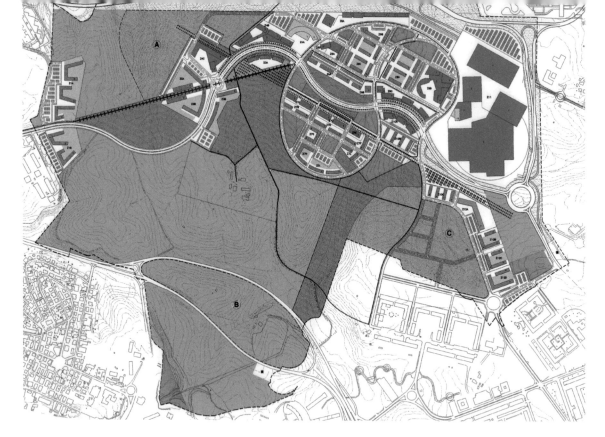

Detail plan of the Bufalotta district, Rome, zoning plan, 2003.

a piece of the *Ager Romanus* invaded by urban sprawl in the case of Bufalotta, therefore requiring a 'foundation' project; and a large abandoned industrial area (Alfa Romeo and Lancia) in the case of Portello, calling for a fundamental process of mending and renewal of already consolidated settlements. In both instances, Valle took an innovative approach to the theme of the 'large scale' of the 'cathedrals of consumption', attempting to soften or even eliminate the risk of an 'off-scale' element in its direct action on the architectural expression of the large object: in Rome as artificial topography and therefore 'landscape', in Milan as 'urban fabric'.

The Bufalotta-Porta di Roma District and the 'private city' of the Roman Developers

The new Bufalotta-Porta di Roma district in Rome is located nine kilometres to the north of the Capitoline Hill in an area previously classified as a 'private services zone' in the Master Plan of 1965, which had envisioned exploitation of the strategic location at the junction of the A1 highway and the 'Grande Raccordo Anulare' (GRA, or orbital motorway) as the arrival and storage point of goods for the city. In 1990 the City of Rome definitively abandoned the hypothesis of a freight terminal, and the land was purchased by a pool of private investors interested in exploiting its excellent location on the expressway by the construction of a new development for 11,000 inhabitants, together with a very large shopping centre that would function as the economic driver for the whole operation. Valle received the commission from the new owners in 1991, but it took many years to complete the complex urban planning process,[2] based on the principles of 'negotiated urbanism' involving the landowners, real estate developers and the municipal administration. Like many other large urban transformation operations in Rome in the 1990s, the Bufalotta-Porta di Roma district was designed as a variant of the current urban planning tools,[3] with a decision-making process unconstrained by the more recent principles of 'sustainable urban growth' formulated in the new Master Plan that was finally approved in 2006.[4] One of the principles of sustainability underlying the new Master Plan was supposed to be the so-called 'iron cure' proposed by the mayor, Francesco Rutelli, during his first term of office (1993–97): it was an ambitious programme of medium- and long-term modernisation of the railway infrastructures, together with extension of the existing metropolitan rail system and the creation of two new lines. In keeping with this principle, no area of urban growth could be more than 500 metres away from a station of the existing rail network or one in planning, while urban densification would be concentrated around railway and metropolitan rail stations. The Bufalotta area, located four kilometres away from the FM1 railway line, therefore represented an open violation of the principle of positioning the new 'centres' along the improved public transport network.[5] The outlining of the Program Agreement, a condition for undertaking the urban transformation, stipulated, in exchange for the generous distribution of development rights of over 2,000,000 cubic metres, that the owners would guarantee not only the road network for the entire sector, but also the creation of two large parks, of approximately 170 hectares, to connect the neighbourhoods and include a mixture of functions so as to guarantee the creation of about 15,000 jobs, as well as provision for 12,000 new residents.

Faced with such a dense, complex urban programme, Valle set out first of all to enhance the landscape qualities of the site, acting on two different levels: the design of the circulation network, and that of the enormous volume of the shopping centre in the most compact form possible. Valle organised the design of the new streets around the undulating landscape of the Roman countryside: he imagined a pattern of curved streets that would gently accompany the topography of the hills, avoiding steep inclines and fissures in the natural terrain, while at the

same time focusing on interesting views of the surrounding landscape. This 'organic' design structured the district in a clear, rational way using three types of streets: a 'boulevard' with a sinusoid form crossing the district lengthways; a 'ring road' with a 'figure-of-eight' form on both sides of the 'boulevard', bordering and enclosing the three main zones of construction; an orthogonal grid for access to the residences within each section. The design of this circulation network exhibits a strong figurative character and, with the clear specification of the height of the buildings,[6] seems sufficient to imbue a formal identity to the urban design, clearly separating the 'constructed' from the 'non-constructed' classified as 'park' (territorial scale) and 'public greenery' (neighbourhood scale). As in a true city, Valle's urban design proposes an intelligent mixture of private and public functions, organised in keeping with criteria of identity and hierarchy.

To design the shopping centre – the largest in Europe – Valle focused first of all on attenuating the presence of this heavy mass in the landscape, to avoid the image of an 'off-scale' object. He thus decided to concentrate all the functions vertically, stacking two parking levels and two floors of shops to avoid spreading 7,500 parking places across the territory. At the same time, he sank the gigantic 'city of consumption' into the ground by excavating to a depth of eleven metres, wider than the building, applying on a more urban scale a principle already used in many industrial buildings: situation of the building inside a moat. Thanks to this strategy, the parking levels receive natural light from the sides, while only the upper floor of the shopping malls emerges above ground level, with three sloping pedestrian plazas that connect the two galleria levels with the large isolated facilities of IKEA and Leroy Merlin, significantly reducing the visual impact of the structure in the landscape.

Besides this action at the level of the overall layout section, Valle also decided to act on the level of the architectural image, carefully choosing the facing materials to create a vivid contrast between the 'heavy' base in panels of tuff-colour concrete

Aerial view of the shopping complex Bufalotta – Porta di Roma, 2009.

and the 'light' top in grey zinc, over which the skylights of the shopping halls stand out with their reflective aluminium roof tiles. The shopping complex asserts itself as a strong presence in the landscape, though its limited height and the use of 'artificial tuff' in the cladding contribute to make it seem more like a compact 'walled city', from whose mass emerges only the tall skylights that illuminate the shopping malls and orient paths of ascent from the underground parking areas. Instead, as opposed to the materiality and 'heaviness' of this 'city of volcanic stone', in the large volume for IKEA Valle added character to the entire structure with an ascending profile and a facade conceived as a dynamic and playful composition of raised three-dimensional volumes: from the main object in blue sheet metal, a screen extends diagonally that surpasses the overhang of

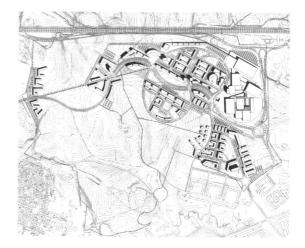

Planivolumetric of the Bufalotta district, Rome, 2003.

the glass mass of the restaurant beneath which the public entrance is placed.[7] This particular way of bending and deforming the cladding, in this case achieving the appearance of an enormous 'wing' or 'ear', had already been successfully applied by Valle in previous industrial and commercial works, particularly in the Bergamin sales centre in Istrana (1995–96) and the Eco Refrigerazione plant at Pocenia (1995–96).

Portello as Urban Mending

In Milan, Valle had already had major opportunities to work on the conversion of large abandoned industrial zones, but it was only with the Portello project, on land belonging to Alfa Romeo and Lancia, that he was able to concretely approach a true urban district. In the Portello area Valle began work on the Master Plan in 1997, after a complex planning process in which Sergio Crotti, Aldo Rossi, Pierluigi Spadolini and Mario Bellini had been involved since 1984. The history of the planning of the area was strongly influenced by the debate on the transformation and development of the Milan Fair.[8] Already in his urban design for the Area Project in 1984, Sergio Crotti had indicated the strategic role of Portello as an 'urban gate' and as a 'metropolitan forum' in the possible improvement of urban services connected with the expansion of the Milan Fair.[9]

As in the Bufalotta project, Valle was asked by the new owners not only to develop an overall Master Plan according to the specifications of the Program Agreement,[10] but first also to design a shopping centre to guarantee financing for the urban transformation. Valle based his project on an interpretation of the complex, fragmented urban landscape, on two different scales of perception: the 'fast' scale of motorists entering the city from the motorways, and the 'slow' scale of the residents of the established neighbourhoods between Via Traiano and Piazzale Accursio. According to this reading, the new urban settlement would have to complete the perceptive sequence of entry in the city, formed by the landmark of Monte Stella and

the 'green city' of QT8, but brutally interrupted by the gigantic pavilions of the Fair and criticised by Valle as being 'decidedly out of scale'.[11] The problem facing Valle was therefore a clear matter of urban mending: how to integrate the 'off-scale' element of the Fair with the new commercial and residential structures; to achieve continuity with the more established urban fabric on the northeastern edge of the area, along Via Traiano and Piazzale Accursio. Valle decided to represent in concrete terms the principle of reconnection with the creation of an artificial landscape of platforms containing all the diagonal crossings of the area, a pedestrian walkway that would make it possible to cross the barrier of the 'internal expressway' of Viale Serra, connecting highly diversified urban places: a sloping pedestrian plaza at the corner of Viale Serra and Viale Scarampo, bordered by three large buildings with a diagonal profile that would emphatically reduce the visual impact of the 'off-scale' element of the Fair; a large seven-hectare park on the other side of Viale Serra, shaped with artificial hills to form a landmark on a geographical scale capable of establishing a dialogue with the nearby Monte Stella and the imposing bulk of Istituto Palazzolo and the Fair; a 'commercial cluster' at the end of the diagonal route towards Piazzale Accursio; new residences were conceived as 'open blocks' to complete the urban fabric along Via Traiano.

The shopping centre was conceived in innovative terms, also due to the new regulations of the municipality of Milan that prevented – unlike Rome – the construction of large shopping malls within the city. Therefore, the proposal focused on the type of so-called 'shopping cluster' that imposed physical separation between the various buildings, joined only by the large continuous slab of the underground parking facility. Rather than a traditional shopping mall closed to the outside and crossed inside by 'streets' and 'plazas' to simulate an urban experience, Valle imagined a structure of streets with porticoes[12] to suggest the commercial spaces of a 'real city' with its mixture of department stores, boutiques, offices, cafes and restaurants. Based on the need to have distinctly

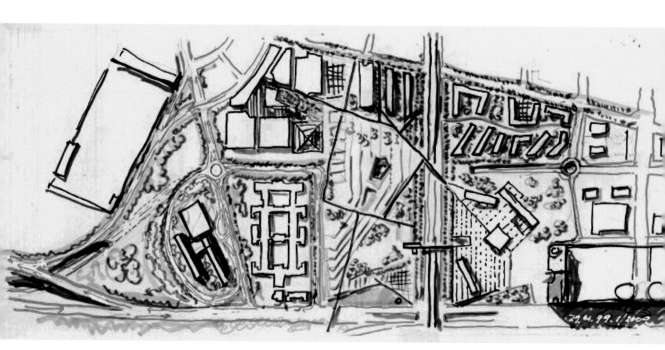

Conversion plan of the former Alfa Romeo area at Portello, planimetric sketch, April 1997.

separate buildings, Valle decided to add a strong individual character to each piece, not only varying the heights of the buildings and porticoes, but also changing the internal layout and the relationships between opaque surfaces and glazing, and introducing exceptional features to create strong visual reference points inside the system of urban routes.

These variations and exceptions – skilfully introduced in the rigorous compositional order imposed by the prefabricated construction system – manage to produce in visitors a pleasant sensation of being in a 'real city'. Organised as 'urban fabric' and not as a traditional introverted 'object', the shopping cluster, completed in 2005, builds physical connections with the existing city, also functioning as a 'gate' of access to the new park. Another access to the park from Via Traiano is provided along the path that cuts diagonally across the interesting residential block designed by Cino Zucchi, completed in 2008, where the tall buildings are not conceived as isolated towers, but instead

as a 'porous' residential tissue that generates a transition between the urban grid and the park.

The project for the plaza and the three linear office buildings was completed by Studio Valle Architetti Associati which, under the guidance of Valle's wife Piera and his son Pietro, has taken on – with great rigour and expertise – the difficult task of finishing and revising the many projects and worksites left in progress[13] when the great master passed away in 2003. Studio Valle has not only controlled the correct implementation of the design for the shopping cluster, already defined in nearly all its constituent parts at the time of Gino's death, but has also autonomously responded to various requests of the client, when construction was in an advanced phase, especially to insert the two new covered galleries that cut diagonally across the two buildings that end along Via Traiano. The same thing has happened with the design of the sloping plaza, where choices made independently, such as that of the curved design of the pavement (developed with the German landscape designers of the Topotek 1 group), the variation of the inclined blocks of the construction system and of the height, have been implemented in a way fully consistent with the principles of Valle's urban design.

Due to its urban and architectural qualities, Portello epitomises Gino Valle's mature expertise, perhaps a testament[14] because it sums up many creative tensions, constructive themes and compositional figures found in his later work. Far from the noise of the increasingly spectacular accents of contemporary architecture, Valle managed to compose, in an apparently 'softer' tone, a true 'city piece' using, as few others have been able, a limited range of standardised construction components – also prefabricated – to build 'real streets with porticoes' and structures capable of expressing a lofty idea of civil architecture. As Fulvio Irace has correctly pointed out, the true novelty of the Portello project lies in its way of presenting itself as a 'normal' city, offering 'a terse alternative to the idea of growth fuelled by media hype around the new "symbols" of an apparently more international Milan, a city that is actually in the grip of a stereotyped idea of modernity represented by ill-advised skyscrapers and superficially fashionable languages'.[15] This appeal to a 'normal' dimension of the city is anything but banal in the case of Portello, for two reasons: first, it was very difficult to intervene in such a heterogeneous, fragmented context, and to manage to construct a clear urban identity so that today, walking in the Portello, it is possible to have a sensation of a unified landscape instead of a basic juxtaposition of fragments; second, Valle knew how to apply, in an innovative way, the great experience he had gained in the field of industrial architecture, transferring it into the realm of commercial architecture and transforming it, to all effects, into 'urban architecture'. In this way, on a larger scale, Valle proposes the same conceptual operation attempted for the first time in the city hall of Casarsa at the end of the 1960s, when the pieces of the 'non-architecture' of the Zanussi equipped axis were deployed in a shrewd 'urban' composition to form a very small 'civic pole' capable of representing the idea of a 'centre' for community life. At Portello the compositional game becomes more refined and detailed, though within the limits of a budget – and a tight one in this case, although it did not prevent Valle from creating 'a landscape enlivened by a sequence

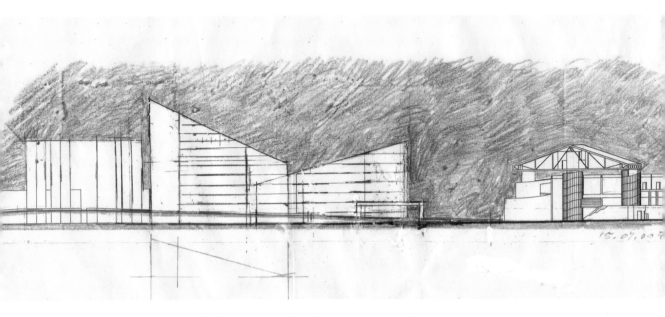

Conversion plan of the former Alfa Romeo area at Portello, project for the plaza and three linear office buildings towards the Fair, facade, July 2002.

View of the constructed complex at Portello, 2014, with the plaza in foreground and the shopping cluster to the rear.

of memorable fragments'.[16] According to this evocative critical interpretation of Alessandro Rocca, it is possible to identify a specific character in these works of 'architecture for commerce', at Portello and at Bufalotta, perhaps not previously explored by Valle in his architecture for industry: a character of 'perhaps rather brutal force' that accepts 'the practicality and economies imposed by the situation as an opportunity to reconstitute a new, ironic and efficient vocabulary for commercial architecture'.[17]

Valle often reminded his students of the importance of thinking of architecture as not only a spatial but also, and above all, a temporal experience, just as the metaphor he liked to use to describe the vision of his work as an 'uninterrupted flow' was also temporal. Years later, the architecture of Gino Valle remains relevant, bearing witness to a rare quality in contemporary production, the capacity to 'last in time' in order to construct authentically urban spaces.

Notes

1   In this quote, Valle curiously associates the question of the client with a film by George Romero: 'As in an American horror film from thirty years ago, called *Night of the Living Dead*, the point is to make culture in spite of the limitations of the client. In that film there were corpses reactivated by the radiation from a missile, which spread terror in the countryside, eating locals and tourists. There was horror, but also a sense of comedy.' See Sandro Marpillero, 'Sandro Marpillero intervista Gino Valle da New York', *Lotus Navigator*, Special Issue on Gino Valle, 1, November 2000, p.79. In the sequel by Romero (*Dawn of the Dead*, 1978) the zombies retreated inside an enormous shopping mall abandoned by consumers, the last refuge of the heroes of the film.

2   In 1993, the municipality identified the zone for an Area Plan, expressing an intention to alter the urban functions specified in the Master Plan. In 1997, with Resolution no. 167 of 13 August 1997, the City of Rome approved the proposal of the Rutelli administration entitled 'Program Agreement for Approval of the Area Project of the Bufalotta Zone', inserting the renewal projects for Bufalotta in those of the 'Roma Capitale' programme (leg. 396 in 1990), as part of the urban recovery and revitalisation of the suburbs through the creation of urban services, and the improvement of badly deteriorated surrounding areas. In 1998, a Program Agreement between the City of Rome, the Lazio Region and ANAS was approved with the Resolution of the City Council no. 167 of 9 September 1998, and in January 2001, the agreement between Società Porta di Roma SRL. and the City of Rome was signed. In April 2001, the worksite for the urban development was established. The IKEA megastore opened on 16 June 2005, while the Porta di Roma shopping centre opened on 25 July 2007.

3   This 'period of new urban planning' of the Rutelli and Veltroni administrations received harsh criticism, also by the media. One of the most critical voices was

that of the urbanist and activist of Italia Nostra, Paolo Berdini. See Paolo Berdini, 'Roma tra pianificazione e contrattazione', *Contesti. Città territori progetti*, the journal of the Department of Urbanism and Territorial Planning of the University of Florence, 2/2008 (Modelli di governo del territorio), Florence, 2009, pp.79–88. See also Paolo Berdini, *La città in vendita*, Editori Riuniti, Rome, 2008, which openly criticises the model of negotiated urbanism.

4   The new Master Plan is the first overall urban planning document since 1965. It was developed by an interdisciplinary group coordinated by Maurizio Marcelloni and approved by the City Council in March 2006 and by the Lazio Region in February 2008.

5   To comply with the stipulations of the Master Plan, and under pressure from many neighbourhood associations, the City adopted the principle of extension of Line B of the metropolitan rail system as far as Bufalotta-Porta di Roma. For a discussion of the case of Bufalotta, see Hélène Nessi and Aurélien Delpirou, 'Les politiques de "développement urbain durable" face aux héritages territoriaux. Regards romains sur la coordination transport/urbanisme', *Flux*, 75, 2009, pp.69–79, with a particular focus on the problem of the relationship between urban development and public transport policy.

6   Maurizio Marcelloni, coordinator of the new Master Plan, points out that Bufalotta 'is one of the few projects for which it has been possible to make a model', which would imply that in many other Roman negotiated urban development operations the urban design was totally lacking. See Maurizio Marcelloni, *Pensare la città contemporanea: il nuovo piano regolatore di Roma*, Laterza, Rome & Bari, 2003, p.140.

7   It was Valle who convinced the management of IKEA to accept this significant change with respect to the standard of its other megastores all over Italy, such as the first IKEA at Anagnina (1998). See Alessandra Criconia,

'Shopping Center, Megastore e altro ancora', *Architetture dello shopping*, Meltemi, Rome, 2009, pp.82–4.

8   Portello and the Fair are two of the most typical places in modern Milan. In historical terms, the *portello* (gate) was a secondary exit opened in the northwestern part of the Spanish walls, near the castle, from which a road extended into the countryside, in the direction of Gallarate. In the early 20th century (1910) the car manufacturer Alfa (Anonima Lombarda Fabbrica Automobili) opened a plant here which grew rapidly: in 1918 Alfa Romeo had an area of 160,000 square metres, which grew to 240,000 in 1940 with the doubling of the facility to the north of Viale Serra. After World War II even these spaces were deemed insufficient. In 1959, it was decided to move Alfa Romeo to a new plant in Arese (2,000,000 square metres), and the first hypotheses for the urban transformation of Portello, linked to the expansion of the Fair, began to be discussed.

9   Submitted in November 1984, the project by Sergio Crotti (coordinated by Andrea Balzani and Alberto Secchi) called for a very compact settlement that would combine, in a single organism, the expansion of the Fair, a convention centre spanning Viale Scarampo, and a hospitality facility with two hotels and a short-term apartment complex. This interesting project was published in the context of a more general investigation of new strategies of urban transformation in Milan: 'I progetti e il piano per Milano', *Casabella*, 508, December 1984, pp.18–29.

10   The Portello areas were acquired by the companies Nuova Portello and Auredia of Gruppo Finiper in 1997, and the Program Agreement with the City and the Region was signed in December 1998. The procedure followed to obtain the urban transformation of the area was that of the Integrated Intervention Program approved in January 2001.

11   Gino Valle, Project Description, 2002.

12   In 2005 Studio Valle added two 'passages' to increase the density and the linear extension of the windows to facilitate the insertion of smaller stores.

13   See the publication Pietro Valle, *Valle Architetti Associati 2003–16*, Libria, Melfi, 2016, with an introductory essay by Giovanni Corbellini.

14   Portello has met with a very positive reception from critics, not just on the level of specialised architectural criticism, but also due to its process of urban transformation. Together with a few French and Spanish examples, the shopping cluster designed by Valle has been cited as one of the few European examples 'that demonstrate how that indifference to the organisation of the city that characterized the better part of shopping centre projects and contributed to deconstruct the territory is being abandoned. Thus conceived, shopping centres can be the lever of a new urban design.' See Maurizio Morandi, 'I centri commerciali nella città diffusa. Le nuove centralità', in Giandomenico Amendola (ed.), *La città vetrina. I luoghi del commercio e le nuove forme del consumo*, Liguori Editore, Napoli, 2006, p.133.

15   Fulvio Irace, 'Milano progetto Portello. Una nuova porta urbana', *Abitare*, 445, December 2004, pp.151–60.

16   Alessandro Rocca, 'Due architetture a Milano, in presa diretta con la città', in Nico Ventura (ed.), *Da, chez, from Gino Valle*, exh. cat., MusArc, Ferrara, 2005, pp.21–5.

17   Rocca also proposes interpreting Valle's works of 'commercial architecture' in a 'polemical' sense: 'we might imagine, certainly in an arbitrary but perhaps not so fantastic way, that such an insistent repertoire of ruthless crudities sets out to unmask the clichés, hypocrisies and taboos on which the artists of architectural composition feed'. Alessandro Rocca, 'Due architetture a Milano', p.23.

Shopping Mall and Urban District

Bufalotta-Porta di Roma

Rome, 1991–2007

The Bufalotta project configures a new urban settlement along the Grande Raccordo Anulare (GRA, orbital motorway) between the neighbourhoods of Val Melaina and Fidene-Castel Giubileo, in a hilly zone of undeveloped countryside. The new city portion takes the landscape as a relational element between the parts of the project, proposing a settlement with a high percentage of green areas accessible to the public (about 50 per cent of the 332 hectares covered by the plan) composed of parks and pathways that adapt to the topography of the terrain. In the park, the 'signs' found in the recent archaeological campaign conducted by the Archaeological Superintendency of Rome (villas, aqueducts) become the reference points of the design, and of the expansion of the new Parco delle Sabine, which penetrates the neighbourhood.

The main axis of the plan is a tree-lined boulevard that crosses the area with a winding route in an east–west direction. This principal sign is repeatedly intersected by secondary streets (ring roads) with the form of a 'figure-of-eight' in the plan, bordering the entire area. The intersections of the two systems form compartments (the neighbourhoods) with different uses, marked by an orthogonal circulation grid that orders the local edification. At the meeting points between the circulatory systems, squares (plazas) host public facilities: a theatre, hotels, a church and a healthcare centre. Office buildings along the main and residential streets of the neighbourhoods reach a height of seven storeys at certain nodal points but are mainly of low density. Particular care has gone into the design of the street sections and

Planimetric study for the Urban Park.

the location of parking to safeguard the presence of greenery and to take maximum advantage of the level shifts to visually connect the underground garages and the outside.

The plan includes a new junction with the GRA at the position of Via Settebagni, acting as the eastern entrance to the neighbourhood. At this intersection stands the Porta di Roma shopping centre, the largest concentration of stores and supermarkets in Europe, containing two parking levels (230,000 square metres) that serve two other levels of shopping malls, a multiplex cinema, a tower with hotel, the buildings of IKEA and Leroy Merlin and three sloping pedestrian plazas in a single structure. Unlike classic shopping malls that have outdoor car parks surrounding an isolated constructed container, it has been decided to concentrate all the functions in a single

Profiles of the complex.

megastructure on multiple levels, surrounded by perimeter roads leading to the parking facilities. The structure, made with prefabricated concrete parts with a grid of eight × eight metres, thus serves four levels, two for parking and two for pedestrian malls. The enormous roof, the fifth facade of the complex, is marked by the presence of pyramidal skylights that bring light to the various internal levels.

Since the death of Gino Valle in 2003, the shopping centre project has been revised, completed and built by Studio Valle Architetti Associati.

The skylights and the large tower at the entrance are also the architectural features that signal the presence of the complex from a distance and orient the public in the path of access to the centre. Approaching by car, the towers can be seen from a distance, and one follows the border of the complex on the perimeter road. The visitor then penetrates the large parking area, open at the sides to allow natural light to enter and to assist orientation.

The facades are made with heavy ochre-colour concrete panels with a very rugged surface displaying a tuff-stone appearance. The panels are used on the covered structures and the terracing of the plazas. The many staircases of the security exits are encased in mesh panels that form a screen around the tuff-concrete and a continuous surface for advertisements. The top of the main volumes at the centre is in matte zinc, luminous, but non-reflective. The groups of skylights form a turreted skyline clad in reflecting aluminium roof tiles that becomes an architectural landmark when seen from afar.

Pietro Valle, 2007

View of the tower and the internal plaza.

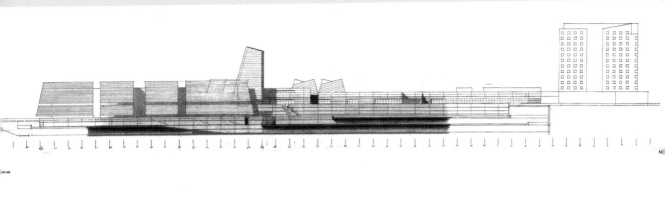

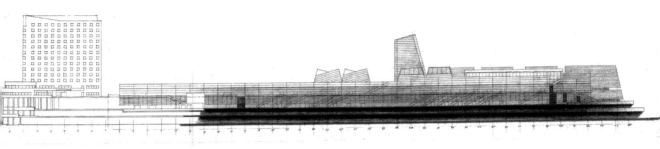

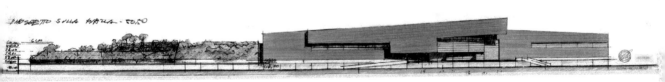

Profiles of the shopping centre: section through three sloping plazas, parking areas and front of the IKEA building.

Plan at the level of the galleria of the shopping centre.

Portello Shopping Cluster

Milan, 2001–2005

The five buildings of the shopping cluster form an urban set that defines the corner between Via Papa, Via Traiano and Via Grosotto, marked by the radial design of the semicircle of Piazzale Accursio. Placed at the northwest corner of the zone involved in the Detail Plan, the complex borders on the park, the new residential block to the east and Istituto Palazzolo to the south. The walkway that connects the new inclined plaza in front of the Fair to the park terminates in the heart of the shopping cluster with a pedestrian plaza covered by a large 'Sail' (a canopy on pillars), 14 metres high, that marks the centre of the complex. Pedestrian paths with porticoes converge on the plaza, with shops and department stores, served by a single, large underground parking facility that joins all the buildings.

Since the death of Gino Valle in 2003, the shopping cluster project has been revised, completed and built by Studio Valle Architetti Associati.

The five buildings that border the plaza with the 'Sail' have similar features but display individual characters, to form a perceptive geography of recognisable places. Buildings 1, 2 and 3, separated by two narrow drives, contain the large retail facilities on the ground floor, while the upper level is for offices, set back from the plaza front. Building 4 also has a single main level occupied by medium and small retail spaces, with porticoes on the north and west sides. On the outer side, along Via Traiano, it has an overhanging triangular volume that contains the offices on the upper level and signals the urban angle where the cluster begins, from a distance. Building 5, at the corner of Via Grosotto and Via Traiano, is the tallest of the complex and features a series of terraced volumes with porticoes and shops on the ground floor, and offices on the three levels above.

All the buildings have a prefabricated structure in reinforced concrete and infill with concrete panels, also precast, in tones of grey and white to form a unified whole. The porticoes, with a height of 3.5 metres, have pairs of metal columns, set eight metres apart, while the 'Sail' has a steel structure clad in aluminium, like the wing of a plane.

The plaza is paved with natural hewn porphyry slabs, in two tones: grey for the pavement under the porticoes, red for the parts in the open air.

The choice of materials (porphyry, concrete with neutral colouring and anodised aluminium) contributes to form a unified and neutral whole that forms a backdrop for events and the store signs.

Pietro Valle, 2003

(*right*) Siteplan.

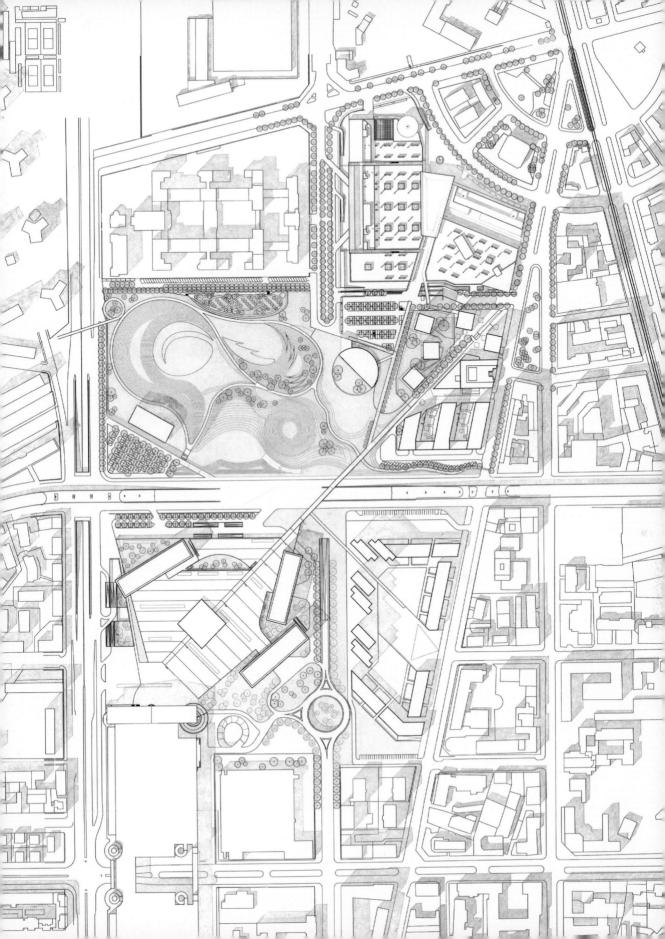

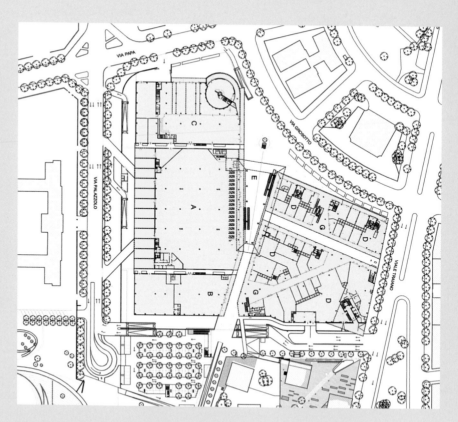

Plan at the level of the ground floor, with the pedestrian paths and the central plaza.

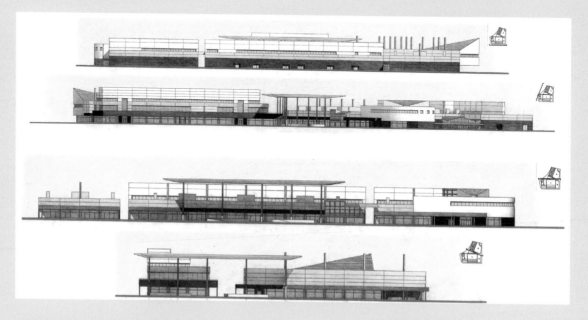

Profiles of the shopping cluster.

Nocturnal view of the sail covering the central plaza.

View of the porticoes around the plaza.

View of the overhang on Via Traiano.

Biographical Notes

1923   Gino Valle is born in Udine.

1948   After experience as a painter (two works selected for the Premio Bergamo in 1943), he takes a degree at the Istituto Universitario di Architettura di Venezia (IUAV, studying with Carlo Scarpa and Giuseppe Samonà); he begins to work in the studio of his father Provino, founding Studio Architetti Valle, later joined by his sister Nani in 1952 (until 1958) and Piera Ricci Menichetti in 1961.

1951   Fulbright Scholarship for the Urban Planning programme at Harvard Graduate School of Design, Cambridge, Massachusetts, USA.

1952   Studies with William L.C. Wheaton and Walter Gropius; Bachelor of City and Regional Planning, and study grant of the Institute for International Education (USA). In this period, among others, he visits the works of Frank Lloyd Wright.

1952–54   Teacher for the courses of the International Summer School of CIAM in Venice.

1954–55   Lecturer for the course in Applications of Descriptive Geometry at IUAV; product design consultant for Solari and Zanussi.

1956   Compasso d'Oro prize for the Cifra 5 Solari electric clock.

1962   Compasso d'Oro prize for the Rex Zanussi stove.

1962–63   Teacher and coordinator of Product Design in the advanced course in Industrial Design in Venice.

1963   Compasso d'Oro prize for the Solari alphanumeric split-flap displays.

1964–67   Member of the Education Working Group of ICSID (International Council of Industrial Designers).

1965   Annual Discourse at Royal Institute of British Architects, London; delivers lectures in Nottingham, Preston, Glasgow, Liverpool, UK

1965–68   Associate at Unimark International, New York, Chicago.

1966   Lecturing post in Elements of Composition.

1967–71   Vice-President of ICSID.

1967–71   Teaching activities at various universities in the USA, South Africa and Europe.

1972–76   Lecturer for the Composition IV course at IUAV.

1975   Member of the Accademia Nazionale di San Luca.

1976–94   Full professor of Architectural and Urban Composition at IUAV.

(*left*) Gino Valle, 1970.

Piera Ricci-Menichetti and Gino Valle in Venice, June 1960.

1983–85	Member of the Gestaltungsbeirat of the City of Salzburg.	1993	Honorary member of AIA (American Institute of Architects).
1988	Antonio Feltrinelli Prize for Architecture assigned by Accademia Nazionale dei Lincei.	1995	Compasso d'Oro career award.
1991	International Stone Architecture Award (second edition) for the Banca Commerciale Italiana building in New York, as best example of a work made with the use of stone.	2002	Receives the diploma 'Medaglia d'argento ai Benemeriti della scuola della cultura e dell'arte' from the Italian President of the Republic.
1991	Premio Piranesi.	2003	Dies in Udine. Studio Valle Architetti Associati continues its activity with Piera Ricci Menichetti, his son Pietro Valle and their staff.

List of Works

Bisaro building (apartments and studio)
Udine, Viale Venezia, 1945–50
with Provino Valle

Project for seasonal rental apartments and Bulian store
Lignano Sabbiadoro (Udine), 1946
with Provino Valle

Margherita cinema-tavern
Tarcento (Udine), 1946–57
  – first phase, 1946–48
  – second phase, 1957
with Provino Valle

Project for Furlanis house
Lignano Sabbiadoro (Udine), 1947
with Provino Valle

Project for Fabro building (four waterfront apartments)
Lignano Sabbiadoro (Udine), 1947
with Provino Valle

Projects for Bevilacqua building and Bevilacqua house
Lignano Sabbiadoro (Udine), 1947–49
with Provino Valle

Vacation residence for Cooperativa Muratori di Udine
Lignano Sabbiadoro (Udine), 1948–49
Degree thesis
Istituto Universitario di Architettura di Venezia

Foghini house
San Giorgio di Nogaro (Udine), 1948–52
with Nani Valle

Project for a pub-restaurant on Lake Cavazzo
Lago di Cavazzo (Udine), 1949
with Provino Valle

Project for the tourism-hotel complex of the Monte Lussari cableway
Ugovizza, Malborghetto-Valbruna (Udine), 1949
with Provino Valle

Project for a covered pedestrian passage between Via Mercatovecchio and Piazza San Cristoforo
Udine, 1949
with Provino Valle

Kindergarten
Fielis (Udine), 1949–50

Project for Moretti ice factory and warehouse
Lignano Sabbiadoro (Udine), 1949–50
with Provino Valle

Project for the 'Istituto tecnico governativo commerciale e per geometri'
Udine, 1950–52
national competition, first prize
revised, 1951–52
with Provino and Nani Valle

Vriz residential and office tower
Trieste, 1950–57
with Provino and Nani Valle
projects for building B, 1956–70
with Piera Ricci Menichetti, Akira Muto
collaborator: Donald D. Appleyard

Ghetti house
Codroipo (Udine), 1951
with Nani Valle

Capannone Migotto
Santa Caterina (Udine), 1952

Veranda of Romanelli house
Udine, 1952–53
with Nani Valle, John R. Myer

Project for Ceretelli house
Lignano Sabbiadoro (Udine), 1953

Project for three Cortolezzis houses
Treppo Carnico (Udine), 1953
with John R. Myer

First project for Nicoletti house
Udine, 1953

Moretti warehouse
Lignano Sabbiadoro (Udine), 1953

Expansion of Nicoletti clinic
Udine, 1953–54
with Provino and Nani Valle

Migotto (now Pozzi) house
Udine, 1953–54
with Provino and Nani Valle

Quaglia house
Sutrio (Udine), 1953–54
with Provino and Nani Valle

Cassa di Risparmio di Udine
Udine, 1953–55
refurbishing of headquarters
with Provino and Nani Valle
collaborators: Giuseppe Baritussio,
John R. Myer

Cassa di Risparmio di Latisana
Latisana (Udine), 1954–56
with Provino and Nani Valle
collaborators: John R. Myer, Dino Basaldella
(sculpture)

Public hospital
Portogruaro (Venice), 1954–68
  – first lot, 1954–57
with Provino and Nani Valle
collaborators: Donald S. Appleyard, Giuseppe
Baritussio
  – fifth and sixth lots, 1966–68
with Nani Valle
collaborator: Carlo Mauro

Project for the Cassa di Risparmio di Gorizia
Gorizia, 1955
invitational competition, second prize
with Nani Valle and Donald S. Appleyard

Project for city hall
Pordenone, 1956
national competition, second prize
with Nani Valle and Aldo Bernardis
collaborator: Donald S. Appleyard

Project for Privileggio building
Udine, 1956
with Donald S. Appleyard

Bellini house
Udine, 1956–57
with Nani Valle, Donald S. Appleyard, Federico
Marconi

Product design for Industrie Zanussi
1956–62
with Gastone Zanello, Tullia Tul Designers and
Ufficio Disegno Industriale Zanussi
  – washing machines: mod. 202, 1957; mod. 211,
  1958; mod. 260, 1961
  – built-in refrigerator, 1959
  – stoves: mod. Rex 700, 1962
  – coordinated kitchen C70, 1967
  – design of televisions, 1960

City hall
Treppo Carnico (Udine), 1956–58
with Nani Valle, Federico Marconi, Giuseppe Zigaina
(mural), Dino Basaldella (bas relief)

Product design for Solari
1956–68
  – Cifra 5, 1954
  – Dator 5, 1958
  – Cifra 3, 1960–66 (with Massimo Vignelli for the
  lettering)
  – Split-flap displays, 1960
  – Dator 6, 1961

Zanussi offices
Porcia (Pordenone), 1957–61
  – first and second project, 1957–59
with Federico Marconi
  – third project, built, 1959–61
collaborator: Alfredo Carnelutti

Elementary school
Sutrio (Udine), 1957–62
with Nani Valle, Federico Marconi, Ken Terris

Project for the municipal theatre
Udine, 1957–64
national competition, first prize
definitive project, 1961–64

Project for the renewal of the historical centre
Udine, 1958
national competition, third prize
with Nani Valle and Federico Marconi

Project for the Istituto psicopedagogico
Adorgnano (Udine), 1958
Triveneto competition second prize
with Nani Valle and Federico Marconi

Project for Zanussi house
Pordenone, 1958
with Nani Valle and Federico Marconi

Residential building on Via Marinoni
Udine, 1958–60
with Firmino Toso

Project for Zanussi guesthouse
Porcia (Pordenone), 1959
with Federico Marconi

Project for the reconstruction of Palazzo Rubazzer
Udine, Piazza Lionello, 1959
with Paolo Pascolo

Arti Grafiche Chiesa plant
Tavagnacco (Udine), 1959–60

Nicoletti house
Udine, 1959–61
collaborators: Alfredo Carnelutti, Carlo Mauro

Monument to the Resistance
Udine, 1959–69
national competition, first prize
revision of the project 1963, construction 1967–69
with Federico Marconi, Giuseppe Baritussio, Adelchi
De Cillia, Carlo Mauro, Dino Basaldella (sculpture),
George Gyssels (landscape)

Hot springs spa
Arta Terme (Udine), 1960–64
collaborators: Lorenzo Giacomuzzi-Moore, Alfredo
Carnelutti, Giuseppe Baritussio, Carlo Mauro

Project for veranda for the Moretti brewery
Udine, Piazza 26 July, 1961

Project for development of the industrial zone Osoppo-Rivoli for Ziro spa
Osoppo (Udine), 1961

Scala ceramics factory
Orcenigo (Pordenone), 1961

Project for the Banca Cattolica
Udine, 1961
national competition, second prize
with Renzo Agosto, F. Anichini, Lorenzo Giacomuzzi-Moore, R. Pannelli

Project for the Cille factory
Trieste, 1961

Urban Design Plan and project for residential building
Piano del Nevegal (Belluno), 1961–68
with Piera Ricci Menichetti
collaborator: Alfredo Carnelutti

Project for the city hall
Jesolo (Venice), 1962

Sipre prefabrication plant
Tavagnacco (Udine), 1962–63

Standard warehouse for Industrie Zanussi-Rex
Porcia (Pordenone), 1963
warehouses built in Bergamo, Milan, Padua, Perugia, Rome

Renovation of Romanelli house
Udine, 1963–64
with Piera Ricci Menichetti
collaborator: Alfredo Carnelutti

Zanussi kitchens factory
Porcia (Udine), 1963–64

Commercial building (Casa Brigo)
Udine, Via Mercatovecchio, 1963–65

collaborators: Alfredo Carnelutti, Giuseppe Baritussio

Chiesa house (addition and renovation)
Udine, 1963–66
with Piera Ricci Menichetti
collaborators: Carlo Mauro, Giuseppe Baritussio

Detail Plan
Caorle – Porto Santa Margherita (Venice), 1963–72
with Lisa Ronchi

Scala ceramics factory
Burgos (Spain), 1964–66

Project for Zanussi administrative centre
Pordenone, Via Montereale, 1965

Manzano house
Udine, 1965–66
collaborators: Alfredo Carnelutti, Carlo Mauro

Project for Residential Tower 140
Chicago, Lake Shore Drive, 1966
with Piera Ricci Menichetti
collaborator: Alfredo Carnelutti

City hall
Casarsa della Delizia (Pordenone), 1966–74
construction 1972–74
with Piera Ricci Menichetti
collaborators: Alfredo Carnelutti, Carlo Mauro, Nelson Zizzutto

Project for plant of Rocky Mountain Dental Products
Denver (Colorado), 1966–68
collaborator: Alfredo Carnelutti

Zanussi equipped axis
Porcia (Pordenone), 1966–70
 – dining hall, 1966
 – DIAD offices, 1967–70
 – human resources offices and central reception
   desk, 1969

Project for Palazzo delle Associazioni Culturali
Udine, Via Manin, 1966–74
   – first project, 1966
   – second project, 1971–74
collaborator: Alfredo Carnelutti

Pighin wine firm
Risano (Udine), 1967
collaborators: Alfredo Carnelutti, Carlo Mauro

Project for the public hospital
Mirano (Venice), 1967
competition, second prize
with Giorgio Bellavittis, Piera Ricci Menichetti and
Nani Valle

Headquarters of the newspaper *Il Messaggero*
Veneto
Udine, 1967–68
with Piera Ricci Menichetti
collaborators: Alfredo Carnelutti, George Gyssels
(landscape)

Detail Plan of the Sitav tourism zone
Saint Vincent (Aosta), 1967–68

Project for the headquarters of La Rinascente
Milan, 1967–72
with Herbert Ohl and Willy Ramstein
collaborator: Alfredo Carnelutti

Project for the Upim shopping centre
Milan, Via Carducci, 1968–69
with Herbert Ohl and Willy Ramstein

Project for a nursery school
Rualis di Cividale (Udine), 1968–69
with Piera Ricci Menichetti

Renovation of Valle house
Udine, Piazza Primo Maggio, 1969
with Piera Ricci Menichetti
collaborator: Adelchi De Cillia

Project for Palazzo della Regione
Udine, 1969–75

with Piera Ricci Menichetti
collaborators: Alfredo Carnelutti, Adelchi De Cillia

Project for the Olivetti factory
Ivrea, 1970
collaborator: Alfredo Carnelutti

INA commercial and residential building
Udine, Via Marinelli, 1970–71
with Piera Ricci Menichetti
collaborators: Alfredo Carnelutti, Carlo Mauro

**Project for parking and refurbishing of Piazza Primo
Maggio**
Udine, 1970–72

Project for the Professional Institute for Commerce
Majano (Udine), 1970–73
with Piera Ricci Menichetti

Project for multisport stadium
Udine, 1971
competition tender, third prize
with Pierluigi Missio

Zanussi electric accounting centre
Pordenone, 1971–73

**Project for traffic terminal and office/shopping
centre**
Trieste, 1972–73

Plan of Laghi di Sibari
Cassano Ionio (Cosenza), 1972–74
with Giorgio Macola

Administrative centre on Galvani area
Pordenone, 1972–82
construction 1979–82
collaborators: Alfredo Carnelutti, Adelchi De Cillia,
Nelson Zizzutto

Fantoni industrial campus
Osoppo (Udine), 1972–96
   – offices and service centre, 1972–75
    (reconstruction after earthquake 1976–78)

– plants, 1974–77/1978/1985
    – MDF plant, 1985–90
with Sergio Marzona
collaborator: Marco Carnelutti
    – entrance (customs, receiving), 1995–96
with Sergio Marzona
collaborator: Gianpietro Franceschinis
    – showroom (auditorium and display space),
      1996
with Mario Broggi, Michael Burckhardt

Warehouse and showroom of Grandi Cucine Geatti
Terenzano (Udine), 1973–74
collaborator: Carlo Mauro

Dapres faced chipboard production plant
Portogruaro (Venice), 1973–74
collaborator: Nelson Zizzutto

Project for the Professional Institute for Commerce, Industry and Crafts
Pordenone, 1973–74
with Piera Ricci Menichetti

City hall
Fontanafredda (Pordenone), 1973–81
addition, 1990
with Giorgio Macola
collaborators: Nelson Zizzutto, Carlo Mauro

Project for residences on the Moretti area
Udine, 1973–76
with Piera Ricci Menichetti
collaborator: Marco Carnelutti

Exhibit design for Venice Biennale
Venice, 1974–76
with Marica Redini, Germano Celant,
Franco Raggi

Valdadige prefabricated schools
1974–84
schools built in Bissuola (Venice), Chirignago
(Venice), Voghera, 1976; San Quirino (Pordenone),
Zelarino (Venice), San Leonardo di Cividale (Udine),
Trasaghis (Udine), 1977; Lurago d'Erba (Como),

Pasian di Prato (Udine), Trofarello (Torino), Cassano
Magnago (Varese), Varese, Forni Avoltri (Udine),
Udine (elementary and middle schools), Lombrugo
(Como), Fontanafredda (Pordenone), Brescia,
Belluno, 1978; Seriate (Bergamo), Fontanafredda
(Pordenone), Chiari (Brescia), Cerro Veronese
(Verona), Albaredo d'Adige (Verona), Villaguardia
(Como), Cavazzo Carnico (Udine), Zuglio (Udine),
Feltre, Bissuola (Venice), 1979; Negrar (Verona),
Castronno (Varese), 1980; Dignano (Udine),
Castiglione Olona (Varese), 1982; Mercallo dei Sassi
(Varese), 1983; Udine, Salboro (Padua), 1984.
with Giorgio Macola
collaborator: Giuliana Ceccotti

Project for the Monument to the Partisans and the Victims of the Massacre at Piazza della Loggia
Brescia, 1975
with Alfredo Carnelutti

Zoppas corporate dining hall
Susegana (Treviso), 1975–76

City hall
Sutrio (Udine), 1975–78
with Giorgio Macola
collaborators: Nelson Zizzutto, Carlo Mauro

Kursaal
Arta Terme (Udine), 1975–78
with Giorgio Macola
collaborators: Nelson Zizzutto, Carlo Mauro

Building for 100 IACP housing units
Udine, 1975–79
with Giorgio Macola, Maria Loretta Tondolo
collaborator: Carlo Mauro

Project for a shopping centre
Arta Terme (Udine), 1976–79
with Piera Ricci Menichetti
collaborator: Adelchi De Cillia

Tomb of Pier Paolo Pasolini
Casarsa della Delizia (Pordenone), 1977

Project for a senior citizens' centre
Buia (Udine), 1977–78
collaborator: Maria Loretta Tondolo

Low-cost housing complex
Santo Stefano di Buia (Udine), 1977–79
with Piera Ricci Menichetti
collaborators: Alfredo Carnelutti, Nelson Zizzutto

Restoration and restructuring of the block of Banca Commerciale Italiana
Milan, 1977–2000
– restoration of Palazzo Besana on Piazzetta
Belgioioso, 1977–81
– restoration of the headquarters on Piazza della
Scala, 1986–2000
with Mario Broggi, Michael Burckhardt
collaborators: Alfredo Carnelutti, Andrea Nulli, Luca Ranza

Banca Commerciale Italiana branch office
Padua, 1977–81
collaboratore: Alessandro Manaigo

Banca Commerciale Italiana branch office
Venice, 1977–81
collaborators: Nelson Zizzutto,
Carlo Mauro

Project for the Brionvega factory
Agrate (Milan), 1978
with Mario Broggi, Michael Burckhardt

Project for 'Teo system' low-cost housing types for Lombardy Region
1978
competition
with Ettore Fermi, Giorgio Macola, Marica Redini,
Piera Ricci Menichetti

Project for IBM facility
Pomezia (Rome), 1978

Project for courthouse
Udine, 1978
competition

with Piera Ricci Menichetti
collaborator: Alfredo Carnelutti

Bergamin Service and Distribution Centre
Portogruaro (Venice), 1978–80
collaborators: Adelchi De Cillia, Nelson Zizzutto

Renovation of Cojazzi house
Udine, 1979
with Piera Ricci Menichetti
collaborators: Nelson Zizzutto, Carlo Mauro

Giovanni Bergamin house
Summaga Portogruaro (Venice), 1979–83
with Piera Ricci Menichetti
collaborator: Nelson Zizzutto

IBM Italia Distribution Centre
Basiano (Milan), 1980–83
collaborators: Alfredo Carnelutti, Sandro Manaigo,
Nelson Zizzutto

Low-cost housing complex at Giudecca
Venice, 1980–86
with Giorgio Macola, Giuseppe Camporini, Maria
Caterina Redini
collaborators: Alfredo Carnelutti, Carlo Mauro,
Gianpietro Franceschinis, Giuliana Ceccotti, Nelson
Zizzutto, Sandro Manaigo

Reconstruction of an urban block
Gemona del Friuli (Udine), 1980–86
with Piera Ricci Menichetti, Alfredo Carnelutti

Reconstruction of an urban block
Santo Stefano di Buia (Udine), 1980–86
with Piera Ricci Menichetti
collaborators: Gianpietro Franceschinis, Nelson
Zizzutto

Project for a multifunctional gymnasium
Martignacco (Udine), 1981

Banca Commerciale Italiana headquarters
New York, One William Street, 1981–86
with Jeremy P. Lang

collaborators: Alfredo Carnelutti,
Marco Carnelutti

Bianca Bergamin house
Portogruaro (Venice), 1982–84
with Piera Ricci Menichetti
collaborator: Nelson Zizzutto

Reconstruction of the urban block no. 2
Venzone (Udine), 1982–86
with Piera Ricci Menichetti
collaborators: Adelchi De Cillia, Carlo Mauro

Headquarters of Cassa Rurale ed Artigiana Monte Magrè
Schio (Vicenza), 1982–87
collaborator: Marco Carnelutti

Project for Piazza San Cristoforo
Udine, 1983
competition
with Piera Ricci Menichetti
collaborators: Marco Carnelutti, Gianpaolo Londero

Project for residential centre
Castelnuovo di Conza (Salerno), 1983
competition tender
with Giorgio Macola

Elementary school
Berlin, Friedrichstrasse, 1983–87
with Mario Broggi, Michael Burckhardt, Walter Hotzel
collaborators: Marcella Rossin, Andrea Nulli, Vincenzo Dato, Renata Murnaghan

Project for residences
Fregnan area, island of Sacca Fisola, Venice, 1984
invitational competition
with Giorgio Macola, Maria Caterina Redini, Giorgio Camporini, Raimund Fein

Installation of exhibition by Emilio Vedova at Museo Correr
Venice, 1984
with Germano Celant

Project for low-cost housing
Vienna, 1984–85
with Franco Fonatti, Piera Ricci Menichetti, Marco Carnelutti

Urban Plan for Dora riverside park
Ivrea, 1984–85
with Sergio Porcellini

Olivetti plants
Ivrea, 1984–86
with Antonio Miliasso
collaborator: Marco Carnelutti

IBM office complex and hotel at La Défense
Paris, 1984–88
with Giorgio Macola, Fernando Urquijo
collaborators: François Cusson, Marco Carnelutti, Nelson Zizzutto, Gianpietro Franceschinis, Raimund Fein, Lorenzo Bader, Susan Franck, Tomas Martinez, Michel Hoelzer

Courthouse
Padua, 1984–90
with Piera Ricci Menichetti
collaborators: Marco Carnelutti, Gianpietro Franceschinis, Nelson Zizzutto, Walter Vidale, Paolo Turco

Project for SNAM offices
San Donato Milanese, 1985
invitational competition
collaborators: Raimund Fein, Marco Carnelutti, Gianpietro Franceschinis, Nelson Zizzutto

Renovation of IBM Italia offices
Milan, Corso Sempione, 1985–87
with Mario Broggi, Michael Burckhardt
collaborators: Andrea Nulli, Luca Ranza

Hotel
Nimes, 1985–87
collaborators: Raimund Fein, Ronald Schulz

Pirelli Bicocca project
Milan, 1985–88

invitational competition
   – first phase, 1985–86
with Aldo Ciocia, Ippolito Pizzetti, Sergio Porcellini,
Piera Ricci Menichetti, Roland Schulz, Raimund Fein
   – second phase, 1987–88
with Ippolito Pizzetti, Sergio Porcellini, Piera Ricci
Menichetti, Roland Schulz, Raimund Fein
collaborators: Adelchi De Cillia, Marco Carnelutti,
Gianpietro Franceschinis, Carlo Mauro, Paolo
Turco, Walter Vidale, Nelson Zizzutto, Robert
Zizzutto

Olivetti managerial offices
Ivrea, 1985–88
collaborators: Marco Carnelutti, Raimund Fein,
Sergio Porcellini

**Restoration of Palazzo Florio for the University of
Udine**
Udine, 1985–88
collaborators: Adelchi De Cillia, Carlo Mauro, Marco
Carnelutti

Elea corporate restaurant
Burolo (Turin), 1985–88
with Antonio Migliasso
collaborators: Raimund Fein, Marco Carnelutti

**Restoration and restructuring of former Olcese
cotton mill for Istituto Universitario di Architettura
di Venezia**
Venice, 1985–89
with Giorgio Macola

Urban design projects
Vicenza, 1985–1995
   – Detail Plan for the 'west shoulder', 1985
collaborators: Raimund Fein, Adelchi De Cillia
   – revision P.P.5, P.P.6, P.P.7, 1995
collaborators: Marco Carnelutti, Adelchi De Cillia,
Gianpietro Franceschinis, Roland Schulz,
Sandro Manaigo, Paolo Turco, Walter Vidale, Piero
Zucchi, Robert Zizzutto

Municipal theatre
Vicenza, 1985–2007

   – first phase, 1985–89
collaborators: Marco Carnelutti, Adelchi De Cillia,
Gianpietro Franceschinis, Roland Schulz,
Sandro Manaigo, Paolo Turco, Walter Vidale, Piero
Zucchi, Robert Zizzutto
   – second phase and construction, 2000–
2007
with Pietro Valle (from 2003), Marco Carnelutti,
Roland Henning
collaborators: Carlo Mauro, Paolo Turco, Walter
Vidale, Robert Zizzutto, Mario Gallinaro (structures),
Glauco Fontanive (physical plant)

Refurbishing of Winkler casino
Salzburg, 1986
invitational competition
collaborators: Raimund Fein, Roland Schulz

**Project for addition and facade of Kulissengebäude
of Staatstheater**
Stuttgart, 1986
invitational competition, third prize
collaborators: Marco Carnelutti, Raimund Fein,
Gianpietro Franceschinis, Roland Schulz,
Robert Zizzutto

**Renovation of Alitalia tower in IBM Italia
headquarters (now INAIL) at EUR**
Rome, 1986–93
construction 1991–93
with Cesare Costantini
collaborators: Gianpietro Franceschinis, Walter
Vidale

Courthouse
Brescia, 1986–2004
   – first project on Via Spalti San Marco, 1986–89,
     construction interrupted in 1990
   – second project on Via Gambara, 1997–2002,
     construction 2002–2004
   – parking on Via Gambara, 1998–2000
with Piera Ricci Menichetti, Pietro Valle, Gianpietro
Franceschinis
collaborators: Marco Carnelutti, Carlo Mauro,
Paolo Turco, Roland Henning, Walter Vidale,
Nelson Zizzutto, Robert Zizzutto

Project for a hotel
Salzburg, 1987
invitational competition
collaborator: Roland Schultz

Project for a museum complex
Vienna, 1987
competition
with Franco Fonati
collaborators: Roland Schulz, Giuliana Ceccotti,
Gianpietro Franceschinis, Walter Vidale

Project for the central square of Scutari
Istanbul, 1987
invitational competition, honorable mention
with Federico Marconi, Piera Ricci Menichetti,
Roland Schulz, Paolo Venturini, Alessio Princic

Project for the renovation of Palais du Trocadéro for Société Générale
Paris, 1987
with Giorgio Macola, Fernando Urquijo, Nicoletta
Macola
collaborators: François Cusson, Pablo Lorenzino,
Philippe Martin

Project for Firenze-Castello shopping centre and parking
Florence, 1987–88
collaborator: Roland Schulz

Project for Alisarda offices
Olbia, 1987–88
collaborators: Marco Carnelutti, Carlo Mauro,
Roland Schulz, Walter Vidale, Nelson Zizzutto, Paolo
Turco

Plan of parking and extension of Piazza Ghiaia
Parma, 1987–88
with Carlo Felice Corini, Gianni De Gregori, Piera
Ricci Menichetti
collaborators: Adelchi De Cillia, Gianpietro
Franceschinis, Sandro Manaigo

Project for former Ilssa-Viola industrial area
Pont Saint Martin (Aosta), 1987–88

with Sergio Porcellini
collaborator: Marco Carnelutti

Headquarters of Cassa Rurale ed Artigiana
Azzano Decimo (Pordenone), 1987–89
Collaborators: Nelson Zizzutto, Leonardo Brosolo,
Carlo Mauro

Project for residential complex
Montpellier le Peyrou, 1988
invitational competition
with Giorgio Macola, Fernando Urquijo, François
Cusson, Nicoletta Macola
collaborators: Stefano Estori, Pablo Lorenzino,
Philippe Martin

Project for ZAC Danton-La Défense
Paris, 1988
competition
with Giorgio Macola, Fernando Urquijo, Nicoletta
Macola
collaborators: Pablo Lorenzino, Philippe Martin,
Roland Shultz

Bergamin Sales Centre
Magnano in Riviera (Udine), 1988–89
with Marco Carnelutti, Adelchi De Cillia, Carlo
Mauro

Bergamin offices
Portogruaro (Venice), 1988–91
with Piera Ricci Menichetti
collaborators: Adelchi De Cillia, Marco Carnelutti,
Ippolito Pizzetti (landscape)

Urban projects for Bergamo south
Bergamo, 1988–96
  – area plan and urban project for the areas of
    the 'south development' in the context of the
    revision of the Master Plan, 1988
with Sergio Porcellini
collaborators: Adelchi De Cillia, Marco
Carnelutti
  – Detail Plan of precinct 8 of variant 35 of Master
    Plan, 1992–96
with Piera Ricci Menichetti

collaborators: Gianpietro Franceschinis, Paolo
Turco, Walter Vidale

Project for Le Triangle de la Folie – La Défense
Paris, 1989
competition
with Giorgio Macola, Fernando Urquijo, Nicoletta
Macola
collaborators: Pablo Lorenzino, Philippe Martin

Project for addition and renovation of Palais d'Iéna
Paris, 1989
invitational competition
with Giorgio Macola, Fernando Urquijo, Nicoletta
Macola
collaborators: Pablo Lorenzino, Philippe Martin

Project for Front de Maine
Angers (France), 1989
invitational competition
with Giorgio Macola, Fernando Urquijo
collaborators: Dimitri De Vecchi, Federico Castro,
Philippe Martin

Project for Mercedes offices and garage
Frankfurt, 1989
competition
with Roland Schulz, Chung Nguyen, Marco
Carnelutti, Gianpietro Franceschinis, Paolo Turco,
Walter Vidale, Nelson Zizzutto, Robert Zizzutto

Project for Bayer offices at Portello
Milan, 1989–90
invitational competition
collaborators: Marco Carnelutti, Gianpietro
Franceschinis, Adelchi De Cillia, Roland Schulz,
Walter Vidale, Robert Zizzutto

Urban projects on Ferrovie Nord areas
Saronno (Milan), 1989–97
  – preliminary architectural and urban design for
    the Saronno-Sud area, 1989–93
  – Detail Plan and definitive project of Saronno-
    Centro, 1994–97
with Piera Ricci Menichetti, Pietro Valle, Elena Carlini
collaborator: Piero Zucchi

Project for the European Patent Office
The Hague, 1989–90
invitational competition (first and second
phases)
with Giorgio Macola, Fernando Urquijo, Nicoletta
Macola
collaborators: Elisabetta Bedeschi, Giorgio Bello,
Dimitri De Vecchi, Stefano Estori, Chung Nguyen,
Philippe Martin, John O'Connor

Project for Société Générale – Gare d'Austerlitz
Paris, 1990
competition
with Giorgio Macola, Fernando Urquijo, Nicoletta
Macola
collaborators: Federico Castro, Philippe Martin,
Pascal Vairon

Project for administrative centre at Ivry
Paris, 1990
competition
with Giorgio Macola, Fernando Urquijo, Nicoletta
Macola
collaborators: Federico Castro, Philippe Martin,
Pascal Vairon

Project for ZAC Reuilly
Paris, 1990
competition
with Giorgio Macola, Fernando Urquijo, Nicoletta
Macola
collaborators: Federico Castro, Philippe Martin,
Pascal Vairon

**Project for the International Tribunal for
the Law of the Sea**
Hamburg, 1990
competition
with Roland Schulz, Chung Nguyen, Marco
Carnelutti, Walter Vidale, Robert Zizzutto

Polis project for port area
Trieste, 1990
with Pietro Valle, Elena Carlini
collaborators: Adelchi De Cillia, Giovanni
Maranzana, Robert Zizzutto

Guideline plan for urban reorganisation of the territory between the Fair, the railway and Via Antonio Grassi
Padua, 1990–95
collaborators: Paolo Turco, Adelchi De Cillia, Robert Zizzutto

Multifunctional centre
San Martino di Lupari (Padua), 1990–98
collaborators: Marco Carnelutti, Carlo Mauro, Chung Nguyen

Project for addition to Mondadori headquarters
Segrate (Milan), 1991
with Piera Ricci Menichetti

Project for renewal of Piazza Ghiaia, former Gondrand area
Parma, 1991–92
Detail Plan of public initiative
with Carlo Felice Corini, Gianni Di Gregorio, Pietro Lunardi (consultant group leader), Gian Luigi Capra, Maurizio Ghillani, Pietro Storchi (for City of Parma), Piera Ricci Menichetti

Renewal of Piazza Venerio and restoration of the church of San Francesco
Udine, 1991
collaborators: Carlo Mauro, Marco Carnelutti

Project for the offices of Olympia & York
London, 1991
collaborators: Marco Carnelutti, Gianpietro Franceschinis, Robert Zizzutto

Project for Piazzale Roma
Venice, 1991
competition
with Giorgio Macola, Giuseppe Camporini, Pietro Valle, Elena Carlini, John O'Connor

Project for Richti-Areal banking offices
Zurich, 1991
competition
with Broggi & Burckhardt Architetti Associati

Project for Hôtel du Département
Marseille, 1991
competition (first and second phases)
with Giorgio Macola, Fernando Urquijo, Daniel Fanzutti, Nicoletta Macola
collaborators: Elisabetta Bedeschi, Chiara Bressan, Giuseppe Camporini, Federico Castro, Dimitri and Stefano De Vecchi, Roberto Driusso, Mara Nave, John O'Connor

Project for Hôtel du Département
Toulouse, 1991–1992
competition (first and second phases)
with Giorgio Macola, Fernando Urquijo, Nicoletta Macola
collaborators: Giuseppe Camporini, Federico Castro, John O'Connor

Bufalotta – Porta di Roma district
Rome, 1991–2007
    – Detail Plan, 1992–97
collaborators: Marco Carnelutti, Sandro Manaigo, Walter Vidale, Paolo Turco, Piero Zucchi
    – Porta di Roma shopping mall, 1997–2007
with Pietro Valle (from 2003), Marco Carnelutti, Walter Vidale, in collaboration with Rosella Capri (Imprese Lamaro), Carlo Costantini (for IKEA)
collaborators: Ugo Tranquillini, Alessandro Manaigo, Piero Zucchi, Nelson Zizzutto

Project for addition to the IBM offices
Segrate, 1992

Project for an exhibition centre
Tashkent (Uzbekistan), 1992
competition
with Giorgio Macola, Nicoletta Macola, Bikan Tugberk
collaborators: Roberto Driusso, John O'Connor

Project for the San Paolo real estate complex
Turin, 1992
development of integrated planning programme

Project for the organisation of the monument and the area of Piazza Vittoria

Bolzano, 1992–95
collaborators: Pietro Valle, Elena Carlini, Paolo
Turco, Walter Vidale

Carabinieri barracks
Padua, 1992–96
collaborators: Marco Carnelutti,
Sandro Manaigo

**Project for the Rosmarinkaree area at
Berlin-Mitte**
Berlin, 1993
competition
with Broggi & Burckhardt Architetti Associati, Walter
Hoetzel

**Renovation of Société Générale office
building**
Paris, Avenue Victor-Hugo, 1993–99
with Giorgio Macola, Nicoletta Macola, Gianluca
Gamberini, Fernando Urquijo
collaborators: Marco Carnelutti, Gianpietro
Franceschinis

**Project for the headquarters of the newspaper
*Sole 24 ore***
Milan, 1994
competition
collaborators: Marco Carnelutti, Gianpietro
Franceschinis, Paolo Turco, Walter Vidale, Robert
Zizzutto

Project for the Borsigarel area at Berlin-Tegel
Berlin, 1994
with Broggi & Burckhardt Architetti Associati, Walter
Hoetzel

Renovation of the Bergamin Sales Centre
Latisana (Udine), 1994–95
collaborators: Marco Carnelutti, Carlo Mauro,
Robert Zizzutto

New university centre
Padua, 1994–2011
    – Department of Psychology 2, 1994–98
with Walter Vidale

collaborators: Carlo Mauro, Paolo Turco
    – Students' Centre, Linguistics Centre and
        Convention Centre, 1994–2011
with Pietro Valle (from 2003), Walter Vidale
collaborators: Francesco De Cillia, Carlo Mauro,
Paolo Turco, Robert Zizzutto

Project for the German government headquarters
Berlin, Spreeinsel, 1995
competition
with Broggi & Burckhardt Architetti Associati, Walter
Hoetzel

**Reorganisation of Piazza Cima and significant
urban spaces**
Conegliano (Treviso), 1995
with Maurizio Dall'Armellina

**Detail Plan of the R56a area and architectural
design of the buildings of Cooperativa**
Bologna, Barca-Casteldebole district, 1990–95
collaborators: Marco Carnelutti, Sandro Manaigo,
Pietro Valle, Elena Carlini, Robert Zizzutto

Eco Refrigerazione plant
Pocenia (Udine), 1995–96
collaborators: Marco Carnelutti, Carlo Mauro,
Walter Vidale

**Renovation of Cinema Nuovo and transformation
as cinema-theatre Pier Paolo Pasolini**
Cervignano del Friuli (Udine), 1995–96
collaborators: Marco Carnelutti, Carlo Mauro

Rhoss plant
Codroipo (Udine), 1995–96
collaborators: Marco Carnelutti, Carlo Mauro

Bergamin Sales Centre and Warehouse
Istrana (Treviso), 1995–96
with Giuseppe Scattolin
collaborators: Marco Carnelutti, Carlo Mauro

'Twin towers' office complex at San Benigno
Genoa, 1995–97
collaborators: Marco Carnelutti, Gianpietro

Franceschinis, Paolo Turco, Walter Vidale,
Robert Zizzutto

**Renovation of Édouard VII block on Boulevard des
Capucines with relocation and reconstruction of
Olympia theatre**
Paris, 1995–99
with Anthony Emmanuel Béchu, Fernando Urquijo,
Giorgio Macola
collaborator: Gianluca Gamberini

Lafarge Plâtres offices and laboratories
Avignon, 1995–2000
with Daniel Fanzutti
collaborators: Marco Carnelutti, Gianluca
Gamberini, Gianpietro Franceschinis, Alessandro
Manaigo, Paolo Turco, Walter Vidale, Robert
Zizzutto

Project for courthouse
Bergamo, 1995–2001
with Piera Ricci Menichetti
collaborators: Marco Carnelutti, Gianpietro
Franceschinis, Paolo Turco, Walter Vidale, Robert
Zizzutto

Nursery school and kindergarten
San Pietro in Casale (Bologna),
1995–2002
with Piera Ricci Menichetti, Gianpietro
Franceschinis
collaborators: Marco Carnelutti, Carlo Mauro,
Robert Zizzutto, Paolo Turco

**Parking facility with shops in the former Cledca
area along the Piovego**
Padua, 1995–2010
with Pietro Valle (from 2003)
collaborators: Marco Carnelutti, Adelchi De Cillia,
Roland Schulz, Roland Henning, Robert Zizzutto,
Walter Vidale

Project for Costantini art museum
Buenos Aires, 1997
competition
with Giorgio Macola, Fernando Urquijo,

Nicoletta Macola
collaborators: Adolfo Zanetti, Carlo Dario

Project for reconstruction of Teatro La Fenice
Venice, 1997
invitational competition
with Giorgio Macola, Nicoletta Macola
collaborators: Marco Carnelutti, Gianpietro
Franceschinis, Paolo Turco, Walter Vidale, Robert
Zizzutto

Urban renewal plan
San Benigno 2 Le Vele Genoa, 1997–2003
with Piera Ricci Menichetti
collaborators: Marco Carnelutti, Roland Henning,
Paolo Turco, Robert Zizzutto

Deutsche Bank headquarters
Milan-Bicocca, 1997–2005
with Pietro Valle (from 2003), Alessandro Manaigo,
with the collaboration of Laura Motta
collaborators: Marco Carnelutti, Gianpietro
Franceschinis, Nelson Zizzutto, Robert Zizzutto,
Paolo Turco, Walter Vidale, Mario Gallinaro
(structures)

Project for a tower at the fair
Basel, 1998
competition
with Broggi & Burckhardt Architetti Associati

Project for the Fusina Terminal
Venice, 1998
competition, honourable mention
with Giorgio Macola, Carlo Dario, Andreas Otto
Kipar, Nicoletta Macola, Adolfo Zanetti, Piero Zucchi

Portello area
Milan, 1998–2014
  – conversion plan Portello area, 1998–2001
collaborators: Marco Carnelutti, Matteo
Franceschin, Roland Henning
  – shopping cluster, design and construction
    2001–2005
with Pietro Valle (from 2003), Piera Ricci
Menichetti

collaborators: Mario Broggi, Elena Carlini, Marco Carnelutti, Francesco De Cillia, Matteo Franceschin, Roland Henning, Alessandro Manaigo, Magda Marchelesio, Paolo Turco, Walter Vidale, Robert Zizzutto
– plaza, offices and parking, 2000–2014
with Pietro Valle (from 2003), Piera Ricci Menichetti, in collaboration with Topotek 1 (landscape)
collaborators: Stefano Bindi, Marco Carnelutti, Francesco De Cillia, Matteo Franceschin, Luisa Foretich, Roland Henning, Magda Marchelesio, Katia Zaffonato

Project for the renewal of three squares
Trieste, 1999
competition
with Erica Scabar
collaborators: Marco Carnelutti, Paolo Turco, Roland Henning, Robert Zizzutto

Project for Palace of Justice
Salerno, 1999
competition
with Giorgio Macola, Luciano Alfano, Michele Valentini, Mario Gallinaro (structures), Glauco Fontanive (physical plant)
collaborators: Nicoletta Macola, Gianpietro Franceschinis, Carlo Dario, Adolfo Zanetti

Montecity urban planning project at Rogoredo
Milan, 1999–2000
with Studio Broggi & Burckhardt Architetti Associati

Coordination of circulation plan in variant to Master Plan
Legnano (Milan), 1999–2000

Detail plan and project for renovation of the Olivetti plant for Telital
Marcianise (Caserta), 1999–2000
with Pietro Valle, Elena Carlini

Rizzani De Eccher headquarters
Udine, 2000–2002
with Marco Carnelutti, Robert Zizzutto

Project for the offices of Lloyd Triestino Evergreen
Trieste, 2001–2002
with Pietro Valle, Elena Carlini

Detail Plan of former school of Via Roma
Cervignano del Friuli (Udine), 2001
with Pietro Valle, Elena Carlini

Preliminary design of SP1 Detail Plan (former Isotta Fraschini area)
Saronno (Varese), 2001

Recreation centre of the port authority in the San Benigno 2 Le Vele renewal plan
Genoa, 2001–2007
Definitive project 2001–2003
collaborators: Marco Carnelutti, Roland Henning, Paolo Turco, Robert Zizzutto
executive project and construction: Impresa Mario Valle (Genoa), 2003–2007

Project for the European Library of Information and Culture (BEIC)
Milan, 2002
competition
with Sergio Pascolo
collaborator: Marco Carnelutti

Detail Plan of the former Socesfin zone
Rome-Fiumicino, 2002–2007
with Pietro Valle, Elena Carlini, Roberto Puciello (from 2003)
collaborators: Marco Carnelutti, Roland Henning

Bocciodromo (bowling ground)
Cussignacco (Udine), 2003–10
with Pietro Valle, Elena Carlini (from 2003)
collaborators: Marco Carnelutti, Francesco De Cillia, Roland Henning, Alessandro Manaigo, Carlo Mauro, Robert Zizzutto

Bibliography

Writings by Gino Valle and Interviews

1952

'La scuola internazionale estiva del CIAM 1952 in Venezia', *Pirelli magazine*, December 1955.

'Applicazione della struttura spaziale continua a ottaedri. La progettazione del velario di copertura del Salone della Cassa di Risparmio di Udine', *Rassegna tecnica della Regione Friuli Venezia Giulia*, 1–2, January–February.

1963

'Friuli Venezia Giulia (Aspetti della regione a statuto speciale e problemi del piano di sviluppo)', with Roberto Costa, *Urbanistica*, 40, p.144.

1965

'Discourse: Gino Valle, summary of the Annual Lectureship at Royal Institute of British Architects, London, 7 April 1965', *RIBA Journal*, May, pp.241–7.

'La funzione dell'industrial designer', *Congresso acciaio*, pp.71–3.

'Otto risposte sui problemi del design'; 'L'educazione dell'industrial designer', *Edilizia Moderna*, 85, pp.21–2, 88–9.

1970

Maria Bottero and Giacomo Scarpini (eds), 'Intervista a Gino Valle', *Zodiac*, 20, December, pp.82–115.

1976

Pier Carlo Santini (ed.), 'Incontro con i protagonisti: Gino Valle', *Ottagono*, 40, March, pp.76–81.

1978

Gino Valle (with Sandro Marpillero), in Lara Vinca Masinia (ed.), *Topologia e morfogenesi. Utopia e crisi dell'antinatura, momenti delle intenzioni architettoniche in Italia*, Edizioni La Biennale di Venezia, pp.156–9.

1979

'L'architettura come pratica progettuale. Intervista a Gino Valle', *Casabella*, 450, September, pp.12–13.

1980

Gino Valle, 'Progetto realizzato', *Polis, quaderni di architettura e urbanistica*, 22, Marsilio, Venice, pp.213–56.

'Progettare il "bianco"', *Domus*, 606, May, pp.50–51.

Lecture at the conference 'Razionalizzazione della produzione e gestione edilizia in rapporto al risparmio energetico', Atti del convegno, Consorzio regionale IACP, Regione Veneto, pp.11–18.

1982

Adalberto Dal Lago (ed.), 'Intervista con Gino Valle', *L'Architettura. Cronache e Storia*, 4, April, pp.278–9.

1983
'Sei posizioni. Progetti di edilizia economica', talk at the conference 'Tecnici per la progettazione edilizia in cooperative di abitazione e strutture di servizio', Pomezia, 15–16 June.

1984
Gianfranco Roccatagliata (ed.), 'Intervista a Gino Valle', *Modulo*, 9, September, pp.871–2.

1985
Pierre-Alain Croset (ed.), 'Una conversazione con Gino Valle', *Casabella*, 519, December, pp.16–17.

1988
Riccardo Roda (ed.), 'Intervista a Gino Valle', *Modulo*, 138, January–February, pp.33–7.
Vittorio Magnago Lampugnani (ed.), 'Gino Valle. Dal luogo alla casa', *Domus*, 692, March, pp.17–24.

1989
Gino Valle, 'Il mestiere più bello del mondo', in Giorgio Ciucci (ed.), *L'architettura italiana oggi. Racconto di una generazione*, Laterza, Bari, pp.275–90.
Fulvio Irace, 'Intervista a Gino Valle', *Abitare*, 275, June 1989, pp.166–71.
Gino Valle, 'Alcune osservazioni sugli ultimi progetti', *Casabella*, 563, December, pp.4–22.

1990
Carla Gilioli (ed.), 'Intervista a Gino Valle', *Costruire in laterizio*, 18, November–December.

1991
Giovanni Vragnaz (ed.), 'Intervista a Gino Valle', in *Piranesi*, 1, January, vol. 1, pp.26–47.
Margherita Petranzan (ed.), 'L'opera in memoria. Intervista dialogo Valle–Petranzan', in 'Gino Valle. Casse rurali e artigiane: Azzano Decimo (Pn)-Monte Magré-Schio (Vi)', monograph, *Anfione Zeto*, 6–7, pp.45–62.

1992
Enzo Volponi and Luigi Soramel (ed.), 'Casa Foghini nei ricordi di Gino Valle', in *Annuario 1992*, Associazione Ad Undecimum, San Giorgio di Nogaro, pp.78–82.

1993
Emilia Bitossi (ed.), 'Gino Valle: architetto e designer', *OFX Office International*, 14, August–September, pp.42–5.

1994
Mario Pisani, 'Dialogo con Gino Valle', *Costruire in laterizio*, 40, July–August, pp.336–9.

1996
Gino Valle, 'Guardare e vedere', *Progetti del laboratorio*, catalogue of the exhibition of CdlA, IUAV Venice, pp.14–15.
'Opinioni e progetti. Gino Valle', *Casabella*, 630–31, January, p.114.

1997
Ado Furlan and Alessio Princic (eds), 'Gino Valle: intervju', *AB Arhitektov Bilten*, 137–8, November, pp.2–13.

1998
'Thoughts on the Public Realm: a Conversation between Peter Smithson and Gino Valle', in *Architecture and Ideas*, 2, Autumn, pp.102–5.

1999
Giovanni Vragnaz (ed.), 'Monumento alla Resistenza a Udine. Intervista a Gino Valle', *Piranesi*, 9–10, Autumn, vol.7, pp.6–27.
Camilla De Mori (ed.), 'Gino Valle: io sono un guardone', *Il Gazzettino*, 22 December, p.XVIII.
Massimo Trevisan (ed.), 'La sottile evidenza della leggerezza. Conversazione con Gino Valle', *Anfione Zeto*, 12.
Massimo Trevisan and Massimo Vedovato, 'Colloquio con Gino Valle', *Anfione Zeto*, 12, pp.81–4.
Davide Ruzzon, 'La sottile evidenza della leggerezza. Dialogo con Gino Valle', *Anfione Zeto*, 12.

2000

'Sandro Marpillero intervista Gino Valle da New York', *Lotus Navigator*, monograph on Gino Valle, November, pp.62–85.

'"Bisogna immergersi nel tempo", conversazione con Gino Valle, Udine, 29 aprile 1995', in Giovanni Corbellini, *Grande & veloce. Strumenti compositivi nei contesti contemporanei*, Officina Edizioni, Rome, pp.224–34.

2001

Erminia Della Frattina (ed.), 'Valle: ricetta Friuli per il paesaggio', *Il Sole-24 Ore nordest*, 30 April, 16, p.3.

2003

Anna Marcolin, 'Gino Valle: l'architettura? Ora è 'vittima' dello star-system', *Realtà industriale*, 1, January, pp.18–22.

Matteo Vercelloni (ed.), 'Gino Valle, l'architetto che guarda', interview from 1991, *Interni*, December.

'Gino Valle. Lezioni di design', www.educational.rai.it/lezionididesign/designers/designers/Valleg.htm.

2009

'Gino Valle. 29 marzo 1988', in Franca Bizzotto and Michela Agazzi (eds), *Colore Segno Progetto Spazio. Giuseppe Mazzariol e gli 'Incontri con gli artisti'*, Il Poligrafo, Padua, pp.135–57.

Writings about Gino Valle

1955

Arturo Manzano, 'Il palazzo della Cassa di Risparmio risanato e adattato alle funzioni dell'Istituto', *Messaggero Veneto*, 6 May.

Giuseppe Samonà, 'Architetture di giovani', *Casabella*, 205, April-May, pp.7–30.

Chino Ermacora and Lino Pilotti (eds), 'Un Palazzo Vivo', *La Panarie*, Udine.

1956

Nani Valle, 'I temi di studio della scuola estiva internazionale di architettura CIAM a Venezia', *Giornale economico*, anno XLI, 9, September, pp.653–60.

'Forma e visione per un orologio', *Stile Industria*, 8, October, pp.34–7.

'Premi alla qualità italiana: i risultati della terza edizione del Premio La Rinascente Compasso d'oro', *Stile industria*, 9, December, pp.6–14.

Francesco Tentori, 'Tre banche dello Studio Valle' (introduction by Ernesto N. Rogers), *Casabella*, 213, December, pp.16–29.

1958

Joseph Rykwert, 'The Work of Studio Architetti Valle', *Architecture and Building*, April, pp.121–39.

Luciano Semerani, 'Una costruzione a Trieste', *Casabella*, 218, April, pp.50–60.

Reyner Banham, 'Tall Block in Trieste', *The Architectural Review*, 742, November, pp.281–2.

Reyner Banham, 'Tornare ai tempi felici', *The Architectural Review*, 742, November, p. 281.

1959

'La distruzione "pianificata". Concorso nazionale per il centro di Udine', *Casabella*, 224, February, pp.40–42.

Francesco Tentori, 'Tre opere e un progetto dello Studio Valle', *Casabella*, 226, April, pp.32–45.

Bruno Zevi, 'Astrattismo contro realismo. Il monumento alla Resistenza di Udine', *L'Espresso*, 10 May.

'Caisse d'Épargne et recette municipale à Latisana. Immeuble d'habitation et de bureau à Trieste', *L'Architecture d'Aujourd'hui*, 78, June, pp.16, 25.

Bruno Zevi, 'Monumento alla Resistenza in Udine', *L'Architettura: Cronache e Storia*, 46, August, p.246.

'Heating in Curtain Wall: Flats and Offices, Trieste, Italy', *Architects Working Details*, 6, Annual Review, pp.138–9.

1960

'Casa a Sutrio, Udine (1953–54). Gino e Nani Valle architetti', in Roberto Aloi, *Ville in Italia*, Hoepli, Milan, pp.33–6.

Konrad Wachsmann, *Wendepunkt Im Bauen*, Krausskopf Verlag, Wiesbaden, 1959 [Italian edition, *Una svolta nelle costruzioni*, Il Saggiatore, Milan, 1960].

Francesco Tentori, 'Dieci anni d'attività dello Studio Architetti Valle', *Casabella*, 246, December, pp.30–49.

1961

Francesco Tentori, 'Quindici anni d'architettura', *Casabella*, 251, May, pp.35–56.

Reyner Banham, 'Studio Valle', *The Architectural Review*, 772, June, p.365.

'House in Sutrio. Udine', *Architectural Design*, 10, October, pp.449–50.

1962

Reyner Banham, 'Rex', *The Architectural Review*, 779, January, p.4.

Roberto Guiducci, 'Presente e futuro dell'architettura industriale in Italia', *Zodiac*, 9, January, pp.127–45.

'The Look of Industry', *The Architectural Forum*, April 1962, pp.78–81.

1963

Gillo Dorfles, *Il disegno industriale e la sua estetica*, Cappelli, Bologna.

'Premio nazionale Aitec 1962. Uffici per le industrie A. Zanussi Rex di Pordenone', *L'industria italiana del cemento*, 1, January, pp.5–39.

'Due realizzazioni delle industrie A. Zanussi di Pordenone', *Casabella*, 277, July, pp.22–8.

'Teleindicatori a palette per aereoporti e stazioni ferroviarie', *Stile Industria*, 41, July, pp.1–11.

Giuseppe Mazzariol, 'Gino Valle', *Zodiac*, 12, October, pp.164–91.

1964

'Uffici per le industrie A. Zanussi Rex, Pordenone', in Giulia Veronesi and Bruno Alfieri (eds), *Lotus Architectural Annual, 1964–65*, Bruno Alfieri Editore, Milan, pp.106–13.

Francesco Tentori, 'Ordine per le coste italiane', *Casabella*, 283, January, pp.5–19.

'Condominio e un alloggio a Udine', *Abitare*, 23, January–February, pp.20–29.

Joseph Rykwert, 'The Work of Gino Valle', *Architectural Design*, March, pp.112–39.

Edward Lucie-Smith, 'The Architectural Imagination', *The Times*, 21 April.

Maria Bottero, 'Italy: The Crisis of a Culture', *World Architecture One*, Studio Books, London, annual magazine, pp.124–39.

1965

'Monumento alla Resistenza a Udine', in Giulia Veronesi and Bruno Alfieri (eds), *Lotus Architectural Annual*, 1965–66, Bruno Alfieri Editore, Milan, pp.204–7.

Dino Dardi, *Dieci profili di artisti nella regione Friuli-Venezia Giulia*, Edizioni della Galleria Il Camino, Pordenone.

'Bureaux Zanussi Rex à Pordenone près d'Udine (1959–61); Etablissement thermal d'Arta (1962–63)', *L'Architecture d'Aujourd'hui*, 48, January, pp.12–13, 18–19.

Maria Bottero, 'Un edificio termale nelle Alpi carniche', *Zodiac*, 14, April, pp.128–45.

Diana Rowntree, 'Gino Valle's Vernacular', *The Guardian*, 8 April, p.8.

Joseph Rykwert, 'Architettura di Gino Valle', *Domus*, 426, May, pp.7–24.

'Stabilimento termale Fonte Pudia ad Arta', *Edilizia Moderna*, special issue 'Architettura italiana 1963', 82–83, November, pp.98–9.

1966

'Un nuovo orologio da tavolo', *Domus*, 437, April, pp.54–5.

1967

Alberto Galardi, *Architettura italiana contemporanea*, Edizioni di Comunità, Milan.

Esther McCoy (ed.), *10 Italian Architects*, Los Angeles County Museum of Art.

'Bâtiment administratif d'une usine, Pordenone, Italie', in *C45-Revue internationale d'amiante-ciment 1*, January, pp.31–2.

Joseph Rykwert, 'Due recenti edifici di Gino Valle', *Domus*, 446, January, pp.1–11.

'Batiment administratif de l'usine Zanussi Rex Pordenone, Italie', *L'Architecture d'Aujourd'hui*, 133, September, p.XXVII.

1968

Vittorio Gregotti, *New Directions in Italian Architecture*, George Brazilier, New York, 1968 [Italian edition, *Orientamenti nuovi nell'architettura italiana*, Electa, Milan, 1969].

Francesco Tentori, 'Il monumento alla Resistenza', *La Panarie*, 3, December, pp.58–64.

1969

Renato Nicolini, 'Gino Valle', in *Dizionario enciclopedico di architettura e urbanistica*, directed by Paolo Portoghesi, vol. 6, Istituto editoriale romano, Rome, pp.367–8.

1970

Comitato esecutivo per l'inaugurazione del monumento alla Resistenza di Udine (ed.), *Nel monumento di Udine la Resistenza in Friuli*, Del Bianco, Udine.

Joseph Rykwert, 'Alle porte di Milano', *Domus*, 486, May, pp.3–7.

Joseph Rykwert, 'Gino Valle: edifici industriali', *Domus*, 492, November, pp.10–16.

1971

'Italian Suavity', *The Architectural Forum*, April, pp.36–8.

1972

'Prefab, Programmi edilizi', *Domus*, 510, May, pp.12–13.

'Büro- und Wohngebäude in Udine', *Werk*, 10, October.

1973

'Offices, Milan', *The Architectural Review*, 911, January, p.25.

1974

'Multipli ufficio', *Architecture intérieure*, 141, June–July, p.81.

'La casa a Sutrio. La casa rossa', *Lotus International*, 8, September.

1975

'Memor Time Clock', *Domus*, 542, January, p.30.

Lorenzo Berni, 'Concorso per il monumento ai partigiani e alle vittime della strage del 28 maggio 1974 a Brescia', *Panorama*, 739, 16 June.

L'Architecture d'Aujourd'hui, special issue 'Italie 75', 181, September–October (Francesco Dal Co and Mario Manieri-Elia, 'La génération de l'incertitude'; 'Gino Valle, Projet pour Murano'; 'Gino Valle ou la technologie du lieu commun', pp.34–56, 69, 87–92.)

1976

La Biennale di Venezia 1976: environment, participation, cultural structures, exh. cat., La Biennale di Venezia, Venice (2 vols).

Manfredo Tafuri and Francesco Dal Co, *Architettura Contemporanea*, Electa, Milan.

Pier Carlo Santini, 'Incontro con i protagonisti: Gino Valle', *Ottagono*, 40, March, pp.76–81.

Francesco Dal Co, 'Gino Valle. La necessità dell'architettura', *Lotus International*, 11, pp.172–89.

1977

Alberto Cavalli, 'La Valdadige per la scuola: il sistema strutturale Ptk', *Modulo*, 4, April, pp.243–8.

Alberto Cavalli, 'La scuola è un contenitore: architettura per la scuola di Gino Valle', *Modulo*, 5, May, pp.340–49.

'Sistema per la scuola', *Domus*, 571, June, pp.24–30.

1978

'Büro-und Geschäftshaus in Udine', in *Neues Bauen in alter Umgebung*, exh. cat., Staatliches Museum für Angewandte Kunst, Munich, pp.36, 43–5, 50, 61.

'Sistema Teo', in *Domus*, special 'Prefab' issue, p.1.

'Zona Peep Udine Est: edificio per 100 alloggi', *Casabella*, 432, January, pp.44–7.

'Osoppo. I mobili Fantoni', *Ricostruire*, 5, June, pp.83–91.

'Concorso per un repertorio di progetti tipo. Lombardia' [competition guideline documents], *Edilizia popolare*, 143, July–August.

'Concorso per l'istituzione del repertorio regionale di progetti tipo della Lombardia. Sistema Teo', *Casabella*, 439, September, pp.18–21.

Caterina Villa Ghezzi and Georgette Illes,
'L'orologio', *Ottagono*, 50, September, pp.48–57.

1979

Gino Valle. Architetto 1950–1978, exh. cat., Padiglione
d'arte contemporanea in Milano, Edizioni PAC
& Idea Editions, Milan (Joseph Rykwert, 'Gino
Valle architetto'; Germano Celant, 'Al limite
dell'avventura').

'Venezia-Scuola media', in *Centro studi per edilizia
scolastica*, exh. cat., Biblioteca Nazionale, Rome
18–23 June, Ministero della pubblica istruzione,
Rome 1979, pp.88–.

'Un sistema per le scuole', *Edilizia scolastica*, 9–10
June, pp.84–94.

Ludovica Scarpa, 'Il duro carattere delle architetture
di Gino Valle', *Paese Sera*, 15 June.

'Uffici e centro servizi della Fantoni Arredamenti
Spa a Osoppo, Udine', *Casabella*, 450, September,
pp.34–51.

Jonathan Glancey, 'Factory, Udine', *The Architectural
Review*, 992, October, pp.253–254.

'Porta rossa per lavorare, porta blu per abitare',
Interni, 295, November, pp.17–21.

'Piani particolareggiati nel Comune di Buia',
Ricostruire, 8–9, pp.33–6.

1980

Gaddo Morpurgo, 'La rappresentazione visiva tra
l'anticipazione e realizzazione del manufatto', in
Fotografia e immagine dell'architettura, exh. cat.,
Galleria d'arte moderna, Bologna.

Guido Canella, 'Figura e funzione nell'architettura
italiana dal dopoguerra agli anni sessanta',
Hinterland, 13–14, January–June.

Andries Van Onck, 'Progettare il "bianco"', *Domus*,
606, May, pp.48–9.

'Case colorate', *Domus*, 609, September, pp.24–7.

Renzo Dubbini, 'Les cendres de Palladio',
L'Architecture d'Aujourd'hui, 211, October,
pp.90–104.

David Morton, 'Fabbrica Fantoni', *Progressive
Architecture*, 9, October, pp.170–.

'Ambito edilizio unitario', in *Ricostruire*, 13–14,
pp.21–3.

1981

Cesare De Seta, *Storia dell'arte in Italia. L'architettura
del Novecento*, Utet, Turin.

Pier Carlo Santini, 'Gino Valle', in *Il materiale delle
arti. Processi tecnici e formativi dell'immagine*,
Punto e Linea, Milan.

'The Greening of Europe', *Life*, March, pp.68–9.

Ornella Selvafolta, 'Colore, parte dell'architettura',
Abitare, 194, May, pp.52–9.

'Quartier résidentiel Santo Stefano di Buia',
L'Architecture d'Aujourd'hui, 216, September,
p.XIX.

Carlo Magnani, Filippo Messina and Gianfranco
Trabucco, 'Neue Projekte für Venedig', *Bauwelt*,
44, November, pp.1977–83.

1982

Vittorio Gregotti, *Il disegno del prodotto industriale.
Italia 1860–1980*, Electa, Milan.

Manfredo Tafuri, 'Architettura italiana 1944–1981', in
Storia dell'arte italiana, parte II, vol. III, Einaudi,
Turin.

'Gino Valle', in *Progetti per la città veneta 1926–1981*,
Neri Pozza Editore, Turin, pp.94–7.

'Gino Valle', in *Wege der Irrwege der Architektur.
Internationale Sommerakademie*, Salzburg, Edition
Tusch, Buch und Kunstverlag GmbH, Vienna,
1983, pp.54–61.

Giacomo Polin, 'Nuove abitazioni popolari a
Venezia', *Casabella*, 478, March, pp.50–61.

Marco Porta, 'Fabbriche nel paesaggio',
L'Architettura: Cronache e Storia, 4, April,
pp.278–87.

Richard A. Etlin, 'The Geometry of Death'; 'David
Morton, Meaning through Precedent', *Progressive
Architecture*, 5, May, pp.134–7, 146–7.

'Centre technique et bureaux de la société Fantoni, à
Udine, Italie', *Techniques & Architecture*, 342, June,
pp.107–9.

'Siège social des meubles Fantoni, Osoppo',
L'Architecture d'Aujourd'hui, 221, June, pp.68–9.

Giandomenico Romanelli, 'Per mettersi in mostra,
La Biennale di Veneziae i suoi allestimenti',
Rassegna, 10, June, pp.14–18.

Kenneth Frampton, 'The ism of Contemporary
Architecture', *Architectural Design*, 52, July–August

(special issue AD Profile 42, 'Modern Architecture and the Critical Present').

'Gino Valle: "...un autorestauro..."', *Interni*, 323, September, pp.18–19.

Giuseppe Camporini and Maria Caterina Redini, 'Intervento residenziale nell'isola della Giudecca a Venezia', *Edilizia popolare*, 168, September–October, pp.48–56.

Lorenzo Berni, 'Complesso uffici Pordenone', *Panorama*, 25 October.

David Morton, 'Coloring Blocks', *Progressive Architecture*, 10, October, pp.94–8.

'Conjunto de viviendas en la isla de Giudecca', *Summarios*, Buenos Aires, 61, November.

'Gino Valle's New York Bank', *Skyline*, November, p.26.

1983

Kenneth Frampton, 'Prospects for a Critical Regionalism', *Perspecta*, 20, pp.147–62.

Sandro Marpillero, 'Grattacielo a metà. Gino Valle: uffici della Banca commerciale italiana a Manhattan', and 'Post scriptum. Produzione del progetto, produzione dell'edificio', *Lotus International*, 37, pp.96–119.

Rosa Maria Rinaldi (ed.), 'Vivere e progettare', *Domus*, 640, June, pp.32–9.

Paolo Fumagalli, 'Architektur jenseits modischer Tendenzen, Arbeiten von Gino Valle', *Werk, Bauen+Wohnen*, 7–8, July.

'Internationale engere Wettbewerb Berlin, Sudliche Friedrichstadt, Block 606', *Bauwelt*, 36, September, p.191.

Pierre-Alain Croset, 'Centro direzionale a Pordenone', *Casabella*, 495, October, pp.50–61.

1984

Sebastiano Brandolini and Pierre-Alain Croset, 'Strategie della modificazione', *Casabella*, 498–499, January–February, pp.40–45.

Pierre-Alain Croset and Giacomo Polin, 'IBM Distribution Center a Basiano', *Casabella*, 500, March, pp.52–63.

'School, Friedrichstrasse: Friedrichstadt', *The Architectural Review*, 1051, September, pp.71–2.

1985

'IBM Distribution Center', in Jean-Paul Robert (ed.), *Vu de l'intérieur. La raison de l'architecture*, catalogue of the 3rd Architectural Biennial of Paris, Editions Pierre Mardaga, Liège.

Amedeo Belluzzi and Claudia Conforti, *Architettura italiana 1944–1984*, Laterza, Rome & Bari.

Maristella Casciato and Giorgio Muratore (eds), 'Centro Galvani, Pordenone', in *Annali dell'architettura italiana contemporanea 1984*, Officina Edizioni, Rome, pp.131–6.

Francesco Dal Co, '1945–1985: Italian Architecture between Innovation and Tradition', in *The European Iceberg*, Art Gallery of Ontario, Toronto and Nuove Edizioni Gabriele Mazzotta, Milan.

Francesco Dal Co, 'Architettura italiana 1960–1980'; Vittorio Gregotti, 'L'esportazione italiana all'estero', in Omar Calabrese (cur.), *Italia moderna 1960–1980. La difficile democrazia*, Electa, Milan.

Marco Pozzetto, 'Note sull'architettura moderna in Friuli', *Parametro*, 135–136, April–May, pp.12–22.

Carlo Magnani and Pierantonio Val, 'La misura del progetto', *Rassegna*, 22 ('Venezia città del moderno'), June, pp.78–83.

'Gino Valle architetto', in *Intart Internationale d'arte*, exh. cat., Künstlerhaus, Klagenfurt, 19 October–9 November.

Carlo Aymonino, 'Giudecca nostra ritrovata', *L'Europeo*, 44, 2 November, p.151.

Pierre-Alain Croset, 'Edifici per Uffici alla Défense a Parigi', *Casabella*, 519, December, pp.4–15.

'New Housing on Giudecca Island', *Architectural Design*, 5–6, v. 55, pp.66–8.

1986

'Residenze a Cannaregio. Intervento di edilizia popolare nell'isola della Giudecca, Venezia', in Maristella Casciato and Giorgio Muratore (eds), *Annali dell'architettura italiana contemporanea 1985*, Officina Edizioni, Rome, pp.248–56.

Bernardo Secchi (ed.), *Progetto Bicocca. Concorso internazionale di progettazione urbanistica e architettonica ideato e realizzato per iniziativa dalle industrie Pirelli*, exh. cat., Triennale di Milano (14 June–28 September 1986), Electa, Milan.

Manfredo Tafuri, *Storia dell'architettura italiana 1944–1985*, Einaudi, Turin.

Marco De Michelis, 'Nuovi progetti alla Giudecca'; Pierre-Alain Croset, 'Sul progetto di Gino Valle alla Giudecca', *Lotus International*, 51, March, pp.78–128.

Bernardo Secchi, Paola Di Biagi, Patrizia Gabellini and Oriol Bohigas, 'Le occasioni del Progetto-Bicocca', *Casabella*, 524, May, pp.4–29.

Dietmar Steiner, 'Nuova edilizia abitativa a Vienna', *Casabella*, 527, September, pp.16–25.

'El trazado exacto de una isla. El área Trevisan, Giudecca', *Arquitectura y Vivienda*, 8, October, pp.48–57.

Pierre-Alain Croset, 'Un immenso appartamento collettivo. 94 case di Gino Valle alla Giudecca', *Casabella*, 528, October, pp.34–5.

Vittorio Gregotti, 'A Venezia qualcosa di nuovo', *Panorama*, 1069, 12 October.

Fulvio Irace, 'Venezia, la Giudecca: nuovo insediamento di edilizia economica popolare', *Abitare*, 248, October, pp.244–55.

'Gino Valle, tovarna "Fantoni" v Osoppu', *ab-Architects bulletin*, November.

David Mangin, 'Terrain ex-Trevisan sur la Giudecca', *L'Architecture d'Aujourd'hui*, 248, December, pp.78–84.

Walter Arno Noebel, 'Alte Architektur für neue Technologien?'; Stefano Boeri, 'Gedanken bei der Wanderung durch die Projekte', *Bauwelt*, 48, 5 December, pp.1752–67.

Ermanno Ranzani and Willem Brouwer, 'Quartiere residenziale, Giudecca (Venezia)', *Domus*, 678, December, pp.38–53.

Francesco Infussi, 'Les stratégies de la modification, 18 projets pour une technopole sur le site des usines Pirelli à Milan', *Faces*, 3, pp.10–17.

1987

'IBM Basiano', in Jacques Ferrier, *Usines*, Electa Moniteur, Paris, pp.8–17.

Romaldo Giurgola, 'Valle Gino', in Ann Lee Morgan and Colin Nayor (eds), *Contemporary Architects,* St James Press, Chicago and London, pp.934–5.

Lorenza Boscetti and Alessandra Chemollo, 'Umnutzung eines Industrieareas', *Werk, Bauen+Wohnen*, 3, March, pp.56–64.

Francesco Moschini, 'Complesso di abitazioni popolari nell'isola della Giudecca', *L'industria delle costruzioni*, 186, April, pp.6–21.

Mirko Zardini, 'Dalla città alla rocca: un concorso a Salisburgo', *Casabella*, 534, April, pp.14–25.

'Haussmann pour IBM à la Défense', *Architecture intérieure cree-Dossier*, 217, April–May, pp.95–100.

Pierre-Alain Croset, 'Continuità e distanza critica. Ultimato l'edificio di Gino Valle a New York', *Casabella*, 535, May, pp.38–9.

Kenneth Frampton, 'Gino Valle, Edificio per uffici, New York', *Domus*, 683, May, pp.25–37.

Oreste Pivetta, 'Milano si rinnova = Renewing Milan', *Arca*, 5, May, pp.54–69.

'Umnutzung eines Industriereals auf der Insel Giudecca in Venedig', *Architektur+Wettbewerbe*, 130, June.

Hans-Michael Herzog, 'Artifizielles auf der Giudecca', *Bauwelt*, 30, August, pp.1100–1108.

Mario Campi, 'Cronaca di un'occasione mancata. Il concorso per l'ampliamento del teatro di stato di Stoccarda', *Casabella*, 538, September.

Engl Romen, 'Wohnquartier auf Giudecca', *Baumeister*, 9, September, pp.26–31.

'Housing in Giudecca, 1986: Gino Valle', *Process: Architecture*, 75, October, pp.126–7.

1988

Riccardo Roda, 'Abitazioni alla Giudecca', *Modulo*, 138, January–February, pp.26–37.

Donatella Smetana, 'Valle's Public Housing in Venice', *Progressive Architecture*, 2, 69, February, pp.32–33.

Dietmar Steiner, 'Il concorso per l'area delle Scuderie Imperiali a Vienna', *Casabella*, 544, March, pp.16–27.

Maria Cristina Tullio, 'I segni e le "tracce". Recenti progetti per spazi pubblici nel Friuli Venezia Giulia', *Arredo urbano*, 25, March–April, pp.62–75.

Tom Fischer and James Murphy, 'Big Blue Designs', *Progressive Architecture*, 6, June, pp.100–103.

Enrico Regazzoni, 'La disfida di Bicocca', *Europeo*, 30, 22 July, pp.104–6.

'Scelto il progetto per il Polo Tecnologico della Bicocca', *Casabella*, 548, July–August, pp.32–33.

Leonardo Benevolo, 'Brescia: prospettive di politica urbana', *Casabella*, 548, July–August, pp.18–23.

Tudy Sammartini, 'Agenda Veneziana: costruire dove non sono ammesse periferie', *Parametro*, 167, July–August, pp.64–9.

'Public Housing Estate, Guidecca Island, Venice, Italy, 1980–86', *GA Houses*, 23, August, pp.174–81.

Pierre-Alain Croset, 'On Gino Valle's Project at the Giudecca', *A+U. Architecture and Urbanism*, 215, August, pp.7–26.

Jean-François Pousse, 'L'ordre parisien. Quartier Michelet, La Défense', *Techniques & Architecture*, 379, August–September, pp.73–9.

Pierre-Alain Croset, *Un 'pezzo di città' alla Défense*, exh. cat., Fondazione Masieri, Venice, September.

Pierre-Alain Croset, 'Un "saggio incompiuto" di architettura urbana', *Casabella* 549, September, pp.30–31.

'Milano, progetto Bicocca: risultati finali del concorso', *Domus*, 698, October, pp.70–80.

Jean-Patrick Fortin, 'Milan La Bicocca', *L'Architecture d'Aujourd'hui*, 259, October, pp.57–69.

'IBM als Bauherr: seine Partnerschaft mit den Architekten', *Baumeister*, 12, December, pp.13–37.

Pierre-Alain Croset, 'Gino Valle. Palazzo di Giustizia di Brescia', *Casabella*, 552, December, pp.56–63.

Robert Walmsley, 'La ville décline ses mémoires: Venise', *Techniques & Architecture*, 381, December–January, pp.139–50.

1989

Pierre-Alain Croset, *Gino Valle. Progetti e architetture*, Electa, Milan.

'Gino Valle: Construire entre le soleil et l'eau', *Techniques & Architecture*, 381, December–January, pp.140–50.

Ermanno Ranzani, 'Gino Valle. Nuova mensa Elea, Burolo (Ivrea)', *Domus*, 701, January, pp.37–46.

Stefano Bronzini, 'Gino Valle, il successo della personalità', *Rassegna Tecnica FVG*, 2, March–April, pp.33–8.

Vittorio Gregotti, 'Il mio lavoro: trovare cose', *Panorama*, n. 1198, 2 April, p.36.

Cesare De Seta, 'Da monte a Valle', *Europeo*, 17–28 April, pp.98–9.

Marina Montuori, '*Gino Valle*. Vicenza, Basilica Palladiana, 17 marzo – 23 aprile; Pierre-Alain Croset, *Gino Valle. Progetti e architetture*', *Selezione della critica d'arte contemporanea*, 75, May, pp.41–4.

Roberto Gabetti, 'Progettare nella terra d'elezione', *L'Indice*, n. 8, October, p.35.

Carlo Olmo, 'A valle di Gino Valle', *Il Giornale dell'Arte*, n. 69, July–August, p.27.

Paolo Fumagalli, 'Eine Gegenarchitektur', *Werk, Bauen+Wohnen*, 5, May, pp.14–15.

'Stabilimento del gruppo Fantoni', *Abitare*, 275, June, pp.162–3.

Fulvio Irace, 'Gino Valle', *Abitare*, 275, June, pp.166–71.

Walter Arno Noebel, 'Piano o progetto? Die Neuebebauung des Bicocca-Areals in Mailand; Gino Valle', *Bauwelt*, 24, June, pp.1134–7, 1144–5.

Jean-Paul Robert, 'Gino Valle', review, '*L'Architecture d'Aujourd'hui*, 263, June, pp.68–70.

'Gino Valle architetto nella Basilica Palladiana', *L'industria delle costruzioni*, 215, September, pp.58–9.

'Pirelli-Gelände "Bicocca" in Mailand, Italien, 2. Stufe', *Architektur + Wettbewerbe*, 140, December, pp.28–35.

Roberto Gabetti, 'Nuovi Uffici Olivetti a Ivrea e altri progetti di Gino Valle', *Casabella*, 563, December, pp.4–22.

Pierluigi Nicolin, 'Il gioco delle somiglianze. Gino Valle alla Défense', *Lotus International*, 61, pp.42–91.

Luciano Semerani, 'Gino Valle, New Housing on Giudecca Island', *Architectural Design Profile*, 59, pp.66–8.

1990

Sandro Marpillero, 'Itinerari nell'architettura', *Casabella*, 564, January, pp.31–2.

Paolo Desideri, 'Pierre-Alain Croset, *Gino Valle. Progetti e architetture*', *Domus*, 713, February, p.XIII.

L. Agostini and S. Guidarini, 'Olivetti e Ivrea', *Domus* itinerary, 713, February, pp.V–X.

Juan Rohe, 'Verwaltungsgebäude in Ivrea', *Baumeister*, 6, June, pp.46–52.

'Convegno Architetti Italiani a Parigi, 11 novembre 1989; Roberto Gabetti, Alla Defense c'è Gino Valle', *Atti e rassegna tecnica della Società Ingegneri e Architetti in Torino*, 11–12, XLIV, November–December, pp.373–92.

La Bayer al Portello, Bayer Italia spa, Milano, Decembre, pp.83–92, 118–19.

V. Travi, 'L'altra faccia della legge', *Costruire per abitare: produzione edilizia: economia e cultura*, 89.

'Gino Valle. Casse rurali e artigiane: Azzano Decimo (Pn)-Monte Magré–Schio (Vi)', *Anfione Zeto*, 6–7, special issue.

Francesco Moschini, 'Gino Valle: l'avventura del collezionista', *Anfione Zeto*, 6–7, pp.55–87.

Giorgio Ciucci and Francesco Dal Co, *Architettura italiana del Novecento*, Electa, Milan.

1991

'Palazzo di Giustizia a Brescia, 1986–89', in *Quinta mostra internazionale di architettura. La Biennale di Venezia 1991*, exh. cat., Electa, Milan, pp.262–3.

'Gino Valle. Uffici della Banca Commerciale Italiana, New York'; Christian Norberg-Schultz, 'Presentazione', in Vincenzo Pavan (ed.), *Il linguaggio della pietra*, Arsenale, Venice, pp.39–55.

Sergio Polano and Marco Mullazzani, *Guida all'architettura italiana del Novecento*, Electa, Milan.

'Il rinnovo delle aree industriali in Valle d'Aosta', *L'Architettura: Cronache e Storia*, 7–8, July–August, pp.640–47.

'Progetto Polis Trieste 1991', *Gb Progetti*, 8–9, July–October, pp.97–101.

'Calme et intemporelle. Banque à Azzano, Italie', *Techniques & Architecture*, 397, August–September, pp.121–3.

'Usine a Osoppo, Italie', *Techniques & Architecture*, 398, October–November, pp.54–6.

1992

Risalire la città: Bergamo Bassa, Bergamo Alta, Premio Schindler, Electa, Milan.

Sergio Polano and Luciano Semerani (eds), *Friuli Venezia Giulia: guida critica all'architettura contemporanea*, Arsenale, Venice.

'Scuola a Berlino di Gino Valle, Mario Broggi & Michael Burckhardt', *Casabella*, 588, March, p.33.

Roberto Gamba, 'La Snam a Metanopoli: nuovi quartieri di espansione', *Industria delle costruzioni*, 245, March, pp.52–3.

Clemens Kusch, 'Architektur ist vorrangig etwas visuelles', *DBZ-Deutsche Bauzeitschrift*, 7, July, pp.1023–31.

'La cifra del tempo', *Modo*, 143, September, pp.74–5.

'Premio Internazionale Architetture di Pietra', *Industria delle costruzioni*, 251, September, pp.59–61.

Rita Capezzuto, 'La ricostruzione urbana come scuola. Valle, Braggi, Burckhardt: intervento in Friedrichstrasse a Berlino', *Lotus International*, 74, November, pp.36–47.

'Trasformazione delle strutture urbane a Genova: Quarto 2', *Edilizia popolare*, 221, pp.13–21.

1993

'Il Concorso per il Casinò di Winkler', in Rita Capezzuto and Mario Lupano (eds), *Salisburgo la verde*, Electa, Milan (Quaderni di Lotus, 19), pp.120–32.

Alessandro Anselmi and Jean-Claude Garcias, 'Tolosa: un concorso verso il decentramento', *Casabella*, 602, June, pp.22–33.

Clemens F. Kusch, 'Grundschule in Berlin', *DBZ-Deutsche Bauzeitschrift*, 6, June, pp.967–72.

Gianni Contessi, 'Architekten im Friul', *Bauwelt*, 25, July, pp.1370–73.

Giampiero Mudanò, 'Cronaca di un insediamento', *Notizie IBM*, 255, October, pp.34–56.

'I nuovi uffici del Dipartimento della Haute Garonne a Tolosa', *Industria delle costruzioni*, 266, December, pp.75–7.

1994

The Italian Metamorphosis 1943–1968, exh. cat., Guggenheim Museum, New York, Progetti Museum Editore, Mondadori Editore.

Monica Quaiattini, 'I racconti architettonici di Gino Valle', *Rassegna Tecnica FVG*, March–April, pp.30–31.

'Grundschule und Sonderschule für Sprachbehinderte, Südliche Friedrichstadt,

Berlin, 1988–1991', *Werk, Bauen+Wohnen*, 4, April, pp.18–21.

'Il talento eclettico di Provino Valle', *Messaggero Veneto*, 6 April.

Alessandro Rocca, 'Zürich, Stuttgart, Paris', *Lotus International*, 83, November, pp.72–9.

1995

Progetto Bicocca: un contributo per Milano policentrica, Electa, Milan.

W. Bigatton, M. Bordugo, G. Lutman and S. Moranduzzo, *Architettura nel Friuli occidentale*, Biblioteca dell'Immagine, Pordenone.

Mario De Micheli, Marina Pizziolo, Marco De Michelis and Marco Pogacnik (eds), 'Monumento alla Resistenza, Udine', in *Le ragioni della libertà a cinquant'anni dalla Resistenza*, exh. cat., Palazzo della Triennale di Milano (25 April–20 May 1995), Vangelista, Milan, pp.220–21.

Alida Moltedo and Paolina La Franca (eds), *Disegni di architetture. Schizzi e studi di opere romane dal dopoguerra agli anni ottanta*, exh. cat., Ministero per i Beni Culturali e Ambientali, Istituto Nazionale per la Grafica, Calcografia, December 1995 – February 1996, Gangemi Editore, Rome.

Annalisa Avon, 'Gino Valla. Industrial design per la casa 1956–75', *Domus*, 769, March, pp.62–70.

Pierre-Alain Croset, 'La metamorfosi di una torre', *La Repubblica*, 27 April.

Pierre-Alain Croset, 'Gino Valle. Trasformazione della torre IBM a Roma', *Casabella*, 622, April, pp.56–66.

Paolo Rosa, 'Un'opera di Gino Valle a Roma: la torre per uffici IBM', *Frames*, 55, April–May, pp.50–57.

Piero Zucchi, 'Valle firma la torre romana IBM', *Il Gazzettino*, 15 May.

Piera Scuri, 'Edifici per uffici: a Roma la torre IBM', *Ufficio stile*, 6, November–December, pp.54–61.

Massimo Faiferri, 'Gino Valle architetto', *D'A: d'architettura*, 14, pp.68–73.

1996

'Solari', in *Nuove contaminazioni*, Galleria d'arte moderna Udine, Edizioni Biblioteca dell'Immagine, Pordenone, pp.108–10.

Giorgio Cacciaguerra (ed.), 'Municipio di Fontanafredda', in *Ordine degli Architetti 50°*.

1946–1996, Ordine degli architetti della provincia di Udine, pp.142–5.

Marco Romanelli and Marta Laudani, *Design Nordest*, Editrice Abitare Segesta, Milan, pp.96–112.

Clemens F. Kusch, 'Dem himmel näher', *DBZ-Deutsche Bauzeitschrift*, 5, May, p.22.

Marco De Michelis, 'Gino Valla. Nuovo palazzo di Giustizia di Padova', *Domus*, 785, September, pp.30–37.

1997

Sergio Polano and Lorenzo Marchetto, 'Architetture del mostrare: cinque allestimenti nella Basilica Palladiana 1986–96', *Casabella*, 642, February, pp.32–45.

Sebastiano Brandolini, 'Public Spirit: New Law Courts, Padua', *World Architecture*, 54, March, pp.60–61.

Francesco Dal Co (ed.), *Storia dell'architettura italiana. Il secondo Novecento*, Electa, Milan.

1998

'Palazzo Uffici 2; Mensa Elea a Burolo', in AA.VV., *Architetture olivettiane a Ivrea*, Gangemi, Rome, pp.130–41, 252–9.

1999

'Cifra "5" clock by Gino Valle', in *100 Designs/100 Years: Innovative Designs of the 20th Century*, Rotovision, Crans-Près-Céligny, pp.144–5.

'Gino Valle. Trasformazione della torre Alitalia a Roma EUR', *Anfione Zeto*, 12, monograph, edited by Margherita Petranzan.

'Gino Valle. Facoltà di Psicologia di Padova', *Lotus International*, 102, September, pp.50–55.

Marc Bédarida, 'La città simulata, tra restituzione e finzione', *Lotus International*, 103, December, pp.6–26.

Sebastiano Brandolini, 'Tre ipotesi per le ceneri della Fenice', *Lotus International*, 103, December, pp.40–57.

Pierre-Alain Croset, 'Attuale oggi un'architettura di ieri', *Abitare*, 390, December, pp.74–83.

'Façades & façadisme; Paris théâtralisé. L'îlot Edouard VII', *Architecture Intérieure Cree*, 289, pp.99–109.

'Progetto Bicocca, 1985–1998', in *I quaderni della Bicocca*, 1, Skira, Milan, pp.54–5.

2000

I progetti per la ricostruzione del teatro La Fenice, 1997, Marsilio, Venice.

'Torre IBM Italia', in Pino Scaglione, *EUR. Controguida d'architettura*, Testo & immagine, Rome.

'Lafarge Plâtres', *Archinews*, August, pp.34–6.

Giovanni Corbellini, 'L'architettura è ciò che il non luogo si aspetta ...', *Architettura/Intersezioni*, 8, October, pp.30–35.

X. H., 'Le modulaire adopté', *Intérieur Systèmes*, 31, October, pp.6–8.

Françoise Arnold, 'Paysage de béton', *D'A: d'architectures*, 106, November, pp.27–8.

Gino Valle, special issue of *Lotus Navigator*, November (Alessandro Rocca, 'Valle ultimo. Fabbriche, uffici e frammenti di città').

'Siège Social Lafarge', in *AMC*, December, pp.28–31.

Paolo Scrivano, 'Caja de ahorros, Udine. Savings Bank, Udine', *2G* (Arquitectura italiana de la posguerra), 15, special issue, pp.100–105.

2001

'Nuova sede Deutsche Bank Italia', in *La Bicocca abitata*, Skira, Milan (I quaderni della Bicocca, 2), pp.74–9.

Ferruccio Luppi, 'I primi progetti per il territorio friulano', in Paola Di Biagi (ed.), *La grande ricostruzione: il piano Ina-Casa e l'Italia degli anni cinquanta*, Donzelli, Rome, pp.365–72.

Ferruccio Luppi and Paolo Nicoloso (eds), *Il Piano Fanfani in Friuli: storia e architettura dell'Ina-Casa*, Leonardo, Pasian di Prato.

Isabella Reale (ed.), *Le arti a Udine nel Novecento*, Marsilio, Venice.

'El conjunto del Puerto obtiene el premio Dé cada 1999–2001', *El Pais*, 12 May.

Enrico Ragazzoni, 'Mestieri in cantiere', *La Repubblica*, 29 June.

'Gino Valle – Progetto Nuovo Portello'; 'Gino Valle – Sede della Deutsche Bank', *Casabella*, 690, June, pp.35–7, 44–7.

Marta Vallribera, 'Connexiò amb l'entorn', *Inde-Informaciò i Debat*, June, p.21.

Gilles Davoine, 'Lafarge Plâtres, au milieu des cyprès', *Le Moniteur*, 5094, 13 July, pp.5–7.

Jacques-Franck Degioanni, 'Déclinaison de bétons', *Le Moniteur*, 27 October, pp.74–5.

Oscar T. Blanca, 'Gino Valle soc un osservador', *Inde-Informaciò i Debat*, pp.20–23.

2002

'Riconoscimenti a Gino Valle', *Corriere della Sera*, 14 April, p.31.

2003

Maurizio Marcelloni, *Pensare la città contemporanea: il nuovo piano regolatore di Roma*, Laterza, Rome & Bari.

Elena Carlini, 'Un circuito ideale, prototipo di sviluppo territoriale integrato e innovativo', *Architettiregione*, 35, March, pp.42–51.

Matteo Vercelloni, 'Portello', *Domus*, 859, May, p.68.

'Gino Valle, 1923–2003', *Arquitectura viva*, 92, September–October, p.21.

G.C. [Gaetano Cola], 'La scomparsa di Gino Valle. Un nome nell'antologia dei grandi architetti'; Sandro Marpillero, 'A Gino Valle dedicato il primo numero di *Lotus Navigator*'; Federico Marconi, 'Nello studio di viale Venezia i tavoli di lavoro di Provino, Nani e Gino'; Argeo Fontana, 'Nel progetto Polis a Trieste, Valle architetto del vento e dell'acqua', *Rassegna Tecnica FVG*, 5, September–October 2003, pp.21–25.

Raimund Fein, 'Gino Valle 1923–2003', *Bauwelt*, 39–40, October, p.5.

Enrico Regazzoni, 'Gino Valle architetto di vento e acqua', *La Repubblica*, 2 October, p.42.

Marco Romanelli, 'Avevano 40 anni, hanno 40 anni', *Abitare*, 432, October, pp.299–315.

'Tarcento. Teatro Margherita, Cervignano. Cinema Teatro Pasolini', *Architettiregione*, 36, November, pp.28–9.

Sebastiano Brandolini, 'Caro Gino Valle', *La Repubblica delle donne*, 22 November, pp.103–7.

Pierre-Alain Croset, 'Gino Valle 1923–2003. Un maestro antidogmatico e anticonformista', *Il Giornale dell'architettura*, 12 November.

Giovanni Vragnaz, 'Lezioni di libertà', *Piranesi*, 17–18, Autumn, pp.5–7.

Marco Elia, 'Il tempo secondo Gino Valle: gli ultimi tremila "Cifra 3" di Solari', *Area*, November–December, pp.186–91.

Fulvio Irace, 'Gino Valle 1923–2003', *Abitare*, December, p.101.

Andreas Kipar, 'Il paesaggio di Gino Valle', *ACER Magazine – Architettura del paesaggio*, December.

Paolo Scrivano, 'Lo scambio inter-atlantico e i suoi attori. Il rapporto tra Stati Uniti e Italia in architettura e urbanistica e il ruolo di Adriano Olivetti', *Mélanges de l'Ecole française de Rome*, 2, 115, pp. 451–73.

2004

Progetto Portello, in Milano e Lombardia. La rinascita del futuro, exh. cat., travelling exhibition, Comune di Milano-Regione Lombardia-Fiera di Milano, Milan, pp.34–7.

Giorgio Ciucci, 'Gino Valle, Uffici Rex-Zanussi, Porcia (Pn)', in Francesca Fabiani (ed.), *Sguardi contemporanei, 50 anni di architettura italiana, 10 critici 10 architetture 10 fotografi*, exh. cat., 9th International Architecture Exhibition of Venice Biennale, Darc, Rome, pp.4–5.

Pierre-Alain Croset, 'Valle Gino. 1923–2003', entry in the *Dizionario dell'architettura del XX secolo*, Istituto della Enciclopedia Italiana Treccani, Rome, pp.2575–81.

Cino Zucchi, 'Gino Valle', *Domus*, 866, January, pp.48–53.

'Gino Valle, Cino Zucchi, Guido Canali, Charles Jencks. "Nuovo Portello Milano"', *Lotus International*, 120, April, pp.114–15.

Boris Podrecca, 'Gino Valle 1923–2003, Ein Requiem', *Architektur-Aktuell*, April, p.6.

Manolo Verga, 'Il principio di individuazione', *Lotus International*, 120, April, pp.114–15.

'Gino Valle. Progetto Fantoni', special issue of the series *Fantoni-Blueindustry*, 7, May.

Andrea Botti, 'La pietra di Botticino e la "Cittadella della Giustizia" di Brescia', *Schegge*, 5, September–October, pp.17–20.

Marco Frusca, 'Il volto urbano della legge', *AB-Atlante Bresciano*, 80, Autumn, pp.66–9.

Fulvio Irace, 'Milano progetto Portello. Una nuova porta urbana', *Abitare*, 445, December, pp.151–160.

Marcella Ottolenghi, 'Gino Valle. Un maestro che non aveva maestri. Anche in un ambito specialistico come quello della prefabbricazione edilizia', *Elite*, 12, pp.64–73.

Frely Sacchi, 'Gino Valle e l'alluminio anodizzato: storia di un felice connubio', *ABCD: Aluminium, Building, Construction, Design*, 16, pp.26–9.

2005

Architetture in montagna. Gino Valle in Carnia, exh. cat., Treppo Carnico, 2 July–25 September 2005, edited by Elena Carlini for Navado Press, Trieste (Alessandro Rocca, 'Meno forma, più concetto. 1960–65: la critica architettonica sull'opera di Gino Valle in Carnia'; Giovanni Corbellini, 'Astratto e contestuale. Gino Valle in Carnia').

Nico Ventura (ed.), *Da, chez, from Gino Valle*, exh. cat., 28 October – 11 December 2005, MusArc, Ferrara (Nico Ventura, 'Principio di deformazione'; Vittorio Gregotti, 'Gino Valle'; Amerigo Restucci, 'Ricerca nella continuità'; Alessandro Rocca, 'Due architetture a Milano, in presa diretta con la città').

Camilla De Mori, 'La Udine di Valle che Udine non ha voluto. I progetti "mancati" della mostra mai nata. Croset: Il Comune scelga un'altra sede. Gli eredi: finita la Deutsche Bank. Firma friulana sull'Ikea da record', *Il Gazzettino*, 23 July.

'Gino Valle in Carnia', *Abitare*, 453, September, p.81.

Pierre-Alain Croset, 'Atmosfera di vera città negli spazi del commercio', *Il Giornale dell'architettura*, 33, October, p.20.

Giovanni Vragnaz, 'Gino Valle in montagna: sperimentalismo senza avanguardia', *Piranesi*, 12, 21–22, Autumn, pp.22–7.

Nino Tenca Montini, 'A bottega in Studio Valle', in Alberto Pratelli (ed.), *Provare con l'architettura*, Forum, Udine, pp.19–22.

Terry Kirk, *The Architecture of Modern Italy, Volume II: Visions of Utopia, 1900–Present*, Princeton Architectural Press, New York, pp.214–17, 234–6.

2006

Leonardo Benevolo, *L'architettura nel nuovo millennio*, Laterza, Bari, pp.44–50.

Maria Rita Censi, Dante Frontero and Angelo Germani, *RM "06". Roma-Architettura contemporanea*, Edizioni Kappa, Rome, pp.13 (1–4), 61 (1–6).

Michele Alberti, 'Una città a tempo di clockwork city. L'aggregato commerciale del nuovo quartiere Portello di Milano', *OfArch*, 88, January–February, pp.70–83.

'Complesso commerciale "Portello" Milan, Italy', *The Plan*, 15, July–August, pp.146–7.

'Architetti Valle', *Costruire in laterizio*, 114, November–December, special issue. (Luka Skansi, 'Materia e spazialità: note sull'architettura di Gino Valle'; Roberto Gamba, 'Architetti Valle, Udine. Pragmatismo e sperimentazione'; Interview with Pietro Valle, by Roberto Gamba).

'Aggregato Commerciale Portello, Milano', in F. Irace (ed.), *Medaglia d'Oro all'Architettura Italiana 2006*, Electa-Mondadori, Milan, pp.38–9.

2007

Pierre Alain Croset, *I costruttori del Novecento. Gino Valle a Udine*, exh. cat., Palazzo Morpurgo in Udine, Mazzotta, Milan.

Vittorio Gregotti, 'A tre anni dalla morte. Gino Valle. Le sue opere per Udine', *La Repubblica*, 19 February.

Alessia Pilotto, 'L'inaugurazione della mostra evento: Le opere di mio padre siano un monito alla città. I disegni di Gino Valle spiegati dal figlio', *Il Gazzettino*, 17 February.

Giorgio Dri, 'Gino Valle nella Galleria d'arte moderna di Udine. Molte idee, tanti progetti', *Rassegna Tecnica del Friuli Venezia Giulia*, 2, March–April, pp.31–5.

Giovanni Corbellini, 'Al palazzo Morpurgo di Udine. Gino Valle oltre il regionalismo', *Il Giornale dell'architettura*, 5 April.

Cesare De Seta, 'Dialogo col paesaggio. L'opera di Gino Valle esprime una poetica sensibilità per il genius loci', *Architectural Digest*, 312, May, pp.68–72.

Laura Della Badia, 'Una città sotto la vela', *Europ'A, Acciaio, Architettura*, Spring–Summer, 5, pp.10–11.

Luka Skansi, 'Un recinto urbano alla Bicocca', *Casabella*, 757, July–August, pp.38–47.

Giovanni Vragnaz, 'Casa Migotto (ora Pozzi) a Udine', *Piranesi*, 25, Autumn, pp.22–9.

'Deutsche Bank'; 'Nuovo Portello', *Lotus International*, 131, pp.16 and 39–56.

AA.VV., 'Gino Valle, Progetto Fantoni', *Fantoni Blueindustry*, 7, Udine, special issue.

2008

Sergio Polano and Donata Battilotti, *Allestimenti tra le quinte di Palladio*, Electa, Milan.

'Aggregato commerciale. Nuovo Portello, Milano', *Ottagono*, 209, April, pp.202–7.

Richard Ingersoll, '"Die ganze Welt ist eine Bühne" – wozu dann ein neues Theater? Die Planungsgeschichte des Städtischen Theaters in Vicenza', *Bauwelt*, 99, 16, 25 April, pp.14–31.

Michele Alberti, 'Il nuovo teatro comunale di Vicenza', *OfArch*, 104, September–October, pp.164–71.

2009

Luka Skansi, *Gino Valle. Deutsche Bank Milano*, Electa, Milan.

'Learning from Gino, colloquio con Pierre-Alain Croset', *Architetti Verona*, 82, May, pp.73–7.

Pietro Valle, 'Oltre le mura scaligere a Vicenza', *Lotus International*, 138, June–July, pp.109–14.

'Nuovo bocciodromo comunale, Cussignacco Udine 2003–2009', *Ottagono*, 223, September.

Paolo Rosa, 'Una "cittadella fortificata". Il centro commerciale Porta di Roma', *Frames*, 142, September, pp.62–7.

Elisa Montalti (ed.), 'Viaggio in Italia: 4. Friuli Venezia Giulia', *Ottagono*, 223, pp.139–78.

2010

Luigi Spinelli, 'Gino Valle: One William Street. NY', *Domus*, 932, January, pp.114–20.

'Nuovo Teatro Comunale/New Municipal Theatre, Vicenza', *Ottagono*, 233, September, p.146.

'Progetto Portello, Milano', in *Ailati, Riflessi dal Futuro*, catalogue of the Italian pavilion at the 12th International Architecture Exhibition – Venice Biennale 2010, p.124–5.

'Quartiere Portello, Milano', in *Superurbano, Sustainable Urban Regeneration*, curated by Andrea Boschetti, Michele De Lucchi, Leopoldo Freyrie and Giovanni Furlan, Padua, pp.95–9.

Pietro Valle, 'Gino Valle, piani Guida per Padova', *Architetti Notizie, Rivista dell'Ordine degli Architetti di Padova*, 4, pp.9–13.

2011

Tomà Berlanda, 'Grattare sul posto', *L'Indice*, 2, February, p.32.

Joseph Rykwert, 'A Powerful Legacy', *Building Design*, 6 May, p.33.

Alessandro Rocca, 'Gino Valle come era lui', *Il Giornale dell'Architettura*, 96, July, p.9.

2013

Marco Biraghi and Silvia Micheli, *Storia dell'Architettura Italiana 1985–2015*, Einaudi, Turin.

Enrico Patti, 'Architettura come Brano di Città', *Architetti*, November–December, pp.6–10.

Diane Ghirardo, *Italy: Modern Architectures in History*, Reaktion Books, London.

Pierre-Alain Croset, 'Uffici Zanussi, Porcia, di Gino Valle', in A. Ferlenga and M. Biraghi (eds), *Architettura del Novecento, III, opere progetti luoghi, L-Z.*, Giulio Einaudi Editore, Turin, pp.725–30.

2014

Luka Skansi, 'Semplici telai: la costruzione a telaio in Italia tra realismo e astrazione', in Maddalena Basso, Jessica Gritti and Orietta Lanzarini (eds), *The Gordian Knot: studi offerti a Richard Schofield*, Campisano, Rome, pp.323–32.

2015

Pietro Valle, 'Studio Valle, Nuovo Polo Universitario di Padova, un pezzo di Città', *Casabella*, 846, February, pp.14–28.

Giuseppe Marinoni and Giovanni Chiaramonte, *Città Europea in Evoluzione – The Evolving European City*, Nuova Portello, Milan, pp.217–29.

Alberto Ferlenga and Marco Biraghi, *Comunità Italia. Architettura / Città / Paesaggio 1945–2000*, exh. cat., Milan Triennale, Milan.

Marco Biraghi, Gabriella Lo Ricco and Silvia Micheli (eds), *Guida all'architettura di Milano 1954–2015: 60 anni di architettura a Milano*, Hoepli, Milan.

2016

Pietro Valle, 'L'Architettura liberata dall'industria, Gino Valle e Zanussi 1956–76', in *Elettrodomesticità, Design e Innovazione nel Nord-Est, Da Zanussi a Electrolux*, exh. cat., Angelo Bertani (cur.), pp.229–69.

Beppe Finessi, *Stanze, Altre Filosofie dell'Abitare – Rooms, Novels, Living Concepts*, exh. cat., Milan, Venice, p.195.

Serena Maffioletti (ed.), *La concretezza sperimentale: l'opera di Nani Valle*, Il poligrafo-IUAV, Padua–Venice, 2016.

Tom Delavan, 'The Clock That Time Cannot Improve', *The New York Times Style Magazine*, 11 September, p.M2100.

Pietro Valle, *Valle Architetti Associati 2003–16* (monograph, in Italian and English with an introductory essay by Giovanni Corbellini), Libria, Melfi.

2017

Valerio Paolo Mosco, *Architettura Italiana, dal Postmoderno a Oggi*, Skira, Milan.

Cesare de Seta, 'Gino Valle: le nuove forme della tecnologia', in Cesare de Seta, *La civiltà architettonica in Italia dal 1945 a oggi*, Longanesi & C., Milan, pp.267–73.

Pietro Valle, 'La Tomba di Pier Paolo Pasolini a Casarsa di Gino Valle 1977 – Pier Paolo Pasolini Tomb in Casarsa by Gino Valle, 1977', in *Pasolini Presente*, exh. cat., Michela Lupieri (cur.), Tolmezzo, pp.56–9.

Luca Molinari, 'The Italian Way to New Brutalism: The Experiences of Vittoriano Viganò, Giancarlo De Carlo and Gino Valle', in *Brutalism, Contributions to the International Symposium in Berlin 2012*, edited by the Wustenrot Foundation, Berlin, pp.85–94.

Pietro Valle, 'Campus Fantoni, Continuità nella Modificazione', *Pièra*, Rivista Semestrale dell'Ordine degli Architetti di Treviso, 6, September, pp.94–107.

Carlo Melograni, 'Un cosmopolita del nord-est', in *Architetture nell'Italia della ricostruzione. Modernità versus modernizzazione 1945–1960*, Quodlibet, Macerata, pp.328–38.

2018

Davide Tommaso Ferrando, 'Gino e Pietro Valle per Fantoni, industriali friulani', *Casabella*, 884, April, pp.16–33.

Index

Note: Page numbers for illustrations appear in *italics*.

Aalto, Alvar 12, 63, 64, 68, 74, 160, 270
Abercrombie, Patrick 15, 34, 73–4
Abraham, Raimund 231
abstract and contextual 32, 61
Adler house 80
advertising function 169
a-formal elements 75
Agosto, Renzo 193
Agrate, Brionvega plant 178–9, *178*
Albini, Franco 63, 90, 138–9
Alfa Romeo area, Portello *296*, *297*
Alisarda offices 271–2, *272*, *273*
Alitalia tower 217–19, *218*, *219*, *220*, 277
Alpine village *58*
American influence 22, 63, 73
André, Carl 179
anti-formalism 12, 75
Appleyard, Donald 26, *44*, 89
Architectural Design 28
    cover *14*
The Architectural Review 15, 18, 109
Ardeatine Caves Memorial 123
Arta Terme spa *6*, *36*, *37*, 111, *126*, 128–9, *130*, 134–5, *134*, *135*, 138, *175*, 176
Arti Grafiche Chiesa plant *43*, 94, *98*, 127
artistic work 31, 59–60, 94

Aulenti, Gae 221
Avellino Duarte house 216–17
Avignon, Lafarge offices and laboratories 274, *274*, *275*, 276
Avon, Annalisa 42
Aymonino, Carlo *45*
Azzano Decimo, Cassa Rurale ed Artigiana 216–17, *217*

Banca Cattolica del Veneto, Tarvisio 64, 138
Banca Commerciale Italiana *212*, 213–16, *214*, *215*, 224, *225*
Banham, Reyner 15, 18, 89, 90, 95, 109
banks
    Cassa di Risparmio di Gorizia 95, *96–7*, 98, *98*
    Cassa di Risparmio di Latisana 80–85, *80*, *81*, *82–3*, 84
    Cassa di Risparmio di Udine 84, *84*, *85*
    Cassa Rurale ed Artigiana 216–17, *217*
    see also Deutsche Bank Italia, Milan
Barcelona, Gran Teatre de Liceu 221
Basaldella, Dino 122, 132
Basiano, IBM Distribution Centre 170–71, *172–3*
Bayer offices 273
Bellini house, Udine *88*, 89, 90–91, *90*, 93–4
Bergamin 180–81, 291
    courtyard of offices *30*

Bergamin (*continued*)
 Distribution Centre and warehouses 169, *171*, 180–81
 offices 181, 190, *190*, *191*
 sales centre *180*, 295
Bergamo
 courthouse 256
 urban project *253*, 256–7
Berlin, elementary school 231, *232*, *233*, *233*
Bevilacqua building, Lignano 61, *61*
Bicocca area, Milan *250*, 251–2, *251*, 276, *278*–9, 284, 291
Bisaro apartment building *20*, 26, 68–9, *71*
Bologna, Barca-Casteldebole *201*, 202
Bottero, Maria 128–9
Brescia
 courthouse *246*, 252–4, *252*, 260, *260*, *261*, 273
 Monument to the Partisans and Victims of the Massacre at Piazza della Loggia 179, *179*
Brionvega plant, Agrate 178–9, *178*
Broggi, Mario 14, 167, 178, 213, 231
Brutalism, New 89–103
Bufalotta-Porta di Roma district 17, 291, 292–5, *292*, *294*, 300, 302–3, *303*, *304*, *305*
Burckhardt, Michael 14, 167, 178, 213, 231

Caccia-Dominioni, Luigi 18, 98
Calamandrei, Piero 121
Calle dei Lavranieri, Giudecca 197, *197*
Campos Venuti, Giuseppe 248
Canova, Antonio 179
Carnelutti, Alfredo 19, 27, 28, 33, 105, 109
Carnelutti, Marco 28
Casabella 16, 18, 95, 98, 168
 cover *15*
Casabella-Continuità 7
'Casa del Viticoltore' 69
Casarsa della Delizia
 city hall *10*, 11, 141, 144–5, *145*, *146*, *147*, 154, *154*, *155*, 160, 167, *175*, 297
 tomb of Pier Paolo Pasolini 179–80, *179*
Cassa di Risparmio di Gorizia Bank 95, *96*–7, 98, *98*

Cassa di Risparmio di Latisana Bank 80–85, *80*, *81*, *82*–3, 84
Cassa di Risparmio di Udine Bank 84, *84*, *85*
Cassa Rurale ed Artigiana 216–17, *217*
Cattinara, hospital 95
Celant, Germano 12, 173
Ceramiche Scala factory, Pordenone 112
Cervignano del Friuli, Cinema-Teatro Pasolini 220, *221*
Chicago, Lake Shore Drive 140–41, *142*–3, *144*
Chiesa house 140, *141*
Chinese gardens 34
Chirignago School *174*
CIAM summer school 46, 74
Cifra 3 *24*
Cifra 5 *25*
Cinema Margherita, Tarcento *63*, 64
Cinema Nuovo (Cervignano del Friuli, Cinema-Teatro Pasolini) 220
city, pieces 199, 202, 231–45, 248, 252, 253, 256, 280
cladding 77, 180, 181, 225, 247, 273, 274
 Bufalotta-Porta di Roma district 294, 295
 Deutsche Bank Italia, Milan 277, 280
 IBM Distribution Centre 170, 172
 Theatre of Vicenza 257, 267
 Valdadige prefabricated schools 171
 Zanussi 169
collage 40, 160, *160*, 220, 238, *239*
Collina di Forni Avoltri, hotel *66*–7
colour, Valle's attitude to 32
complex geometry 148, 214, 236, 276
constructive grammar 111, 114, 173
constructive language 21, 89, 114, 273
constructive poetics 167
context 7, 32, 37, 65, 68, 75, 248
 Banca Commerciale Italiana 215, 270
 Bicocca area 251, 276, 277, 284
 Cassa Rurale ed Artigiana 216, 217
 and character 61
 La Defense office complex 233, 237, 269
 Fantoni offices 169
 and historic city 36, 95, 98, 138, 141, 145

and language 94
and low-cost housing 193, 194
Pordenone 160, 162
Portello, Milan shopping cluster 297
Quaglia house 79
schools 173, 175
Société Générale 220
Sutrio 109, 177, 178
Vicenza, Municipal Theatre 257
Vienna, Imperial Stables, project for a museum complex 252
Vriz complex 92
Zanussi 105, 116
Cooperativa Muratori of Udine 61, 62, *62*
Corbellini, Giovanni 35, 40
Cortolezzis houses, Treppo Carnico *79*, 80
Costantini, Carlo 218
critical regionalism 37
crossing, path of 122, 123, 132, 141, 175
Crotti, Sergio 295
culture of Udine and Friuli 34
curved development 154, 218, 257, 269, 274, 293, 296-7
    Alisarda offices 272
    Cassa Rurale ed Artigiana 216
    Olivetti offices 282
    San Donato Milanese 271

'Da, chez, from Gino Valle', exhibition 8
Dal Co, Francesco 29, 38, 169
Dapres factory 169, *170*
Dator 6 horizontal *25*
Dator 10 *25*
De Carlo, Giancarlo *44*, 68
De Cillia, Adelchi 28
De Cillia, Francesco 28
La Défense office complex *15*, 233-7, *234-5*, *236*, *237*, 242, *242*, *243*, 248, 269, 277
deformations 154, 181, 199, 216, 271
De Michelis, Marco 202
Denver, Colorado, production plant *126*, *128-9*, 130, *130*, 159
design education 46

de Sola-Morales, Ignasi 221
Deutsche Bank Italia, Milan 11, *11*, *268*, 276-80, *277*, *278-9*, 284, *285*, *286*, *287*, *288-9*, 291
dialogue 79, 94, 193, 231, 257, 260, 295
    at Banca Commerciale Italiana 214
    with cladding 77
    and geographical scale of the landscape 194
    at Giudecca 198, 199
    with Monte Stella 157
    at Olivetti offices 269, 270
    at Sutrio 176
Dilme, Lluis 221
D'Olivo, Marcello 59
Duchamp, Marcel 31, 113
Dudok, Willem Marinus 63

eclecticism 40
Eco Refrigerazione facility 181, *181*, 295
Édouard VII block, Paris *230*, 238-9, *238*, *241*, 244, *245*
Education Working Group of ICSID 46
Eisenman, Peter *45*
environment 15, 34-7, 73-4, 93, 94, 95
    and foundation idea of architecture 127
    Valdadige schools 173, 175
equipped axis *113*, 114, 116, 141, 144, 167, 297
Etlin, Richard A. 179
excavation 139, 158, 159, 160, 253, 256, 262, 276
exceptions 178, 181, 199, 200, 215, 233, 236, 296

Fabiani, Max 236
Fabio Filzi district, Milan 68-9
Fabre, Xavier 221
Fabro house *60*, 61
façadisme 238
Fagnoni, Raffaello 46-7
Fair, Milan 295
Fantoni industrial complex 34, *35*, *41*, 42, *166*, 167-70, *183*, 184, *185*, *186-7*, *188*, *189*
Fanzutti, Daniel 274
Fehn, Sverre 18
Feng Shui 15, 34, 73-4, 121-2

Figini, Gino 19
figurative gestures 69
'finding things' 15–16
Fiorentino, Mario 123
Foghini house, San Giorgio di Nogaro 69
Fontanafredda, city hall *176*, 177–8
formative experiences 59–71
Forni Avoltri, hotel 65
Frampton, Kenneth 18, 37, 215
Frankfurt, Mercedes offices and garage 273
Frankl, Wolfgang 90
Fraticelli, Vanna *45*
'Fronte Nuovo delle Arti' 60
Fuller Buckminster, Richard 38, 84

Gabetti, Roberto 236–7
Gardella, Ignazio 69, 77
Geatti plant, Terenzano *33*, *168*, 169
generative grammar 175, 199
Ghetti house, Codroipo *68*, 69
'Gino Valle Architetto', exhibition *12*
'Gino Valle in Carnia', exhibition 8
'Gino Valle: progetti e architetture per Udine,
    1948–2003', exhibition 8
Giudecca, low-cost housing complex *192*, *196*,
    197–202, *197*, 206–7, *206*, *207*, 208–9, *210*, *211*, 271
Goodman, Nelson 42
Gorizia, Cassa di Risparmio 95, 96–7
Gran Teatre de Liceu, Barcelona 221
Gregotti, Vittorio 17, 42, 105, 145, 251–2, 291
Gregotti Associati 276, 284
Gropius, Walter 45–6, 73
Gutkind, Erwin 74
Gyssels, George 32

Hamburg, International Tribunal for the Law of the
    Sea 254, *255*, 256
Haring, Keith 238
Harvard Graduate School of Design 22, 45, 73
    visiting professor 46
Hejduk, John 231
Hertzberger, Herman 231

Hilversum, city hall 64
Howard, Ebenezer 74

IACP housing 193–4, *194*, 204, *204*, *205*
IBM
    addition to Segrate offices 273–4, *273*
    Alitalia tower, Rome 217–19, *218*, *219*, 220, 277
    Distribution Centre 170–71, *172–3*
    office complex and hotel, La Défense, Paris 15,
        233–7, *234–5*, *236*, *237*, 242, *242*, *243*, 248, 269,
        277
ICSID conference, Bruges 46
identity, changing 40
IG Farben Building 280
IKEA 294–5, 302
INA building, Udine *136*, 145–6, *148*
INA-Casa plan 68, 193
industrial objects 17, 23, 42, 167–91
infill panels 112, 114, 138, 152
intellectual curiosity 25
Internationale Bauausstellung (IBA) 231
Irace, Fulvio 14–15, 297
Istituto statale d'arte, Venice 46
Istituto tecnico, Udine, competition project 69, *69*
Istrana, Bergamin sales centre 181
IUAV, Venice 45, 46–7, 59
    thesis examination 62–3
Ivrea, Olivetti headquarters 269–71, *270*, 273, 276, 280,
    282, *282*, *283*

James, Henry 200
Jesolo, city hall 16, *109*, 111
Jewish Museum, Berlin 231
JFK Airport, TWA terminal *24*

Kahn, Louis 40, 73, 80, 90, 109
Kimball, Francis M. 214, 224
Kindergarten, Fielis 64–5, *64*, *65*
Kleihues, Josef Paul 231
Kollhoff, Hans 231
Koolhaas, Rem 231
Krier, Rob 231

Lafarge offices and laboratories 274, *274, 275*, 276
landscape 34, 37, 127, 130, 169, 170–71, 270–71
 Alisarda offices 272
 Bufalotta district, Rome 292, 293
 Deutsche Bank Italia, Milan 276, 284
 Lafarge offices and laboratories 274
 shopping cluster, Portello 297, 300
 SNAM offices 271
Latisana
 Bergamin sales centre *180*, 295
 Cassa di Risparmio 80–85, *80, 81, 82–3*, 84
Le Corbusier, Charles-Edouard Jeanneret-Gris 8, 26,
  29, 36, *44*, 74, 193
Libera, Adalberto 176, 257
Libeskind, Daniel 231
Lignano Sabbiadoro 60–62
linguistic austerity 280
'linguistic baggage' 38, 40
linguistic differentiation 277
linguistic elements 270
linguistic interpretation 38–40
linguistic 'neutrality' 167
linguistic sources 68
Lisbon, Chiado area 239
London, residential project at Golden Lane *194*
Loos, Adolf 9, 216
Lotus Navigator 8
low-cost housing 193–211
Loyer, Francois 238

Macola, Giorgio 14, 171, 193, 219, 238
Magnani, Carlo *45*
major urban transformations 148, 184
Maldonado, Tomás 157
Mangiarotti, Angelo 90
Manieri-Elia, Mario 29
mannerism 111
Manzano house 139–40, *139, 140*
Marconi, Federico 26, 105, 121
Margherita cinema, Tarcento *63*, 64
Marpillero, Sandro 21, 39, 213–14, *215*
Masieri, Angelo 64, 73

mat building 198, 199, 200
Matta-Clark, Gordon 32
Mattioni, Emilio 193
Mazzariol, Giuseppe 12, 34–5, 75
Merleau-Ponty, Maurice 175
memory 128–9, 130, 137, 138, 169, 236, 271
Menichetti, Piera Ricci 13, 25, 140, 141, 145
Mercedes offices and garage 273, *273*
Il Messaggero Veneto 144, *144*
metamorphosis 217–20
Michelucci, Giovanni 138
Midena, Ermes 220
Mies van der Rohe, Ludwig 45
Migotto house 75–7, *76*
Milan
 Bayer offices, Portello *273*
 Bicocca area *250*, 251–2, *251*, 276, *278–9*, 284, 291
 Deutsche Bank headquarters 11, *11, 268*, 276–80,
  277, 278–9, 284, *285, 286, 287, 288–9*, 291
 Palazzo Besana restoration 213, *216*
 La Rinascente 138–9, 145, 157–9, *158*, 291
 shopping cluster, Portello 17, *290*, 291, 292,
  295–300, *296, 298–9*, 306–9, *307, 308, 309*
Minimal Art 11, 175–8, 181
Mirano hospital *145*
modernity 138, 297
Molino Stucky 197
Mondrian, Piet 31
Moneo, Rafael *45*
montage 43, *128*, 141, 168, 252
Monte Lussari, tourism complex 65
Monte Stella 157, 295
monument 7, 18, 32, 121, 122–3, 127, 132, *133*, 179, 180,
  238, 247, 269
Monument to the Resistance of Udine *15*, 18, *27*, 32,
  118, 121–7, *121, 122, 123*, 124–5, 132, *132, 133*
 sketch on envelope *31*
Morandi, Giorgio 60
Morassutti, Bruno 14, *42*
Morris, Robert 175
Moschini, Francesco 17, 216
'Mostra di architettura moderna', exhibition 63

Mulas, Ugo 178
Mumford, Lewis 74
musical 'score' 42–3
Myer, John *44*, 89

National Pensions Institute, Helsinki 270
Navy, Pula 59
Neutra, Richard 26, 63
New York, Banca Commerciale Italiana *212*, 213–14,
    214, *215*, 224, *225*, 270
Nicoletti house, Udine 77, *77*, 93, 94, *100*, *101*
Nicolin, Pierluigi 17, 237
Niemeyer, Oscar 273
non-architecture 16, 111, 112–13, 114, 137, 141, 144,
    297
Noorda, Bob 28
Nordic architecture 68

office buildings 269–89
Ohl, Herbert 167
Olbia, Alisarda offices 271–2, 273
Olivetti offices 269–71, *270*, 273, 276, 280, 282, *282*,
    283
Olympia theatre 238, 239, 244, *244*
Osborn, Frederick James 74
Osoppo, Fantoni industrial complex *35*, *41*, *166*,
    167–70, *183*, 184, *185*, *186–7*, *188*, *189*

Padua
    courthouse 247–8, *248*, 249, 277
    guideline plan for urban reorganisation of the
        territory between the Fair, the railroad and Via
        Antonio Grassi *248*
    new university campus 256–7, 262, *262*, *263*
Paestum, temples 169
Palazzo Besana 213, *216*
Palazzo dell'Acqua e della Luce 123, 127
Palazzo della Regione 146, 148, *149*
Palazzo delle Associazioni Culturali 145, *150*, *151*
Palazzo delle Poste
    Naples 280
    Rome 257

Paris
    Edouard VII block and Olympia theatre 230, 238–9,
        238, *241*, 244, *244*, *245*
    IBM office complex and hotel, La Défense 233–7,
        234–5, *236*, *237*, 242, *242*, *243*, 248, 269, 277
    Société Générale 219–20, *220*, 226, *226*, *227*, *228–9*
Pasolini, Pier Paolo 179–80
Pasolini cinema-theatre 220, *221*
Pastor, Valeriano *45*
path of crossing 122, 123, 132, 141, 175
Peep-est Master Plan 193
People's Savings Bank, Cedar Rapids, Iowa 217
Perspecta 73
'phenomenology of perception' 175
Philippe, Gerard *44*
Piazza Primo Maggio 28–9, 159, *161*
Picasso, Pablo 7
pictorial gestures 31, 218
Pirelli, Leopoldo 251, 252
Pizzetti, Ippolito 32, 47, 181, 191, 251
Pocenia, Eco Refrigerazione facility 181, *181*, 295
Podrecca, Boris 20–21
Poelzig, Hans 280
'poetics of tension' 146
'poetics of the box' 176
Polesello, Gianugo 193
Ponti, Giò 5
Porcia
    Zanussi equipped axis *113*, 114, 116, 141, 144, 167,
        297
    Zanussi offices 14, 16, 18, 20–21, 25, 32, *34*, *104*,
        106–8, *114*, *115*, 116–19, *117–19*
Pordenone
    administrative centre 11, *156*, 159–60, *160*, 162–5,
        162, *163*, *164–5*, 175, 199, 236
    Ceramiche Scala factory 112
    city hall *91*, 95
    Villa Zanussi *72*, *79*, 80
    Zanussi electric accounting centre 167, *169*
Poretti, Sergio 18, 20
Portello, Milan shopping cluster 17, *290*, 291, 292,
    295–300, *296*, *298–9*, 306–9, *307*, *308*, *309*

Portogruaro
  Bergamin Distribution Centre and warehouses
    169, *171*, 180–81
  Bergamin offices 181, 190, *190*, *191*
  Dapres factory 169, *170*
  hospital 92–3, *93*, 127
prefabrication 41–2, 43, 112, 167, 168, 171, 194
  shopping cluster, Portello 297, 306
Premio Bergamo, 5th 59–60
product design 17, 23, 105
A propos de Venise (Le Corbusier) 44, 74
'Prospects for a Critical Regionalism' (Frampton) 18

Quaglia house 40, 77, *78*, 79, *79*, *80* 23

'ready-made' 113
reconstruction 213–16, 219–21, 226, 244
'recycling' 217–18
renovation 244
representational value of architecture 216, 217, 220,
  231
'residential mat' 199
Resistance of Udine, monument, competition
    project *15*, 18, *27*, 32, *118*, 121–7, *121*, *122*, *123*,
    124–5, 132, *132*, *133*
  sketch on envelope *31*
restoring 40, 213–29
restructuring 140, 213–29, *231*, *238*
retail architecture 291–309
reusing 213–29
RIBA, London, Annual Lecture 16, 95
ribbon windows 271, 280
Ricci Menichetti, Piera 13, 25, 140, 141, 145
Richardson, Henry Hobson 63
Ridolfi, Mario 90
La Rinascente 138–9, 145, 157–9, *158*, 291
Rocca, Alessandro 28–9, 32, 35, 94–5, 167, 280, 300
Rogers, Ernesto Nathan 63, 74, 95
Romanelli House, Udine 79, *87*
  veranda *40*
Rome
  Alitalia tower 217–19, *218*, *219*, 220, 277

Bufalotta-Porta di Roma district 17, 291, 292–5,
    292, *294*, 300, 302–3, *303*, *304*, *305*
Rossi, Aldo 221
Royal College of Art, London 6, 95
Rudolph, Paul 73
Rutelli, Francesco 293
Rykwert, Joseph 10, 12, 18, 28, 34, 35, 89, 95
  on culture of Udine and Friuli 34
  on La Rinascente 158
  on Valdadige schools 173

Sacca Fisola 197, *198*, *200*, 202, *207*
Samona, Giuseppe 63, 69, 74
San Donato Milanese, SNAM offices 271, *271*
San Quirino School *174*
Santini, Pier Carlo 23
Santo Stefano di Buia, low-cost housing complex
    194, *195*, 197, 199
Säynätsalo City Hall 74
Scarpa, Carlo *44*, 63, 79
Scharoun, Hans 26, 63
schools 171, 173, *174*, 175, 231, *232*, 233, *233*
Secchi, Bernardo 248, 254, 256
Second World War 59
Segrate, IBM offices, addition 273–4, *273*
Semerani, Luciano *44*, 95
Serra, Richard 32
shopping centres 17, *290*, 291–309, *294*, *303*, *304*, *305*
Sipre 41–2
site specific 32
Siza, Álvaro 216–17, 239
Smithson, Peter and Alison 193, 194
Smithson, Robert 175
SNAM offices 271, *271*
Snozzi, Luigi 40
Société Générale 219–20, *220*, 226, *226*, *227*, 228–9
Solà-Morales, Ignasi 221
Solari 17, 23
  alphanumeric split-flap displays *24*
solitude 25
space 12, 30, 31, 33, 74, 80
  at Arta Terme spa 134

space (*continued*)
   at Casarsa della Delizia city hall 154
   at Cassa di Risparmio di Udine Bank 84
   at La Défense 242
   at Deutsche Bank Italia, Milan 276
   and low-cost housing 199
   monumental 32
   and object 175
   at Olympia Theatre 244
   at Padua 247, 256
   public and private 238
   at Theatre of Vicenza 257, 265
   at Zanussi offices 116
spatial experience 10
Stirling, James 40, 248
Studio Architetti Valle 8, 13–14, 26, *26, 28*–9
   exhibition, poster *13*
Stuttgart
   Staatsgalerie 248
   Staatstheater 222
Sullivan, Louis Henry 217
Sutrio
   city hall 176–7, *177,* 178
   Quaglia house 40, 77, *77, 78,* 79, *79, 80*
   school 109–11, *110,* 127

Tafuri, Manfredo 17, 18, 123, 138, 248, 251
Tamaro, Gigetta 95
Tarcento, Cinema Margherita *63*
Tavagnacco-Molin Nuovo, Arti Grafiche Chiesa plant *43, 98,* 127
teaching 45–7
Teatro La Fenice, Venice 220–21, *223*
temporal flow 9
Tenca Montini, Nino 33
Tentori, Francesco 26, 75, 80, 94, 127
'Teo system' 199
Terenzano, Geatti *168,* 169
testimony 7, 12, 40, 148
Toso, Firmino 98
Treppo Carnico
   city hall 9, 34, 94, *94, 102, 103*

   Cortolezzis houses *79,* 80
Trieste, Vriz residential and office tower 15, 18, 91–2, *91, 92,* 95
Turcato, Giulio 60

Udine
   Arti Grafiche Chiesa plant *43,* 94, *98,* 127
   Banca Cattolica 64, 138
   Bellini house *88,* 89, 90–91, *90, 93*–4
   Cassa di Risparmio 84, *84, 85*
   Chiesa house 140, *141*
   IACP housing 193–4, *194,* 204, *204, 205*
   INA commercial and residential building on Via Marinelli *136,* 145–6, *148*
   Istituto tecnico, Udine, competition project 69, *69*
   Manzano house 139–40, *139, 140*
   Il Messaggero Veneto 144, *144*
   Monument to the Resistance 15, 18, 27, *31,* 32, *118,* 121–7, *121, 122, 123, 124–5,* 132, *132, 133*
   Moretti area residences 159, *159*
   Nicoletti house 77, *77,* 93, 94, *100, 101*
   offices and residences on Via Marinoni 95, 98, *99*
   Palazzo delle Associazioni Culturali, Via Manin 145, *150, 151*
   Piazza Primo Maggio 28–9, 159, *161*
   project for renewal of historic centre 137
   projects for Palazzo della Regione 146, 148, *149*
   Romanelli House 40, 79, *87*
   stadium, competition project 19, 159, *161*
   theatre project 137, *138*
   Via Mercatovecchio building 39, 137–9, *139,* 152, *152, 153,* 214
Ungers, Oswald Mathias 18
Unimark International 28
Unite d'habitation 193
upgrading 23
urban design 17, 18, 23, 202, 247, 248, 251, 252, 256, 257, 291, 293, 295, 297
urban fabric 162, 175, 233, 254, 257, 292, 295, 296
urbanism, negotiated 291, 292
Urquijo, Fernando 219, 238
Utzon, Jørn 18

vacation housing 62

Vaccaro, Giuseppe 280

Valdadige prefabricated schools 171, 173, *174*, 175

Valle, Gino
    pictured at Cinema Margherita, 1946–48 *63*
    pictured with his father Provino, late 1940s *22*
    pictured with his sister Nani, late 1940s *23*
    pictured in Salem, winter 1951–52 *50*
    pictured at Le Corbusier lecture, 1952 *44*
    pictured with his sister Nani meeting Ernest
        Hemingway, 1954 *23*
    pictured at Cassa di Risparmio di Latisana Bank,
        1955 *81*
    pictured at Arta Terme, 1964 *130*
    pictured at Royal College of Art, London, 1964 *6*
    pictured at the seminar in Ulm, 1965 *46*
    pictured in 1966 *48*
    pictured in 1970 *310*
    pictured at design seminar at IUAV, 1979 *45*
    pictured in the studio on Piazza 1° Maggio, Udine,
        1982 *28*

Valle, Nani 22, *23*, 26, *44*, *45*, 59, 68, 92, 105

Valle, Pietro 13

Valle, Provino 22, 26, 59, 60
    archive 8
    pictured with Gino, late 1940s *22*
    portrait, 1945 *58*

Vedova, Emilio 31, 60

Venice
    Istituto statale d'arte 46
    low-cost housing on Giudecca *192*, *196*, 197–202,
        197, 206–7, *206*, *207*, *208–9*, *210*, *211*, 271
    Sacca Fisola 197, *198*, *200*, 202, *207*
    Teatro La Fenice 220–21, *223*

Venice Biennale 173, 175, *178*

Vicenza, Municipal Theatre *256*, 257, *257*, 264–5, *264*,
    265, *266–7*

Vienna, Imperial Stables, project for a museum
    complex *252*, *259*

Viganò, Vittoriano 90

Vignelli, Massimo 4, 28

Villa Zanussi, Pordenone *72*, *79*, 80

Vriz residential and office tower *15*, 18, 91–2, *91*, *92*, 95

Wachsmann, Konrad 84

watercolour painting 31

windows, ribbon 271, 280

Wright, Frank Lloyd 63, 65, 68, 73, 129

Zanuso, Marco 90, 273, 274

Zanussi 17, 23, 105–9, 112–19
    electric accounting centre 167, *169*
    equipped axis *113*, 114, 116, 141, 144, 167, 297
    offices *14*, 16, 18, *20–21*, 25, *32*, 34, *104*, *106–8*, *114*,
        115, *117–19*, 127
    production plant, stoves *112*
    warehouses 41–2, *111*, 113, 169

Zanussi-Rex *111*

Zevi, Bruno 17–18

Zizzutto, Nelson 28

Zizzutto, Robert 28

Zodiac 16
    cover *14*

Zucchi, Cino 296

Illustration Credits